Your Literacy Standards Companion
at a Glance

Indexes Cross-Referencing Your State Standards with the Common Core appear at the front of the book.

Specific strands and standards are listed for each state.

Each state and grade level is listed at the top for easy reference.

The gist of each standard is succinctly summarized.

This column shows where to find instructional guidance for each standard.

Indexes Cross-Referencing Your State Standards

Alaska, Grades 9–10

Alaska Strand/Standard	Focus of Alaska Standard	For More Information
Reading Literature		
RL.1	Cite strong and thorough textual evidence to support analysis of what the text says explicitly and implicitly	R1 pp. 6–11
RL.2	Determine a theme or central idea of a text and analyze its development and how it is shaped by specific details; summarize the text	R2 pp. 12–17
RL.3	Analyze how characters develop, interact, and advance the plot or develop the theme	R3 pp. 18–23
RL.4	Determine the meaning of words and phrases as they are used in a text, including figurative and connotative meanings; analyze the cumulative impact of word choice on meaning and tone	R4 pp. 24–29
RL.5	Analyze how an author's choices regarding structure, the order of events, and manipulating time create such effects as mystery, tension, or surprise	R5 pp. 30–35
RL.6	Analyze a point of view, perspective, or cultural experience reflected in a piece of literature	R6 pp. 36–41
RL.7	Analyze the representation of a subject or scene in two different artistic mediums, including what is emphasized or absent in each treatment	R7 pp. 42–47
RL.8	NA	
RL.9	Analyze how an author draws on and transforms source material	R9 pp. 54–59
RL.10	Read literature of appropriate complexity independently with proficiency	R10 pp. 60–65
Reading Informational Text		
RI.1	Cite strong and thorough textual evidence to support analysis of what the text says explicitly and implicitly	R1 pp. 6–11
RI.2	Determine the central idea of a text and analyze its development; summarize main ideas or events	R2 pp. 12–17
RI.3	Analyze how the author structures an analysis or series of ideas or events, including the order, how they are developed, and the connections between them	R3 pp. 18–23
RI.4	Determine the meaning of words and phrases in a text; analyze the cumulative impact of specific word choices	R4 pp. 24–29
RI.5	Analyze in detail how ideas or claims are developed by particular sentences, paragraphs, or larger portions of text	R5 pp. 30–35
RI.6	Analyze how an author uses rhetoric to advance a point of view, perspective, or purpose	R6 pp. 36–41
RI.7	Analyze various accounts of a subject told in different mediums	R7 pp. 42–47
RI.8	Evaluate the argument in a text; assess reasoning and evidence; identify false statements and fallacious reasoning	R8 pp. 48–53
RI.9	Analyze U.S. documents of historical and literary significance, noting how they address related themes and concepts	R9 pp. 54–59
RI.10	Read and comprehend appropriately complex informational texts independently and proficiently	R10 pp. 60–65
Writing		
W.1	Write arguments to support claims, using valid reasoning and relevant and sufficient evidence	W1 pp. 70–77
W.2	Write informative/explanatory texts to effectively examine and convey complex ideas, concepts, and information	W2 pp. 78–85
W.3	Write narratives to develop real or imagined experiences or events using effective technique, well-chosen details, and well-structured event sequences	W3 pp. 86–91
W.4	Produce writing in which the development, organization, style, and features are appropriate to the task, genre, purpose, and audience	W4 pp. 92–97

(Continued)

Alaska Strand/Standard	Focus of Alaska Standard	For More Information
Writing		
W.5	Develop and strengthen writing as needed by planning, revising, and editing, rewriting, or trying a new approach	W5 pp. 98–103
W.6	Use technology to produce, publish, and update individual or shared writing projects	W6 pp. 104–109
W.7	Conduct research projects to answer a question or solve a problem; synthesize multiple sources; demonstrate understanding of the subject	W7 pp. 110–115
W.8	Gather information from multiple sources, using advanced searches effectively; assess usefulness of sources, integrate information, avoiding plagiarism	W8 pp. 116–121
W.9	Draw evidence from texts to support analysis, reflection, research, and/or synthesis	W9 pp. 122–127
W.10	Write routinely over shorter and extended time frames for a range of audiences, tasks, and purposes	W10 pp. 128–133
Speaking and Listening		
SL.1	Engage effectively in a range of collaborative discussions with diverse partners, building on others' ideas and expressing their own clearly and persuasively	SL1 pp. 138–143
SL.2	Integrate multiple sources of information presented in diverse media or formats; evaluate credibility and accuracy of sources and noting discrepancies	SL2 pp. 144–149
SL.3	Evaluate a speaker's point of view, reasoning, and use of evidence and rhetoric; identify fallacious reasoning or exaggerated or distorted evidence	SL3 pp. 150–155
SL.4	Present information clearly, concisely, and logically; ensure organization, development, substance, and style are appropriate to purpose, audience, and task	SL4 pp. 156–161
SL.5	Make strategic use of digital media in presentations to enhance understanding and to add interest	SL5 pp. 162–167
SL.6	Adapt speech to a variety of contexts and tasks; demonstrate a command of formal English when appropriate	SL6 pp. 168–173
Language		
L.1	Demonstrate command of the conventions of standard English grammar and usage when writing or speaking	L1 pp. 178–183
L.2	Demonstrate command of the conventions of standard English capitalization, punctuation, and spelling when writing	L2 pp. 184–189
L.3	Apply knowledge of language to make effective choices for meaning or style, to comprehend more fully when reading or listening, and to write and edit so that it conforms to the guidelines in a style manual appropriate for the writing type	L3 pp. 190–195
L.4	Determine or clarify the meaning of unknown and multiple-meaning words and phrases, choosing flexibly from an array of strategies	L4 pp. 196–201
L.5	Demonstrate understanding of figurative language, word relationships, and nuances in word meanings	L5 pp. 202–207
L.6	Acquire and use accurately general academic and domain-specific words and phrases; demonstrate independence in gathering vocabulary knowledge	L6 pp. 208–213
Reading History/Social Studies		
R.1	Cite specific textual evidence to support analysis of primary and secondary sources	R1 pp. 6–11
R.2	Determine central ideas or information of a primary or secondary source; summarize how they develop	R2 pp. 12–17
R.3	Analyze in detail a series of events; determine whether earlier events caused later ones	R3 pp. 18–23
R.4	Determine the meaning of words and phrases, including vocabulary describing political, social, or economic aspects of history/social studies	R4 pp. 24–29
R.5	Analyze how a text uses structure to emphasize key points or advance an explanation or analysis	R5 pp. 30–35
R.6	Compare the point of view of two or more authors for how they treat the same or similar topics	R6 pp. 36–41
R.7	Integrate quantitative or technical analysis with qualitative analysis	R7 pp. 42–47
R.8	Assess the extent to which reasoning and evidence support the author's claim	R8 pp. 48–53
R.9	Compare and contrast treatment of the same topic in several primary and secondary sources	R9 pp. 54–59
R.10	Read and comprehend history/social studies texts of appropriate complexity	R10 pp. 60–65

Shaded bands highlight the overarching strands.

Each standard under the strand is specifically called out.

Each section begins with a restatement of the official anchor standards as they appear in the actual Common Core State Standards document.

College and Career Readiness Anchor Standards for

Reading 9–12

Source: Common Core State Standards

The grades 6–12 standards on the following pages define what students should understand and be able to do by the end of each grade. They correspond to the College and Career Readiness (CCR) anchor standards by number. The CCR and grade-specific standards are necessary complements—the former providing broad standards, the latter providing additional specificity—that together define the skills and understandings that all students must demonstrate.

Key Ideas and Details

1. Read closely to determine what the text says explicitly and to make logical inferences from it; cite specific textual evidence when writing or speaking to support conclusions drawn from the text.
2. Determine central ideas or themes of a text and analyze their development; summarize the key supporting details and ideas.
3. Analyze how and why individuals, events, and ideas develop and interact over the course of a text.

Craft and Structure

4. Interpret words and phrases as they are used in a text, including determining technical, connotative, and figurative meanings, and analyze how specific word choices shape meaning or tone.
5. Analyze the structure of texts, including how specific sentences, paragraphs, and larger portions of the text (e.g., a section, chapter, scene, or stanza) relate to one another and the whole.
6. Assess how point of view or purpose shapes the content and style of a text.

Integration of Knowledge and Ideas

7. Integrate and evaluate content presented in diverse formats and media, including visually and quantitatively, as well as in words.*
8. Delineate and evaluate the argument and specific claims in a text, including the validity of the reasoning as well as the relevance and sufficiency of the evidence.
9. Analyze how two or more texts address similar themes or topics to build knowledge or to compare the approaches the authors take.

Range of Reading and Level of Text Complexity

10. Read and comprehend complex literary and informational texts independently and proficiently.

Note on Range and Content of Student Reading

To become college and career ready, students must grapple with works of exceptional craft and thought whose range extends across genres, cultures, and centuries. Such works offer profound insights into the human condition and serve as models for students' thinking and writing. Along with high-quality contemporary works, these texts should be chosen from among seminal U.S. documents, the classics of American literature, and the timeless dramas of Shakespeare. Through wide and deep reading of literature and literary nonfiction of steadily increasing sophistication, students gain a reservoir of literary and cultural knowledge, references, and images; the ability to evaluate intricate arguments; and the capacity to surmount the challenges posed by complex texts.

* Please consult the full Common Core State Standards document (and all updates and appendices) at http://www.corestandards.org/ELA-Literacy. See "Research to Build Knowledge" in the Writing section and "Comprehension and Collaboration" in the Speaking and Listening section for additional standards relevant to gathering, assessing, and applying information from print and digital sources.

Source: Copyright © 2010. National Governors Association Center for Best Practices and Council of Chief State School Officers. All rights reserved.

College and Career Readiness Anchor Standards for

Reading

The College and Career Readiness (CCR) anchor standards are the same for all middle and high school students, regardless of subject area or grade level. What varies is the specific content at each grade level, most notably the level of complexity of the texts, skills, and knowledge at each subsequent grade level in each disciplinary domain. The guiding principle here is that the core reading skills should not change as students advance; rather, the level at which they learn and can perform those skills should increase in complexity as students move from one grade to the next.

Key Ideas and Details

This first strand of reading standards emphasizes students' ability to identify key ideas and themes in a text, whether literary, informational, primary, or foundational and whether in print, graphic, quantitative, or mixed media formats. The focus of this first set of standards is on *reading to understand*, during which students focus on *what the text says*. The premise is that students cannot delve into the deeper (implicit) meaning of any text if they cannot first grasp the surface (explicit) meaning of that text. Beyond merely identifying these ideas, readers must learn to see how these ideas and themes, or the story's characters and events, develop and evolve over the course of a text. Such reading demands that students know how to identify, evaluate, assess, and analyze the elements of a text for their importance, function, and meaning within the text.

Craft and Structure

The second set of standards builds on the first, focusing not on *what the text says* but *how it says it*, the emphasis here being on analyzing how texts are made to serve a function or achieve a purpose. These standards ask readers to examine the choices the author makes in terms of words and sentence and paragraph structure and how these choices contribute to the meaning of the text and the author's larger purpose. Inherent in the study of craft and structure is how these elements interact with and influence the ideas and details outlined in the first three standards.

Integration of Knowledge and Ideas

This third strand might be summed up as *reading to extend* or *deepen one's knowledge* of a subject by comparing what a range of sources have said about it over time and across different media. In addition, these standards emphasize the importance of being able to read the arguments; that is, they look at how to identify the claims the texts make and evaluate the evidence used to support those claims regardless of the media. Finally, these standards ask students to analyze the choice of means and medium the author chooses and the effect those choices have on ideas and details. Thus, if a writer integrates words, images, and video in a mixed media text, readers should be able to examine how and why the author did that for stylistic and rhetorical purposes.

Range of Reading and Level of Text Complexity

The Common Core State Standards document itself offers the most useful explanation of what this last standard means in a note titled "Note on range and content of student reading," which accompanies the reading standards:

To become college and career ready, students must grapple with works of exceptional craft and thought whose range extends across genres, cultures, and centuries. Such works offer profound insights into the human condition and serve as models for students' own thinking and writing. Along with high-quality contemporary works, these texts should be chosen from among seminal U.S. documents, the classics of American literature, and the timeless dramas of Shakespeare. Through wide and deep reading of literature and literary nonfiction of steadily increasing sophistication, students gain a reservoir of literary and cultural knowledge, references, and images; the ability to evaluate intricate arguments; and the capacity to surmount the challenges posed by complex texts. (CCSS 2010, p. 35)

On the facing page, a user-friendly "translation" of each standard gives you a fuller sense of the big picture and big objectives as you consider how it relates to your state's standards.

Built-in tabs facilitate navigation.

The actual CCSS Anchor Standard is included for easy reference.

Bold type spotlighting what's different across grade spans specifically identifies what students must learn within each class and across subjects.

The specific strand situates you within the larger context of the standards.

On this page you'll find accessible translations of the standards at your left so you can better grasp what they mean.

The emphasis now is on what students should do, utilizing the same grade-level and subject-area structure at your left.

Comprehension questions are included for helping students master thinking moves and skills behind each standard; all can be adapted to a range of class texts and topics or to needs specific to your particular state standards.

Reading Standards   *Key Ideas and Details*

Reading 1: Read closely to determine what the text says explicitly and to make logical inferences from it; cite specific textual evidence when writing or speaking to support conclusions drawn from the text.

9–10 Literature
Cite strong and thorough textual evidence to support analysis of what the text says explicitly as well as inferences drawn from the text.

11–12 Literature
Cite strong and thorough textual evidence to support analysis of what the text says explicitly as well as inferences drawn from the text, **including determining where the text leaves matters uncertain.**

9–10 Informational Text
Cite strong and thorough textual evidence to support analysis of what the text says explicitly as well as inferences drawn from the text.

11–12 Informational Text
Cite strong and thorough textual evidence to support analysis of what the text says explicitly as well as inferences drawn from the text, **including determining where the text leaves matters uncertain.**

9–10 History/Social Studies
Cite specific textual evidence to support analysis of primary and secondary sources, attending to such features as the date and origin of information.

11–12 History/Social Studies
Cite specific textual evidence to support analysis of primary and secondary sources, **connecting insights gained from specific details to an understanding of the text as a whole.**

9–10 Science/Technical Subjects
Cite specific textual evidence to support analysis of science and technical texts, attending to the precise details of explanations or descriptions.

11–12 Science/Technical Subjects
Cite specific textual evidence to support analysis of science and technical texts, attending to **important distinctions the author makes and to any gaps or inconsistencies in the account.**

Source: Copyright © 2010. National Governors Association Center for Best Practices and Council of Chief State School Officers. All rights reserved.

Common Core Reading Standard 1

What the Student Does

9–10 Literature
Gist: Literal comprehension accompanied by evidence from the text. Say what happens in the story or what the poem says based on evidence from the text, without making personal connections or commentary.
- What happens in this story, play, or poem?
- Which specific details are most important to mention?
- What is the setting (time, place, atmosphere)?
- Who is involved? What do they say, do, think, and feel?
- How specific and detailed is the evidence drawn from the text?

11–12 Literature
Gist: Literal comprehension supported with evidence. Report the events of the story or what the poem says based on details from the text, without explaining what the text means or why it is important; note those places where the text is ambiguous or unclear.
- What happens in this story, play, or poem?
- Which specific details are most important to cite?
- What is the setting (time, place, atmosphere)?
- Who is involved? What do they say, do, think, and feel?
- Which parts of the text are ambiguous or vague?

9–10 Informational Text
Gist: Literal comprehension accompanied by evidence from the text. Say what happens in the text or what the poem says based on evidence from the text, without making personal connections or commentary.
- What is the subject—and what does it say about that?
- Which specific details are most important to mention?
- What is the setting (time, place, atmosphere)?
- Who is involved? What do they say, do, think, and feel?
- How specific and detailed is the evidence drawn from the text?

11–12 Informational Text
Gist: Literal comprehension supported with evidence. Report the events of the story or what the poem says based on details from the text, without explaining what the text means or why it is important; note those places where the text is ambiguous or unclear.
- What is the subject—and what does it say about that?
- Which specific details are most important to cite?
- What is the setting (time, place, atmosphere)?
- Who is involved? What do they say, do, think, and feel?
- Which parts of the text are ambiguous or vague?

9–10 History/Social Studies
Gist: Literal comprehension supported with evidence. Say what the primary source says about its subject and what secondary sources say about that same subject and/or the primary source, using evidence from the texts to support your statements.
- What type of text is this: primary or secondary?
- What are the subject and the source of information of the text?
- What does the text say or suggest about this subject?
- Who is the author or speaker of the text?
- How specific, detailed, and accurate is my textual evidence?

11–12 History/Social Studies
Gist: Literal comprehension supported with evidence. Report in precise detail what the primary source and secondary sources say about their subject (or the texts the secondary sources may discuss), using evidence from these texts to support your assertions. Include in your retelling of the text any insights about the text and how these contribute to your understanding of these texts when considered together.
- What type of text is this: primary or secondary?
- What are the subject and the source of information of the text?
- What does the text say or suggest about this subject?
- How specific, detailed, and accurate is my textual evidence?
- How do my revelations about the text and its contents add to my understanding of the text itself?

9–10 Science/Technical Subjects
Gist: Literal comprehension supported with precise details from the text. Sum up what the text says in precise detail and language, using evidence from the text to support your statements. Look closely at the words used to describe or explain when analyzing the text.
- What type of text is this?
- What is the subject of this text?
- What does the text say about this subject?
- Which precise details/data are important to mention?
- How precise, accurate, and detailed is my textual evidence?

11–12 Science/Technical Subjects
Gist: Literal comprehension backed up with precise details from the text. Report in detail what the text says, indicating those areas where the author emphasizes the difference between key elements or causes inconsistencies by leaving out key information when describing what they did or discovered.
- What is the subject of this text?
- What does the text say about this subject?
- Which precise details/data are important to mention?
- How precise, accurate, and detailed is my textual evidence?
- What key distinctions or inconsistencies should I report?

Horizontal and vertical views enable you to consider how the standards change across grade levels for a given subject or down a given grade level in all subjects.

Standards for each discipline are featured on a single page for easy cross-departmental collaboration.

The right-hand page utilizes the very same cross-discipline and grade-level format to provide two distinct visual paths for understanding the standards.

"Gist" sections provide plain-English synopses of the standards so you can put them to immediate use.

Featured on a separate page are specific teaching techniques for realizing each standard. Applicable to all subjects across grades 9–12, these strategies focus on what works in the classroom, based on Jim's own experience and recent content-area research.

What the **Teacher** Does

To teach students how to "read closely," do the following:

- Provide students access to the text—via tablet or photocopy—so they can annotate it as directed.
- Model close reading for students by thinking aloud as you go through the text with them or displaying your annotations on a tablet via an LCD projector; show them how to examine a text by scrutinizing its words, sentence structures, or any other details needed to understand its explicit meaning.
- Display the text via tablet or computer as you direct students' attention—by highlighting, circling, or otherwise drawing their attention—to specific words, sentences, or paragraphs that are essential to the meaning of the text; as you do this, ask them to explain what a word means or how it is used in that sentence or how a specific sentence contributes to the meaning of the larger text.
- Pose questions—about words, actions, details—that require students to look closely at the text for answers.

To get students to determine "what the text says explicitly," do the following:

- Ask students to "say what it says"—not what it means, since the emphasis here is on its literal meaning.
- Offer students an example of what it means to read explicitly and support your inferences with evidence; then tell them what a passage explicitly says, asking them to find evidence inside the text to support their statement about its meaning.
- Give students several pieces of evidence and ask them to determine what explicit idea in the text the evidence supports.

To develop students' ability to "cite specific textual evidence," do the following:

- Offer them a set of samples of evidence of different degrees of specificity and quality to evaluate, requiring them to choose the one that is best and provide a rationale for their choice.
- Show students how you would choose evidence from the text to support your inference; discuss with them the questions you would ask to arrive at that selection.

To "make logical inferences," ask students to do the following:

- Add what they *learned* (from the text about this subject) compared to what they already *know* (about that subject); then, have students *confirm* that their reasoning is sound by finding evidence for their inferences.
- Think aloud (with your guidance) about the process and how they make such inferences, and then have students find and use evidence to support their inferences.

To identify "uncertainties," "gaps," or "inconsistencies," students can try the following:

- Read—or *reread*—key sections that focus on reasoning or evidence, and ask, "So what?" or any of the reporter's questions (who, what, when, where, why, how) that seem appropriate to the text or topic, looking for those spots that cannot answer these basic questions logically or fully.

To help your English Language Learners, try this strategy:

- Repeat the process used to make such inferences, verbally labeling each step as you demonstrate it; then ask them to demonstrate their ability to do it on their own or with your prompting. Post the steps (e.g., "Inferences = What You Know + What You Learned") with an example on a poster or handout they can reference on their own as needed.

Notes

You can record notes here as you prepare to teach. Additional copies can be made if you'd like to adapt the pages to your school's instructional planning processes.

A dedicated academic vocabulary section offers a quick-reference glossary of key words and phrases for each standard.

In this last worksheet, you can record your final teaching plan.

Common Core Reading Standard 1

Academic Vocabulary: Key Words and Phrases

Analysis of primary and secondary sources: Primary sources are those accounts recorded from people who witnessed or participated in the event themselves; these sources include journals, letters, oral history recordings; secondary sources are those written by others *based on* primary sources and the opinions of scholars past and present.

Attending to such features: Close reading demands paying attention to any features, such as format, source, or date published, that might add subtle but noteworthy meaning to the document.

Cite specific textual evidence: All claims, assertions, or arguments about what a text means or says require evidence from within the text itself, not the reader's opinion or experience; students should be able to quote or refer to a specific passage from the text to support their idea.

Conclusions drawn from the text: Readers take a group of details (different findings, series of events, related examples) and draw from them an insight or understanding about their meaning or importance within the passage or the text as a whole.

Connecting insights gained from specific details to an understanding of the text as a whole: It is not enough to discern the meaning of a small detail; close reading demands connecting all the dots to reveal how these small details contribute to the meaning of the larger text.

Explicitly: Clearly stated in great or precise detail; may suggest factual information or literal meaning, though not necessarily the case.

Gaps or inconsistencies in the account: Some gaps are intentional, meant to leave room for interpretation or allow for some ambiguity that adds depth and complexity to a text; unintended gaps or inconsistencies undermine the credibility of the work or author by raising questions about the accuracy or reliability of the information.

Important distinctions the author makes: Authors draw a line at times between ideas, categories, or

certain elements, attributing more meaning or importance to one than another.

Informational text: These include nonfiction texts from a range of sources and written for a variety of purposes; everything from essays to advertisements, historical documents to op-ed pieces. Informational texts include written arguments as well as infographics.

Literature: This text can include not only fiction, poetry, drama, and graphic stories but also artworks, such as master paintings or works by preeminent photographers.

Logical inferences: To infer, readers add what they *learned* from the text to what they already *know* about the subject; however, for the inference to be logical, it must be based on evidence *from the text.*

Read closely (or close reading): Reading that emphasizes not only surface details but the deeper meaning and larger connections between words, sentences, and the full text; this also demands scrutiny of craft, including arguments and style used by the author.

Strong and thorough textual evidence: Not all evidence is created equal; students need to choose those examples or quotations that provide the best example of what they are saying or most compelling quotation to support their assertion.

Support conclusions: Related to citing textual evidence, this phrase requires readers to back up their claims about what a text says with evidence, such as examples, details, or quotations.

Text: In its broadest meaning, a text is whatever one is trying to read: a poem, essay, essay, or article; in its more modern sense, a text can also be an image, an artwork, speech, or multimedia format such as a website, film, or social media message, such as a Tweet.

Where the text leaves matters uncertain: The writer may intend to be ambiguous or unclear to imply a lack of clarity or resolution about this subject; it can also mean the writer did not tie up loose ends, thus, creating a weak link in an argument or narrative.

Planning to Teach
What to Do—and How

Clearly worded entries decode each word or phrase according to the particular way it is used in a given standard.

Your Literacy Standards Companion, Grades 9–12

YOUR LITERACY STANDARDS COMPANION, GRADES 9–12

What They Mean and How to Teach Them

Jim Burke

resources.corwin.com/literacycompanion9-12

| Name: _____ |
| Department: _____ |
| Learning Team: _____ |

FOR INFORMATION:

Corwin

A SAGE Company

2455 Teller Road

Thousand Oaks, California 91320

(800) 233-9936

www.corwin.com

SAGE Publications Ltd.

1 Oliver's Yard

55 City Road

London EC1Y 1SP

United Kingdom

SAGE Publications India Pvt. Ltd.

B 1/I 1 Mohan Cooperative Industrial Area

Mathura Road, New Delhi 110 044

India

SAGE Publications Asia-Pacific Pte. Ltd.

3 Church Street

#10-04 Samsung Hub

Singapore 049483

Copyright © 2017 by Corwin

All rights reserved. When forms and sample documents are included, their use is authorized only by educators, local school sites, and/or noncommercial or nonprofit entities that have purchased the book. Except for that usage, no part of this book may be reproduced or utilized in any form or by any means, electronic or mechanical, including photocopying, recording, or by any information storage and retrieval system, without permission in writing from the publisher.

National Governors Association Center for Best Practices, Council of Chief State School Officers, Common Core State Standards, English Language Arts Standards. Publisher: National Governors Association Center for Best Practices, Council of Chief State School Officers, Washington, DC. Copyright 2010. For more information, visit http://www.corestandards.org/ELA-Literacy.

Printed in the United States of America

ISBN 978-1-5063-8552-5

This book is printed on acid-free paper.

Publisher and Senior Program Director: Lisa Luedeke

Editorial Development Manager: Julie Nemer

Editorial Assistant: Nicole Shade

Production Editor: Melanie Birdsall

Copy Editors: Codi Bowman and Deanna Noga

Typesetter: C&M Digitals (P) Ltd.

Proofreaders: Wendy Jo Dymond and Laura Webb

Cover Designer: Scott Van Atta

Interior Designer: Auburn Associates, Inc.

Marketing Manager: Rebecca Eaton

19 20 21 10 9 8 7 6 5 4 3 2

Contents

Visit the companion website at
resources.corwin.com/literacycompanion9-12
for downloadable versions of the
Indexes Cross-Referencing Your State Standards.

Note: For the complete Common Core standards document, please visit corestandards.org.

Introduction

Turning Standards Into Daily Teaching

People can't live with change if there's not a changeless core inside them. The key to the ability to change is a changeless sense of who you are, what you are about, and what you value.

—Stephen Covey

Moving Forward—Together

An excellent education should not be an accident; it should be a right, though nowhere in the U.S. Constitution or any of our other founding documents do we find that right listed. Across the nation, state academic standards address that omission and challenge us all—administrators and teachers, parents and children, politicians and the public at large, professors and student teachers—to commit ourselves anew to the success of our children and our country.

In my nearly 25 years in education, I have been involved with many efforts to develop standards. I have had the honor of sitting alongside some of our country's greatest educational innovators and leaders to help develop the College Board's Pre-AP English Language Arts Framework, the National Board for Professional Teaching Standards for Adolescent Literacy, the National Council of Teachers of English Language Arts Standards, the framework for the Advanced Placement English Literature and Composition, the California Standards for English Language Arts, and, to the extent that such books serve as a form of literacy standards, the Holt McDougal 6–12 language arts textbooks. But the standards movement today is different: it comes with a level of support, a degree of commitment from leaders at all levels of government and business, and a sense of urgency that the other efforts could not or cannot claim.

There is a sense that we are all at some crucial inflection point in our national story, one that provides an opportunity we must not squander if our children are to help make this story we are trying to write about our country come true. I am often struck, listening to my mother-in-law, who has lived with us for many years, by her description of the country during the Depression and World War II, both of which she endured while living in the house she now shares with us. Almost any story she tells conveys a sense of shared commitment to the good of the community and country, that vital sense of mission that everyone was in it together, even—or especially—when the work was difficult and demanded some sacrifice.

It is not just the country and students that stand to benefit from the new commitment to standards, but teachers, too, for as Calkins, Ehrenworth, and Lehman (2012) argue, teaching to standards can "deepen the reading skills of adults as well." It is this same sense of mutual benefit that Carol Jago (2005) calls to mind in her allusion to the old U.S. Navy watchword of "one hand for the ship, one hand for yourself" (p. 101), because everything I have done to better understand and implement the standards has only made me more aware of my teaching, and improved it, by making it more "*intentional* [and challenging me to] establish an environment conducive for learning by setting objectives, reinforcing effort, and providing recognition" (Kendall, 2011, p. 28).

Arthur Applebee (2013), in writing more specifically about the Common Core State Standards, offered a detailed analysis that illustrates and confirms "that aligning our teaching [to standards] does not mean we need to abandon all that we have learned about effective curriculum and instruction." Applebee spends much of this journal article analyzing lessons from my own class, which I described in *What's the Big Idea? Question-Driven Units to Motivate Reading, Writing, and Thinking* (Burke, 2010). In his analysis, Applebee notes the following:

> Burke's lessons are quite overtly aligned to standards. Rather than teaching to the tests, these lessons focus on engaging students in cognitively and linguistically challenging tasks in the course of which they will gain the knowledge and skills that the standards require.

> Units with the richness and imagination of those that Burke describes in *What's the Big Idea?* reflect a coming together of the wisdom of practice with the best of current research and theory on the teaching of English language arts. Such teaching does not offer the simple prescriptions that guide classrooms that focus curriculum and instruction more directly on the standards and the tests that accompany them. But the paradox is that by not teaching to the test, students in classrooms like Burke's will do better on tests in general, and at the same time develop the knowledge and skills to do well in other contexts of schooling, life and work. And schools will be much more interesting places to be, for teachers and students alike. (p. 33)

A Brief Orientation to *Your Literacy Standards Companion, Grades 9–12*

One cannot benefit from or use a standards document that demands more time than a teacher or administrator has each day; thus, I seek here to share with you, my fellow educators, these indispensable resources: concise translations of the standards I currently use in my classroom in California, the Common Core standards, along with detailed correlation indexes showing readers in key non–Common Core states exactly which pages of this book have relevant information for them. I created this book in part for myself, to make my job easier as I plan my lessons every evening, write my books, or prepare the workshops I give around the country.

What I offer you here is a compass of sorts to help you—whether you are an administrator or teacher, department chair or district curriculum supervisor, a professor, or a student teacher training to join us in this richly rewarding enterprise called education—understand and make better use of your standards. Here you will find several features I have designed and refined with the help of many teachers, curriculum supervisors, and superintendents with whom I have met and worked around the country in recent years. Because California has adopted the Common Core standards, these standards are naturally the basis for my plan. Still, I think you'll find the features, in combination with the correlation indexes at the front of this book, will provide you with a working compass to navigate your own state standards.

Additional key features, each developed with you in mind, include the following:

A one-page overview of *all* the Common Core anchor standards. The anchor standards form the spine that holds the K–12 ELA standards together. The anchor standards encompass each aspect of English Language Arts: reading, writing, speaking and listening, and language. Beginning in kindergarten and running through grade 12, each grade-specific standard builds incrementally to college and career readiness. If you are in a non–Common Core state, your state standards will be different in specifics, but their purpose and organization are similar. Designed for quick reference, this one-page document offers all users an overview—a place where you can get the lay of the land, no matter what state you're in or what grade you teach.

Side-by-side anchor standards translation. How do anchor standards translate to the classroom? The anchor standards for each category—reading, writing, speaking and listening, and language—appear at the start of each section as a two-page spread with the original Common Core anchor standards on the left and, on the right, their matching translations in more accessible, classroom-friendly language. While the specifics of your standards may differ, you'll undoubtedly find the real-world explications relevant and useful to your situation.

A new user-friendly format for each standard. Instead of the four reading standard domains—literature, informational, social studies, and science and technical subjects— spread throughout the Common Core State Standards document, here you will find the first reading standard for grades 9–10 and 11–12 and the four different domains, for example, all on one page. This allows you to use the book to see at a glance what Reading Standard 1 looks like in grades 9–10 across different text types and subject areas, but also, equally important, shows you what that same informational text standard looks like across grade levels from 9–12 to be sure your curriculum honors the challenge to increase complexity as students move from grade to grade. If you are in a non–Common Core state, the indexes cross-referencing your state standards will point you to the relevant pages.

Parallel translation/what students do. Each standard opens to a two-page spread that has the original Common Core standards on the left (all gathered on that one page for each standard) and a parallel translation of each standard mirrored on the right in more accessible language (referred to on these pages as the "Gist") so you can concentrate on how to *teach* the standards instead of how to understand them, for while they are admirably concise in their original form, they are, nonetheless, remarkably dense texts once you start trying to grasp exactly what they say. These Gist pages align themselves with the original Common Core, so you can move between the two without turning a page as you think about what they mean and how to teach them. Also, beneath each translation of a standard appears a brief but carefully developed list of questions you can teach your students to ask as a way for them to meet that standard. These are meant to be very practical questions students can ask themselves or which you, in the course of teaching them, can pose. Note also that the more advanced requirements added to the 11–12 grade standards are **bolded** for emphasis, quick reference, and ease of use. Again, if you are in a non–Common Core state, the indexes cross-referencing your state standards will direct you to the pages directly relevant to you.

Instructional techniques/what the teacher does. These methods and activities, based on current literacy research, offer teachers across subject areas specific, if concise, suggestions for how to teach that specific standard, the activities specifically linked to the demands of the standard.

Academic vocabulary: key words and phrases. Each standard comes with a unique glossary since words used in more than one standard have a unique meaning in each. Any word or phrase that seemed a source of possible confusion is defined in some detail.

Planning notes/teaching notes. Each standard offers two pages designed to give you a place to transition your curriculum over to your new standards or to make notes about what to teach and how. These pages can serve as a place to capture ideas for yourself or for grade-level teams, departments, schools, and district curriculum offices or for students, teachers, and their professors in a methods class at the university. They can also be copied for additional planning.

How to Use This Book

As each school or department has its own culture, I am reluctant to say what you should do or how you should use *Your Literacy Standards Companion*. Still, a few ideas suggest themselves, which you should adapt, adopt, or avoid as you see fit:

- Provide all teachers in a department or school with a copy to establish a common text to work from and refer to throughout your planning and instructional design work.
- Bring your *Companion* to all meetings for quick reference or planning with colleagues in the school or your department or grade-level team.
- Use your *Companion* to aid in the transition from what you were doing to what you will be doing, treating the planning pages that accompany each standard as a place to note what you do.
- Begin or end meetings with a brief but carefully planned sample lesson or instructional connection, asking one or more colleagues in the school or

department to present and lead a discussion of how it might apply to other classes, grade levels, or subject areas.

- Use the *Companion* in conjunction with your professional learning community (PLC) to add further cohesion and consistency between all your ideas and plans.
- Begin slowly, proceed incrementally, giving it first to key instructional leaders—department chairs, instructional coaches, PLC, or other team leaders—to figure out how best to roll it out to the larger faculty or integrate into teams examining student work or creating new standards-aligned units.

Accepting the Invitation

When I began teaching in the late 1980s, I asked my new department chair what I would be teaching. He smiled and handed me a single sheet of paper with a list of titles on it and wished me luck (always making time to help me if I had questions). Years later, many districts, mine included, had thick binders, binders so heavy with so many standards that they were all ignored since they did not come with the time to read and think about how to teach them. Now we have a new set of standards, which come just as a large group of teachers will retire, leaving an equally large group of new teachers feeling a bit up the river without a paddle, as the saying goes. This book is meant to be that oar or a map you or your faculty or colleagues can use to guide you through the curriculum (which derives from the words *current* and *course*).

These new standards offer me a view of the territory I have crossed to arrive here, having been the first in my family to graduate from college. In a section titled "A Country Called School" from my book *School Smarts: The Four Cs of Academic Success* (Burke, 2004), I wrote of my experience of being a student:

Learning is natural; schooling is not. Schools are countries to which we send our children, expecting these places and the people who work there to help draw out and shape our children into the successful adults we want them to become. As with travel to other countries, however, people only truly benefit from the time spent there to the extent that they can and do participate. If someone doesn't know the language, the customs, the culture—well, that person will feel like the outsider they are. As Gerald Graff, author of *Clueless in Academe* (2003) puts it, "schooling takes students who are perfectly street-smart and exposes them to the life of the mind in ways that make them feel dumb" (p. 2).

This is precisely how I felt when I arrived at college. I lacked any understanding of the language. The culture of academics confused me. The conventions that governed students' behaviors and habits were invisible to me. Those who thrived in school seemed to have been born into the culture, have heard the language all their life, and knew inherently what mattered, what was worth paying attention to, how much effort was appropriate. Teachers somehow seemed to expect that we all came equipped with the same luggage, all of which contained the necessary tools and strategies that would ensure our success in their classes and, ultimately, school. It wasn't so. (p. 1)

When I enrolled in a community college all those years ago, I was placed in a remedial writing class, highlighted whole chapters of textbooks, and had no idea what to say or how to enter class discussions. School extended an invitation to me then that I did not know at first how to accept, so disoriented was I by its demands. Across the country, new state standards extend a similar invitation—and challenge—to us all, teachers and administrators, and all others engaged in the very serious business of educating middle and high school students. It is an invitation I have already accepted on behalf of my students and myself.

Reading these standards, I am reminded of a passage from a wonderful book by Magdalene Lampert (2001) titled *Teaching Problems and the Problems of Teaching*. In that book, she has a chapter titled "Teaching Students to Be People Who Study in School," in which she says of students not unlike the one I was and many of those I teach:

Some students show up at school as "intentional learners"—people who are already interested in doing whatever they need to do to learn academic subjects— they are the exception rather than the rule. Even if they are disposed to study, they probably need to learn how. But more fundamental than knowing how is developing a sense of oneself as a learner that makes it socially acceptable to engage in academic work. The goal of school is not to turn all students into people who see themselves as professional academics, but to enable all of them to include a disposition toward productive study of academic subjects among the personality traits they exhibit while they are in the classroom. If the young people who come to school do not see themselves as learners, they are not going to act like learners even if that would help them to be successful in school. It is the teacher's job to help them change their sense of themselves so that studying is not a self-contradictory activity. (p. 265)

Lampert's statement goes to the core of our work as teachers and these standards, as well. The work ahead will be difficult, as nearly all important work is, because it often asks more of us than we knew we had to give, yet doing the work will give us the strength we need to succeed in the future we are called to create for ourselves and our country. The word "education" stems from the Latin word *educare*, meaning to draw out that which is within, to lead. This is what we must do. I offer you this book to help you do that work and wish you all the strength and patience your two hands can hold.

References

Applebee, A. (2013). Common Core State Standards: The promise and the peril in a national palimpsest. *English Journal, 103*(1), 25–33.

Burke, J. (2004). *School smarts: The four Cs of academic success*. Portsmouth, NH: Heinemann.

Burke, J. (2010). *What's the big idea? Question-driven units to motivate reading, writing, and thinking*. Portsmouth, NH: Heinemann.

Calkins, L., Ehrenworth, M., & Lehman, C. (2012). *Pathways to the common core: Accelerating achievement*. Portsmouth, NH: Heinemann.

Graff, G. (2003). *Clueless in academe: How schooling obscures the life of the mind.* New Haven, CT: Yale University Press.

Jago, C. (2005). *Papers, papers, papers: An English teacher's survival guide.* Portsmouth, NH: Heinemann.

Kendall, J. (2011). *Understanding common core state standards.* Alexandria, VA: Association for Supervision and Curriculum Development.

Lampert, M. (2001). *Teaching problems and the problems of teaching.* New Haven, CT: Yale University Press.

Reading

Key Ideas and Details

1. Read closely to determine what the text says explicitly and to make logical inferences from it; cite specific textual evidence when writing or speaking to support conclusions drawn from the text.

2. Determine central ideas or themes of a text and analyze their development; summarize the key supporting details and ideas.

3. Analyze how and why individuals, events, and ideas develop and interact over the course of a text.

Craft and Structure

4. Interpret words and phrases as they are used in a text, including determining technical, connotative, and figurative meanings, and analyze how specific word choices shape meaning or tone.

5. Analyze the structure of texts, including how specific sentences, paragraphs, and larger portions of the text (e.g., a section, chapter, scene, or stanza) relate to each other and the whole.

6. Assess how point of view or purpose shapes the content and style of a text.

Integration of Knowledge and Ideas

7. Integrate and evaluate content presented in diverse formats and media, including visually and quantitatively, as well as in words.

8. Delineate and evaluate the argument and specific claims in a text, including the validity of the reasoning as well as the relevance and sufficiency of the evidence.

9. Analyze how two or more texts address similar themes or topics to build knowledge or to compare the approaches the authors take.

Range of Reading and Level of Text Complexity

10. Read and comprehend complex literary and informational texts independently and proficiently.

Writing

Text Types and Purposes*

1. Write arguments to support claims in an analysis of substantive topics or texts, using valid reasoning and relevant and sufficient evidence.

2. Write informative/explanatory texts to examine and convey complex ideas and information clearly and accurately through the effective selection, organization, and analysis of content.

3. Write narratives to develop real or imagined experiences or events using effective technique, well-chosen details, and well-structured event sequences.

Production and Distribution of Writing

4. Produce clear and coherent writing in which the development, organization, and style are appropriate to task, purpose, and audience.

5. Develop and strengthen writing as needed by planning, revising, editing, rewriting, or trying a new approach.

6. Use technology, including the Internet, to produce and publish writing and to interact and collaborate with others.

Research to Build and Present Knowledge

7. Conduct short as well as more sustained research projects based on focused questions, demonstrating understanding of the subject under investigation.

8. Gather relevant information from multiple print and digital sources, assess the credibility and accuracy of each source, and integrate the information while avoiding plagiarism.

9. Draw evidence from literary or informational texts to support analysis, reflection, and research.

Range of Writing

10. Write routinely over extended time frames (time for research, reflection, and revision) and shorter time frames (a single sitting or a day or two) for a range of tasks, purposes, and audiences.

Speaking and Listening

Comprehension and Collaboration

1. Prepare for and participate effectively in a range of conversations and collaborations with diverse partners, building on others' ideas and expressing their own clearly and persuasively.

2. Integrate and evaluate information presented in diverse media and formats, including visually, quantitatively, and orally.

3. Evaluate a speaker's point of view, reasoning, and use of evidence and rhetoric.

Presentation of Knowledge and Ideas

4. Present information, findings, and supporting evidence such that listeners can follow the line of reasoning and the organization, development, and style are appropriate to task, purpose, and audience.

5. Make strategic use of digital media and visual displays of data to express information and enhance understanding of presentations.

6. Adapt speech to a variety of contexts and communicative tasks, demonstrating command of formal English when indicated or appropriate.

Language

Conventions of Standard English

1. Demonstrate command of the conventions of standard English grammar and usage when writing or speaking.

2. Demonstrate command of the conventions of standard English capitalization, punctuation, and spelling when writing.

Knowledge of Language

3. Apply knowledge of language to understand how language functions in different contexts, to make effective choices for meaning or style, and to comprehend more fully when reading or listening.

Vocabulary Acquisition and Use

4. Determine or clarify the meaning of unknown and multiple-meaning words and phrases by using context clues, analyzing meaningful word parts, and consulting general and specialized reference materials, as appropriate.

5. Demonstrate understanding of figurative language, word relationships, and nuances in word meanings.

6. Acquire and use accurately a range of general academic and domain-specific words and phrases sufficient for reading, writing, speaking, and listening at the college and career readiness level; demonstrate independence in gathering vocabulary knowledge when considering a word or phrase important to comprehension or expression.

Source: Designed by Jim Burke. Visit www.englishcompanion.com for more information.

Note: For the complete Common Core standards document, please visit corestandards.org.

*These broad types of writing include many subgenres. See Appendix A for definitions of key writing types.

Quick Reference: Common Core State Standards, 6–12 English Language Arts in History/Social Studies, Science, and Technical Subjects

Reading

Key Ideas and Details

1. Read closely to determine what the text says explicitly and to make logical inferences from it; cite specific textual evidence when writing or speaking to support conclusions drawn from the text.

2. Determine central ideas or themes of a text and analyze their development; summarize the key supporting details and ideas.

3. Analyze how and why individuals, events, or ideas develop and interact over the course of a text.

Craft and Structure

4. Interpret words and phrases as they are used in a text, including determining technical, connotative, and figurative meanings, and analyze how specific word choices shape meaning or tone.

5. Analyze the structure of texts, including how specific sentences, paragraphs, and larger portions of the text (e.g., a section, chapter, scene, or stanza) relate to each other and the whole.

6. Assess how point of view or purpose shapes the content and style of a text.

Integration of Knowledge and Ideas

7. Integrate and evaluate content presented in diverse formats and media, including visually and quantitatively, as well as in words.

8. Delineate and evaluate the argument and specific claims in a text, including the validity of the reasoning as well as the relevance and sufficiency of the evidence.

9. Analyze how two or more texts address similar themes or topics in order to build knowledge or to compare the approaches the authors take.

Range of Reading and Level of Text Complexity

10. Read and comprehend complex literary and informational texts independently and proficiently.

Writing

Text Types and Purposes*

1. Write arguments to support claims in an analysis of substantive topics or texts using valid reasoning and relevant and sufficient evidence.

2. Write informative/explanatory texts to examine and convey complex ideas and information clearly and accurately through the effective selection, organization, and analysis of content.

3. Write narratives to develop real or imagined experiences or events using effective technique, well-chosen details, and well-structured event sequences.

Production and Distribution of Writing

4. Produce clear and coherent writing in which the development, organization, and style are appropriate to task, purpose, and audience.

5. Develop and strengthen writing as needed by planning, revising, editing, rewriting, or trying a new approach.

6. Use technology, including the Internet, to produce and publish writing and to interact and collaborate with others.

Research to Build and Present Knowledge

7. Conduct short as well as more sustained research projects based on focused questions, demonstrating understanding of the subject under investigation.

8. Gather relevant information from multiple print and digital sources, assess the credibility and accuracy of each source, and integrate the information while avoiding plagiarism.

9. Draw evidence from literary or informational texts to support analysis, reflection, and research.

Range of Writing

10. Write routinely over extended time frames (time for research, reflection, and revision) and shorter time frames (a single sitting or a day or two) for a range of tasks, purposes, and audiences.

Source: Designed by Jim Burke. Visit www.englishcompanion.com for more information.

Note: For the complete Common Core standards document, please visit corestandards.org.

*These broad types of writing include many subgenres. See Appendix A for definitions of key writing types.

Indexes Cross-Referencing Your State Standards

 Available for download at **resources.corwin.com/literacycompanion9-12**

Alaska, Grades 9–10

Alaska Strand/Standard	Focus of Alaska Standard	For More Information
Reading Literature		
RL.1	Cite strong and thorough textual evidence to support analysis of what the text says explicitly and implicitly	R1 pp. 6–11
RL.2	Determine a theme or central idea of a text and analyze its development and how it is shaped by specific details; summarize the text	R2 pp. 12–17
RL.3	Analyze how characters develop, interact, and advance the plot or develop the theme	R3 pp. 18–23
RL.4	Determine the meaning of words and phrases as they are used in a text, including figurative and connotative meanings; analyze the cumulative impact of word choice on meaning and tone	R4 pp. 24–29
RL.5	Analyze how an author's choices regarding structure, the order of events, and manipulating time create such effects as mystery, tension, or surprise	R5 pp. 30–35
RL.6	Analyze a point of view, perspective, or cultural experience reflected in a piece of literature	R6 pp. 36–41
RL.7	Analyze the representation of a subject or scene in two different artistic mediums, including what is emphasized or absent in each treatment	R7 pp. 42–47
RL.8	NA	
RL.9	Analyze how an author draws on and transforms source material	R9 pp. 54–59
RL.10	Read literature of appropriate complexity independently with proficiency	R10 pp. 60–65
Reading Informational Text		
RI.1	Cite strong and thorough textual evidence to support analysis of what the text says explicitly and implicitly	R1 pp. 6–11
RI.2	Determine the central idea of a text and analyze its development; summarize main ideas or events	R2 pp. 12–17
RI.3	Analyze how the author structures an analysis or series of ideas or events, including the order, how they are developed, and the connections between them	R3 pp. 18–23
RI.4	Determine the meaning of words and phrases in a text; analyze the cumulative impact of specific word choices	R4 pp. 24–29
RI.5	Analyze in detail how ideas or claims are developed by particular sentences, paragraphs, or larger portions of text	R5 pp. 30–35
RI.6	Analyze how an author uses rhetoric to advance a point of view, perspective, or purpose	R6 pp. 36–41
RI.7	Analyze various accounts of a subject told in different mediums	R7 pp. 42–47
RI.8	Evaluate the argument in a text; assess reasoning and evidence; identify false statements and fallacious reasoning	R8 pp. 48–53
RI.9	Analyze U.S. documents of historical and literary significance, noting how they address related themes and concepts	R9 pp. 54–59
RI.10	Read and comprehend appropriately complex informational texts independently and proficiently	R10 pp. 60–65
Writing		
W.1	Write arguments to support claims, using valid reasoning and relevant and sufficient evidence	W1 pp. 70–77
W.2	Write informative/explanatory texts to effectively examine and convey complex ideas, concepts, and information	W2 pp. 78–85
W.3	Write narratives to develop real or imagined experiences or events using effective technique, well-chosen details, and well-structured event sequences	W3 pp. 86–91

(Continued)

Alaska Strand/Standard	Focus of Alaska Standard	For More Information
Writing		
W.4	Produce writing in which the development, organization, style, and features are appropriate to the task, genre, purpose, and audience	W4 pp. 92–97
W.5	Develop and strengthen writing as needed by planning, revising, and editing, rewriting, or trying a new approach	W5 pp. 98–103
W.6	Use technology to produce, publish, and update individual or shared writing projects	W6 pp. 104–109
W.7	Conduct research projects to answer a question or solve a problem; synthesize multiple sources; demonstrate understanding of the subject	W7 pp. 110–115
W.8	Gather information from multiple sources, using advanced searches effectively; assess usefulness of sources; integrate information, avoiding plagiarism	W8 pp. 116–121
W.9	Draw evidence from texts to support analysis, reflection, research, and/or synthesis	W9 pp. 122–127
W.10	Write routinely over shorter and extended time frames for a range of audiences, tasks, and purposes	W10 pp. 128–133
Speaking and Listening		
SL.1	Engage effectively in a range of collaborative discussions with diverse partners, building on others' ideas and expressing their own clearly and persuasively	SL1 pp. 138–143
SL.2	Integrate multiple sources of information presented in diverse media or formats; evaluate credibility and accuracy of sources and noting discrepancies	SL2 pp. 144–149
SL.3	Evaluate a speaker's point of view, reasoning, and use of evidence and rhetoric; identify fallacious reasoning or exaggerated or distorted evidence	SL3 pp. 150–155
SL.4	Present information clearly, concisely, and logically; ensure organization, development, substance, and style are appropriate to purpose, audience, and task	SL4 pp. 156–161
SL.5	Make strategic use of digital media in presentations to enhance understanding and to add interest	SL5 pp. 162–167
SL.6	Adapt speech to a variety of contexts and tasks; demonstrate a command of formal English when appropriate	SL6 pp. 168–173
Language		
L.1	Demonstrate command of the conventions of standard English grammar and usage when writing or speaking	L1 pp. 178–183
L.2	Demonstrate command of the conventions of standard English capitalization, punctuation, and spelling when writing	L2 pp. 184–189
L.3	Apply knowledge of language to make effective choices for meaning or style, to comprehend more fully when reading or listening, and to write and edit so that it conforms to the guidelines in a style manual appropriate for the writing type	L3 pp. 190–195
L.4	Determine or clarify the meaning of unknown and multiple-meaning words and phrases, choosing flexibly from an array of strategies	L4 pp. 196–201
L.5	Demonstrate understanding of figurative language, word relationships, and nuances in word meanings	L5 pp. 202–207
L.6	Acquire and use accurately general academic and domain-specific words and phrases; demonstrate independence in gathering vocabulary knowledge	L6 pp. 208–213
Reading History/Social Studies		
R.1	Cite specific textual evidence to support analysis of primary and secondary sources	R1 pp. 6–11
R.2	Determine central ideas or information of a primary or secondary source; summarize how they develop	R2 pp. 12–17
R.3	Analyze in detail a series of events; determine whether earlier events caused later ones	R3 pp. 18–23
R.4	Determine the meaning of words and phrases, including vocabulary describing political, social, or economic aspects of history/social studies	R4 pp. 24–29
R.5	Analyze how a text uses structure to emphasize key points or advance an explanation or analysis	R5 pp. 30–35
R.6	Compare the point of view of two or more authors for how they treat the same or similar topics	R6 pp. 36–41
R.7	Integrate quantitative or technical analysis with qualitative analysis	R7 pp. 42–47
R.8	Assess the extent to which reasoning and evidence support the author's claim	R8 pp. 48–53
R.9	Compare and contrast treatment of the same topic in several primary and secondary sources	R9 pp. 54–59
R.10	Read and comprehend history/social studies texts of appropriate complexity	R10 pp. 60–65

Alaska Strand/Standard	Focus of Alaska Standard	For More Information
Reading Science/Technical Subjects		
R.1	Cite specific textual evidence to support analysis of science and technical texts	R1 pp. 6–11
R.2	Determine central ideas or conclusions; trace the explanation of a complex process; provide an accurate summary	R2 pp. 12–17
R.3	Follow precisely a complex multistep procedure, attending to special cases or exceptions defined in the text	R3 pp. 18–23
R.4	Determine the meaning of domain-specific words and phrases as they are used in a special scientific or technical context	R4 pp. 24–29
R.5	Analyze the structure of relationships among concepts in a text	R5 pp. 30–35
R.6	Analyze the author's purpose in providing an explanation, describing a procedure, or discussing an experiment	R6 pp. 36–41
R.7	Translate quantitative or technical information expressed in words into visual form, and translate information expressed visually into words	R7 pp. 42–47
R.8	Assess the extent to which reasoning and evidence support the author's claim or recommendation for solving a problem	R8 pp. 48–53
R.9	Compare and contrast findings presented in a text to those from other sources, noting where they support or contradict previous explanations	R9 pp. 54–59
R.10	Read and comprehend science/technical texts of appropriate complexity	R10 pp. 60–65
Writing History/Social Studies, Science and Technical Subjects		
W.1	Write arguments focused on disciple-specific content	W1 pp. 70–77
W.2	Write informative/explanatory texts, including the narration of historical events, scientific procedures, or technical processes	W2 pp. 78–85
W.3	NA	W3 pp. 86–91
W.4	Produce clear and coherent writing in which the development, organization, and style are appropriate to task, purpose, and audience	W4 pp. 92–97
W.5	Develop and strengthen writing as needed by planning, revising, editing, rewriting, or trying a new approach	W5 pp. 98–103
W.6	Use technology to produce, publish, and update individual or shared writing projects	W6 pp. 104–109
W.7	Conduct research projects to answer a question or solve a problem; synthesize multiple sources, demonstrating understanding of the subject	W7 pp. 110–115
W.8	Gather relevant information from multiple print and digital sources; assess the usefulness of each source; integrate information, avoiding plagiarism	W8 pp. 116–121
W.9	Draw evidence from informational texts to support analysis, reflection, and research	W9 pp. 122–127
W.10	Write routinely for a range of discipline-specific tasks, purposes, and audiences	W10 pp. 128–133

Alaska, Grades 11–12

Alaska Strand/Standard	Focus of Alaska Standard	For More Information
Reading Literature		
RL.1	Cite strong and thorough textual evidence to support analysis of what the text says explicitly and implicitly	R1 pp. 6–11
RL.2	Determine two or more themes or central ideas and analyze their development; restate and summarize main ideas or events	R2 pp. 12–17
RL.3	Analyze how characters develop, interact, and advance the plot or develop the theme	R3 pp. 18–23
RL.4	Determine the meaning of words and phrases as they are used in a text, including figurative and connotative meanings; analyze the cumulative impact of word choice on meaning and tone	R4 pp. 24–29
RL.5	Analyze how an author's choices concerning how to structure specific parts of the text contribute to its overall structure and meaning	R5 pp. 30–35

(Continued)

Alaska Strand/Standard	Focus of Alaska Standard	For More Information
Reading Literature		
RL.6	Analyze a case in which grasping point of view requires distinguishing what is directly stated from what is really meant	R6 pp. 36–41
RL.7	Analyze multiple representations of a story, drama, or poem, evaluating how each interprets the source text	R7 pp. 42–47
RL.8	NA	
RL.9	Demonstrate knowledge of 18th, 19th, and early 20th century foundational works of American literature	R9 pp. 54–59
RL.10	Read and comprehend a range of literature from a variety of cultures	R10 pp. 60–65
Reading Informational Text		
RI.1	Cite strong and thorough textual evidence to support analysis of what the text says explicitly and implicitly, including where the text leaves matters uncertain	R1 pp. 6–11
RI.2	Determine two or more central ideas of a text and analyze their development; restate or summarize main ideas or events	R2 pp. 12–17
RI.3	Analyze a complex set of ideas or sequence of events and explain how specific individuals, ideas, or events interact and develop	R3 pp. 18–23
RI.4	Determine the meaning of words and phrases in a text; analyze how an author uses and refines the meaning of key terms over the course of a text	R4 pp. 24–29
RI.5	Analyze and evaluate the effectiveness of the structure in an exposition or argument	R5 pp. 30–35
RI.6	Analyze how an author's style and content contribute to the power, persuasiveness, or impact of the text	R6 pp. 36–41
RI.7	Integrate and evaluate multiple sources of information presented in different media or formats in order to address a question or solve a problem	R7 pp. 42–47
RI.8	Delineate and evaluate the reasoning in seminal U.S. texts, including the application of constitutional principles and use of legal reasoning, and the premises, purposes, and arguments in works of public policy	R8 pp. 48–53
RI.9	Analyze 17th, 18th, and 19th century foundational U.S. and world documents of literary significance	R9 pp. 54–59
RI.10	Read and comprehend literary nonfiction independently and proficiently	R10 pp. 60–65
Writing		
W.1	Write arguments to support claims, using valid reasoning and relevant and sufficient evidence	W1 pp. 70–77
W.2	Write informative/explanatory texts to examine and convey complex ideas, concepts, and information clearly and accurately	W2 pp. 78–85
W.3	Write narratives to develop real or imagined experiences or events using effective technique, well-chosen details, and well-structured event sequences	W3 pp. 86–91
W.4	Produce writing in which the development, organization, style, and features are appropriate to the task, genre, purpose, and audience	W4 pp. 92–97
W.5	Develop and strengthen writing as needed by planning, revising, and editing, rewriting, or trying a new approach	W5 pp. 98–103
W.6	Use technology to produce, publish, and update individual or shared writing projects	W6 pp. 104–109
W.7	Conduct research projects to answer a question or solve a problem; synthesize multiple sources; demonstrate understanding of the subject	W7 pp. 110–115
W.8	Gather information from multiple sources, using advanced searches effectively; assess strengths and limitations of sources; integrate information, avoiding plagiarism and overreliance on any one source	W8 pp. 116–121
W.9	Draw evidence from texts to support analysis, reflection, and research	W9 pp. 122–127
W.10	Write routinely over shorter and extended time frames for a range of audiences, tasks, and purposes	W10 pp. 128–133
Speaking and Listening		
SL.1	Engage effectively in a range of collaborative discussions with diverse partners, building on others' ideas and expressing their own clearly and persuasively	SL1 pp. 138–143
SL.2	Integrate multiple sources of information presented in diverse media or formats; evaluate credibility and accuracy of sources and note discrepancies	SL2 pp. 144–149
SL.3	Evaluate a speaker's point of view, reasoning, and use of evidence and rhetoric; assess the stance, premises, link among ideas, word choice, emphasis, and tone	SL3 pp. 150–155

Alaska Strand/Standard	Focus of Alaska Standard	For More Information
Speaking and Listening		
SL.4	Present information, conveying a clear and distinct perspective, address alternative viewpoints; presentation is appropriate to purpose, audience, and task	SL4 pp. 156–161
SL.5	Make strategic use of digital media in presentations to enhance understanding and to add interest	SL5 pp. 162–167
SL.6	Adapt speech to a variety of contexts and tasks; demonstrate a command of formal English when appropriate	SL6 pp. 168–173
Language		
L.1	Demonstrate command of the conventions of standard English grammar and usage when writing or speaking	L1 pp. 178–183
L.2	Demonstrate command of the conventions of standard English capitalization, punctuation, and spelling when writing	L2 pp. 184–189
L.3	Apply knowledge of language to make effective choices for meaning or style, and to comprehend more fully when reading or listening	L3 pp. 190–195
L.4	Determine or clarify the meaning of unknown and multiple-meaning words and phrases, choosing flexibly from an array of strategies	L4 pp. 196–201
L.5	Demonstrate understanding of figurative language, word relationships, and nuances in word meanings	L5 pp. 202–207
L.6	Acquire and use accurately general academic and domain-specific words and phrases; demonstrate independence in gathering vocabulary knowledge	L6 pp. 208–213
Reading History/Social Studies		
R.1	Cite specific textual evidence to support analysis of primary and secondary sources	R1 pp. 6–11
R.2	Determine central ideas or information of a primary or secondary source; summarize how they develop	R2 pp. 12–17
R.3	Evaluate explanations for actions or events and determine which best accords with textual evidence	R3 pp. 18–23
R.4	Determine the meaning of words and phrases, including figurative and connotative meanings; analyze the impact of specific word choices	R4 pp. 24–29
R.5	Analyze in detail how a complex primary source is structured	R5 pp. 30–35
R.6	Evaluate authors' differing points of view on the same historical event	R6 pp. 36–41
R.7	Integrate and evaluate multiple sources of information presented in diverse formats and media in order to address a question or solve a problem	R7 pp. 42–47
R.8	Evaluate an author's premises, claims, and evidence by corroborating or challenging them	R8 pp. 48–53
R.9	Integrate information from diverse sources into a coherent understanding of an idea or event	R9 pp. 54–59
R.10	Read and comprehend history/social studies texts of appropriate complexity	R10 pp. 60–65
Reading Science/Technical Subjects		
R.1	Cite specific textual evidence to support analysis of science and technical texts	R1 pp. 6–11
R.2	Determine central ideas or conclusions; summarize complex concepts by paraphrasing into simpler but accurate terms	R2 pp. 12–17
R.3	Follow precisely a complex multistep procedure; analyze the results based on explanations in the text	R3 pp. 18–23
R.4	Determine the meaning of domain-specific words and phrases as they are used in a special scientific or technical context	R4 pp. 24–29
R.5	Analyze how the text structures information into categories or hierarchies, demonstrating understanding	R5 pp. 30–35
R.6	Analyze the author's purpose in providing an explanation, describing a procedure, or discussing an experiment	R6 pp. 36–41
R.7	Integrate and evaluate multiple sources of information presented in diverse formats and media in order to address a question or solve a problem	R7 pp. 42–47
R.8	Evaluate the hypotheses, data, analysis, and conclusions in a science or technical text, corroborating or challenging conclusions	R8 pp. 48–53
R.9	Synthesize information from a range of sources into a coherent understanding, resolving conflicting information when possible	R9 pp. 54–59
R.10	Read and comprehend science/technical texts of appropriate complexity	R10 pp. 60–65

(Continued)

Alaska Strand/Standard	Focus of Alaska Standard	For More Information
Writing History/Social Studies, Science and Technical Subjects		
W.1	Write arguments focused on disciple-specific content	W1 pp. 70–77
W.2	Write informative/explanatory texts, including the narration of historical events, scientific procedures, or technical processes	W2 pp. 78–85
W.3	NA	
W.4	Produce clear and coherent writing in which the development, organization, and style are appropriate to task, purpose, and audience	W4 pp. 92–97
W.5	Develop and strengthen writing as needed by planning, revising, editing, rewriting, or trying a new approach	W5 pp. 98–103
W.6	Use technology to produce, publish, and update individual or shared writing projects	W6 pp. 104–109
W.7	Conduct research projects to answer a question or solve a problem; synthesize multiple sources, demonstrating understanding of the subject	W7 pp. 110–115
W.8	Gather relevant information from multiple print and digital sources; assess the usefulness of each source; integrate information, avoiding plagiarism and overreliance on any one source	W8 pp. 116–121
W.9	Draw evidence from informational texts to support analysis, reflection, and research	W9 pp. 122–127
W.10	Write routinely for a range of discipline-specific tasks, purposes, and audiences	W10 pp. 128–133

Arizona, Grades 9–10

Arizona Strand/Standard	Focus of Arizona Standard	For More Information
Reading Literature		
RL.1	Cite strong and thorough textual evidence to support analysis of what the text says explicitly and implicitly	R1 pp. 6–11
RL.2	Determine a theme or central idea of a text and analyze its development and how it is shaped by specific details; summarize the text	R2 pp. 12–17
RL.3	Analyze how characters develop, interact, and advance the plot or develop the theme	R3 pp. 18–23
RL.4	Determine the meaning of words and phrases as they are used in a text, including figurative and connotative meanings; analyze the cumulative impact of word choice on meaning and tone	R4 pp. 24–29
RL.5	Analyze how an author's choices regarding structure, the order of events, and manipulating time create such effects as mystery, tension, or surprise	R5 pp. 30–35
RL.6	Analyze a point of view, perspective, or cultural experience reflected in a piece of literature	R6 pp. 36–41
RL.7	Analyze the representation of a subject or scene in two different artistic mediums, including what is emphasized or absent in each treatment	R7 pp. 42–47
RL.8	NA	
RL.9	Analyze how an author draws on and transforms source material	R9 pp. 54–59
RL.10	Read literature of appropriate complexity independently with proficiency	R10 pp. 60–65
Reading Informational Text		
RI.1	Cite strong and thorough textual evidence to support analysis of what the text says explicitly and implicitly	R1 pp. 6–11
RI.2	Determine the central idea of a text and analyze its development; summarize main ideas or events	R2 pp. 12–17
RI.3	Analyze how the author structures an analysis or series of ideas or events, including the order, how they are developed, and the connections between them	R3 pp. 18–23
RI.4	Determine the meaning of words and phrases in a text; analyze the cumulative impact of specific word choices	R4 pp. 24–29
RI.5	Analyze in detail how ideas or claims are developed by particular sentences, paragraphs, or larger portions of text	R5 pp. 30–35
RI.6	Analyze how an author uses rhetoric to advance a point of view, perspective, or purpose	R6 pp. 36–41

Arizona Strand/Standard	Focus of Arizona Standard	For More Information
Reading Informational Text		
RI.7	Analyze various accounts of a subject told in different mediums	R7 pp. 42–47
RI.8	Evaluate the argument in a text; assess reasoning and evidence; identify false statements and fallacious reasoning	R8 pp. 48–53
RI.9	Analyze U.S. documents of historical and literary significance, noting how they address related themes and concepts	R9 pp. 54–59
RI.10	Read and comprehend appropriately complex informational texts independently and proficiently	R10 pp. 60–65
Writing		
W.1	Write arguments to support claims, using valid reasoning and relevant and sufficient evidence	W1 pp. 70–77
W.2	Write informative/explanatory texts to effectively examine and convey complex ideas, concepts, and information	W2 pp. 78–85
W.3	Write narratives to develop real or imagined experiences or events using effective technique, well-chosen details, and well-structured event sequences	W3 pp. 86–91
W.4	Produce writing in which the development, organization, style, and features are appropriate to the task, genre, purpose, and audience	W4 pp. 92–97
W.5	Develop and strengthen writing as needed by planning, revising, and editing, rewriting, or trying a new approach	W5 pp. 98–103
W.6	Use technology to produce, publish, and update individual or shared writing projects	W6 pp. 104–109
W.7	Conduct research projects to answer a question or solve a problem; synthesize multiple sources; demonstrate understanding of the subject	W7 pp. 110–115
W.8	Gather information from multiple sources, using advanced searches effectively; assess usefulness of sources; integrate information, avoiding plagiarism	W8 pp. 116–121
W.9	Draw evidence from texts to support analysis, reflection, research, and/or synthesis	W9 pp. 122–127
W.10	Write routinely over short and extended time frames for a range of audiences, tasks, and purposes	W10 pp. 128–133
Speaking and Listening		
SL.1	Engage effectively in a range of collaborative discussions with diverse partners, building on others' ideas and expressing their own clearly and persuasively	SL1 pp. 138–143
SL.2	Integrate multiple sources of information presented in diverse media or formats; evaluate credibility and accuracy of sources and noting discrepancies	SL2 pp. 144–149
SL.3	Evaluate a speaker's point of view, reasoning, and use of evidence and rhetoric; identify fallacious reasoning or exaggerated or distorted evidence	SL3 pp. 150–155
SL.4	Present information clearly, concisely, and logically; ensure organization, development, substance, and style are appropriate to purpose, audience, and task	SL4 pp. 156–161
SL.5	Make strategic use of digital media in presentations to enhance understanding and to add interest	SL5 pp. 162–167
SL.6	Adapt speech to a variety of contexts and tasks; demonstrate a command of formal English when appropriate	SL6 pp. 168–173
Language		
L.1	Demonstrate command of the conventions of standard English grammar and usage when writing or speaking	L1 pp. 178–183
L.2	Demonstrate command of the conventions of standard English capitalization, punctuation, and spelling when writing	L2 pp. 184–189
L.3	Apply knowledge of language to make effective choices for meaning or style, and to comprehend more fully when reading or listening	L3 pp. 190–195
L.4	Determine or clarify the meaning of unknown and multiple-meaning words and phrases, choosing flexibly from an array of strategies	L4 pp. 196–201
L.5	Demonstrate understanding of figurative language, word relationships, and nuances in word meanings	L5 pp. 202–207
L.6	Acquire and use accurately general academic and domain-specific words and phrases; demonstrate independence in gathering vocabulary knowledge	L6 pp. 208–213

(Continued)

Arizona Strand/Standard	Focus of Arizona Standard	For More Information
Reading History/Social Studies		
RH.1	Cite specific textual evidence to support analysis of primary and secondary sources	R1 pp. 6–11
RH.2	Determine central ideas or information of a primary or secondary source; summarize how they develop	R2 pp. 12–17
RH.3	Analyze in detail a series of events; determine whether earlier events caused later ones	R3 pp. 18–23
RH.4	Determine the meaning of words and phrases, including vocabulary describing political, social, or economic aspects of history/social studies	R4 pp. 24–29
RH.5	Analyze how a text uses structure to emphasize key points or advance an explanation or analysis	R5 pp. 30–35
RH.6	Compare the point of view of two or more authors for how they treat the same or similar topics	R6 pp. 36–41
RH.7	Integrate quantitative or technical analysis with qualitative analysis	R7 pp. 42–47
RH.8	Assess the extent to which reasoning and evidence support the author's claim	R8 pp. 48–53
RH.9	Compare and contrast treatment of the same topic in several primary and secondary sources	R9 pp. 54–59
RH.10	Read and comprehend history/social studies texts of appropriate complexity	R10 pp. 60–65
Reading Science/Technical Subjects		
RST.1	Cite specific textual evidence to support analysis of science and technical texts	R1 pp. 6–11
RST.2	Determine central ideas or conclusions; trace the explanation of a complex process; provide an accurate summary	R2 pp. 12–17
RST.3	Follow precisely a complex multistep procedure, attending to special cases or exceptions defined in the text	R3 pp. 18–23
RST.4	Determine the meaning of domain-specific words and phrases as they are used in a special scientific or technical context	R4 pp. 24–29
RST.5	Analyze the structure of relationships among concepts in a text	R5 pp. 30–35
RST.6	Analyze the author's purpose in providing an explanation, describing a procedure, or discussing an experiment	R6 pp. 36–41
RST.7	Translate quantitative or technical information expressed in words into visual form, and translate information expressed visually into words	R7 pp. 42–47
RST.8	Assess the extent to which reasoning and evidence support the author's claim or recommendation for solving a problem	R8 pp. 48–53
RST.9	Compare and contrast findings presented in a text to those from other sources, noting where they support or contradict previous explanations	R9 pp. 54–59
RST.10	Read and comprehend science/technical texts of appropriate complexity	R10 pp. 60–65
Writing History/Social Studies, Science and Technical Subjects		
WHST.1	Write arguments focused on disciple-specific content	W1 pp. 70–77
WHST.2	Write informative/explanatory texts, including the narration of historical events, scientific procedures, or technical processes	W2 pp. 78–85
WHST.3	NA	
WHST.4	Produce clear and coherent writing in which the development, organization, and style are appropriate to task, purpose, and audience	W4 pp. 92–97
WHST.5	Develop and strengthen writing as needed by planning, revising, editing, rewriting, or trying a new approach	W5 pp. 98–103
WHST.6	Use technology to produce, publish, and update individual or shared writing projects	W6 pp. 104–109
WHST.7	Conduct research projects to answer a question or solve a problem; synthesize multiple sources, demonstrating understanding of the subject	W7 pp. 110–115
WHST.8	Gather relevant information from multiple print and digital sources; assess the usefulness of each source; integrate information, avoiding plagiarism	W8 pp. 116–121
WHST.9	Draw evidence from informational texts to support analysis, reflection, and research	W9 pp. 122–127
WHST.10	Write routinely for a range of discipline-specific tasks, purposes, and audiences	W10 pp. 128–133

Arizona, Grades 11–12

Arizona Strand/Standard	Focus of Arizona Standard	For More Information
Reading Literature		
RL.1	Cite strong and thorough textual evidence to support analysis of what the text says explicitly and implicitly	R1 pp. 6–11
RL.2	Determine two or more themes or central ideas and analyze their development; restate and summarize main ideas or events	R2 pp. 12–17
RL.3	Analyze the impact of the author's choices regarding how to develop and relate elements of a story	R3 pp. 18–23
RL.4	Determine the meaning of words and phrases as they are used in a text, including figurative and connotative meanings; analyze the cumulative impact of word choice on meaning and tone	R4 pp. 24–29
RL.5	Analyze how an author's choices concerning how to structure specific parts of the text contribute to its overall structure and meaning	R5 pp. 30–35
RL.6	Analyze a case in which grasping point of view requires distinguishing what is directly stated from what is really meant	R6 pp. 36–41
RL.7	Analyze multiple representations of a story, drama, or poem, evaluating how each interprets the source text	R7 pp. 42–47
RL.8	NA	
RL.9	Demonstrate knowledge of 18th, 19th, and early 20th century foundational works of American literature	R9 pp. 54–59
RL.10	Read and comprehend a range of literature from a variety of cultures	R10 pp. 60–65
Reading Informational Text		
RI.1	Cite strong and thorough textual evidence to support analysis of what the text says explicitly and implicitly, including where the text leaves matters uncertain	R1 pp. 6–11
RI.2	Determine two or more central ideas of a text and analyze their development; restate or summarize main ideas or events	R2 pp. 12–17
RI.3	Analyze a complex set of ideas or sequence of events and explain how specific individuals, ideas, or events interact and develop	R3 pp. 18–23
RI.4	Determine the meaning of words and phrases in a text; analyze how an author uses and refines the meaning of key terms over the course of a text	R4 pp. 24–29
RI.5	Analyze and evaluate the effectiveness of the structure in an exposition or argument	R5 pp. 30–35
RI.6	Analyze how an author's style and content contribute to the power, persuasiveness, or impact of the text	R6 pp. 36–41
RI.7	Integrate and evaluate multiple sources of information presented in different media or formats in order to address a question or solve a problem	R7 pp. 42–47
RI.8	Delineate and evaluate the reasoning in seminal U.S. texts, including the application of constitutional principles and use of legal reasoning, and the premises, purposes, and arguments in works of public policy	R8 pp. 48–53
RI.9	Analyze 17th, 18th, and 19th century foundational U.S. and world documents of literary significance	R9 pp. 54–59
RI.10	Read and comprehend literary nonfiction independently and proficiently	R10 pp. 60–65
Writing		
W.1	Write arguments to support claims, using valid reasoning and relevant and sufficient evidence	W1 pp. 70–77
W.2	Write informative/explanatory texts to examine and convey complex ideas, concepts, and information clearly and accurately	W2 pp. 78–85
W.3	Write narratives to develop real or imagined experiences or events using effective technique, well-chosen details, and well-structured event sequences	W3 pp. 86–91
W.4	Produce writing in which the development, organization, style, and features are appropriate to the task, genre, purpose, and audience	W4 pp. 92–97
W.5	Develop and strengthen writing as needed by planning, revising, and editing, rewriting, or trying a new approach	W5 pp. 98–103
W.6	Use technology to produce, publish, and update individual or shared writing projects	W6 pp. 104–109

(Continued)

Arizona Strand/Standard	Focus of Arizona Standard	For More Information
Writing		
W.7	Conduct research projects to answer a question or solve a problem; synthesize multiple sources; demonstrate understanding of the subject	W7 pp. 110–115
W.8	Gather information from multiple sources, using advanced searches effectively; assess strengths and limitations of sources; integrate information, avoiding plagiarism and overreliance on any one source	W8 pp. 116–121
W.9	Draw evidence from texts to support analysis, reflection, and research	W9 pp. 122–127
W.10	Write routinely over short and extended time frames for a range of audiences, tasks, and purposes	W10 pp. 128–133
Speaking and Listening		
SL.1	Engage effectively in a range of collaborative discussions with diverse partners, building on others' ideas and expressing their own clearly and persuasively	SL1 pp. 138–143
SL.2	Integrate multiple sources of information presented in diverse media or formats; evaluate credibility and accuracy of sources and note discrepancies	SL2 pp. 144–149
SL.3	Evaluate a speaker's point of view, reasoning, and use of evidence and rhetoric; assess the stance, premises, link among ideas, word choice, emphasis, and tone	SL3 pp. 150–155
SL.4	Present information, conveying a clear and distinct perspective, address alternative viewpoints; presentation is appropriate to purpose, audience, and task	SL4 pp. 156–161
SL.5	Make strategic use of digital media in presentations to enhance understanding and to add interest	SL5 pp. 162–167
SL.6	Adapt speech to a variety of contexts and tasks; demonstrate a command of formal English when appropriate	SL6 pp. 168–173
Language		
L.1	Demonstrate command of the conventions of standard English grammar and usage when writing or speaking	L1 pp. 178–183
L.2	Demonstrate command of the conventions of standard English capitalization, punctuation, and spelling when writing	L2 pp. 184–189
L.3	Apply knowledge of language to make effective choices for meaning or style, and to comprehend more fully when reading or listening	L3 pp. 190–195
L.4	Determine or clarify the meaning of unknown and multiple-meaning words and phrases, choosing flexibly from an array of strategies	L4 pp. 196–201
L.5	Demonstrate understanding of figurative language, word relationships, and nuances in word meanings	L5 pp. 202–207
L.6	Acquire and use accurately general academic and domain-specific words and phrases; demonstrate independence in gathering vocabulary knowledge	L6 pp. 208–213
Reading History/Social Studies		
RH.1	Cite specific textual evidence to support analysis of primary and secondary sources	R1 pp. 6–11
RH.2	Determine central ideas or information of a primary or secondary source; summarize how they develop	R2 pp. 12–17
RH.3	Evaluate explanations for actions or events and determine which best accords with textual evidence	R3 pp. 18–23
RH.4	Determine the meaning of words and phrases, including figurative and connotative meanings; analyze the impact of specific word choices	R4 pp. 24–29
RH.5	Analyze in detail how a complex primary source is structured	R5 pp. 30–35
RH.6	Evaluate authors' differing points of view on the same historical event	R6 pp. 36–41
RH.7	Integrate and evaluate multiple sources of information presented in diverse formats and media in order to address a question or solve a problem	R7 pp. 42–47
RH.8	Evaluate an author's premises, claims, and evidence by corroborating or challenging them	R8 pp. 48–53
RH.9	Integrate information from diverse sources into a coherent understanding of an idea or event	R9 pp. 54–59
RH.10	Read and comprehend history/social studies texts of appropriate complexity	R10 pp. 60–65
Reading Science/Technical Subjects		
RST.1	Cite specific textual evidence to support analysis of science and technical texts	R1 pp. 6–11
RST.2	Determine central ideas or conclusions; summarize complex concepts by paraphrasing into simpler but accurate terms	R2 pp. 12–17

Arizona Strand/Standard	Focus of Arizona Standard	For More Information
Reading Science/Technical Subjects		
RST.3	Follow precisely a complex multistep procedure; analyze the results based on explanations in the text	R3 pp. 18–23
RST.4	Determine the meaning of domain-specific words and phrases as they are used in a special scientific or technical context	R4 pp. 24–29
RST.5	Analyze how the text structures information into categories or hierarchies, demonstrating understanding	R5 pp. 30–35
RST.6	Analyze the author's purpose in providing an explanation, describing a procedure, or discussing an experiment	R6 pp. 36–41
RST.7	Integrate and evaluate multiple sources of information presented in diverse formats and media in order to address a question or solve a problem	R7 pp. 42–47
RST.8	Evaluate the hypotheses, data, analysis, and conclusions in a science or technical text, corroborating or challenging conclusions	R8 pp. 48–53
RST.9	Synthesize information from a range of sources into a coherent understanding, resolving conflicting information when possible	R9 pp. 54–59
RST.10	Read and comprehend science/technical texts of appropriate complexity	R10 pp. 60–65
Writing History/Social Studies, Science and Technical Subjects		
WHST.1	Write arguments focused on discipline-specific content	W1 pp. 70–77
WHST.2	Write informative/explanatory texts, including the narration of historical events, scientific procedures, or technical processes	W2 pp. 78–85
WHST.3	NA	
WHST.4	Produce clear and coherent writing in which the development, organization, and style are appropriate to task, purpose, and audience	W4 pp. 92–97
WHST.5	Develop and strengthen writing as needed by planning, revising, editing, rewriting, or trying a new approach	W5 pp. 98–103
WHST.6	Use technology to produce, publish, and update individual or shared writing projects	W6 pp. 104–109
WHST.7	Conduct research projects to answer a question or solve a problem; synthesize multiple sources, demonstrating understanding of the subject	W7 pp. 110–115
WHST.8	Gather relevant information from multiple print and digital sources; assess the usefulness of each source; integrate information, avoiding plagiarism and overreliance on any one source	W8 pp. 116–121
WHST.9	Draw evidence from informational texts to support analysis, reflection, and research	W9 pp. 122–127
WHST.10	Write routinely for a range of discipline-specific tasks, purposes, and audiences	W10 pp. 128–133

Arkansas, Grades 9–10

Arkansas Strand/Standard	Focus of Arkansas Standard	For More Information
Reading Literature		
RL.1	Cite strong and thorough textual evidence to support analysis of what the text says explicitly and implicitly	R1 pp. 6–11
RL.2	Determine a theme of a text and analyze its development; provide a summary	R2 pp. 12–17
RL.3	Analyze how characters develop, interact, and advance the plot or develop the theme	R3 pp. 18–23
RL.4	Determine the meaning of words and phrases as they are used in a text, including figurative and connotative meanings; analyze the cumulative impact of word choice on meaning and tone	R4 pp. 24–29
RL.5	Analyze how an author's choices regarding structure, the order of events, and manipulating time create such effects as mystery, tension, or surprise	R5 pp. 30–35
RL.6	Analyze a point of view, perspective, or cultural experience reflected in a piece of literature	R6 pp. 36–41
RL.7	Analyze the representation of a subject in two different artistic mediums	R7 pp. 42–47

(Continued)

Arkansas Strand/Standard	Focus of Arkansas Standard	For More Information
Reading Literature		
RL.8	NA	
RL.9	Analyze how an author draws on and transforms source material	R9 pp. 54–59
RL.10	Read literature of appropriate complexity independently with proficiency	R10 pp. 60–65
Reading Informational Text		
RI.1	Cite strong and thorough textual evidence to support analysis of what the text says explicitly and implicitly	R1 pp. 6–11
RI.2	Determine the main idea of a text and analyze its development; provide a summary	R2 pp. 12–17
RI.3	Analyze how the author structures an analysis or series of ideas or events, including the order, how they are developed, and the connections between them	R3 pp. 18–23
RI.4	Determine the meaning of words and phrases in a text; analyze the cumulative impact of specific word choices	R4 pp. 24–29
RI.5	Analyze in detail how ideas or claims are developed by particular sentences, paragraphs, or larger portions of text	R5 pp. 30–35
RI.6	Analyze how an author uses rhetoric to advance a point of view, perspective, or purpose	R6 pp. 36–41
RI.7	Analyze various accounts of a subject told in different mediums	R7 pp. 42–47
RI.8	Evaluate the argument in a text; assess reasoning and evidence; identify false statements and fallacious reasoning	R8 pp. 48–53
RI.9	Analyze documents of historical and literary significance, noting how they address related themes and concepts	R9 pp. 54–59
RI.10	Read and comprehend appropriately complex informational texts independently and proficiently	R10 pp. 60–65
Writing		
W.1	Write arguments to support claims, using valid reasoning and relevant and sufficient evidence	W1 pp. 70–77
W.2	Write effective informative/explanatory texts effectively examine and convey complex ideas, concepts, and information	W2 pp. 78–85
W.3	Write narratives to develop real or imagined experiences or events using effective technique, well-chosen details, and well-structured event sequences	W3 pp. 86–91
W.4	Produce writing in which the development and organization are appropriate to the task and purpose	W4 pp. 92–97
W.5	Develop and strengthen writing as needed by planning, revising, and editing, or trying a new approach	W5 pp. 98–103
W.6	Use technology to produce, publish, and update individual or shared writing projects	W6 pp. 104–109
W.7	Conduct research projects to answer a question or solve a problem; synthesize multiple sources; demonstrate understanding	W7 pp. 110–115
W.8	Recall information from experiences or gather information from print and digital sources	W8 pp. 116–121
W.9	Draw evidence from texts to support analysis, reflection, research, and/or synthesis	W9 pp. 122–127
W.10	Write routinely over shorter and extended time frames	W10 pp. 128–133
Speaking and Listening		
SL.1	Engage effectively in a range of collaborative discussions with diverse partners, building on others' ideas and expressing their own clearly	SL1 pp. 138–143
SL.2	Integrate multiple sources of information gained by means other than reading; evaluate credibility and accuracy of sources	SL2 pp. 144–149
SL.3	Evaluate a speaker's perspective, reasoning, and use of evidence and rhetoric; identify fallacious reasoning	SL3 pp. 150–155
SL.4	Present information clearly, concisely, and logically; ensure organization, development, substance, and style are appropriate to purpose, audience, and task	SL4 pp. 156–161
SL.5	Make strategic use of digital media in presentations to enhance understanding and to add interest	SL5 pp. 162–167
SL.6	Adapt speech to a variety of contexts and tasks; demonstrate a command of formal English when appropriate	SL6 pp. 168–173

Arkansas Strand/Standard	Focus of Arkansas Standard	For More Information
Language		
L.1	Demonstrate command of the conventions of standard English grammar and usage when writing or speaking	L1 pp. 178–183
L.2	Demonstrate command of the conventions of standard English capitalization, punctuation, and spelling when writing	L2 pp. 184–189
L.3	Apply knowledge of language to make effective choices for meaning or style, and to comprehend more fully when reading or listening	L3 pp. 190–195
L.4	Determine or clarify the meaning of unknown and multiple-meaning words and phrases, choosing flexibly from an array of strategies	L4 pp. 196–201
L.5	Demonstrate understanding of figurative language, word relationships, and nuances in word meanings	L5 pp. 202–207
L.6	Acquire and use accurately general academic and domain-specific words and phrases; demonstrate independence in gathering vocabulary knowledge	L6 pp. 208–213

Arkansas, Grades 11–12

Arkansas Strand/Standard	Focus of Arkansas Standard	For More Information
Reading Literature		
RL.1	Cite strong and thorough textual evidence to support analysis of what the text says explicitly and implicitly	R1 pp. 6–11
RL.2	Determine two or more themes of a text and analyze their development; provide a summary	R2 pp. 12–17
RL.3	Analyze how characterization, plot, setting, and other elements interact and contribute to the development of a text	R3 pp. 18–23
RL.4	Determine the meaning of words and phrases as they are used in a text, including figurative and connotative meanings; analyze the cumulative impact of word choice on meaning and tone	R4 pp. 24–29
RL.5	Analyze how an author's choices regarding how to structure specific parts of a text contribute to its overall structure and meaning	R5 pp. 30–35
RL.6	Analyze a case where grasping perspective and/or purpose requires distinguishing what is directly stated from what is really meant	R6 pp. 36–41
RL.7	Analyze the representation of a subject in two different artistic mediums	R7 pp. 42–47
RL.8	NA	
RL.9	Analyze how two or more influential literary works from the same time period address similar themes	R9 pp. 54–59
RL.10	Read literature of appropriate complexity independently with proficiency	R10 pp. 60–65
Reading Informational Text		
RI.1	Cite strong and thorough textual evidence to support analysis of what the text says explicitly and implicitly	R1 pp. 6–11
RI.2	Determine two or more central ideas of a text and analyze their development; provide a summary	R2 pp. 12–17
RI.3	Analyze and explain how individuals, ideas, or events interact and develop over the course of a text	R3 pp. 18–23
RI.4	Determine the meaning of words and phrases in a text; analyze how an author uses and refines the meaning of key terms over the course of a text	R4 pp. 24–29
RI.5	Analyze in detail how ideas or claims are developed by particular sentences, paragraphs, or larger portions of text	R5 pp. 30–35
RI.6	Evaluate the effectiveness of the text's structure, including whether the structure makes points clear, convincing, and engaging	R6 pp. 36–41
RI.7	Integrate and evaluate multiple sources of information presented in diverse media or formats	R7 pp. 42–47
RI.8	Evaluate the reasoning, premises, purposes, and arguments in texts such as works of public advocacy	R8 pp. 48–53

(Continued)

Arkansas Strand/Standard	Focus of Arkansas Standard	For More Information
Reading Informational Text		
RI.9	Analyze documents of historical and literary significance, for their themes, purposes, and rhetorical features	R9 pp. 54–59
RI.10	Read and comprehend appropriately complex informational texts independently and proficiently	R10 pp. 60–65
Writing		
W.1	Write arguments to support claims, using valid reasoning and relevant and sufficient evidence	W1 pp. 70–77
W.2	Write effective informative/explanatory texts; effectively examine and convey complex ideas, concepts, and information	W2 pp. 78–85
W.3	Write narratives to develop real or imagined experiences or events using effective technique, well-chosen details, and well-structured event sequences	W3 pp. 86–91
W.4	Produce clear, coherent writing in which the development and organization are appropriate to the task and purpose	W4 pp. 92–97
W.5	Develop and strengthen writing as needed by planning, revising, and editing, or trying a new approach	W5 pp. 98–103
W.6	Use technology to produce, publish, and update individual or shared writing projects	W6 pp. 104–109
W.7	Conduct research projects to answer a question or solve a problem; synthesize multiple sources; demonstrate understanding	W7 pp. 110–115
W.8	Gather, assess, and integrate relevant information from multiple print and digital sources, using advanced searches effectively	W8 pp. 116–121
W.9	Draw evidence from texts to support analysis, reflection, research, and/or synthesis	W9 pp. 122–127
W.10	Write routinely over shorter and extended time frames	W10 pp. 128–133
Speaking and Listening		
SL.1	Engage effectively in a range of collaborative discussions with diverse partners, building on others' ideas and expressing their own persuasively	SL1 pp. 138–143
SL.2	Integrate multiple sources of information gained by means other than reading; evaluate credibility and accuracy of sources, and note discrepancies	SL2 pp. 144–149
SL.3	Evaluate a speaker's perspective, reasoning, and use of evidence and rhetoric; assess stance, premises, word choice, points of emphasis, and tone	SL3 pp. 150–155
SL.4	Present information, conveying a clear perspective, addressing alternative perspectives; organization, substance, style are appropriate to purpose, audience, and task	SL4 pp. 156–161
SL.5	Make strategic use of digital media in presentations to enhance understanding and to add interest	SL5 pp. 162–167
SL.6	Adapt speech to a variety of contexts and tasks; demonstrate a command of formal English when appropriate	SL6 pp. 168–173
Language		
L.1	Demonstrate command of the conventions of standard English grammar and usage when writing or speaking	L1 pp. 178–183
L.2	Demonstrate command of the conventions of standard English capitalization, punctuation, and spelling when writing	L2 pp. 184–189
L.3	Apply knowledge of language to make effective choices for meaning or style, and to comprehend more fully when reading or listening	L3 pp. 190–195
L.4	Determine or clarify the meaning of unknown and multiple-meaning words and phrases, choosing flexibly from an array of strategies	L4 pp. 196–201
L.5	Demonstrate understanding of figurative language, word relationships, and nuances in word meanings	L5 pp. 202–207
L.6	Acquire and use accurately general academic and domain-specific words and phrases; demonstrate independence in gathering vocabulary knowledge	L6 pp. 208–213

Colorado, Grade 9

Colorado Strand/Standard	Focus of Colorado Standard	For More Information
Oral Expression and Listening		
1	Oral presentations require effective preparation strategies	SL5 pp. 162–167 SL6 pp. 168–173
2	Listening critically to comprehend a speaker's message requires mental and physical strategies to direct and maintain attention	SL1 pp. 138–143 SL2 pp. 144–149
Reading for All Purposes		
1	Increasingly complex literary element in traditional and contemporary works of literature require scrutiny and comparison	R2 pp. 12–17 R3 pp. 18–23 R5 pp. 30–35 R6 pp. 36–41 R9 pp. 54–59 R10 pp. 60–65
2	Increasingly complex informational texts require mature interpretation and study	R2 pp. 12–17 R3 pp. 18–23 R5 pp. 30–35 R6 pp. 36–41 R8 pp. 48–53 R10 pp. 60–65
Writing and Composition		
1	Literary and narrative texts develop a controlling idea or theme with descriptive and expressive language	W3 pp. 86–91
2	Informational and persuasive texts develop a topic and establish a controlling idea or theme with relevant support	W1 pp. 70–77
3	Writing for grammar, usage, mechanics, and clarity requires ongoing refinements and revisions	L2 pp. 184–189 L4 pp. 196–201 L5 pp. 202–207 L6 pp. 208–213
Research and Reasoning		
1	Informational materials, including electronic sources, need to be collected, evaluated, and analyzed for accuracy, relevance, and effectiveness in answering research questions	NA
2	Effective problem-solving strategies require high-quality reasoning	NA

Colorado, Grade 10

Colorado Strand/Standard	Focus of Colorado Standard	For More Information
Oral Expression and Listening		
1	Content that is gathered carefully and organized will successfully influences an audience	SL4 pp. 156–161
2	Effectively operating in small and large groups to accomplish a goal requires active listening	SL1 pp. 138–143 SL3 pp. 150–155
Reading for All Purposes		
1	Literary and historical influences determine the meaning of traditional and contemporary literary texts	R1 pp. 6–11 R4 pp. 24–29 R5 pp. 30–35 R7 pp. 42–47 R10 pp. 60–65

(Continued)

Colorado Strand/Standard	Focus of Colorado Standard	For More Information
Reading for All Purposes		
2	The development of new ideas and concepts within informational and persuasive manuscripts	R1 pp. 6–11 R4 pp. 24–29 R7 pp. 42–47 R9 pp. 54–59 R10 pp. 60–65
3	Context, parts of speech, grammar, and word choice influence the understanding of literary, persuasive, and informational texts	L4 pp. 196–201 L5 pp. 202–207 L6 pp. 208–213
Writing and Composition		
1	Literary and narrative genres feature a variety of stylistic devices to engage or entertain an audience	W3 pp. 86–91
2	Organizational writing patterns inform or persuade an audience	W2 pp. 78–85
3	Grammar, language usage, mechanics, and clarity are the basis of ongoing refinements and revisions within the writing process	L1 pp. 178–183 L2 pp. 184–189 L3 pp. 190–195 W4 pp. 92–97 W5 pp. 98–103 W6 pp. 104–109
Research and Reasoning		
1	Collect, analyze, and evaluate information obtained from multiple sources to answer a question, propose solutions, or share findings and conclusions	W7 pp. 110–115 W8 pp. 116–121 W9 pp. 122–127
2	An author's reasoning is the essence of legitimate writing and requires evaluating text for validity and accuracy	NA

Colorado, Grade 11

Colorado Strand/Standard	Focus of Colorado Standard	For More Information
Oral Expression and Listening		
1	Verbal and nonverbal cues impact the intent of communication	NA
2	Validity of a message is determined by its accuracy and relevance	SL1 pp. 138–143 SL2 pp. 144–149 SL3 pp. 150–155
Reading for All Purposes		
1	Complex literary texts require critical reading approaches to effectively interpret and evaluate meaning	R1 pp. 6–11 R2 pp. 12–17 R3 pp. 18–23 R4 pp. 24–29 R6 pp. 36–41 R7 pp. 42–47 R9 pp. 54–59 R10 pp. 60–65
2	Ideas synthesized from informational texts serve a specific purpose	R1 pp. 6–11 R2 pp. 12–17 R3 pp. 18–23 R4 pp. 24–29 R5 pp. 30–35 R8 pp. 48–53 R9 pp. 54–59 R10 pp. 60–65
3	Knowledge of language, including syntax and grammar, influence the understanding of literary, persuasive, and informational texts	L3 pp. 190–195 L4 pp. 196–201 L5 pp. 202–207 L6 pp. 208–213

Colorado Strand/Standard	Focus of Colorado Standard	For More Information
Writing and Composition		
1	Stylistic and thematic elements of literary or narrative texts can be refined to engage or entertain an audience	W3 pp. 86–91
2	Elements of informational and persuasive texts can be refined to inform or influence an audience	W1 pp. 70–77 W2 pp. 78–85
3	Writing demands ongoing revisions and refinements for grammar, usage, mechanics, and clarity	L1 pp. 178–183 L2 pp. 184–189 W4 pp. 92–97 W5 pp. 98–103 W6 pp. 104–109
Research and Reasoning		
1	Self-designed research provides insightful information, conclusions, and possible outcomes	W7 pp. 110–115 W8 pp. 116–121 W9 pp. 122–127
2	An author's reasoning is the essence of legitimate writing; complex situations require critical thinking across disciplines	NA
3	Evaluating quality reasoning includes the value of intellectual character such as humility, empathy, and confidence	NA

Colorado, Grade 12

Colorado Strand/Standard	Focus of Colorado Standard	For More Information
Oral Expression and Listening		
1	Effective speaking in formal and informal settings requires appropriate use of methods and audience awareness	SL4 pp. 156–161 SL5 pp. 162–167 SL6 pp. 168–173
2	Effective collaborative groups accomplish goals	SL1 pp. 138–143
Reading for All Purposes		
1	Literary criticism of complex texts requires the use of analysis, interpretive, and evaluative strategies	R5 pp. 30–35 R10 pp. 60–65
2	Interpreting and evaluating complex informational texts require the understanding of rhetoric, critical reading, and analysis skills	R6 pp. 36–41 R7 pp. 42–47 R10 pp. 60–65
Writing and Composition		
1	Style, detail, expressive language, and genre create a well-crafted statement directed at an intended audience and purpose	NA
2	Ideas, evidence, structure, and style create persuasive, academic, and technical texts for particular audiences and specific purposes	NA
3	Standard English conventions effectively communicate to targeted audiences and purposes	NA
Research and Reasoning		
1	Independent research designs articulate and defend information, conclusions, and solutions that address specific contexts and purposes	NA
2	Logical arguments distinguish facts from opinions; and evidence defines reasoned judgement	NA

Florida, Grades 9–10

Florida Strand/Standard	Focus of Florida Standard	For More Information
Reading Literature		
RL.1.1	Cite strong and thorough textual evidence to support analysis of what the text says explicitly and implicitly	R1 pp. 6–11
RL.1.2	Determine a theme of a text and analyze its development; summarize the text	R2 pp. 12–17
RL.1.3	Analyze how characters develop, interact, and advance the plot or develop the theme	R3 pp. 18–23
RL.2.4	Determine the meaning of words and phrases as they are used in a text, including figurative and connotative meanings; analyze the cumulative impact of word choice on meaning and tone	R4 pp. 24–29
RL.2.5	Analyze how an author's choices regarding structure, the order of events, and manipulating time create such effects as mystery, tension, or surprise	R5 pp. 30–35
RL.2.6	Analyze a point of view, perspective, or cultural experience reflected in a work of literature from outside the U.S.	R6 pp. 36–41
RL.3.7	Analyze the representation of a subject or scene in two different artistic mediums	R7 pp. 42–47
RL.8	NA	
RL.3.9	Analyze how an author draws on and transforms source material	R9 pp. 54–59
RL.4.10	Read and comprehend literature of appropriate complexity independently with proficiency	R10 pp. 60–65
Reading Informational Text		
RI.1.1	Cite strong and thorough textual evidence to support analysis of what the text says explicitly and implicitly	R1 pp. 6–11
RI.1.2	Determine the central idea of a text and analyze its development; summarize the text	R2 pp. 12–17
RI.1.3	Analyze how the author unfolds an analysis or series of ideas or events, including the order, how they are developed, and the connections between them	R3 pp. 18–23
RI.2.4	Determine the meaning of words and phrases in a text; analyze the cumulative impact of specific word choices on meaning and tone	R4 pp. 24–29
RI.2.5	Analyze in detail how ideas or claims are developed by particular sentences, paragraphs, or larger portions of text	R5 pp. 30–35
RI.2.6	Analyze how an author uses rhetoric to advance a point of view, perspective, or purpose	R6 pp. 36–41
RI.3.7	Analyze various accounts of a subject told in different mediums	R7 pp. 42–47
RI.3.8	Delineate and evaluate the argument in a text; assess reasoning and evidence; identify false statements and fallacious reasoning	R8 pp. 48–53
RI.3.9	Analyze U.S. documents of historical and literary significance, noting how they address related themes and concepts	R9 pp. 54–59
RI.4.10	Read and comprehend appropriately complex literary nonfiction independently and proficiently	R10 pp. 60–65
Writing		
W.1.1	Write arguments to support claims, using valid reasoning and relevant and sufficient evidence	W1 pp. 70–77
W.1.2	Write informative/explanatory texts to effectively examine and convey complex ideas, concepts, and information	W2 pp. 78–85
W.1.3	Write narratives to develop real or imagined experiences or events using effective technique, well-chosen details, and well-structured event sequences	W3 pp. 86–91
W.2.4	Produce writing in which the development, organization, and style are appropriate to the task, genre, purpose, and audience	W4 pp. 92–97
W.2.5	Develop and strengthen writing as needed by planning, revising, and editing, rewriting, or trying a new approach	W5 pp. 98–103

Florida Strand/Standard	Focus of Florida Standard	For More Information
Writing		
W.2.6	Use technology to produce, publish, and update individual or shared writing projects	W6 pp. 104–109
W.3.7	Conduct research projects to answer a question or solve a problem; synthesize multiple sources; demonstrate understanding of the subject	W7 pp. 110–115
W.3.8	Gather information from multiple sources, using advanced searches effectively; assess usefulness of sources; integrate information, avoiding plagiarism	W8 pp. 116–121
W.3.9	Draw evidence from texts to support analysis, reflection, and research	W9 pp. 122–127
W.4.10	Write routinely over shorter and extended time frames for a range of audiences, tasks, and purposes	W10 pp. 128–133
Speaking and Listening		
SL.1.1	Engage effectively in a range of collaborative discussions with diverse partners, building on others' ideas and expressing their own clearly and persuasively	SL1 pp. 138–143
SL.1.2	Integrate multiple sources of information presented in diverse media or formats; evaluate credibility and accuracy of sources and noting discrepancies	SL2 pp. 144–149
SL.1.3	Evaluate a speaker's point of view, reasoning, and use of evidence and rhetoric; identify fallacious reasoning	SL3 pp. 150–155
SL.2.4	Present information clearly, concisely, and logically; ensure organization, development, substance, and style are appropriate to purpose, audience, and task	SL4 pp. 156–161
SL.2.5	Make strategic use of digital media in presentations to enhance understanding and to add interest	SL5 pp. 162–167
SL.2.6	Adapt speech to a variety of contexts and tasks; demonstrate a command of formal English when appropriate	SL6 pp. 168–173
Language		
L.1.1	Demonstrate command of the conventions of standard English grammar and usage when writing or speaking	L1 pp. 178–183
L.1.2	Demonstrate command of the conventions of standard English capitalization, punctuation, and spelling when writing	L2 pp. 184–189
L.2.3	Apply knowledge of language to make effective choices for meaning or style, and to comprehend more fully when reading or listening	L3 pp. 190–195
L.3.4	Determine or clarify the meaning of unknown and multiple-meaning words and phrases, choosing flexibly from an array of strategies	L4 pp. 196–201
L.3.5	Demonstrate understanding of figurative language, word relationships, and nuances in word meanings	L5 pp. 202–207
L.3.6	Acquire and use accurately general academic and domain-specific words and phrases; demonstrate independence in gathering vocabulary knowledge	L6 pp. 208–213
Reading History/Social Studies		
RH.1.1	Cite specific textual evidence to support analysis of primary and secondary sources	R1 pp. 6–11
RH.1.2	Determine central ideas or information of a primary or secondary source; summarize how they develop	R2 pp. 12–17
RH.1.3	Analyze in detail a series of events; determine whether earlier events caused later ones	R3 pp. 18–23
RH.2.4	Determine the meaning of words and phrases, including vocabulary describing political, social, or economic aspects of history/social science	R4 pp. 24–29
RH.2.5	Analyze how a text uses structure to emphasize key points or advance an explanation or analysis	R5 pp. 30–35
RH.2.6	Compare the point of view of two or more authors for how they treat the same or similar topics	R6 pp. 36–41
RH.3.7	Integrate quantitative or technical analysis with qualitative analysis	R7 pp. 42–47

(Continued)

Florida Strand/Standard	Focus of Florida Standard	For More Information
Reading History/Social Studies		
RH.3.8	Assess the extent to which reasoning and evidence support the author's claim	R8 pp. 48–53
RH.3.9	Compare and contrast treatment of the same topic in several primary and secondary sources	R9 pp. 54–59
RH.4.10	Read and comprehend history/social studies texts of appropriate complexity	R10 pp. 60–65
Reading Science/Technical Subjects		
RST.1.1	Cite specific textual evidence to support analysis of science and technical texts	R1 pp. 6–11
RST.1.2	Determine central ideas or conclusions; trace the explanation of a complex process; provide an accurate summary	R2 pp. 12–17
RST.1.3	Follow precisely a complex multistep procedure, attending to special cases or exceptions defined in the text	R3 pp. 18–23
RST.2.4	Determine the meaning of domain-specific words and phrases as they are used in a special scientific or technical context	R4 pp. 24–29
RST.2.5	Analyze the structure of relationships among concepts in a text	R5 pp. 30–35
RST.2.6	Analyze the author's purpose in providing an explanation, describing a procedure, or discussing an experiment	R6 pp. 36–41
RST.3.7	Translate quantitative or technical information expressed in words into visual form, and translate information expressed visually into words	R7 pp. 42–47
RST.3.8	Assess the extent to which reasoning and evidence support the author's claim or recommendation for solving a problem	R8 pp. 48–53
RST.3.9	Compare and contrast findings presented in a text to those from other sources, noting where they support or contradict previous explanations	R9 pp. 54–59
RST.4.10	Read and comprehend science/technical texts of appropriate complexity	R10 pp. 60–65
Writing History/Social Studies, Science and Technical Subjects		
WHST.1.1	Write arguments focused on disciple-specific content	W1 pp. 70–77
WHST.1.2	Write informative/explanatory texts, including the narration of historical events, scientific procedures, or technical processes	W2 pp. 78–85
WHST.1.3	NA	W3 pp. 86–91
WHST.2.4	Produce clear and coherent writing in which the development, organization, and style are appropriate to task, purpose, and audience	W4 pp. 92–97
WHST.2.5	Develop and strengthen writing as needed by planning, revising, editing, rewriting, or trying a new approach	W5 pp. 98–103
WHST.2.6	Use technology to produce, publish, and update individual or shared writing projects	W6 pp. 104–109
WHST.3.7	Conduct research projects to answer a question or solve a problem; synthesize multiple sources, demonstrating understanding of the subject	W7 pp. 110–115
WHST.3.8	Gather relevant information from multiple print and digital sources; assess the usefulness of each source; integrate information, avoiding plagiarism	W8 pp. 116–121
WHST.3.9	Draw evidence from informational texts to support analysis, reflection, and research	W9 pp. 122–127
WHST.4.10	Write routinely for a range of discipline-specific tasks, purposes, and audiences	W10 pp. 128–133

Florida, Grades 11–12

Florida Strand/Standard	Focus of Florida Standard	For More Information
Reading Literature		
RL.1.1	Cite strong and thorough textual evidence to support analysis of what the text says explicitly and implicitly	R1 pp. 6–11
RL.1.2	Determine two or more themes or central ideas and analyze their development; summarize the text	R2 pp. 12–17
RL.1.3	Analyze the impact of the author's choices regarding how to develop and relate elements of a story or drama	R3 pp. 18–23
RL.2.4	Determine the meaning of words and phrases as they are used in a text, including figurative and connotative meanings; analyze the cumulative impact of word choice on meaning and tone	R4 pp. 24–29
RL.2.5	Analyze how an author's choices concerning how to structure specific parts of the text contribute to its overall structure and meaning	R5 pp. 30–35
RL.2.6	Analyze a case in which grasping point of view requires distinguishing what is directly stated from what is really meant	R6 pp. 36–41
RL.3.7	Analyze multiple representations of a story, drama, or poem, evaluating how each interprets the source text	R7 pp. 42–47
RL.8	NA	
RL.3.9	Demonstrate knowledge of 18th, 19th, and early 20th century foundational works of American literature	R9 pp. 54–59
RL.4.10	Read and comprehend a range of literature at an appropriate level of complexity	R10 pp. 60–65
Reading Informational Text		
RI.1.1	Cite strong and thorough textual evidence to support analysis of what the text says explicitly and implicitly, including where the text leaves matters uncertain	R1 pp. 6–11
RI.1.2	Determine two or more central ideas of a text and analyze their development; summarize the text	R2 pp. 12–17
RI.1.3	Analyze a complex set of ideas or sequence of events and explain how specific individuals, ideas, or events interact and develop	R3 pp. 18–23
RI.2.4	Determine the meaning of words and phrases in a text; analyze how an author uses and refines the meaning of key terms over the course of a text	R4 pp. 24–29
RI.2.5	Analyze and evaluate the effectiveness of the structure in an exposition or argument	R5 pp. 30–35
RI.2.6	Analyze how an author's style and content contribute to the power, persuasiveness, or beauty of the text	R6 pp. 36–41
RI.3.7	Integrate and evaluate multiple sources of information presented in different media or formats in order to address a question or solve a problem	R7 pp. 42–47
RI.3.8	Delineate and evaluate the reasoning in seminal U.S. texts, including the application of constitutional principles and use of legal reasoning, and the premises, purposes, and arguments in works of public advocacy	R8 pp. 48–53
RI.3.9	Analyze 17th, 18th, and 19th century foundational U.S. and world documents of literary significance for their themes, purposes, and rhetorical features	R9 pp. 54–59
RI.4.10	Read and comprehend literary nonfiction independently and proficiently	R10 pp. 60–65
Writing		
W.1.1	Write arguments to support claims, using valid reasoning and relevant and sufficient evidence	W1 pp. 70–77
W.1.2	Write informative/explanatory texts to examine and convey complex ideas, concepts, and information clearly and accurately	W2 pp. 78–85
W.1.3	Write narratives to develop real or imagined experiences or events using effective technique, well-chosen details, and well-structured event sequences	W3 pp. 86–91

(Continued)

Florida Strand/Standard	Focus of Florida Standard	For More Information
Writing		
W.2.4	Produce writing in which the development, organization, and style are appropriate to the task, genre, purpose, and audience	W4 pp. 92–97
W.2.5	Develop and strengthen writing as needed by planning, revising, and editing, rewriting, or trying a new approach	W5 pp. 98–103
W.2.6	Use technology to produce, publish, and update individual or shared writing projects	W6 pp. 104–109
W.3.7	Conduct research projects to answer a question or solve a problem; synthesize multiple sources; demonstrate understanding of the subject	W7 pp. 110–115
W.3.8	Gather information from multiple sources, using advanced searches effectively; assess strengths and limitations of sources; integrate information, avoiding plagiarism and overreliance on any one source	W8 pp. 116–121
W.3.9	Draw evidence from texts to support analysis, reflection, and research	W9 pp. 122–127
W.4.10	Write routinely over shorter and extended time frames for a range of audiences, tasks, and purposes	W10 pp. 128–133
Speaking and Listening		
SL.1.1	Engage effectively in a range of collaborative discussions with diverse partners, building on others' ideas and expressing their own clearly and persuasively	SL1 pp. 138–143
SL.1.2	Integrate multiple sources of information presented in diverse media or formats; evaluate credibility and accuracy of sources and note discrepancies	SL2 pp. 144–149
SL.1.3	Evaluate a speaker's point of view, reasoning, and use of evidence and rhetoric; assess the stance, premises, link among ideas, word choice, emphasis, and tone	SL3 pp. 150–155
SL.2.4	Present information, findings, and supporting evidence, conveying a clear and distinct perspective; address alternative viewpoints; ensure presentation is appropriate to purpose, audience, and task	SL4 pp. 156–161
SL.2.5	Make strategic use of digital media in presentations to enhance understanding and to add interest	SL5 pp. 162–167
SL.2.6	Adapt speech to a variety of contexts and tasks; demonstrate a command of formal English when appropriate	SL6 pp. 168–173
Language		
L.1.1	Demonstrate command of the conventions of standard English grammar and usage when writing or speaking	L1 pp. 178–183
L.1.2	Demonstrate command of the conventions of standard English capitalization, punctuation, and spelling when writing	L2 pp. 184–189
L.2.3	Apply knowledge of language to make effective choices for meaning or style, and to comprehend more fully when reading or listening	L3 pp. 190–195
L.3.4	Determine or clarify the meaning of unknown and multiple-meaning words and phrases, choosing flexibly from an array of strategies	L4 pp. 196–201
L.3.5	Demonstrate understanding of figurative language, word relationships, and nuances in word meanings	L5 pp. 202–207
L.3.6	Acquire and use accurately general academic and domain-specific words and phrases; demonstrate independence in gathering vocabulary knowledge	L6 pp. 208–213
Reading History/Social Studies		
RH.1.1	Cite specific textual evidence to support analysis of primary and secondary sources	R1 pp. 6–11
RH.1.2	Determine central ideas or information of a primary or secondary source; summarize how they develop	R2 pp. 12–17
RH.1.3	Evaluate explanations for actions or events and determine which best accords with textual evidence	R3 pp. 18–23
RH.2.4	Determine the meaning of words and phrases in a text, including how an author uses and refines the meaning of a key term	R4 pp. 24–29

Florida Strand/Standard	Focus of Florida Standard	For More Information
Reading History/Social Studies		
RH.2.5	Analyze in detail how a complex primary source is structured	R5 pp. 30–35
RH.2.6	Evaluate authors' differing points of view on the same historical event	R6 pp. 36–41
RH.3.7	Integrate and evaluate multiple sources of information presented in diverse formats and media in order to address a question or solve a problem	R7 pp. 42–47
RH.3.8	Evaluate an author's premises, claims, and evidence by corroborating or challenging them	R8 pp. 48–53
RH.3.9	Integrate information from diverse sources into a coherent understanding of an idea or event	R9 pp. 54–59
RH.4.10	Read and comprehend history/social studies texts of appropriate complexity	R10 pp. 60–65
Reading Science/Technical Subjects		
RST.1.1	Cite specific textual evidence to support analysis of science and technical texts	R1 pp. 6–11
RST.1.2	Determine central ideas or conclusions; summarize complex concepts by paraphrasing in simpler but accurate terms	R2 pp. 12–17
RST.1.3	Follow precisely a complex multistep procedure; analyze the results based on explanations in the text	R3 pp. 18–23
RST.2.4	Determine the meaning of domain-specific words and phrases as they are used in a special scientific or technical context	R4 pp. 24–29
RST.2.5	Analyze how the text structures information into categories or hierarchies, demonstrating understanding	R5 pp. 30–35
RST.2.6	Analyze the author's purpose in providing an explanation, describing a procedure, or discussing an experiment	R6 pp. 36–41
RST.3.7	Integrate and evaluate multiple sources of information presented in diverse formats and media in order to address a question or solve a problem	R7 pp. 42–47
RST.3.8	Evaluate the hypotheses, data, analysis, and conclusions in a science or technical text, corroborating or challenging conclusions	R8 pp. 48–53
RST.3.9	Synthesize information from a range of sources into a coherent understanding, resolving conflicting information when possible	R9 pp. 54–59
RST.4.10	Read and comprehend science/technical texts of appropriate complexity	R10 pp. 60–65
Writing History/Social Studies, Science and Technical Subjects		
WHST.1.1	Write arguments focused on disciple-specific content	W1 pp. 70–77
WHST.1.2	Write informative/explanatory texts, including the narration of historical events, scientific procedures, or technical processes	W2 pp. 78–85
WHST.1.3	NA	
WHST.2.4	Produce clear and coherent writing in which the development, organization, and style are appropriate to task, purpose, and audience	W4 pp. 92–97
WHST.2.5	Develop and strengthen writing as needed by planning, revising, editing, rewriting, or trying a new approach	W5 pp. 98–103
WHST.2.6	Use technology to produce, publish, and update individual or shared writing projects	W6 pp. 104–109
WHST.3.7	Conduct research projects to answer a question or solve a problem; synthesize multiple sources, demonstrating understanding of the subject	W7 pp. 110–115
WHST.3.8	Gather relevant information from multiple print and digital sources; assess the usefulness of each source; integrate information, avoiding plagiarism and overreliance on any one source	W8 pp. 116–121
WHST.3.9	Draw evidence from informational texts to support analysis, reflection, and research	W9 pp. 122–127
WHST.4.10	Write routinely for a range of discipline-specific tasks, purposes, and audiences	W10 pp. 128–133

Georgia, Grades 9–10

Georgia Strand/Standard	Focus of Georgia Standard	For More Information
Reading Literature		
RL.1	Cite strong and thorough textual evidence to support analysis of what the text says explicitly and implicitly	R1 pp. 6–11
RL.2	Determine a theme or central idea of a text and analyze its development and how it is shaped by specific details; summarize the text	R2 pp. 12–17
RL.3	Analyze how characters develop, interact, and advance the plot or develop the theme	R3 pp. 18–23
RL.4	Determine the meaning of words and phrases as they are used in a text, including figurative and connotative meanings; analyze the cumulative impact of word choice on meaning and tone	R4 pp. 24–29
RL.5	Analyze how an author's choices regarding structure, the order of events, and manipulating time create such effects as mystery, tension, or surprise	R5 pp. 30–35
RL.6	Analyze a point of view, perspective, or cultural experience reflected in a piece of literature	R6 pp. 36–41
RL.7	Analyze the representation of a subject or scene in two different artistic mediums, including what is emphasized or absent in each treatment	R7 pp. 42–47
RL.8	NA	
RL.9	Analyze how an author draws on and transforms source material	R9 pp. 54–59
RL.10	Read literature of appropriate complexity independently with proficiency	R10 pp. 60–65
Reading Informational Text		
RI.1	Cite strong and thorough textual evidence to support analysis of what the text says explicitly and implicitly	R1 pp. 6–11
RI.2	Determine the central idea of a text and analyze its development; summarize main ideas or events	R2 pp. 12–17
RI.3	Analyze how the author structures an analysis or series of ideas or events, including the order, how they are developed, and the connections between them	R3 pp. 18–23
RI.4	Determine the meaning of words and phrases in a text; analyze the cumulative impact of specific word choices	R4 pp. 24–29
RI.5	Analyze in detail how ideas or claims are developed by particular sentences, paragraphs, or larger portions of text	R5 pp. 30–35
RI.6	Analyze how an author uses rhetoric to advance a point of view, perspective, or purpose	R6 pp. 36–41
RI.7	Analyze various accounts of a subject told in different mediums	R7 pp. 42–47
RI.8	Evaluate the argument in a text; assess reasoning and evidence; identify false statements and fallacious reasoning	R8 pp. 48–53
RI.9	Analyze U.S. documents of historical and literary significance, noting how they address related themes and concepts	R9 pp. 54–59
RI.10	Read and comprehend appropriately complex informational texts independently and proficiently	R10 pp. 60–65
Writing		
W.1	Write arguments to support claims, using valid reasoning and relevant and sufficient evidence	W1 pp. 70–77
W.2	Write informative/explanatory texts to effectively examine and convey complex ideas, concepts, and information	W2 pp. 78–85
W.3	Write narratives to develop real or imagined experiences or events using effective technique, well-chosen details, and well-structured event sequences	W3 pp. 86–91
W.4	Produce writing in which the development, organization, style, and features are appropriate to the task, genre, purpose, and audience	W4 pp. 92–97

Georgia Strand/Standard	Focus of Georgia Standard	For More Information
Writing		
W.5	Develop and strengthen writing as needed by planning, revising, and editing, rewriting, or trying a new approach	W5 pp. 98–103
W.6	Use technology to produce, publish, and update individual or shared writing projects	W6 pp. 104–109
W.7	Conduct research projects to answer a question or solve a problem; synthesize multiple sources; demonstrate understanding of the subject	W7 pp. 110–115
W.8	Gather information from multiple sources, using advanced searches effectively; assess usefulness of sources; integrate information, avoiding plagiarism	W8 pp. 116–121
W.9	Draw evidence from texts to support analysis, reflection, research, and/or synthesis	W9 pp. 122–127
W.10	Write routinely over shorter and extended time frames for a range of audiences, tasks, and purposes	W10 pp. 128–133
Speaking and Listening		
SL.1	Engage effectively in a range of collaborative discussions with diverse partners, building on others' ideas and expressing their own clearly and persuasively	SL1 pp. 138–143
SL.2	Integrate multiple sources of information presented in diverse media or formats; evaluate credibility and accuracy of sources and noting discrepancies	SL2 pp. 144–149
SL.3	Evaluate a speaker's point of view, reasoning, and use of evidence and rhetoric; identify fallacious reasoning or exaggerated or distorted evidence	SL3 pp. 150–155
SL.4	Present information clearly, concisely, and logically; ensure organization, development, substance, and style are appropriate to purpose, audience, and task	SL4 pp. 156–161
SL.5	Make strategic use of digital media in presentations to enhance understanding and to add interest	SL5 pp. 162–167
SL.6	Adapt speech to a variety of contexts and tasks; demonstrate a command of formal English when appropriate	SL6 pp. 168–173
Language		
L.1	Demonstrate command of the conventions of standard English grammar and usage when writing or speaking	L1 pp. 178–183
L.2	Demonstrate command of the conventions of standard English capitalization, punctuation, and spelling when writing	L2 pp. 184–189
L.3	Apply knowledge of language to make effective choices for meaning or style, to comprehend more fully when reading or listening, and to write and edit so that it conforms to the guidelines in a style manual appropriate for the writing type	L3 pp. 190–195
L.4	Determine or clarify the meaning of unknown and multiple-meaning words and phrases, choosing flexibly from an array of strategies	L4 pp. 196–201
L.5	Demonstrate understanding of figurative language, word relationships, and nuances in word meanings	L5 pp. 202–207
L.6	Acquire and use accurately general academic and domain-specific words and phrases; demonstrate independence in gathering vocabulary knowledge	L6 pp. 208–213
Reading History/Social Studies		
RH.1	Cite specific textual evidence to support analysis of primary and secondary sources	R1 pp. 6–11
RH.2	Determine central ideas or information of a primary or secondary source; summarize how they develop	R2 pp. 12–17
RH.3	Analyze in detail a series of events; determine whether earlier events caused later ones	R3 pp. 18–23
RH.4	Determine the meaning of words and phrases, including vocabulary describing political, social, or economic aspects of history/social studies	R4 pp. 24–29
RH.5	Analyze how a text uses structure to emphasize key points or advance an explanation or analysis	R5 pp. 30–35
RH.6	Compare the point of view of two or more authors for how they treat the same or similar topics	R6 pp. 36–41

(Continued)

Georgia Strand/Standard	Focus of Georgia Standard	For More Information
Reading History/Social Studies		
RH.7	Integrate quantitative or technical analysis with qualitative analysis	R7 pp. 42–47
RH.8	Assess the extent to which reasoning and evidence support the author's claim	R8 pp. 48–53
RH.9	Compare and contrast treatment of the same topic in several primary and secondary sources	R9 pp. 54–59
RH.10	Read and comprehend history/social studies texts of appropriate complexity	R10 pp. 60–65
Reading Science/Technical Subjects		
RST.1	Cite specific textual evidence to support analysis of science and technical texts	R1 pp. 6–11
RST.2	Determine central ideas or conclusions; trace the explanation of a complex process; provide an accurate summary	R2 pp. 12–17
RST.3	Follow precisely a complex multistep procedure, attending to special cases or exceptions defined in the text	R3 pp. 18–23
RST.4	Determine the meaning of domain-specific words and phrases as they are used in a special scientific or technical context	R4 pp. 24–29
RST.5	Analyze the structure of relationships among concepts in a text	R5 pp. 30–35
RST.6	Analyze the author's purpose in providing an explanation, describing a procedure, or discussing an experiment	R6 pp. 36–41
RST.7	Translate quantitative or technical information expressed in words into visual form, and translate information expressed visually into words	R7 pp. 42–47
RST.8	Assess the extent to which reasoning and evidence support the author's claim or recommendation for solving a problem	R8 pp. 48–53
RST.9	Compare and contrast findings presented in a text to those from other sources, noting where they support or contradict previous explanations	R9 pp. 54–59
RST.10	Read and comprehend science/technical texts of appropriate complexity	R10 pp. 60–65
Writing History/Social Studies, Science and Technical Subjects		
WHST.1	Write arguments focused on disciple-specific content	W1 pp. 70–77
WHST.2	Write informative/explanatory texts, including the narration of historical events, scientific procedures, or technical processes	W2 pp. 78–85
WHST.3	NA	W3 pp. 86–91
WHST.4	Produce clear and coherent writing in which the development, organization, and style are appropriate to task, purpose, and audience	W4 pp. 92–97
WHST.5	Develop and strengthen writing as needed by planning, revising, editing, rewriting, or trying a new approach	W5 pp. 98–103
WHST.6	Use technology to produce, publish, and update individual or shared writing projects	W6 pp. 104–109
WHST.7	Conduct research projects to answer a question or solve a problem; synthesize multiple sources, demonstrating understanding of the subject	W7 pp. 110–115
WHST.8	Gather relevant information from multiple print and digital sources; assess the usefulness of each source; integrate information, avoiding plagiarism	W8 pp. 116–121
WHST.9	Draw evidence from informational texts to support analysis, reflection, and research	W9 pp. 122–127
WHST.10	Write routinely for a range of discipline-specific tasks, purposes, and audiences	W10 pp. 128–133

Georgia, Grades 11–12

Georgia Strand/Standard	Focus of Georgia Standard	For More Information
Reading Literature		
RL.1	Cite strong and thorough textual evidence to support analysis of what the text says explicitly and implicitly	R1 pp. 6–11
RL.2	Determine two or more themes or central ideas and analyze their development; restate and summarize main ideas or events	R2 pp. 12–17
RL.3	Analyze how characters develop, interact, and advance the plot or develop the theme	R3 pp. 18–23
RL.4	Determine the meaning of words and phrases as they are used in a text, including figurative and connotative meanings; analyze the cumulative impact of word choice on meaning and tone	R4 pp. 24–29
RL.5	Analyze how an author's choices concerning how to structure specific parts of the text contribute to its overall structure and meaning	R5 pp. 30–35
RL.6	Analyze a case in which grasping point of view requires distinguishing what is directly stated from what is really meant	R6 pp. 36–41
RL.7	Analyze multiple representations of a story, drama, or poem, evaluating how each interprets the source text	R7 pp. 42–47
RL.8	NA	
RL.9	Demonstrate knowledge of 18th, 19th, and early 20th century foundational works of literature, including how two or more texts from the same period treat similar themes or topics	R9 pp. 54–59
RL.10	Read and comprehend a range of literature from a variety of cultures	R10 pp. 60–65
Reading Informational Text		
RI.1	Cite strong and thorough textual evidence to support analysis of what the text says explicitly and implicitly, including where the text leaves matters uncertain	R1 pp. 6–11
RI.2	Determine two or more central ideas of a text and analyze their development; restate or summarize main ideas or events	R2 pp. 12–17
RI.3	Analyze a complex set of ideas or sequence of events and explain how specific individuals, ideas, or events interact and develop	R3 pp. 18–23
RI.4	Determine the meaning of words and phrases in a text; analyze how an author uses and refines the meaning of key terms over the course of a text	R4 pp. 24–29
RI.5	Analyze and evaluate the effectiveness of the structure in an exposition or argument	R5 pp. 30–35
RI.6	Analyze how an author's style and content contribute to the power, persuasiveness, or impact of the text	R6 pp. 36–41
RI.7	Integrate and evaluate multiple sources of information presented in different media or formats in order to address a question or solve a problem	R7 pp. 42–47
RI.8	Delineate and evaluate the reasoning in seminal U.S. texts, including the application of constitutional principles and use of legal reasoning, and the premises, purposes, and arguments in works of public advocacy	R8 pp. 48–53
RI.9	Analyze foundational U.S. documents of historical and literary significance for their themes, purposes, and rhetorical features	R9 pp. 54–59
RI.10	Read and comprehend literary nonfiction independently and proficiently	R10 pp. 60–65
Writing		
W.1	Write arguments to support claims, using valid reasoning and relevant and sufficient evidence	W1 pp. 70–77
W.2	Write informative/explanatory texts to examine and convey complex ideas, concepts, and information clearly and accurately	W2 pp. 78–85

(Continued)

Georgia Strand/Standard	Focus of Georgia Standard	For More Information
Writing		
W.3	Write narratives to develop real or imagined experiences or events using effective technique, well-chosen details, and well-structured event sequences	W3 pp. 86–91
W.4	Produce writing in which the development, organization, style, and features are appropriate to the task, genre, purpose, and audience	W4 pp. 92–97
W.5	Develop and strengthen writing as needed by planning, revising, and editing, rewriting, or trying a new approach	W5 pp. 98–103
W.6	Use technology to produce, publish, and update individual or shared writing projects	W6 pp. 104–109
W.7	Conduct research projects to answer a question or solve a problem; synthesize multiple sources; demonstrate understanding of the subject	W7 pp. 110–115
W.8	Gather information from multiple sources, using advanced searches effectively; assess strengths and limitations of sources; integrate information, avoiding plagiarism and overreliance on any one source	W8 pp. 116–121
W.9	Draw evidence from texts to support analysis, reflection, and research	W9 pp. 122–127
W.10	Write routinely over shorter and extended time frames for a range of audiences, tasks, and purposes	W10 pp. 128–133
Speaking and Listening		
SL.1	Engage effectively in a range of collaborative discussions with diverse partners, building on others' ideas and expressing their own clearly and persuasively	SL1 pp. 138–143
SL.2	Integrate multiple sources of information presented in diverse media or formats; evaluate credibility and accuracy of sources and note discrepancies	SL2 pp. 144–149
SL.3	Evaluate a speaker's point of view, reasoning, and use of evidence and rhetoric; assess the stance, premises, link among ideas, word choice, emphasis, and tone	SL3 pp. 150–155
SL.4	Present information, conveying a clear and distinct perspective, address alternative viewpoints; presentation is appropriate to purpose, audience, and task	SL4 pp. 156–161
SL.5	Make strategic use of digital media in presentations to enhance understanding and to add interest	SL5 pp. 162–167
SL.6	Adapt speech to a variety of contexts and tasks; demonstrate a command of formal English when appropriate	SL6 pp. 168–173
Language		
L.1	Demonstrate command of the conventions of standard English grammar and usage when writing or speaking	L1 pp. 178–183
L.2	Demonstrate command of the conventions of standard English capitalization, punctuation, and spelling when writing	L2 pp. 184–189
L.3	Apply knowledge of language to make effective choices for meaning or style, and to comprehend more fully when reading or listening	L3 pp. 190–195
L.4	Determine or clarify the meaning of unknown and multiple-meaning words and phrases, choosing flexibly from an array of strategies	L4 pp. 196–201
L.5	Demonstrate understanding of figurative language, word relationships, and nuances in word meanings	L5 pp. 202–207
L.6	Acquire and use accurately general academic and domain-specific words and phrases; demonstrate independence in gathering vocabulary knowledge	L6 pp. 208–213
Reading History/Social Studies		
RH.1	Cite specific textual evidence to support analysis of primary and secondary sources	R1 pp. 6–11
RH.2	Determine central ideas or information of a primary or secondary source; summarize how they develop	R2 pp. 12–17
RH.3	Evaluate explanations for actions or events and determine which best accords with textual evidence	R3 pp. 18–23

Georgia Strand/Standard	Focus of Georgia Standard	For More Information
Reading History/Social Studies		
RH.4	Determine the meaning of words and phrases in a text, including figurative and connotative meanings; analyze the impact of specific word choices	R4 pp. 24–29
RH.5	Analyze in detail how a complex primary source is structured	R5 pp. 30–35
RH.6	Evaluate authors' differing points of view on the same historical event	R6 pp. 36–41
RH.7	Integrate and evaluate multiple sources of information presented in diverse formats and media in order to address a question or solve a problem	R7 pp. 42–47
RH.8	Evaluate an author's premises, claims, and evidence by corroborating or challenging them	R8 pp. 48–53
RH.9	Integrate information from diverse sources into a coherent understanding of an idea or event	R9 pp. 54–59
RH.10	Read and comprehend history/social studies texts of appropriate complexity	R10 pp. 60–65
Reading Science/Technical Subjects		
RST.1	Cite specific textual evidence to support analysis of science and technical texts	R1 pp. 6–11
RST.2	Determine central ideas or conclusions; summarize complex concepts by paraphrasing in simpler but accurate terms	R2 pp. 12–17
RST.3	Follow precisely a complex multistep procedure; analyze the results based on explanations in the text	R3 pp. 18–23
RST.4	Determine the meaning of domain-specific words and phrases as they are used in a special scientific or technical context	R4 pp. 24–29
RST.5	Analyze how the text structures information into categories or hierarchies, demonstrating understanding	R5 pp. 30–35
RST.6	Analyze the author's purpose in providing an explanation, describing a procedure, or discussing an experiment	R6 pp. 36–41
RST.7	Integrate and evaluate multiple sources of information presented in diverse formats and media in order to address a question or solve a problem	R7 pp. 42–47
RST.8	Evaluate the hypotheses, data, analysis, and conclusions in a science or technical text, corroborating or challenging conclusions	R8 pp. 48–53
RST.9	Synthesize information from a range of sources into a coherent understanding, resolving conflicting information when possible	R9 pp. 54–59
RST.10	Read and comprehend science/technical texts of appropriate complexity	R10 pp. 60–65
Writing History/Social Studies, Science and Technical Subjects		
WHST.1	Write arguments focused on disciple-specific content	W1 pp. 70–77
WHST.2	Write informative/explanatory texts, including the narration of historical events, scientific procedures, or technical processes	W2 pp. 78–85
WHST.3	NA	
WHST.4	Produce clear and coherent writing in which the development, organization, and style are appropriate to task, purpose, and audience	W4 pp. 92–97
WHST.5	Develop and strengthen writing as needed by planning, revising, editing, rewriting, or trying a new approach	W5 pp. 98–103
WHST.6	Use technology to produce, publish, and update individual or shared writing projects	W6 pp. 104–109
WHST.7	Conduct research projects to answer a question or solve a problem; synthesize multiple sources, demonstrating understanding of the subject	W7 pp. 110–115
WHST.8	Gather relevant information from multiple print and digital sources; assess the usefulness of each source; integrate information, avoiding plagiarism and overreliance on any one source	W8 pp. 116–121
WHST.9	Draw evidence from informational texts to support analysis, reflection, and research	W9 pp. 122–127
WHST.10	Write routinely for a range of discipline-specific tasks, purposes, and audiences	W10 pp. 128–133

Indiana, Grades 9–10

Indiana Strand/Standard	Focus of Indiana Standard	For More Information
Reading Literature		
RL.1	Read a variety of literature within an appropriate range of complexity	R10 pp. 60–65
RL.2.1	Cite strong and thorough textual evidence to support analysis of what the text says explicitly and implicitly	R1 pp. 6–11
RL.2.2	Analyze the development of two or more themes or central ideas and how they are shaped by specific details	R2 pp. 12–17
RL.2.3	Analyze how characters develop, interact, and advance the plot or develop the theme	R3 pp. 18–23
RL.3.1	Analyze how an author's choices regarding structure, the order of events, and manipulating time create such effects as mystery, tension, or surprise	R5 pp. 30–35
RL.3.2	Analyze how the author creates such effects as suspense and humor	NA
RL.4.1	Analyze multiple interpretations of a text, evaluating how each interprets the source	R7 pp. 42–47
RL.4.2	Analyze how works of literary or cultural significance draw on and transform source material	R9 pp. 54–59
Reading Nonfiction		
RN.1	Read a variety of nonfiction within an appropriate range of complexity	R10 pp. 60–65
RN.2.1	Cite strong and thorough textual evidence to support analysis of what the text says explicitly and implicitly	R1 pp. 6–11
RN.2.2	Analyze the development of the central idea and how they are shaped by specific details	R2 pp. 12–17
RN.2.3	Analyze how the author unfolds a series of ideas or events and the connections drawn between them	R3 pp. 18–23
RN.3.2	Analyze in detail how ideas or claims are developed by particular sentences, paragraphs, or larger portions of text	R5 pp. 30–35
RN.3.3	Analyze how an author uses rhetoric to advance a point of view, perspective, or purpose	R6 pp. 36–41
RN.4.1	Evaluate the argument in a text; assess reasoning and evidence; identify false statements and fallacious reasoning	R8 pp. 48–53
RN.4.2	Analyze various accounts of a subject told in different mediums	R7 pp. 42–47
RN.4.3	Analyze U.S. documents of historical and literary significance, noting how they address related themes and concepts	R9 pp. 54–59
Reading Vocabulary		
RV.1	Acquire and use accurately general academic and domain-specific words and phrases; demonstrate independence in gathering vocabulary knowledge	L6 pp. 208–213
RV.2.1	Use context to determine or clarify the meaning of words and phrases	L4 pp. 196–201
RV.2.3	Analyze nuances in the meaning of words	L5 pp. 202–207
RV.2.4	Identify and correctly use patterns of word changes	L4 pp. 196–201
RV.2.5	Select and use appropriate reference materials	L4 pp. 196–201
RV.3.1	Analyze the meaning of words and phrases as they are used in works of literature	R4 pp. 24–29
RV.3.2	Determine the meaning of words and phrases as they are used in a nonfiction text	R4 pp. 24–29
RV.3.3	Interpret figures of speech and analyze their role in the text	L5 pp. 202–207

Indiana Strand/Standard	Focus of Indiana Standard	For More Information
Writing		
W.1	Write routinely over short and extended time frames for a range of audiences, tasks, and purposes	W9 pp. 122–127 W10 pp. 128–133
W.3.1	Write arguments to support claims, using valid reasoning and relevant and sufficient evidence	W1 pp. 70–77
W.3.2	Write informative/explanatory texts to effectively examine and convey complex ideas, concepts, and information	W2 pp. 78–85
W.3.3	Write narratives to develop real or imagined experiences or events using effective technique, well-chosen details, and well-structured event sequences	W3 pp. 86–91
W.4	Apply the writing process to develop, draft, revise, rewrite, try a new approach, and edit to produce writing that is clear and coherent; use technology to produce, publish, and update writing	W5 pp. 98–103 W6 pp. 104–109
W.5	Conduct research assignments to build knowledge about the process and the topics	W7 pp. 110–115 W8 pp. 116–121
W.6.1	Demonstrate command of the conventions of standard English grammar and usage when writing or speaking	L1 pp. 178–183
W.6.2	Demonstrate command of the conventions of standard English capitalization, punctuation, and spelling when writing	L2 pp. 184–189
Speaking and Listening		
SL.1	Listen actively and adjust the use of spoken language to communicate effectively	SL6 pp. 168–173
SL.2.1	Engage effectively in a range of collaborative discussions with diverse partners, building on others' ideas and expressing their own clearly and persuasively	SL1 pp. 138–143
SL.2.2	Support or refute points under discussion by providing specific evidence	SL1 pp. 138–143
SL.2.3	Work with peers to set rules for discussions and decision-making	SL1 pp. 138–143
SL.2.4	Pose and respond to questions that relate discussions to broader themes; incorporate others into the discussion; clarify, verify, or challenge ideas	SL1 pp. 138–143
SL.2.5	Respond thoughtfully to multiple perspectives	SL1 pp. 138–143
SL.3.1	Integrate multiple sources of information presented in diverse media or formats; evaluate credibility and accuracy of sources and noting discrepancies	SL2 pp. 144–149
SL.3.2	Evaluate a speaker's point of view, reasoning, and use of evidence and rhetoric; identify fallacious reasoning or exaggerated or distorted evidence	SL3 pp. 150–155
SL.4.1	Present information clearly, concisely, and logically; ensure organization, development, substance, and style are appropriate to purpose, audience, and task	SL4 pp. 156–161
SL.4.2	Make strategic use of digital media in presentations to enhance understanding and to add interest	SL5 pp. 162–167
History/Social Studies		
LH.1.1	Read and comprehend history/social studies texts of appropriate complexity	R10 pp. 60–65
LH.1.2	Write routinely for a range of discipline-specific tasks, purposes, and audiences	W10 pp. 128–133
LH.2.1	Cite specific textual evidence to support analysis of primary and secondary sources	R1 pp. 6–11
LH.2.2	Determine central ideas or information of a primary or secondary source; summarize how they develop	R2 pp. 12–17
LH.2.3	Analyze in detail a series of events; determine whether earlier events caused later ones	R3 pp. 18–23
LH.3.1	Determine the meaning of words and phrases, including vocabulary describing political, social, or economic aspects of history/social studies	R4 pp. 24–29
LH.3.2	Analyze how a text uses structure to emphasize key points or advance an explanation or analysis	R5 pp. 30–35
LH.3.3	Compare the point of view of two or more authors for how they treat the same or similar topics	R6 pp. 36–41
LH.4.1	Integrate quantitative or technical analysis with qualitative analysis	R7 pp. 42–47

(Continued)

Indiana Strand/Standard	Focus of Indiana Standard	For More Information
History/Social Studies		
LH.4.2	Assess the extent to which reasoning and evidence support the author's claim	R8 pp. 48–53
LH.4.3	Compare and contrast treatment of the same topic in several primary and secondary sources	R9 pp. 54–59
LH.5.1	Write arguments focused on disciple-specific content	W1 pp. 70–77
LH.5.2	Write informative/explanatory texts, including the narration of historical events, scientific procedures, or technical processes	W2 pp. 78–85
LH.6.1	Produce clear and coherent writing in which the development, organization, and style are appropriate to task, purpose, and audience; develop and strengthen writing as needed by planning, revising, editing, rewriting, or trying a new approach	W4 pp. 92–97 W5 pp. 98–103
LH.6.2	Use technology to produce, publish, and update individual or shared writing projects	W6 pp. 104–109
LH.7.1	Conduct research projects to answer a question or solve a problem; synthesize multiple sources, demonstrating understanding of the subject	W7 pp. 110–115
LH.7.2	Gather relevant information from multiple print and digital sources; assess the usefulness of each source; integrate information, avoiding plagiarism and overreliance on any one source	W8 pp. 116–121
LH.7.3	Draw evidence from informational texts to support analysis, reflection, and research	W9 pp. 122–127
Science/Technical Subjects		
LST.1.1	Read and comprehend science/technical texts of appropriate complexity	R10 pp. 60–65
LST.1.2	Write routinely for a range of discipline-specific tasks, purposes, and audiences	W10 pp. 128–133
LST.2.1	Cite specific textual evidence to support analysis of science and technical texts	R1 pp. 6–11
LST.2.2	Determine central ideas or conclusions; trace the explanation of a complex process; provide an accurate summary	R2 pp. 12–17
LST.2.3	Follow precisely a complex multistep procedure; analyze the results based on explanations in the text	R3 pp. 18–23
LST.3.1	Determine the meaning of domain-specific words and phrases as they are used in a special scientific or technical context	R4 pp. 24–29
LST.3.2	Analyze the structure of relationships among concepts in a text	R5 pp. 30–35
LST.3.3	Analyze the author's purpose in providing an explanation, describing a procedure, or discussing an experiment	R6 pp. 36–41
LST.4.1	Translate quantitative or technical information expressed in words into visual form, and translate information expressed visually into words	R7 pp. 42–47
LST.4.2	Assess the extent to which reasoning and evidence support the author's claim or recommendation for solving a problem	R8 pp. 48–53
LST.4.3	Compare and contrast findings presented in a text to those from other sources, noting where they support or contradict previous explanations	R9 pp. 54–59
LST.5.1	Write arguments focused on discipline-specific content	W1 pp. 70–77
LST.5.2	Write informative/explanatory texts, including the narration of historical events, scientific procedures, or technical processes	W2 pp. 78–85
LST.6.1	Produce clear and coherent writing in which the development, organization, and style are appropriate to task, purpose, and audience; develop and strengthen writing as needed by planning, revising, editing, rewriting, or trying a new approach	W4 pp. 92–97 W5 pp. 98–103
LST.6.2	Use technology to produce, publish, and update individual or shared writing projects	W6 pp. 104–109
LST.7.1	Conduct research projects to answer a question or solve a problem; synthesize multiple sources, demonstrating understanding of the subject	W7 pp. 110–115
LST.7.2	Gather relevant information from multiple print and digital sources; assess the usefulness of each source; integrate information, avoiding plagiarism and overreliance on any one source	W8 pp. 116–121
LST.7.3	Draw evidence from informational texts to support analysis, reflection, and research	W9 pp. 122–127

Indiana, Grades 11–12

Indiana Strand/Standard	Focus of Indiana Standard	For More Information
Reading Literature		
RL.1	Read and comprehend a range of literature from a variety of cultures	R10 pp. 60–65
RL.2.1	Cite strong and thorough textual evidence to support analysis of what the text says explicitly and implicitly	R1 pp. 6–11
RL.2.2	Determine two or more themes or central ideas and analyze their development; restate and summarize main ideas or events	R2 pp. 12–17
RL.2.3	Analyze the impact of the author's choices regarding how to develop and relate elements of a story	R3 pp. 18–23
RL.3.1	Analyze how an author's choices regarding structure, the order of events, and manipulating time create such effects as mystery, tension, or surprise	R5 pp. 30–35
RL.3.2	Analyze a work in which grasping point of view requires distinguishing what is directly stated from what is really meant	R6 pp. 36–41
RL.4.1	Analyze multiple interpretations of a text, evaluating how each interprets the source	R7 pp. 42–47
RL.4.2	Analyze how works of literary or cultural significance use archetypes drawn from myths, traditional stories, or religious works	R9 pp. 54–59
Reading Nonfiction		
RN.1	Read a variety of nonfiction within an appropriate range of complexity	R10 pp. 60–65
RN.2.1	Cite strong and thorough textual evidence to support analysis of what the text says explicitly and implicitly	R1 pp. 6–11
RN.2.2	Compare and contrast the development of similar central ideas across two or more texts	R2 pp. 12–17
RN.2.3	Analyze a complex set of ideas or sequence of events and explain how specific individuals, ideas, or events interact and develop	R3 pp. 18–23
RN.3.2	Analyze and evaluate the effectiveness of the structure in an exposition or argument	R5 pp. 30–35
RN.3.3	Analyze how an author's style and content contribute to the power, persuasiveness, or impact of the text	R6 pp. 36–41
RN.4.1	Delineate and evaluate the reasoning in seminal U.S. texts, including the application of constitutional principles and use of legal reasoning, and the premises, purposes, and arguments in works of public advocacy	R8 pp. 48–53
RN.4.2	Synthesize and evaluate multiple sources of information presented in different media or formats in order to address a question or solve a problem	R7 pp. 42–47
RN.4.3	Analyze and synthesize U.S. and world documents of historical and literary significance, noting how they address related themes and concepts	R9 pp. 54–59
Reading Vocabulary		
RV.1	Acquire and use accurately general academic and domain-specific words and phrases; demonstrate independence in gathering vocabulary knowledge	L6 pp. 208–213
RV.2.1	Use context to determine or clarify the meaning of words and phrases	L4 pp. 196–201
RV.2.3	Analyze nuances in the meaning of words	L5 pp. 202–207
RV.2.4	Identify and correctly use patterns of word changes	L4 pp. 196–201
RV.2.5	Select and use appropriate reference materials	L4 pp. 196–201
RV.3.1	Analyze the meaning of words and phrases as they are used in works of literature	R4 pp. 24–29
RV.3.2	Determine the meaning of words and phrases as they are used in a nonfiction text	R4 pp. 24–29
RV.3.3	Interpret figures of speech and analyze their role in the text	L5 pp. 202–207

(Continued)

Indiana Strand/Standard	Focus of Indiana Standard	For More Information
Writing		
W.1	Write routinely over short and extended time frames for a range of audiences, tasks, and purposes	W9 pp. 122–127 W10 pp. 128–133
W.3.1	Write arguments to support claims, using valid reasoning and relevant and sufficient evidence	W1 pp. 70–77
W.3.2	Write informative/explanatory texts to effectively examine and convey complex ideas, concepts, and information	W2 pp. 78–85
W.3.3	Write narratives to develop real or imagined experiences or events using effective technique, well-chosen details, and well-structured event sequences	W3 pp. 86–91 W4 pp. 92–97
W.4	Apply the writing process to develop, draft, revise, rewrite, try a new approach, and edit to produce writing that is clear and coherent; use technology to produce, publish, and update writing	W5 pp. 98–103 W6 pp. 104–109
W.5	Conduct research assignments to build knowledge about the process and the topics	W7 pp. 110–115 W8 pp. 116–121
W.6.1	Demonstrate command of the conventions of standard English grammar and usage when writing or speaking	L1 pp. 178–183
W.6.2	Demonstrate command of the conventions of standard English capitalization, punctuation, and spelling when writing	L2 pp. 184–189
Speaking and Listening		
SL.1	Listen actively and adjust the use of spoken language to communicate effectively	SL6 pp. 168–173
SL.2.1	Engage effectively in a range of collaborative discussions with diverse partners, building on others' ideas and expressing their own clearly and persuasively	SL1 pp. 138–143
SL.2.2	Stimulate a thoughtful, well-reasoned debate and exchange of ideas by referring to specific evidence	SL1 pp. 138–143
SL.2.3	Work with peers to promote collegial discussions and decision-making	SL1 pp. 138–143
SL.2.4	Pose and respond to questions that probe reasoning and evidence; clarify, verify, or challenge ideas; promote divergent and creative perspectives	SL1 pp. 138–143
SL.2.5	Conduct debate and discussion to allow all views to be presented	SL1 pp. 138–143
SL.3.1	Integrate multiple sources of information presented in diverse media or formats; evaluate credibility and accuracy of sources and noting discrepancies	SL2 pp. 144–149
SL.3.2	Evaluate a speaker's point of view, reasoning, and use of evidence and rhetoric, assessing the stance, points of emphasis, and tone	SL3 pp. 150–155
SL.4.1	Present information, conveying a clear and distinct perspective, address alternative viewpoints; presentation is appropriate to purpose, audience, and task	SL4 pp. 156–161
SL.4.2	Make strategic use of digital media in presentations to enhance understanding and to add interest	SL5 pp. 162–167
History/Social Studies		
LH.1.1	Read and comprehend history/social studies texts of appropriate complexity	R10 pp. 60–65
LH.1.2	Write routinely for a range of discipline-specific tasks, purposes, and audiences	W10 pp. 128–133
LH.2.1	Cite specific textual evidence to support analysis of primary and secondary sources	R1 pp. 6–11
LH.2.2	Determine central ideas or information of a primary or secondary source; summarize how they develop	R2 pp. 12–17
LH.2.3	Evaluate explanations for actions or events and determine which best accords with textual evidence	R3 pp. 18–23
LH.3.1	Determine the meaning of words and phrases, including figurative and connotative meanings; analyze the impact of specific word choices	R4 pp. 24–29
LH.3.2	Analyze in detail how a complex primary source is structured	R5 pp. 30–35
LH.3.3	Evaluate authors' differing points of view on the same historical event	R6 pp. 36–41
LH.4.1	Integrate and evaluate multiple sources of information presented in diverse formats and media in order to address a question or solve a problem	R7 pp. 42–47

Indiana Strand/Standard	Focus of Indiana Standard	For More Information
History/Social Studies		
LH.4.2	Evaluate an author's premises, claims, and evidence by corroborating or challenging them	R8 pp. 48–53
LH.4.3	Integrate information from diverse sources into a coherent understanding of an idea or event	R9 pp. 54–59
LH.5.1	Write arguments focused on disciple-specific content	W1 pp. 70–77
LH.5.2	Write informative/explanatory texts, including the narration of historical events, scientific procedures, or technical processes	W2 pp. 78–85
LH.6.1	Produce clear and coherent writing in which the development, organization, and style are appropriate to task, purpose, and audience; develop and strengthen writing as needed by planning, revising, editing, rewriting, or trying a new approach	W4 pp. 92–97 W5 pp. 98–103
LH.6.2	Use technology to produce, publish, and update individual or shared writing projects	W6 pp. 104–109
LH.7.1	Conduct research projects to answer a question or solve a problem; synthesize multiple sources, demonstrating understanding of the subject	W7 pp. 110–115
LH.7.2	Gather relevant information from multiple print and digital sources; assess the usefulness of each source; integrate information, avoiding plagiarism and overreliance on any one source	W8 pp. 116–121
LH.7.3	Draw evidence from informational texts to support analysis, reflection, and research	W9 pp. 122–127
Science/Technical Subjects		
LST.1.1	Read and comprehend science/technical texts of appropriate complexity	R10 pp. 60–65
LST.1.2	Write routinely for a range of discipline-specific tasks, purposes, and audiences	W10 pp. 128–133
LST.2.1	Cite specific textual evidence to support analysis of science and technical texts	R1 pp. 6–11
LST.2.2	Determine central ideas or conclusions; summarize complex concepts by paraphrasing into simpler but accurate terms	R2 pp. 12–17
LST.2.3	Follow precisely a complex multistep procedure; analyze the results based on explanations in the text	R3 pp. 18–23
LST.3.1	Determine the meaning of domain-specific words and phrases as they are used in a special scientific or technical context	R4 pp. 24–29
LST.3.2	Analyze how the text structures information into categories or hierarchies, demonstrating understanding	R5 pp. 30–35
LST.3.3	Analyze the author's purpose in providing an explanation, describing a procedure, or discussing an experiment	R6 pp. 36–41
LST.4.1	Integrate and evaluate multiple sources of information presented in diverse formats and media in order to address a question or solve a problem	R7 pp. 42–47
LST.4.2	Evaluate the hypotheses, data, analysis, and conclusions in a science or technical text, corroborating or challenging conclusions	R8 pp. 48–53
LST.4.3	Synthesize information from a range of sources into a coherent understanding, resolving conflicting information when possible	R9 pp. 54–59
LST.5.1	Write arguments focused on discipline-specific content	W1 pp. 70–77
LST.5.2	Write informative/explanatory texts, including the narration of historical events, scientific procedures, or technical processes	W2 pp. 78–85
LST.6.1	Produce clear and coherent writing in which the development, organization, and style are appropriate to task, purpose, and audience; develop and strengthen writing as needed by planning, revising, editing, rewriting, or trying a new approach	W4 pp. 92–97 W5 pp. 98–103
LST.6.2	Use technology to produce, publish, and update individual or shared writing projects	W6 pp. 104–109
LST.7.1	Conduct research projects to answer a question or solve a problem; synthesize multiple sources, demonstrating understanding of the subject	W7 pp. 110–115
LST.7.2	Gather relevant information from multiple print and digital sources; assess the usefulness of each source; integrate information, avoiding plagiarism and overreliance on any one source	W8 pp. 116–121
LST.7.3	Draw evidence from informational texts to support analysis, reflection, and research	W9 pp. 122–127

Iowa, Grades 9–10

Iowa Strand/Standard	Focus of Iowa Standard	For More Information
Reading Literature		
RL.1	Cite strong and thorough textual evidence to support analysis of what the text says explicitly and implicitly	R1 pp. 6–11
RL.2	Determine a theme or central idea of a text and analyze its development and how it is shaped by specific details; summarize the text	R2 pp. 12–17
RL.3	Analyze how characters develop, interact, and advance the plot or develop the theme	R3 pp. 18–23
RL.IA.1	Employ the full range of reading comprehension strategies	NA
RL.IA.2	Read on-level text at an appropriate rate, with accuracy and fluency	NA
RL.4	Determine the meaning of words and phrases as they are used in a text, including figurative and connotative meanings; analyze the cumulative impact of word choice on meaning and tone	R4 pp. 24–29
RL.5	Analyze how an author's choices regarding structure, the order of events, and manipulating time create such effects as mystery, tension, or surprise	R5 pp. 30–35
RL.6	Analyze a point of view, perspective, or cultural experience reflected in a piece of literature	R6 pp. 36–41
RL.7	Analyze the representation of a subject or scene in two different artistic mediums, including what is emphasized or absent in each treatment	R7 pp. 42–47
RL.8	NA	
RL.9	Analyze how an author draws on and transforms source material	R9 pp. 54–59
RL.10	Read literature of appropriate complexity independently with proficiency	R10 pp. 60–65
Reading Informational Text		
RI.1	Cite strong and thorough textual evidence to support analysis of what the text says explicitly and implicitly	R1 pp. 6–11
RI.2	Determine the central idea of a text and analyze its development; summarize main ideas or events	R2 pp. 12–17
RI.3	Analyze how the author structures an analysis or series of ideas or events, including the order, how they are developed, and the connections between them	R3 pp. 18–23
RI.IA.1	Employ the full range of reading comprehension strategies	NA
RI.IA.2	Read on-level text at an appropriate rate, with accuracy and fluency	NA
RI.4	Determine the meaning of words and phrases in a text; analyze the cumulative impact of specific word choices	R4 pp. 24–29
RI.5	Analyze in detail how ideas or claims are developed by particular sentences, paragraphs, or larger portions of text	R5 pp. 30–35
RI.6	Analyze how an author uses rhetoric to advance a point of view, perspective, or purpose	R6 pp. 36–41
RI.7	Analyze various accounts of a subject told in different mediums	R7 pp. 42–47
RI.8	Evaluate the argument in a text; assess reasoning and evidence; identify false statements and fallacious reasoning	R8 pp. 48–53
RI.9	Analyze U.S. documents of historical and literary significance, noting how they address related themes and concepts	R9 pp. 54–59
RI.10	Read and comprehend appropriately complex informational texts independently and proficiently	R10 pp. 60–65
Writing		
W.1	Write arguments to support claims, using valid reasoning and relevant and sufficient evidence	W1 pp. 70–77
W.2	Write informative/explanatory texts to effectively examine and convey complex ideas, concepts, and information	W2 pp. 78–85

Iowa Strand/Standard	Focus of Iowa Standard	For More Information
Writing		
W.3	Write narratives to develop real or imagined experiences or events using effective technique, well-chosen details, and well-structured event sequences	W3 pp. 86–91
W.4	Produce writing in which the development, organization, style, and features are appropriate to the task, genre, purpose, and audience	W4 pp. 92–97
W.5	Develop and strengthen writing as needed by planning, revising, and editing, rewriting, or trying a new approach	W5 pp. 98–103
W.6	Use technology to produce, publish, and update individual or shared writing projects	W6 pp. 104–109
W.7	Conduct research projects to answer a question or solve a problem; synthesize multiple sources; demonstrate understanding of the subject	W7 pp. 110–115
W.8	Gather information from multiple sources, using advanced searches effectively; assess usefulness of sources; integrate information, avoiding plagiarism	W8 pp. 116–121
W.9	Draw evidence from texts to support analysis, reflection, research, and/or synthesis	W9 pp. 122–127
W.10	Write routinely over short and extended time frames for a range of audiences, tasks, and purposes	W10 pp. 128–133
Speaking and Listening		
SL.1	Engage effectively in a range of collaborative discussions with diverse partners, building on others' ideas and expressing their own clearly and persuasively	SL1 pp. 138–143
SL.2	Integrate multiple sources of information presented in diverse media or formats; evaluate credibility and accuracy of sources and noting discrepancies	SL2 pp. 144–149
SL.3	Evaluate a speaker's point of view, reasoning, and use of evidence and rhetoric; identify fallacious reasoning or exaggerated or distorted evidence	SL3 pp. 150–155
SL.4	Present information clearly, concisely, and logically; ensure organization, development, substance, and style are appropriate to purpose, audience, and task	SL4 pp. 156–161
SL.5	Make strategic use of digital media in presentations to enhance understanding and to add interest	SL5 pp. 162–167
SL.6	Adapt speech to a variety of contexts and tasks; demonstrate a command of formal English when appropriate	SL6 pp. 168–173
SL.IA.5	Prepare and conduct interviews	NA
SL.IA.6	Participate in public performances	NA
SL.IA.7	Debate an issue from the other side	NA
Language		
L.1	Demonstrate command of the conventions of standard English grammar and usage when writing or speaking	L1 pp. 178–183
L.2	Demonstrate command of the conventions of standard English capitalization, punctuation, and spelling when writing	L2 pp. 184–189
L.3	Apply knowledge of language to make effective choices for meaning or style, and to comprehend more fully when reading or listening	L3 pp. 190–195
L.4	Determine or clarify the meaning of unknown and multiple-meaning words and phrases, choosing flexibly from an array of strategies	L4 pp. 196–201
L.5	Demonstrate understanding of figurative language, word relationships, and nuances in word meanings	L5 pp. 202–207
L.6	Acquire and use accurately general academic and domain-specific words and phrases; demonstrate independence in gathering vocabulary knowledge	L6 pp. 208–213
Reading History/Social Studies		
RH.1	Cite specific textual evidence to support analysis of primary and secondary sources	R1 pp. 6–11
RH.2	Determine central ideas or information of a primary or secondary source; summarize how they develop	R2 pp. 12–17

(Continued)

Iowa Strand/Standard	Focus of Iowa Standard	For More Information
Reading History/Social Studies		
RH.3	Analyze in detail a series of events; determine whether earlier events caused later ones	R3 pp. 18–23
RH.4	Determine the meaning of words and phrases, including vocabulary describing political, social, or economic aspects of history/social studies	R4 pp. 24–29
RH.5	Analyze how a text uses structure to emphasize key points or advance an explanation or analysis	R5 pp. 30–35
RH.6	Compare the point of view of two or more authors for how they treat the same or similar topics	R6 pp. 36–41
RH.7	Integrate quantitative or technical analysis with qualitative analysis	R7 pp. 42–47
RH.8	Assess the extent to which reasoning and evidence support the author's claim	R8 pp. 48–53
RH.9	Compare and contrast treatment of the same topic in several primary and secondary sources	R9 pp. 54–59
RH.10	Read and comprehend history/social studies texts of appropriate complexity	R10 pp. 60–65
Reading Science/Technical Subjects		
RST.1	Cite specific textual evidence to support analysis of science and technical texts	R1 pp. 6–11
RST.2	Determine central ideas or conclusions; trace the explanation of a complex process; provide an accurate summary	R2 pp. 12–17
RST.3	Follow precisely a complex multistep procedure, attending to special cases or exceptions defined in the text	R3 pp. 18–23
RST.4	Determine the meaning of domain-specific words and phrases as they are used in a special scientific or technical context	R4 pp. 24–29
RST.5	Analyze the structure of relationships among concepts in a text	R5 pp. 30–35
RST.6	Analyze the author's purpose in providing an explanation, describing a procedure, or discussing an experiment	R6 pp. 36–41
RST.7	Translate quantitative or technical information expressed in words into visual form, and translate information expressed visually into words	R7 pp. 42–47
RST.8	Assess the extent to which reasoning and evidence support the author's claim or recommendation for solving a problem	R8 pp. 48–53
RST.9	Compare and contrast findings presented in a text to those from other sources, noting where they support or contradict previous explanations	R9 pp. 54–59
RST.10	Read and comprehend science/technical texts of appropriate complexity	R10 pp. 60–65
Writing History/Social Studies, Science and Technical Subjects		
WHST.1	Write arguments focused on disciple-specific content	W1 pp. 70–77
WHST.2	Write informative/explanatory texts, including the narration of historical events, scientific procedures, or technical processes	W2 pp. 78–85
WHST.3	NA	W3 pp. 86–91
WHST.4	Produce clear and coherent writing in which the development, organization, and style are appropriate to task, purpose, and audience	W4 pp. 92–97
WHST.5	Develop and strengthen writing as needed by planning, revising, editing, rewriting, or trying a new approach	W5 pp. 98–103
WHST.6	Use technology to produce, publish, and update individual or shared writing projects	W6 pp. 104–109
WHST.7	Conduct research projects to answer a question or solve a problem; synthesize multiple sources, demonstrating understanding of the subject	W7 pp. 110–115
WHST.8	Gather relevant information from multiple print and digital sources; assess the usefulness of each source; integrate information, avoiding plagiarism	W8 pp. 116–121
WHST.9	Draw evidence from informational texts to support analysis, reflection, and research	W9 pp. 122–127
WHST.10	Write routinely for a range of discipline-specific tasks, purposes, and audiences	W10 pp. 128–133

Iowa, Grades 11–12

Iowa Strand/Standard	Focus of Iowa Standard	For More Information
Reading Literature		
RL.1	Cite strong and thorough textual evidence to support analysis of what the text says explicitly and implicitly	R1 pp. 6–11
RL.2	Determine two or more themes or central ideas and analyze their development; restate and summarize main ideas or events	R2 pp. 12–17
RL.3	Analyze the impact of the author's choices regarding how to develop and relate elements of a story	R3 pp. 18–23
RL.IA.1	Employ the full range of reading comprehension strategies	NA
RL.IA.2	Read on-level text at an appropriate rate, with accuracy and fluency	NA
RL.4	Determine the meaning of words and phrases as they are used in a text, including figurative and connotative meanings; analyze the cumulative impact of word choice on meaning and tone	R4 pp. 24–29
RL.5	Analyze how an author's choices concerning how to structure specific parts of the text contribute to its overall structure and meaning	R5 pp. 30–35
RL.6	Analyze a case in which grasping point of view requires distinguishing what is directly stated from what is really meant	R6 pp. 36–41
RL.7	Analyze multiple representations of a story, drama, or poem, evaluating how each interprets the source text	R7 pp. 42–47
RL.8	NA	
RL.9	Demonstrate knowledge of 18th, 19th, and early 20th century foundational works of American literature	R9 pp. 54–59
RL.10	Read and comprehend a range of literature from a variety of cultures	R10 pp. 60–65
Reading Informational Text		
RI.1	Cite strong and thorough textual evidence to support analysis of what the text says explicitly and implicitly, including where the text leaves matters uncertain	R1 pp. 6–11
RI.2	Determine two or more central ideas of a text and analyze their development; restate or summarize main ideas or events	R2 pp. 12–17
RI.3	Analyze a complex set of ideas or sequence of events and explain how specific individuals, ideas, or events interact and develop	R3 pp. 18–23
RI.IA.1	Employ the full range of reading comprehension strategies	NA
RI.IA.2	Read on-level text at an appropriate rate, with accuracy and fluency	NA
RI.4	Determine the meaning of words and phrases in a text; analyze how an author uses and refines the meaning of key terms over the course of a text	R4 pp. 24–29
RI.5	Analyze and evaluate the effectiveness of the structure in an exposition or argument	R5 pp. 30–35
RI.6	Analyze how an author's style and content contribute to the power, persuasiveness, or impact of the text	R6 pp. 36–41
RI.7	Integrate and evaluate multiple sources of information presented in different media or formats in order to address a question or solve a problem	R7 pp. 42–47
RI.8	Delineate and evaluate the reasoning in seminal U.S. texts, including the application of constitutional principles and use of legal reasoning, and the premises, purposes, and arguments in works of public policy	R8 pp. 48–53
RI.9	Analyze 17th, 18th, and 19th century foundational U.S. and world documents of literary significance	R9 pp. 54–59
RI.10	Read and comprehend literary nonfiction independently and proficiently	R10 pp. 60–65
Writing		
W.1	Write arguments to support claims, using valid reasoning and relevant and sufficient evidence	W1 pp. 70–77
W.2	Write informative/explanatory texts to examine and convey complex ideas, concepts, and information clearly and accurately	W2 pp. 78–85

(Continued)

Iowa Strand/Standard	Focus of Iowa Standard	For More Information
Writing		
W.3	Write narratives to develop real or imagined experiences or events using effective technique, well-chosen details, and well-structured event sequences	W3 pp. 86–91
W.4	Produce writing in which the development, organization, style, and features are appropriate to the task, genre, purpose, and audience	W4 pp. 92–97
W.5	Develop and strengthen writing as needed by planning, revising, and editing, rewriting, or trying a new approach	W5 pp. 98–103
W.6	Use technology to produce, publish, and update individual or shared writing projects	W6 pp. 104–109
W.7	Conduct research projects to answer a question or solve a problem; synthesize multiple sources; demonstrate understanding of the subject	W7 pp. 110–115
W.8	Gather information from multiple sources, using advanced searches effectively; assess strengths and limitations of sources; integrate information, avoiding plagiarism and overreliance on any one source	W8 pp. 116–121
W.9	Draw evidence from texts to support analysis, reflection, and research	W9 pp. 122–127
W.10	Write routinely over shorter and extended time frames for a range of audiences, tasks, and purposes	W10 pp. 128–133
Speaking and Listening		
SL.1	Engage effectively in a range of collaborative discussions with diverse partners, building on others' ideas and expressing their own clearly and persuasively	SL1 pp. 138–143
SL.2	Integrate multiple sources of information presented in diverse media or formats; evaluate credibility and accuracy of sources and note discrepancies	SL2 pp. 144–149
SL.3	Evaluate a speaker's point of view, reasoning, and use of evidence and rhetoric; assess the stance, premises, link among ideas, word choice, emphasis, and tone	SL3 pp. 150–155
SL.4	Present information, conveying a clear and distinct perspective, address alternative viewpoints; presentation is appropriate to purpose, audience, and task	SL4 pp. 156–161
SL.5	Make strategic use of digital media in presentations to enhance understanding and to add interest	SL5 pp. 162–167
SL.6	Adapt speech to a variety of contexts and tasks; demonstrate a command of formal English when appropriate	SL6 pp. 168–173
SL.IA.5	Prepare and conduct interviews	NA
SL.IA.6	Participate in public performances	NA
SL.IA.7	Debate an issue from the other side	NA
Language		
L.1	Demonstrate command of the conventions of standard English grammar and usage when writing or speaking	L1 pp. 178–183
L.2	Demonstrate command of the conventions of standard English capitalization, punctuation, and spelling when writing	L2 pp. 184–189
L.3	Apply knowledge of language to make effective choices for meaning or style, and to comprehend more fully when reading or listening	L3 pp. 190–195
L.4	Determine or clarify the meaning of unknown and multiple-meaning words and phrases, choosing flexibly from an array of strategies	L4 pp. 196–201
L.5	Demonstrate understanding of figurative language, word relationships, and nuances in word meanings	L5 pp. 202–207
L.6	Acquire and use accurately general academic and domain-specific words and phrases; demonstrate independence in gathering vocabulary knowledge	L6 pp. 208–213
Reading History/Social Studies		
RH.1	Cite specific textual evidence to support analysis of primary and secondary sources	R1 pp. 6–11
RH.2	Determine central ideas or information of a primary or secondary source; summarize how they develop	R2 pp. 12–17
RH.3	Evaluate explanations for actions or events and determine which best accords with textual evidence	R3 pp. 18–23

Iowa Strand/Standard	Focus of Iowa Standard	For More Information
Reading History/Social Studies		
RH.4	Determine the meaning of words and phrases, including figurative and connotative meanings; analyze the impact of specific word choices	R4 pp. 24–29
RH.5	Analyze in detail how a complex primary source is structured	R5 pp. 30–35
RH.6	Evaluate authors' differing points of view on the same historical event	R6 pp. 36–41
RH.7	Integrate and evaluate multiple sources of information presented in diverse formats and media in order to address a question or solve a problem	R7 pp. 42–47
RH.8	Evaluate an author's premises, claims, and evidence by corroborating or challenging them	R8 pp. 48–53
RH.9	Integrate information from diverse sources into a coherent understanding of an idea or event	R9 pp. 54–59
RH.10	Read and comprehend history/social studies texts of appropriate complexity	R10 pp. 60–65
Reading Science/Technical Subjects		
RST.1	Cite specific textual evidence to support analysis of science and technical texts	R1 pp. 6–11
RST.2	Determine central ideas or conclusions; summarize complex concepts by paraphrasing into simpler but accurate terms	R2 pp. 12–17
RST.3	Follow precisely a complex multistep procedure; analyze the results based on explanations in the text	R3 pp. 18–23
RST.4	Determine the meaning of domain-specific words and phrases as they are used in a special scientific or technical context	R4 pp. 24–29
RST.5	Analyze how the text structures information into categories or hierarchies, demonstrating understanding	R5 pp. 30–35
RST.6	Analyze the author's purpose in providing an explanation, describing a procedure, or discussing an experiment	R6 pp. 36–41
RST.7	Integrate and evaluate multiple sources of information presented in diverse formats and media in order to address a question or solve a problem	R7 pp. 42–47
RST.8	Evaluate the hypotheses, data, analysis, and conclusions in a science or technical text, corroborating or challenging conclusions	R8 pp. 48–53
RST.9	Synthesize information from a range of sources into a coherent understanding, resolving conflicting information when possible	R9 pp. 54–59
RST.10	Read and comprehend science/technical texts of appropriate complexity	R10 pp. 60–65
Writing History/Social Studies, Science and Technical Subjects		
WHST.1	Write arguments focused on disciple-specific content	W1 pp. 70–77
WHST.2	Write informative/explanatory texts, including the narration of historical events, scientific procedures, or technical processes	W2 pp. 78–85
WHST.3	NA	
WHST.4	Produce clear and coherent writing in which the development, organization, and style are appropriate to task, purpose, and audience	W4 pp. 92–97
WHST.5	Develop and strengthen writing as needed by planning, revising, editing, rewriting, or trying a new approach	W5 pp. 98–103
WHST.6	Use technology to produce, publish, and update individual or shared writing projects	W6 pp. 104–109
WHST.7	Conduct research projects to answer a question or solve a problem; synthesize multiple sources, demonstrating understanding of the subject	W7 pp. 110–115
WHST.8	Gather relevant information from multiple print and digital sources; assess the usefulness of each source; integrate information, avoiding plagiarism and overreliance on any one source	W8 pp. 116–121
WHST.9	Draw evidence from informational texts to support analysis, reflection, and research	W9 pp. 122–127
WHST.10	Write routinely for a range of discipline-specific tasks, purposes, and audiences	W10 pp. 128–133

Kansas, Grades 9–10

Kansas Strand/Standard	Focus of Kansas Standard	For More Information
Reading Literature		
RL.1	Cite strong and thorough textual evidence to support analysis of what the text says explicitly and implicitly	R1 pp. 6–11
RL.2	Determine a theme or central idea of a text and analyze its development and how it is shaped by specific details; summarize the text	R2 pp. 12–17
RL.3	Analyze how characters develop, interact, and advance the plot or develop the theme	R3 pp. 18–23
RL.4	Determine the meaning of words and phrases as they are used in a text, including figurative and connotative meanings; analyze the cumulative impact of word choice on meaning and tone	R4 pp. 24–29
RL.5	Analyze how an author's choices regarding structure, the order of events, and manipulating time create such effects as mystery, tension, or surprise	R5 pp. 30–35
RL.6	Analyze a point of view, perspective, or cultural experience reflected in a piece of literature	R6 pp. 36–41
RL.7	Analyze the representation of a subject or scene in two different artistic mediums, including what is emphasized or absent in each treatment	R7 pp. 42–47
RL.8	NA	
RL.9	Analyze how an author draws on and transforms source material	R9 pp. 54–59
RL.10	Read literature of appropriate complexity independently with proficiency	R10 pp. 60–65
Reading Informational Text		
RI.1	Cite strong and thorough textual evidence to support analysis of what the text says explicitly and implicitly	R1 pp. 6–11
RI.2	Determine the central idea of a text and analyze its development; summarize main ideas or events	R2 pp. 12–17
RI.3	Analyze how the author structures an analysis or series of ideas or events, including the order, how they are developed, and the connections between them	R3 pp. 18–23
RI.4	Determine the meaning of words and phrases in a text; analyze the cumulative impact of specific word choices	R4 pp. 24–29
RI.5	Analyze in detail how ideas or claims are developed by particular sentences, paragraphs, or larger portions of text	R5 pp. 30–35
RI.6	Analyze how an author uses rhetoric to advance a point of view, perspective, or purpose	R6 pp. 36–41
RI.7	Analyze various accounts of a subject told in different mediums	R7 pp. 42–47
RI.8	Evaluate the argument in a text; assess reasoning and evidence; identify false statements and fallacious reasoning	R8 pp. 48–53
RI.9	Analyze U.S. documents of historical and literary significance, noting how they address related themes and concepts	R9 pp. 54–59
RI.10	Read and comprehend appropriately complex informational texts independently and proficiently	R10 pp. 60–65
Writing		
W.1	Write arguments to support claims, using valid reasoning and relevant and sufficient evidence	W1 pp. 70–77
W.2	Write informative/explanatory texts to effectively examine and convey complex ideas, concepts, and information	W2 pp. 78–85
W.3	Write narratives to develop real or imagined experiences or events using effective technique, well-chosen details, and well-structured event sequences	W3 pp. 86–91
W.4	Produce writing in which the development, organization, style, and features are appropriate to the task, genre, purpose, and audience	W4 pp. 92–97

Kansas Strand/Standard	Focus of Kansas Standard	For More Information
Writing		
W.5	Develop and strengthen writing as needed by planning, revising, and editing, rewriting, or trying a new approach	W5 pp. 98–103
W.6	Use technology to produce, publish, and update individual or shared writing projects	W6 pp. 104–109
W.7	Conduct research projects to answer a question or solve a problem; synthesize multiple sources; demonstrate understanding of the subject	W7 pp. 110–115
W.8	Gather information from multiple sources, using advanced searches effectively; assess usefulness of sources; integrate information, avoiding plagiarism	W8 pp. 116–121
W.9	Draw evidence from texts to support analysis, reflection, research, and/or synthesis	W9 pp. 122–127
W.10	Write routinely over short and extended time frames for a range of audiences, tasks, and purposes	W10 pp. 128–133
Speaking and Listening		
SL.1	Engage effectively in a range of collaborative discussions with diverse partners, building on others' ideas and expressing their own clearly and persuasively	SL1 pp. 138–143
SL.2	Integrate multiple sources of information presented in diverse media or formats; evaluate credibility and accuracy of sources and noting discrepancies	SL2 pp. 144–149
SL.3	Evaluate a speaker's point of view, reasoning, and use of evidence and rhetoric; identify fallacious reasoning or exaggerated or distorted evidence	SL3 pp. 150–155
SL.4	Present information clearly, concisely, and logically; ensure organization, development, substance, and style are appropriate to purpose, audience, and task	SL4 pp. 156–161
SL.5	Make strategic use of digital media in presentations to enhance understanding and to add interest	SL5 pp. 162–167
SL.6	Adapt speech to a variety of contexts and tasks; demonstrate a command of formal English when appropriate	SL6 pp. 168–173
Language		
L.1	Demonstrate command of the conventions of standard English grammar and usage when writing or speaking	L1 pp. 178–183
L.2	Demonstrate command of the conventions of standard English capitalization, punctuation, and spelling when writing	L2 pp. 184–189
L.3	Apply knowledge of language to make effective choices for meaning or style, and to comprehend more fully when reading or listening	L3 pp. 190–195
L.4	Determine or clarify the meaning of unknown and multiple-meaning words and phrases, choosing flexibly from an array of strategies	L4 pp. 196–201
L.5	Demonstrate understanding of figurative language, word relationships, and nuances in word meanings	L5 pp. 202–207
L.6	Acquire and use accurately general academic and domain-specific words and phrases; demonstrate independence in gathering vocabulary knowledge	L6 pp. 208–213
Reading History/Social Studies		
RH.1	Cite specific textual evidence to support analysis of primary and secondary sources	R1 pp. 6–11
RH.2	Determine central ideas or information of a primary or secondary source; summarize how they develop	R2 pp. 12–17
RH.3	Analyze in detail a series of events; determine whether earlier events caused later ones	R3 pp. 18–23
RH.4	Determine the meaning of words and phrases, including vocabulary describing political, social, or economic aspects of history/social studies	R4 pp. 24–29
RH.5	Analyze how a text uses structure to emphasize key points or advance an explanation or analysis	R5 pp. 30–35
RH.6	Compare the point of view of two or more authors for how they treat the same or similar topics	R6 pp. 36–41

(Continued)

Kansas Strand/Standard	Focus of Kansas Standard	For More Information
Reading History/Social Studies		
RH.7	Integrate quantitative or technical analysis with qualitative analysis	R7 pp. 42–47
RH.8	Assess the extent to which reasoning and evidence support the author's claim	R8 pp. 48–53
RH.9	Compare and contrast treatment of the same topic in several primary and secondary sources	R9 pp. 54–59
RH.10	Read and comprehend history/social studies texts of appropriate complexity	R10 pp. 60–65
Reading Science/Technical Subjects		
RST.1	Cite specific textual evidence to support analysis of science and technical texts	R1 pp. 6–11
RST.2	Determine central ideas or conclusions; trace the explanation of a complex process; provide an accurate summary	R2 pp. 12–17
RST.3	Follow precisely a complex multistep procedure, attending to special cases or exceptions defined in the text	R3 pp. 18–23
RST.4	Determine the meaning of domain-specific words and phrases as they are used in a special scientific or technical context	R4 pp. 24–29
RST.5	Analyze the structure of relationships among concepts in a text	R5 pp. 30–35
RST.6	Analyze the author's purpose in providing an explanation, describing a procedure, or discussing an experiment	R6 pp. 36–41
RST.7	Translate quantitative or technical information expressed in words into visual form, and translate information expressed visually into words	R7 pp. 42–47
RST.8	Assess the extent to which reasoning and evidence support the author's claim or recommendation for solving a problem	R8 pp. 48–53
RST.9	Compare and contrast findings presented in a text to those from other sources, noting where they support or contradict previous explanations	R9 pp. 54–59
RST.10	Read and comprehend science/technical texts of appropriate complexity	R10 pp. 60–65
Writing History/Social Studies, Science and Technical Subjects		
WHST.1	Write arguments focused on disciple-specific content	W1 pp. 70–77
WHST.2	Write informative/explanatory texts, including the narration of historical events, scientific procedures, or technical processes	W2 pp. 78–85
WHST.3	NA	
WHST.4	Produce clear and coherent writing in which the development, organization, and style are appropriate to task, purpose, and audience	W4 pp. 92–97
WHST.5	Develop and strengthen writing as needed by planning, revising, editing, rewriting, or trying a new approach	W5 pp. 98–103
WHST.6	Use technology to produce, publish, and update individual or shared writing projects	W6 pp. 104–109
WHST.7	Conduct research projects to answer a question or solve a problem; synthesize multiple sources, demonstrating understanding of the subject	W7 pp. 110–115
WHST.8	Gather relevant information from multiple print and digital sources; assess the usefulness of each source; integrate information, avoiding plagiarism	W8 pp. 116–121
WHST.9	Draw evidence from informational texts to support analysis, reflection, and research	W9 pp. 122–127
WHST.10	Write routinely for a range of discipline-specific tasks, purposes, and audiences	W10 pp. 128–133

Kansas, Grades 11–12

Kansas Strand/Standard	Focus of Kansas Standard	For More Information
Reading Literature		
RL.1	Cite strong and thorough textual evidence to support analysis of what the text says explicitly and implicitly	R1 pp. 6–11
RL.2	Determine two or more themes or central ideas and analyze their development; restate and summarize main ideas or events	R2 pp. 12–17
RL.3	Analyze the impact of the author's choices regarding how to develop and relate elements of a story	R3 pp. 18–23
RL.4	Determine the meaning of words and phrases as they are used in a text, including figurative and connotative meanings; analyze the cumulative impact of word choice on meaning and tone	R4 pp. 24–29
RL.5	Analyze how an author's choices concerning how to structure specific parts of the text contribute to its overall structure and meaning	R5 pp. 30–35
RL.6	Analyze a case in which grasping point of view requires distinguishing what is directly stated from what is really meant	R6 pp. 36–41
RL.7	Analyze multiple representations of a story, drama, or poem, evaluating how each interprets the source text	R7 pp. 42–47
RL.8	NA	
RL.9	Demonstrate knowledge of 18th, 19th, and early 20th century foundational works of American literature	R9 pp. 54–59
RL.10	Read and comprehend a range of literature from a variety of cultures	R10 pp. 60–65
Reading Informational Text		
RI.1	Cite strong and thorough textual evidence to support analysis of what the text says explicitly and implicitly, including where the text leaves matters uncertain	R1 pp. 6–11
RI.2	Determine two or more central ideas of a text and analyze their development; restate or summarize main ideas or events	R2 pp. 12–17
RI.3	Analyze a complex set of ideas or sequence of events and explain how specific individuals, ideas, or events interact and develop	R3 pp. 18–23
RI.4	Determine the meaning of words and phrases in a text; analyze how an author uses and refines the meaning of key terms over the course of a text	R4 pp. 24–29
RI.5	Analyze and evaluate the effectiveness of the structure in an exposition or argument	R5 pp. 30–35
RI.6	Analyze how an author's style and content contribute to the power, persuasiveness, or impact of the text	R6 pp. 36–41
RI.7	Integrate and evaluate multiple sources of information presented in different media or formats in order to address a question or solve a problem	R7 pp. 42–47
RI.8	Delineate and evaluate the reasoning in seminal U.S. texts, including the application of constitutional principles and use of legal reasoning, and the premises, purposes, and arguments in works of public policy	R8 pp. 48–53
RI.9	Analyze 17th, 18th, and 19th century foundational U.S. and world documents of literary significance	R9 pp. 54–59
RI.10	Read and comprehend literary nonfiction independently and proficiently	R10 pp. 60–65
Writing		
W.1	Write arguments to support claims, using valid reasoning and relevant and sufficient evidence	W1 pp. 70–77
W.2	Write informative/explanatory texts to examine and convey complex ideas, concepts, and information clearly and accurately	W2 pp. 78–85
W.3	Write narratives to develop real or imagined experiences or events using effective technique, well-chosen details, and well-structured event sequences	W3 pp. 86–91

(Continued)

Kansas Strand/Standard	Focus of Kansas Standard	For More Information
Writing		
W.4	Produce writing in which the development, organization, style, and features are appropriate to the task, genre, purpose, and audience	W4 pp. 92–97
W.5	Develop and strengthen writing as needed by planning, revising, and editing, rewriting, or trying a new approach	W5 pp. 98–103
W.6	Use technology to produce, publish, and update individual or shared writing projects	W6 pp. 104–109
W.7	Conduct research projects to answer a question or solve a problem; synthesize multiple sources; demonstrate understanding of the subject	W7 pp. 110–115
W.8	Gather information from multiple sources, using advanced searches effectively; assess strengths and limitations of sources; integrate information, avoiding plagiarism and overreliance on any one source	W8 pp. 116–121
W.9	Draw evidence from texts to support analysis, reflection, and research	W9 pp. 122–127
W.10	Write routinely over shorter and extended time frames for a range of audiences, tasks, and purposes	W10 pp. 128–133
Speaking and Listening		
SL.1	Engage effectively in a range of collaborative discussions with diverse partners, building on others' ideas and expressing their own clearly and persuasively	SL1 pp. 138–143
SL.2	Integrate multiple sources of information presented in diverse media or formats; evaluate credibility and accuracy of sources and note discrepancies	SL2 pp. 144–149
SL.3	Evaluate a speaker's point of view, reasoning, and use of evidence and rhetoric; assess the stance, premises, link among ideas, word choice, emphasis, and tone	SL3 pp. 150–155
SL.4	Present information, conveying a clear and distinct perspective, address alternative viewpoints; presentation is appropriate to purpose, audience, and task	SL4 pp. 156–161
SL.5	Make strategic use of digital media in presentations to enhance understanding and to add interest	SL5 pp. 162–167
SL.6	Adapt speech to a variety of contexts and tasks; demonstrate a command of formal English when appropriate	SL6 pp. 168–173
Language		
L.1	Demonstrate command of the conventions of standard English grammar and usage when writing or speaking	L1 pp. 178–183
L.2	Demonstrate command of the conventions of standard English capitalization, punctuation, and spelling when writing	L2 pp. 184–189
L.3	Apply knowledge of language to make effective choices for meaning or style, and to comprehend more fully when reading or listening	L3 pp. 190–195
L.4	Determine or clarify the meaning of unknown and multiple-meaning words and phrases, choosing flexibly from an array of strategies	L4 pp. 196–201
L.5	Demonstrate understanding of figurative language, word relationships, and nuances in word meanings	L5 pp. 202–207
L.6	Acquire and use accurately general academic and domain-specific words and phrases; demonstrate independence in gathering vocabulary knowledge	L6 pp. 208–213
Reading History/Social Studies		
RH.1	Cite specific textual evidence to support analysis of primary and secondary sources	R1 pp. 6–11
RH.2	Determine central ideas or information of a primary or secondary source; summarize how they develop	R2 pp. 12–17
RH.3	Evaluate explanations for actions or events and determine which best accords with textual evidence	R3 pp. 18–23
RH.4	Determine the meaning of words and phrases, including figurative and connotative meanings; analyze the impact of specific word choices	R4 pp. 24–29

Kansas Strand/Standard	Focus of Kansas Standard	For More Information
Reading History/Social Studies		
RH.5	Analyze in detail how a complex primary source is structured	R5 pp. 30–35
RH.6	Evaluate authors' differing points of view on the same historical event	R6 pp. 36–41
RH.7	Integrate and evaluate multiple sources of information presented in diverse formats and media in order to address a question or solve a problem	R7 pp. 42–47
RH.8	Evaluate an author's premises, claims, and evidence by corroborating or challenging them	R8 pp. 48–53
RH.9	Integrate information from diverse sources into a coherent understanding of an idea or event	R9 pp. 54–59
RH.10	Read and comprehend history/social studies texts of appropriate complexity	R10 pp. 60–65
Reading Science/Technical Subjects		
RST.1	Cite specific textual evidence to support analysis of science and technical texts	R1 pp. 6–11
RST.2	Determine central ideas or conclusions; summarize complex concepts by paraphrasing into simpler but accurate terms	R2 pp. 12–17
RST.3	Follow precisely a complex multistep procedure; analyze the results based on explanations in the text	R3 pp. 18–23
RST.4	Determine the meaning of domain-specific words and phrases as they are used in a special scientific or technical context	R4 pp. 24–29
RST.5	Analyze how the text structures information into categories or hierarchies, demonstrating understanding	R5 pp. 30–35
RST.6	Analyze the author's purpose in providing an explanation, describing a procedure, or discussing an experiment	R6 pp. 36–41
RST.7	Integrate and evaluate multiple sources of information presented in diverse formats and media in order to address a question or solve a problem	R7 pp. 42–47
RST.8	Evaluate the hypotheses, data, analysis, and conclusions in a science or technical text, corroborating or challenging conclusions	R8 pp. 48–53
RST.9	Synthesize information from a range of sources into a coherent understanding, resolving conflicting information when possible	R9 pp. 54–59
RST.10	Read and comprehend science/technical texts of appropriate complexity	R10 pp. 60–65
Writing History/Social Studies, Science and Technical Subjects		
WHST.1	Write arguments focused on disciple-specific content	W1 pp. 70–77
WHST.2	Write informative/explanatory texts, including the narration of historical events, scientific procedures, or technical processes	W2 pp. 78–85
WHST.3	NA	
WHST.4	Produce clear and coherent writing in which the development, organization, and style are appropriate to task, purpose, and audience	W4 pp. 92–97
WHST.5	Develop and strengthen writing as needed by planning, revising, editing, rewriting, or trying a new approach	W5 pp. 98–103
WHST.6	Use technology to produce, publish, and update individual or shared writing projects	W6 pp. 104–109
WHST.7	Conduct research projects to answer a question or solve a problem; synthesize multiple sources, demonstrating understanding of the subject	W7 pp. 110–115
WHST.8	Gather relevant information from multiple print and digital sources; assess the usefulness of each source; integrate information, avoiding plagiarism and overreliance on any one source	W8 pp. 116–121
WHST.9	Draw evidence from informational texts to support analysis, reflection, and research	W9 pp. 122–127
WHST.10	Write routinely for a range of discipline-specific tasks, purposes, and audiences	W10 pp. 128–133

Louisiana, Grades 9–10

Louisiana Strand/Standard	Focus of Louisiana Standard	For More Information
Reading Literature		
RL.1	Cite relevant and thorough textual evidence to support analysis of what the text says explicitly and implicitly	R1 pp. 6–11
RL.2	Determine a theme or central idea of a text and analyze its development and how it is shaped by specific details; summarize the text	R2 pp. 12–17
RL.3	Analyze how characters develop, interact, and advance the plot or develop the theme	R3 pp. 18–23
RL.4	Determine the meaning of words and phrases as they are used in a text, including figurative and connotative meanings; analyze the cumulative impact of word choice on meaning and tone	R4 pp. 24–29
RL.5	Analyze how an author's choices regarding structure, the order of events, and manipulating time create such effects as mystery, tension, or surprise	R5 pp. 30–35
RL.6	Analyze a point of view, perspective, or cultural experience reflected in works of literature	R6 pp. 36–41
RL.7	Analyze the representation of a subject or scene in two different artistic mediums, including what is emphasized or absent in each treatment	R7 pp. 42–47
RL.8	NA	
RL.9	Analyze how an author draws on and transforms source material	R9 pp. 54–59
RL.10	Read literature of appropriate complexity independently with proficiency	R10 pp. 60–65
Reading Informational Text		
RI.1	Cite relevant and thorough textual evidence to support analysis of what the text says explicitly and implicitly	R1 pp. 6–11
RI.2	Determine the central idea of a text and analyze its development; summarize main ideas or events	R2 pp. 12–17
RI.3	Analyze how the author structures an analysis or series of ideas or events, including the order, how they are developed, and the connections between them	R3 pp. 18–23
RI.4	Determine the meaning of words and phrases in a text; analyze the cumulative impact of specific word choices	R4 pp. 24–29
RI.5	Analyze in detail how ideas or claims are developed by particular sentences, paragraphs, or larger portions of text	R5 pp. 30–35
RI.6	Analyze how an author uses rhetoric to advance a point of view, perspective, or purpose	R6 pp. 36–41
RI.7	Analyze various accounts of a subject told in different mediums	R7 pp. 42–47
RI.8	Evaluate the argument in a text; assess reasoning and evidence; identify false statements and fallacious reasoning	R8 pp. 48–53
RI.9	Analyze U.S. documents of historical and literary significance, noting how they address related themes and concepts	R9 pp. 54–59
RI.10	Read and comprehend appropriately complex informational texts independently and proficiently	R10 pp. 60–65
Writing		
W.1	Write arguments to support claims, using valid reasoning and relevant and sufficient evidence	W1 pp. 70–77
W.2	Write informative/explanatory texts to effectively examine and convey complex ideas, concepts, and information	W2 pp. 78–85
W.3	Write narratives to develop real or imagined experiences or events using effective technique, well-chosen details, and well-structured event sequences	W3 pp. 86–91
W.4	Produce writing in which the development, organization, style, and features are appropriate to the task, genre, purpose, and audience	W4 pp. 92–97
W.5	Develop and strengthen writing as needed by planning, revising, and editing, rewriting, or trying a different approach	W5 pp. 98–103

Louisiana Strand/Standard	Focus of Louisiana Standard	For More Information
Writing		
W.6	Use technology to produce, publish, and update individual or shared writing projects	W6 pp. 104–109
W.7	Conduct research projects to answer a question or solve a problem; synthesize multiple sources; demonstrate understanding of the subject	W7 pp. 110–115
W.8	Gather information from multiple sources, using advanced searches effectively; assess usefulness of sources; integrate information, avoiding plagiarism and overreliance on any one source	W8 pp. 116–121
W.9	Draw relevant evidence from texts to support analysis, reflection, research, and/or synthesis	W9 pp. 122–127
W.10	Write routinely over shorter and extended time frames for a range of audiences, tasks, and purposes	W10 pp. 128–133
Speaking and Listening		
SL.1	Engage effectively in a range of collaborative discussions with diverse partners, building on others' ideas and expressing their own clearly and persuasively	SL1 pp. 138–143
SL.2	Integrate multiple sources of information presented in diverse media or formats; evaluate credibility and accuracy of sources and noting discrepancies	SL2 pp. 144–149
SL.3	Evaluate a speaker's point of view, reasoning, and use of evidence and rhetoric; identify fallacious reasoning or exaggerated or distorted evidence	SL3 pp. 150–155
SL.4	Present information clearly, concisely, and logically; ensure organization, development, substance, and style are appropriate to purpose, audience, and task	SL4 pp. 156–161
SL.5	Make strategic use of digital media in presentations to enhance understanding and to add interest	SL5 pp. 162–167
SL.6	Adapt speech to a variety of contexts, audiences, and tasks; demonstrate a command of formal English when appropriate	SL6 pp. 168–173
Language		
L.1	Demonstrate command of the conventions of standard English grammar and usage when writing or speaking	L1 pp. 178–183
L.2	Demonstrate command of the conventions of standard English capitalization, punctuation, and spelling when writing	L2 pp. 184–189
L.3	Apply knowledge of language to make effective choices for meaning or style, to comprehend more fully when reading or listening, and to write and edit so that it conforms to the guidelines in a style manual appropriate for the writing type	L3 pp. 190–195
L.4	Determine or clarify the meaning of unknown and multiple-meaning words and phrases, choosing flexibly from an array of strategies	L4 pp. 196–201
L.5	Demonstrate understanding of figurative language, word relationships, and nuances in word meanings	L5 pp. 202–207
L.6	Acquire and use accurately general academic and domain-specific words and phrases; demonstrate independence in gathering vocabulary knowledge	L6 pp. 208–213
Reading History/Social Studies		
R.1	Cite specific textual evidence to support analysis of primary and secondary sources	R1 pp. 6–11
R.2	Determine central ideas or information of a primary or secondary source; summarize how they develop	R2 pp. 12–17
R.3	Analyze in detail a series of events; determine whether earlier events caused later ones	R3 pp. 18–23
R.4	Determine the meaning of words and phrases, including vocabulary describing political, social, or economic aspects of history/social studies	R4 pp. 24–29
R.5	Analyze how a text uses structure to emphasize key points or advance an explanation or analysis	R5 pp. 30–35
R.6	Compare the point of view of two or more authors for how they treat the same or similar topics	R6 pp. 36–41
R.7	Integrate quantitative or technical analysis with qualitative analysis	R7 pp. 42–47

(Continued)

Louisiana Strand/Standard	Focus of Louisiana Standard	For More Information
Reading History/Social Studies		
R.8	Assess the extent to which reasoning and evidence support the author's claim	R8 pp. 48–53
R.9	Compare and contrast treatment of the same topic in several primary and secondary sources	R9 pp. 54–59
R.10	Read and comprehend history/social studies texts of appropriate complexity	R10 pp. 60–65
Reading Science/Technical Subjects		
R.1	Cite specific textual evidence to support analysis of science and technical texts	R1 pp. 6–11
R.2	Determine central ideas or conclusions; trace the explanation of a complex process; provide an accurate summary	R2 pp. 12–17
R.3	Follow precisely a complex multistep procedure, attending to special cases or exceptions defined in the text	R3 pp. 18–23
R.4	Determine the meaning of domain-specific words and phrases as they are used in a special scientific or technical context	R4 pp. 24–29
R.5	Analyze the structure of relationships among concepts in a text	R5 pp. 30–35
R.6	Analyze the author's purpose in providing an explanation, describing a procedure, or discussing an experiment	R6 pp. 36–41
R.7	Translate quantitative or technical information expressed in words into visual form, and translate information expressed visually into words	R7 pp. 42–47
R.8	Assess the extent to which reasoning and evidence support the author's claim or recommendation for solving a problem	R8 pp. 48–53
R.9	Compare and contrast findings presented in a text to those from other sources, noting where they support or contradict previous explanations	R9 pp. 54–59
R.10	Read and comprehend science/technical texts of appropriate complexity	R10 pp. 60–65
Writing History/Social Studies, Science and Technical Subjects		
W.1	Write arguments focused on disciple-specific content	W1 pp. 70–77
W.2	Write informative/explanatory texts, including the narration of historical events, scientific procedures, or technical processes	W2 pp. 78–85
W.3	NA	W3 pp. 86–91
W.4	Produce clear and coherent writing in which the development, organization, and style are appropriate to task, purpose, and audience	W4 pp. 92–97
W.5	Develop and strengthen writing as needed by planning, revising, editing, rewriting, or trying a new approach	W5 pp. 98–103
W.6	Use technology to produce, publish, and update individual or shared writing projects	W6 pp. 104–109
W.7	Conduct research projects to answer a question or solve a problem; synthesize multiple sources, demonstrating understanding of the subject	W7 pp. 110–115
W.8	Gather relevant information from multiple print and digital sources; assess the usefulness of each source; integrate information, avoiding plagiarism	W8 pp. 116–121
W.9	Draw evidence from informational texts to support analysis, reflection, and research	W9 pp. 122–127
W.10	Write routinely for a range of discipline-specific tasks, purposes, and audiences	W10 pp. 128–133

Louisiana, Grades 11–12

Louisiana Strand/Standard	Focus of Louisiana Standard	For More Information
Reading Literature		
RL.1	Cite strong, thorough, and relevant textual evidence to support analysis of what the text says explicitly and implicitly	R1 pp. 6–11
RL.2	Determine two or more themes or central ideas and analyze their development; restate and summarize main ideas or events	R2 pp. 12–17
RL.3	Analyze the impact of the author's choices regarding how to develop and relate elements of a story or drama	R3 pp. 18–23
RL.4	Determine the meaning of words and phrases as they are used in a text, including figurative and connotative meanings; analyze the cumulative impact of word choice on meaning and tone	R4 pp. 24–29
RL.5	Analyze how an author's choices concerning how to structure specific parts of the text contribute to its overall structure and meaning	R5 pp. 30–35
RL.6	Analyze a case in which grasping point of view requires distinguishing what is directly stated from what is really meant	R6 pp. 36–41
RL.7	Analyze multiple representations of a story, drama, or poem, evaluating how each interprets the source text	R7 pp. 42–47
RL.8	NA	
RL.9	Demonstrate knowledge of foundational works of U.S. and world literature	R9 pp. 54–59
RL.10	Read and comprehend a range of literature from a variety of cultures	R10 pp. 60–65
Reading Informational Text		
RI.1	Cite strong, thorough, and relevant textual evidence to support analysis of what the text says explicitly and implicitly, including where the text leaves matters uncertain	R1 pp. 6–11
RI.2	Determine two or more central ideas of a text and analyze their development; restate or summarize main ideas or events	R2 pp. 12–17
RI.3	Analyze a complex set of ideas or sequence of events and explain how specific individuals, ideas, or events interact and develop	R3 pp. 18–23
RI.4	Determine the meaning of words and phrases in a text; analyze how an author uses and refines the meaning of key terms over the course of a text	R4 pp. 24–29
RI.5	Analyze and evaluate the effectiveness of the structure in an exposition or argument	R5 pp. 30–35
RI.6	Analyze how an author's style and content contribute to the reader's interpretation of the power, persuasiveness, or impact of the text	R6 pp. 36–41
RI.7	Integrate and evaluate multiple sources of information presented in different media or formats in order to address a question or solve a problem	R7 pp. 42–47
RI.8	Delineate and evaluate the reasoning in seminal U.S. texts, including the application of constitutional principles and use of legal reasoning, and the premises, purposes, and arguments in works of public policy	R8 pp. 48–53
RI.9	Analyze foundational U.S. and world documents of literary significance	R9 pp. 54–59
RI.10	Read and comprehend literary nonfiction independently and proficiently	R10 pp. 60–65
Writing		
W.1	Write arguments to support claims, using valid reasoning and relevant and sufficient evidence	W1 pp. 70–77
W.2	Write informative/explanatory texts to examine and convey complex ideas, concepts, and information clearly and accurately	W2 pp. 78–85
W.3	Write narratives to develop real or imagined experiences or events using effective technique, well-chosen details, and well-structured event sequences	W3 pp. 86–91

(Continued)

Louisiana Strand/Standard	Focus of Louisiana Standard	For More Information
Writing		
W.4	Produce writing in which the development, organization, style, and features are appropriate to the task, genre, purpose, and audience	W4 pp. 92–97
W.5	Develop and strengthen writing as needed by planning, revising, and editing, rewriting, or trying a new approach	W5 pp. 98–103
W.6	Use technology to produce, publish, and update individual or shared writing projects	W6 pp. 104–109
W.7	Conduct research projects to answer a question or solve a problem; synthesize multiple sources; demonstrate understanding of the subject	W7 pp. 110–115
W.8	Gather information from multiple sources, using advanced searches effectively; assess strengths and limitations of sources; integrate information, avoiding plagiarism and overreliance on any one source	W8 pp. 116–121
W.9	Draw evidence from texts to support analysis, reflection, and research	W9 pp. 122–127
W.10	Write routinely over shorter and extended time frames for a range of audiences, tasks, and purposes	W10 pp. 128–133
Speaking and Listening		
SL.1	Engage effectively in a range of collaborative discussions with diverse partners, building on others' ideas and expressing their own clearly and persuasively	SL1 pp. 138–143
SL.2	Integrate multiple sources of information presented in diverse media or formats; evaluate credibility and accuracy of sources and note discrepancies	SL2 pp. 144–149
SL.3	Evaluate a speaker's point of view, reasoning, and use of evidence and rhetoric; assess the stance, premises, link among ideas, word choice, emphasis, and tone	SL3 pp. 150–155
SL.4	Present information, conveying a clear and distinct perspective; address alternative viewpoints; presentation is appropriate to purpose, audience, and task	SL4 pp. 156–161
SL.5	Make strategic use of digital media in presentations to enhance understanding and to add interest	SL5 pp. 162–167
SL.6	Adapt speech to a variety of contexts, audiences, and tasks; demonstrate a command of formal English when appropriate	SL6 pp. 168–173
Language		
L.1	Demonstrate command of the conventions of standard English grammar and usage when writing or speaking	L1 pp. 178–183
L.2	Demonstrate command of the conventions of standard English capitalization, punctuation, and spelling when writing	L2 pp. 184–189
L.3	Apply knowledge of language to make effective choices for meaning or style, and to comprehend more fully when reading or listening	L3 pp. 190–195
L.4	Determine or clarify the meaning of unknown and multiple-meaning words and phrases, choosing flexibly from an array of strategies	L4 pp. 196–201
L.5	Demonstrate understanding of figurative language, word relationships, and nuances in word meanings	L5 pp. 202–207
L.6	Acquire and use accurately general academic and domain-specific words and phrases; demonstrate independence in gathering vocabulary knowledge	L6 pp. 208–213
Reading History/Social Studies		
R.1	Cite specific textual evidence to support analysis of primary and secondary sources	R1 pp. 6–11
R.2	Determine central ideas or information of a primary or secondary source; summarize how they develop	R2 pp. 12–17
R.3	Evaluate explanations for actions or events and determine which best accords with textual evidence	R3 pp. 18–23
R.4	Determine the meaning of words and phrases, including figurative and connotative meanings; analyze the impact of specific word choices	R4 pp. 24–29

Louisiana Strand/Standard	Focus of Louisiana Standard	For More Information
Reading History/Social Studies		
R.5	Analyze in detail how a complex primary source is structured	R5 pp. 30–35
R.6	Evaluate authors' differing points of view on the same historical event	R6 pp. 36–41
R.7	Integrate and evaluate multiple sources of information presented in diverse formats and media in order to address a question or solve a problem	R7 pp. 42–47
R.8	Evaluate an author's premises, claims, and evidence by corroborating or challenging them	R8 pp. 48–53
R.9	Integrate information from diverse sources into a coherent understanding of an idea or event	R9 pp. 54–59
R.10	Read and comprehend history/social studies texts of appropriate complexity	R10 pp. 60–65
Reading Science/Technical Subjects		
R.1	Cite specific textual evidence to support analysis of science and technical texts	R1 pp. 6–11
R.2	Determine central ideas or conclusions; summarize complex concepts by paraphrasing into simpler but accurate terms	R2 pp. 12–17
R.3	Follow precisely a complex multistep procedure; analyze the results based on explanations in the text	R3 pp. 18–23
R.4	Determine the meaning of domain-specific words and phrases as they are used in a special scientific or technical context	R4 pp. 24–29
R.5	Analyze how the text structures information into categories or hierarchies, demonstrating understanding	R5 pp. 30–35
R.6	Analyze the author's purpose in providing an explanation, describing a procedure, or discussing an experiment	R6 pp. 36–41
R.7	Integrate and evaluate multiple sources of information presented in diverse formats and media in order to address a question or solve a problem	R7 pp. 42–47
R.8	Evaluate the hypotheses, data, analysis, and conclusions in a science or technical text, corroborating or challenging conclusions	R8 pp. 48–53
R.9	Synthesize information from a range of sources into a coherent understanding, resolving conflicting information when possible	R9 pp. 54–59
R.10	Read and comprehend science/technical texts of appropriate complexity	R10 pp. 60–65
Writing History/Social Studies, Science and Technical Subjects		
W.1	Write arguments focused on disciple-specific content	W1 pp. 70–77
W.2	Write informative/explanatory texts, including the narration of historical events, scientific procedures, or technical processes	W2 pp. 78–85
W.3	NA	
W.4	Produce clear and coherent writing in which the development, organization, and style are appropriate to task, purpose, and audience	W4 pp. 92–97
W.5	Develop and strengthen writing as needed by planning, revising, editing, rewriting, or trying a new approach	W5 pp. 98–103
W.6	Use technology to produce, publish, and update individual or shared writing projects	W6 pp. 104–109
W.7	Conduct research projects to answer a question or solve a problem; synthesize multiple sources, demonstrating understanding of the subject	W7 pp. 110–115
W.8	Gather relevant information from multiple print and digital sources; assess the usefulness of each source; integrate information, avoiding plagiarism and overreliance on any one source	W8 pp. 116–121
W.9	Draw evidence from informational texts to support analysis, reflection, and research	W9 pp. 122–127
W.10	Write routinely for a range of discipline-specific tasks, purposes, and audiences	W10 pp. 128–133

Maryland, Grades 9–10

Maryland Strand/Standard	Focus of Maryland Standard	For More Information
Reading Literature		
RL.1	Cite strong and thorough textual evidence to support analysis of what the text says explicitly and implicitly	R1 pp. 6–11
RL.2	Determine a theme or central idea of a text and analyze its development and how it is shaped by specific details; summarize the text	R2 pp. 12–17
RL.3	Analyze how characters develop, interact, and advance the plot or develop the theme	R3 pp. 18–23
RL.4	Determine the meaning of words and phrases as they are used in a text, including figurative and connotative meanings; analyze the cumulative impact of word choice on meaning and tone	R4 pp. 24–29
RL.5	Analyze how an author's choices regarding structure, the order of events, and manipulating time create such effects as mystery, tension, or surprise	R5 pp. 30–35
RL.6	Analyze a point of view, perspective, or cultural experience reflected in a piece of literature	R6 pp. 36–41
RL.7	Analyze the representation of a subject or scene in two different artistic mediums, including what is emphasized or absent in each treatment	R7 pp. 42–47
RL.8	NA	
RL.9	Analyze how an author draws on and transforms source material	R9 pp. 54–59
RL.10	Read literature of appropriate complexity independently with proficiency	R10 pp. 60–65
Reading Informational Text		
RI.1	Cite strong and thorough textual evidence to support analysis of what the text says explicitly and implicitly	R1 pp. 6–11
RI.2	Determine the central idea of a text and analyze its development; summarize main ideas or events	R2 pp. 12–17
RI.3	Analyze how the author structures an analysis or series of ideas or events, including the order, how they are developed, and the connections between them	R3 pp. 18–23
RI.4	Determine the meaning of words and phrases in a text; analyze the cumulative impact of specific word choices	R4 pp. 24–29
RI.5	Analyze in detail how ideas or claims are developed by particular sentences, paragraphs, or larger portions of text	R5 pp. 30–35
RI.6	Analyze how an author uses rhetoric to advance a point of view, perspective, or purpose	R6 pp. 36–41
RI.7	Analyze various accounts of a subject told in different mediums	R7 pp. 42–47
RI.8	Evaluate the argument in a text; assess reasoning and evidence; identify false statements and fallacious reasoning	R8 pp. 48–53
RI.9	Analyze U.S. documents of historical and literary significance, noting how they address related themes and concepts	R9 pp. 54–59
RI.10	Read and comprehend appropriately complex informational texts independently and proficiently	R10 pp. 60–65
Writing		
W.1	Write arguments to support claims, using valid reasoning and relevant and sufficient evidence	W1 pp. 70–77
W.2	Write informative/explanatory texts to effectively examine and convey complex ideas, concepts, and information	W2 pp. 78–85
W.3	Write narratives to develop real or imagined experiences or events using effective technique, well-chosen details, and well-structured event sequences	W3 pp. 86–91
W.4	Produce writing in which the development, organization, style, and features are appropriate to the task, genre, purpose, and audience	W4 pp. 92–97
W.5	Develop and strengthen writing as needed by planning, revising, and editing, rewriting, or trying a new approach	W5 pp. 98–103
W.6	Use technology to produce, publish, and update individual or shared writing projects	W6 pp. 104–109
W.7	Conduct research projects to answer a question or solve a problem; synthesize multiple sources; demonstrate understanding of the subject	W7 pp. 110–115
W.8	Gather information from multiple sources, using advanced searches effectively; assess usefulness of sources; integrate information, avoiding plagiarism	W8 pp. 116–121

Maryland Strand/Standard	Focus of Maryland Standard	For More Information
Writing		
W.9	Draw evidence from texts to support analysis, reflection, research, and/or synthesis	W9 pp. 122–127
W.10	Write routinely over short and extended time frames for a range of audiences, tasks, and purposes	W10 pp. 128–133
Speaking and Listening		
SL.1	Engage effectively in a range of collaborative discussions with diverse partners, building on others' ideas and expressing their own clearly and persuasively	SL1 pp. 138–143
SL.2	Integrate multiple sources of information presented in diverse media or formats; evaluate credibility and accuracy of sources and noting discrepancies	SL2 pp. 144–149
SL.3	Evaluate a speaker's point of view, reasoning, and use of evidence and rhetoric; identify fallacious reasoning or exaggerated or distorted evidence	SL3 pp. 150–155
SL.4	Present information clearly, concisely, and logically; ensure organization, development, substance, and style are appropriate to purpose, audience, and task	SL4 pp. 156–161
SL.5	Make strategic use of digital media in presentations to enhance understanding and to add interest	SL5 pp. 162–167
SL.6	Adapt speech to a variety of contexts and tasks; demonstrate a command of formal English when appropriate	SL6 pp. 168–173
Language		
L.1	Demonstrate command of the conventions of standard English grammar and usage when writing or speaking	L1 pp. 178–183
L.2	Demonstrate command of the conventions of standard English capitalization, punctuation, and spelling when writing	L2 pp. 184–189
L.3	Apply knowledge of language to make effective choices for meaning or style, and to comprehend more fully when reading or listening	L3 pp. 190–195
L.4	Determine or clarify the meaning of unknown and multiple-meaning words and phrases, choosing flexibly from an array of strategies	L4 pp. 196–201
L.5	Demonstrate understanding of figurative language, word relationships, and nuances in word meanings	L5 pp. 202–207
L.6	Acquire and use accurately general academic and domain-specific words and phrases; demonstrate independence in gathering vocabulary knowledge	L6 pp. 208–213
Reading History/Social Studies		
RH.1	Cite specific textual evidence to support analysis of primary and secondary sources	R1 pp. 6–11
RH.2	Determine central ideas or information of a primary or secondary source; summarize how they develop	R2 pp. 12–17
RH.3	Analyze in detail a series of events; determine whether earlier events caused later ones	R3 pp. 18–23
RH.4	Determine the meaning of words and phrases, including vocabulary describing political, social, or economic aspects of history/social studies	R4 pp. 24–29
RH.5	Analyze how a text uses structure to emphasize key points or advance an explanation or analysis	R5 pp. 30–35
RH.6	Compare the point of view of two or more authors for how they treat the same or similar topics	R6 pp. 36–41
RH.7	Integrate quantitative or technical analysis with qualitative analysis	R7 pp. 42–47
RH.8	Assess the extent to which reasoning and evidence support the author's claim	R8 pp. 48–53
RH.9	Compare and contrast treatment of the same topic in several primary and secondary sources	R9 pp. 54–59
RH.10	Read and comprehend history/social studies texts of appropriate complexity	R10 pp. 60–65
Reading Science/Technical Subjects		
RST.1	Cite specific textual evidence to support analysis of science and technical texts	R1 pp. 6–11
RST.2	Determine central ideas or conclusions; trace the explanation of a complex process; provide an accurate summary	R2 pp. 12–17
RST.3	Follow precisely a complex multistep procedure, attending to special cases or exceptions defined in the text	R3 pp. 18–23
RST.4	Determine the meaning of domain-specific words and phrases as they are used in a special scientific or technical context	R4 pp. 24–29

(Continued)

Maryland Strand/Standard	Focus of Maryland Standard	For More Information
Reading Science/Technical Subjects		
RST.5	Analyze the structure of relationships among concepts in a text	R5 pp. 30–35
RST.6	Analyze the author's purpose in providing an explanation, describing a procedure, or discussing an experiment	R6 pp. 36–41
RST.7	Translate quantitative or technical information expressed in words into visual form, and translate information expressed visually into words	R7 pp. 42–47
RST.8	Assess the extent to which reasoning and evidence support the author's claim or recommendation for solving a problem	R8 pp. 48–53
RST.9	Compare and contrast findings presented in a text to those from other sources, noting where they support or contradict previous explanations	R9 pp. 54–59
RST.10	Read and comprehend science/technical texts of appropriate complexity	R10 pp. 60–65
Writing History/Social Studies, Science and Technical Subjects		
WHST.1	Write arguments focused on disciple-specific content	W1 pp. 70–77
WHST.2	Write informative/explanatory texts, including the narration of historical events, scientific procedures, or technical processes	W2 pp. 78–85
WHST.3	NA	
WHST.4	Produce clear and coherent writing in which the development, organization, and style are appropriate to task, purpose, and audience	W4 pp. 92–97
WHST.5	Develop and strengthen writing as needed by planning, revising, editing, rewriting, or trying a new approach	W5 pp. 98–103
WHST.6	Use technology to produce, publish, and update individual or shared writing projects	W6 pp. 104–109
WHST.7	Conduct research projects to answer a question or solve a problem; synthesize multiple sources, demonstrating understanding of the subject	W7 pp. 110–115
WHST.8	Gather relevant information from multiple print and digital sources; assess the usefulness of each source; integrate information, avoiding plagiarism	W8 pp. 116–121
WHST.9	Draw evidence from informational texts to support analysis, reflection, and research	W9 pp. 122–127
WHST.10	Write routinely for a range of discipline-specific tasks, purposes, and audiences	W10 pp. 128–133

Maryland, Grades 11–12

Maryland Strand/Standard	Focus of Maryland Standard	For More Information
Reading Literature		
RL.1	Cite strong and thorough textual evidence to support analysis of what the text says explicitly and implicitly	R1 pp. 6–11
RL.2	Determine two or more themes or central ideas and analyze their development; restate and summarize main ideas or events	R2 pp. 12–17
RL.3	Analyze the impact of the author's choices regarding how to develop and relate elements of a story	R3 pp. 18–23
RL.4	Determine the meaning of words and phrases as they are used in a text, including figurative and connotative meanings; analyze the cumulative impact of word choice on meaning and tone	R4 pp. 24–29
RL.5	Analyze how an author's choices concerning how to structure specific parts of the text contribute to its overall structure and meaning	R5 pp. 30–35
RL.6	Analyze a case in which grasping point of view requires distinguishing what is directly stated from what is really meant	R6 pp. 36–41
RL.7	Analyze multiple representations of a story, drama, or poem, evaluating how each interprets the source text	R7 pp. 42–47
RL.8	NA	

Maryland Strand/Standard	Focus of Maryland Standard	For More Information
Reading Literature		
RL.9	Demonstrate knowledge of 18th, 19th, and early 20th century foundational works of American literature	R9 pp. 54–59
RL.10	Read and comprehend a range of literature from a variety of cultures	R10 pp. 60–65
Reading Informational Text		
RI.1	Cite strong and thorough textual evidence to support analysis of what the text says explicitly and implicitly, including where the text leaves matters uncertain	R1 pp. 6–11
RI.2	Determine two or more central ideas of a text and analyze their development; restate or summarize main ideas or events	R2 pp. 12–17
RI.3	Analyze a complex set of ideas or sequence of events and explain how specific individuals, ideas, or events interact and develop	R3 pp. 18–23
RI.4	Determine the meaning of words and phrases in a text; analyze how an author uses and refines the meaning of key terms over the course of a text	R4 pp. 24–29
RI.5	Analyze and evaluate the effectiveness of the structure in an exposition or argument	R5 pp. 30–35
RI.6	Analyze how an author's style and content contribute to the power, persuasiveness, or impact of the text	R6 pp. 36–41
RI.7	Integrate and evaluate multiple sources of information presented in different media or formats in order to address a question or solve a problem	R7 pp. 42–47
RI.8	Delineate and evaluate the reasoning in seminal U.S. texts, including the application of constitutional principles and use of legal reasoning, and the premises, purposes, and arguments in works of public policy	R8 pp. 48–53
RI.9	Analyze 17th, 18th, and 19th century foundational U.S. and world documents of literary significance	R9 pp. 54–59
RI.10	Read and comprehend literary nonfiction independently and proficiently	R10 pp. 60–65
Writing		
W.1	Write arguments to support claims, using valid reasoning and relevant and sufficient evidence	W1 pp. 70–77
W.2	Write informative/explanatory texts to examine and convey complex ideas, concepts, and information clearly and accurately	W2 pp. 78–85
W.3	Write narratives to develop real or imagined experiences or events using effective technique, well-chosen details, and well-structured event sequences	W3 pp. 86–91
W.4	Produce writing in which the development, organization, style, and features are appropriate to the task, genre, purpose, and audience	W4 pp. 92–97
W.5	Develop and strengthen writing as needed by planning, revising, and editing, rewriting, or trying a new approach	W5 pp. 98–103
W.6	Use technology to produce, publish, and update individual or shared writing projects	W6 pp. 104–109
W.7	Conduct research projects to answer a question or solve a problem; synthesize multiple sources; demonstrate understanding of the subject	W7 pp. 110–115
W.8	Gather information from multiple sources, using advanced searches effectively; assess strengths and limitations of sources; integrate information, avoiding plagiarism and overreliance on any one source	W8 pp. 116–121
W.9	Draw evidence from texts to support analysis, reflection, and research	W9 pp. 122–127
W.10	Write routinely over shorter and extended time frames for a range of audiences, tasks, and purposes	W10 pp. 128–133
Speaking and Listening		
SL.1	Engage effectively in a range of collaborative discussions with diverse partners, building on others' ideas and expressing their own clearly and persuasively	SL1 pp. 138–143
SL.2	Integrate multiple sources of information presented in diverse media or formats; evaluate credibility and accuracy of sources and note discrepancies	SL2 pp. 144–149
SL.3	Evaluate a speaker's point of view, reasoning, and use of evidence and rhetoric; assess the stance, premises, link among ideas, word choice, emphasis, and tone	SL3 pp. 150–155
SL.4	Present information, conveying a clear and distinct perspective, address alternative viewpoints; presentation is appropriate to purpose, audience, and task	SL4 pp. 156–161

(Continued)

Maryland Strand/Standard	Focus of Maryland Standard	For More Information
Speaking and Listening		
SL.5	Make strategic use of digital media in presentations to enhance understanding and to add interest	SL5 pp. 162–167
SL.6	Adapt speech to a variety of contexts and tasks; demonstrate a command of formal English when appropriate	SL6 pp. 168–173
Language		
L.1	Demonstrate command of the conventions of standard English grammar and usage when writing or speaking	L1 pp. 178–183
L.2	Demonstrate command of the conventions of standard English capitalization, punctuation, and spelling when writing	L2 pp. 184–189
L.3	Apply knowledge of language to make effective choices for meaning or style, and to comprehend more fully when reading or listening	L3 pp. 190–195
L.4	Determine or clarify the meaning of unknown and multiple-meaning words and phrases, choosing flexibly from an array of strategies	L4 pp. 196–201
L.5	Demonstrate understanding of figurative language, word relationships, and nuances in word meanings	L5 pp. 202–207
L.6	Acquire and use accurately general academic and domain-specific words and phrases; demonstrate independence in gathering vocabulary knowledge	L6 pp. 208–213
Reading History/Social Studies		
RH.1	Cite specific textual evidence to support analysis of primary and secondary sources	R1 pp. 6–11
RH.2	Determine central ideas or information of a primary or secondary source; summarize how they develop	R2 pp. 12–17
RH.3	Evaluate explanations for actions or events and determine which best accords with textual evidence	R3 pp. 18–23
RH.4	Determine the meaning of words and phrases, including figurative and connotative meanings; analyze the impact of specific word choices	R4 pp. 24–29
RH.5	Analyze in detail how a complex primary source is structured	R5 pp. 30–35
RH.6	Evaluate authors' differing points of view on the same historical event	R6 pp. 36–41
RH.7	Integrate and evaluate multiple sources of information presented in diverse formats and media in order to address a question or solve a problem	R7 pp. 42–47
RH.8	Evaluate an author's premises, claims, and evidence by corroborating or challenging them	R8 pp. 48–53
RH.9	Integrate information from diverse sources into a coherent understanding of an idea or event	R9 pp. 54–59
RH.10	Read and comprehend history/social studies texts of appropriate complexity	R10 pp. 60–65
Reading Science/Technical Subjects		
RST.1	Cite specific textual evidence to support analysis of science and technical texts	R1 pp. 6–11
RST.2	Determine central ideas or conclusions; summarize complex concepts by paraphrasing into simpler but accurate terms	R2 pp. 12–17
RST.3	Follow precisely a complex multistep procedure; analyze the results based on explanations in the text	R3 pp. 18–23
RST.4	Determine the meaning of domain-specific words and phrases as they are used in a special scientific or technical context	R4 pp. 24–29
RST.5	Analyze how the text structures information into categories or hierarchies, demonstrating understanding	R5 pp. 30–35
RST.6	Analyze the author's purpose in providing an explanation, describing a procedure, or discussing an experiment	R6 pp. 36–41
RST.7	Integrate and evaluate multiple sources of information presented in diverse formats and media in order to address a question or solve a problem	R7 pp. 42–47
RST.8	Evaluate the hypotheses, data, analysis, and conclusions in a science or technical text, corroborating or challenging conclusions	R8 pp. 48–53
RST.9	Synthesize information from a range of sources into a coherent understanding, resolving conflicting information when possible	R9 pp. 54–59
RST.10	Read and comprehend science/technical texts of appropriate complexity	R10 pp. 60–65

Maryland Strand/Standard	Focus of Maryland Standard	For More Information
Writing History/Social Studies, Science and Technical Subjects		
WHST.1	Write arguments focused on disciple-specific content	W1 pp. 70–77
WHST.2	Write informative/explanatory texts, including the narration of historical events, scientific procedures, or technical processes	W2 pp. 78–85
WHST.3	NA	
WHST.4	Produce clear and coherent writing in which the development, organization, and style are appropriate to task, purpose, and audience	W4 pp. 92–97
WHST.5	Develop and strengthen writing as needed by planning, revising, editing, rewriting, or trying a new approach	W5 pp. 98–103
WHST.6	Use technology to produce, publish, and update individual or shared writing projects	W6 pp. 104–109
WHST.7	Conduct research projects to answer a question or solve a problem; synthesize multiple sources, demonstrating understanding of the subject	W7 pp. 110–115
WHST.8	Gather relevant information from multiple print and digital sources; assess the usefulness of each source; integrate information, avoiding plagiarism and overreliance on any one source	W8 pp. 116–121
WHST.9	Draw evidence from informational texts to support analysis, reflection, and research	W9 pp. 122–127
WHST.10	Write routinely for a range of discipline-specific tasks, purposes, and audiences	W10 pp. 128–133

Minnesota, Grades 9–10

Minnesota Strand/Standard	Focus of Minnesota Standard	For More Information
Reading Literature		
4.1.1	Cite strong and thorough textual evidence to support analysis of what the text says explicitly and implicitly	R1 pp. 6–11
4.2.2	Determine a theme or central idea of a text and analyze its development and how it is shaped by specific details; summarize the text	R2 pp. 12–17
4.3.3	Analyze how characters develop, interact, and advance the plot or develop the theme	R3 pp. 18–23
4.4.4	Determine the meaning of words and phrases as they are used in a text, including figurative and connotative meanings; analyze the cumulative impact of word choice on meaning and tone	R4 pp. 24–29
4.5.5	Analyze how an author's choices regarding structure, the order of events, and manipulating time create such effects as mystery, tension, or surprise	R5 pp. 30–35
4.6.6	Analyze a point of view, perspective, or cultural experience reflected in a piece of literature	R6 pp. 36–41
4.7.7	Analyze the representation of a subject or scene in two different artistic mediums, including what is emphasized or absent in each treatment	R7 pp. 42–47
4.8.8	NA	
4.9.9	Analyze how an author draws on and transforms source material	R9 pp. 54–59
4.10.10	Read literature and other texts of appropriate complexity independently with proficiency	R10 pp. 60–65
Read Informational Texts		
5.1.1	Cite strong and thorough textual evidence to support analysis of what the text says explicitly and implicitly	R1 pp. 6–11
5.2.2	Determine the central idea of a text and analyze its development; summarize main ideas or events	R2 pp. 12–17
5.3.3	Analyze how the author structures an analysis or series of ideas or events, including the order, how they are developed, and the connections between them	R3 pp. 18–23
5.4.4	Determine the meaning of words and phrases in a text; analyze the cumulative impact of specific word choices	R4 pp. 24–29
5.5.5	Analyze in detail how ideas or claims are developed by particular sentences, paragraphs, or larger portions of text	R5 pp. 30–35

(Continued)

Minnesota Strand/Standard	Focus of Minnesota Standard	For More Information
Read Informational Texts		
5.6.6	Analyze how an author uses rhetoric to advance a point of view, perspective, or purpose	R6 pp. 36–41
5.7.7	Analyze various accounts of a subject told in different mediums	R7 pp. 42–47
5.8.8	Evaluate the argument in a text; assess reasoning and evidence; identify false statements and fallacious reasoning	R8 pp. 48–53
5.9.9	Analyze U.S. documents of historical and literary significance, noting how they address related themes and concepts	R9 pp. 54–59
5.10.10	Read and comprehend appropriately complex informational texts independently and proficiently	R10 pp. 60–65
Writing		
7.1.1	Write arguments to support claims, using valid reasoning and relevant and sufficient evidence	W1 pp. 70–77
7.2.2	Write informative/explanatory texts to effectively examine and convey complex ideas, concepts, and information	W2 pp. 78–85
7.3.3	Write narratives to develop real or imagined experiences or events using effective technique, well-chosen details, and well-structured event sequences	W3 pp. 86–91
7.4.4	Produce writing in which the development, organization, style, and features are appropriate to the task, genre, purpose, and audience	W4 pp. 92–97
7.5.5	Use a writing process to develop and strengthen writing as needed by planning, revising, and editing, rewriting, or trying a new approach	W5 pp. 98–103
7.6.6	Use technology to produce, publish, and update individual or shared writing projects	W6 pp. 104–109
7.7.7	Conduct research projects to answer a question or solve a problem; synthesize multiple sources; demonstrate understanding of the subject	W7 pp. 110–115
7.8.8	Gather information from multiple sources, using advanced searches effectively; assess usefulness of sources; integrate information, avoiding plagiarism	W8 pp. 116–121
7.9.9	Draw evidence from texts to support analysis, reflection, research, and/or synthesis	W9 pp. 122–127
7.10.10	Write routinely over short and extended time frames for a range of audiences, tasks, and purposes	W10 pp. 128–133
Speaking, Viewing, Listening, and Media Literacy		
9.1.1	Engage effectively in a range of collaborative discussions with diverse partners, building on others' ideas and expressing their own clearly and persuasively	SL1 pp. 138–143
9.2.2	Integrate multiple sources of information presented in diverse media or formats; evaluate credibility and accuracy of sources and noting discrepancies	SL2 pp. 144–149
9.3.3	Evaluate a speaker's point of view, reasoning, and use of evidence and rhetoric; identify fallacious reasoning or exaggerated or distorted evidence	SL3 pp. 150–155
9.4.4	Present information clearly, concisely, and logically; ensure organization, development, substance, and style are appropriate to purpose, audience, and task	SL4 pp. 156–161
9.5.5	Make strategic use of digital media in presentations to enhance understanding and to add interest	SL5 pp. 162–167
9.6.6	Adapt speech to a variety of contexts and tasks; demonstrate a command of formal English when appropriate	SL6 pp. 168–173
9.7.7	Understand, analyze, evaluate, and use different types of media	NA
9.8.8	Create a multimedia work, a remix, or a piece of digital communication for a specific purpose	NA
Language		
11.1.1	Demonstrate command of the conventions of standard English grammar and usage when writing or speaking	L1 pp. 178–183
11.2.2	Demonstrate command of the conventions of standard English capitalization, punctuation, and spelling when writing	L2 pp. 184–189

Minnesota Strand/Standard	Focus of Minnesota Standard	For More Information
Language		
11.3.3	Apply knowledge of language to make effective choices for meaning or style, and to comprehend more fully when reading or listening	L3 pp. 190–195
11.4.4	Determine or clarify the meaning of unknown and multiple-meaning words and phrases, choosing flexibly from an array of strategies	L4 pp. 196–201
11.5.5	Demonstrate understanding of figurative language, word relationships, and nuances in word meanings	L5 pp. 202–207
11.6.6	Acquire and use accurately general academic and domain-specific words and phrases; demonstrate independence in gathering vocabulary knowledge	L6 pp. 208–213
Literacy in History/Social Studies		
12.1.1	Cite specific textual, visual, or physical evidence to support analysis of primary and secondary sources	R1 pp. 6–11
12.2.2	Determine central ideas or information of a primary or secondary source; summarize how they develop	R2 pp. 12–17
12.3.3	Analyze in detail a series of events; determine whether earlier events caused later ones	R3 pp. 18–23
12.4.4	Determine the meaning of words and phrases, including vocabulary describing political, social, or economic aspects of history/social studies	R4 pp. 24–29
12.5.5	Analyze how a text uses structure to emphasize key points or advance an explanation or analysis	R5 pp. 30–35
12.6.6	Compare the point of view of two or more authors for how they treat the same or similar topics	R6 pp. 36–41
12.7.7	Integrate quantitative or technical analysis with qualitative analysis	R7 pp. 42–47
12.8.8	Assess the extent to which reasoning and evidence support the author's claim	R8 pp. 48–53
12.9.9	Compare and contrast treatment of the same topic in several primary and secondary sources	R9 pp. 54–59
12.10.10	Read and comprehend history/social studies texts of appropriate complexity	R10 pp. 60–65
Reading Science/Technical Subjects		
13.1.1	Cite specific textual evidence to support analysis of science and technical texts	R1 pp. 6–11
13.2.2	Determine central ideas or conclusions; trace the explanation of a complex process; provide an accurate summary	R2 pp. 12–17
13.3.3	Follow precisely a complex multistep procedure, attending to special cases or exceptions defined in the text	R3 pp. 18–23
13.4.4	Determine the meaning of domain-specific words and phrases as they are used in a special scientific or technical context	R4 pp. 24–29
13.5.5	Analyze the structure of relationships among concepts in a text	R5 pp. 30–35
13.6.6	Analyze the author's purpose in providing an explanation, describing a procedure, or discussing an experiment	R6 pp. 36–41
13.7.7	Translate quantitative or technical information expressed in words into visual form, and translate information expressed visually into words	R7 pp. 42–47
13.8.8	Assess the extent to which reasoning and evidence support the author's claim or recommendation for solving a problem	R8 pp. 48–53
13.9.9	Compare and contrast findings presented in a text to those from other sources, noting where they support or contradict previous explanations	R9 pp. 54–59
13.10.10	Read and comprehend science/technical texts of appropriate complexity	R10 pp. 60–65
Writing History/Social Studies, Science and Technical Subjects		
14.1.1	Write arguments focused on disciple-specific content	W1 pp. 70–77
14.2.2	Write informative/explanatory texts as they apply to each discipline and reporting format, including the narration of historical events, scientific procedures, or technical processes	W2 pp. 78–85

(Continued)

Minnesota Strand/Standard	Focus of Minnesota Standard	For More Information
Writing History/Social Studies, Science and Technical Subjects		
14.3.3	NA	
14.4.4	Produce clear and coherent writing in which the development, organization, and style are appropriate to task, purpose, and audience	W4 pp. 92–97
14.5.5	Use a writing process to develop and strengthen writing as needed by planning, revising, editing, rewriting, or trying a new approach	W5 pp. 98–103
14.6.6	Use technology to produce, publish, and update individual or shared writing projects	W6 pp. 104–109
14.7.7	Conduct research projects to answer a question or solve a problem; synthesize multiple sources, demonstrating understanding of the subject	W7 pp. 110–115
14.8.8	Gather relevant information from multiple print and digital sources; assess the usefulness of each source; integrate information, avoiding plagiarism	W8 pp. 116–121
14.9.9	Draw evidence from informational texts to support analysis, reflection, and research	W9 pp. 122–127
14.10.10	Write routinely for a range of discipline-specific tasks, purposes, and audiences	W10 pp. 128–133

Minnesota, Grades 11–12

Minnesota Strand/Standard	Focus of Minnesota Standard	For More Information
Reading Literature		
4.1.1	Cite strong and thorough textual evidence to support analysis of what the text says explicitly and implicitly	R1 pp. 6–11
4.2.2	Determine two or more themes or central ideas and analyze their development; restate and summarize main ideas or events	R2 pp. 12–17
4.3.3	Analyze the impact of the author's choices regarding how to develop and relate elements of a story	R3 pp. 18–23
4.4.4	Determine the meaning of words and phrases as they are used in a text, including figurative and connotative meanings; analyze the cumulative impact of word choice on meaning and tone	R4 pp. 24–29
4.5.5	Analyze how an author's choices concerning how to structure specific parts of the text contribute to its overall structure and meaning	R5 pp. 30–35
4.6.6	Analyze a case in which grasping point of view requires distinguishing what is directly stated from what is really meant	R6 pp. 36–41
4.7.7	Analyze multiple representations of a story, drama, or poem, evaluating how each interprets the source text	R7 pp. 42–47
4.8.8	NA	
4.9.9	Demonstrate knowledge of 18th, 19th, and early 20th century foundational works of American literature	R9 pp. 54–59
4.10.10	Read and comprehend a range of literature from a variety of cultures	R10 pp. 60–65
Read Informational Texts		
5.1.1	Cite strong and thorough textual evidence to support analysis of what the text says explicitly and implicitly, including where the text leaves matters uncertain	R1 pp. 6–11
5.2.2	Determine two or more central ideas of a text and analyze their development; restate or summarize main ideas or events	R2 pp. 12–17
5.3.3	Analyze a complex set of ideas or sequence of events and explain how specific individuals, ideas, or events interact and develop	R3 pp. 18–23

Minnesota Strand/Standard	Focus of Minnesota Standard	For More Information
Read Informational Texts		
5.4.4	Determine the meaning of words and phrases in a text; analyze how an author uses and refines the meaning of key terms over the course of a text	R4 pp. 24–29
5.5.5	Analyze and evaluate the effectiveness of the structure in an exposition or argument	R5 pp. 30–35
5.6.6	Analyze how an author's style and content contribute to the power, persuasiveness, or impact of the text	R6 pp. 36–41
5.7.7	Evaluate the argument in a text; assess reasoning and evidence; identify false statements and fallacious reasoning	R7 pp. 42–47
5.8.8	Delineate and evaluate the reasoning in seminal U.S. texts, including the application of constitutional principles and use of legal reasoning, and the premises, purposes, and arguments in works of public policy	R8 pp. 48–53
5.9.9	Analyze 17th, 18th, and 19th century foundational U.S. and world documents of literary significance	R9 pp. 54–59
5.10.10	Read and comprehend literary nonfiction independently and proficiently	R10 pp. 60–65
Writing		
7.1.1	Write arguments to support claims, using valid reasoning and relevant and sufficient evidence	W1 pp. 70–77
7.2.2	Write informative/explanatory texts to examine and convey complex ideas, concepts, and information clearly and accurately	W2 pp. 78–85
7.3.3	Write narratives to develop real or imagined experiences or events using effective technique, well-chosen details, and well-structured event sequences	W3 pp. 86–91
7.4.4	Produce writing in which the development, organization, style, and features are appropriate to the task, genre, purpose, and audience	W4 pp. 92–97
7.5.5	Use a writing process to develop and strengthen writing as needed by planning, revising, and editing, rewriting, or trying a new approach	W5 pp. 98–103
7.6.6	Use technology to produce, publish, and update individual or shared writing projects	W6 pp. 104–109
7.7.7	Conduct research projects to answer a question or solve a problem; synthesize multiple sources; demonstrate understanding of the subject	W7 pp. 110–115
7.8.8	Gather information from multiple sources, using advanced searches effectively; assess strengths and limitations of sources; integrate information, avoiding plagiarism and overreliance on any one source	W8 pp. 116–121
7.9.9	Draw evidence from texts to support analysis, reflection, research, and/or synthesis	W9 pp. 122–127
7.10.10	Write routinely over short and extended time frames for a range of audiences, tasks, and purposes	W10 pp. 128–133
Speaking, Viewing, Listening, and Media Literacy		
9.1.1	Engage effectively in a range of collaborative discussions with diverse partners, building on others' ideas and expressing their own clearly and persuasively	SL1 pp. 138–143
9.2.2	Integrate multiple sources of information presented in diverse media or formats; evaluate credibility and accuracy of sources and noting discrepancies	SL2 pp. 144–149
9.3.3	Evaluate a speaker's point of view, reasoning, and use of evidence and rhetoric; assess the stance, premises, link among ideas, word choice, emphasis, and tone	SL3 pp. 150–155
9.4.4	Present information, conveying a clear and distinct perspective, address alternative viewpoints; presentation is appropriate to purpose, audience, and task	SL4 pp. 156–161
9.5.5	Make strategic use of digital media in presentations to enhance understanding and to add interest	SL5 pp. 162–167
9.6.6	Adapt speech to a variety of contexts and tasks; demonstrate a command of formal English when appropriate	SL6 pp. 168–173
9.7.7	Understand, analyze, evaluate, and use different types of media	NA
9.8.8	Create a multimedia work, a remix, or a piece of digital communication for a specific purpose	NA

(Continued)

Minnesota Strand/Standard	Focus of Minnesota Standard	For More Information
Language		
11.1.1	Demonstrate command of the conventions of standard English grammar and usage when writing or speaking	L1 pp. 178–183
11.2.2	Demonstrate command of the conventions of standard English capitalization, punctuation, and spelling when writing	L2 pp. 184–189
11.3.3	Apply knowledge of language to make effective choices for meaning or style, and to comprehend more fully when reading or listening	L3 pp. 190–195
11.4.4	Determine or clarify the meaning of unknown and multiple-meaning words and phrases, choosing flexibly from an array of strategies	L4 pp. 196–201
11.5.5	Demonstrate understanding of figurative language, word relationships, and nuances in word meanings	L5 pp. 202–207
11.6.6	Acquire and use accurately general academic and domain-specific words and phrases; demonstrate independence in gathering vocabulary knowledge	L6 pp. 208–213
Literacy in History/Social Studies		
12.1.1	Cite specific textual, visual, or physical evidence to support analysis of primary and secondary sources	R1 pp. 6–11
12.2.2	Determine central ideas or information of a primary or secondary source; summarize how they develop	R2 pp. 12–17
12.3.3	Evaluate explanations for actions or events and determine which best accords with textual evidence	R3 pp. 18–23
12.4.4	Determine the meaning of words and phrases, including figurative and connotative meanings; analyze the impact of specific word choices	R4 pp. 24–29
12.5.5	Analyze in detail how a complex primary source is structured	R5 pp. 30–35
12.6.6	Evaluate authors' differing points of view on the same historical event	R6 pp. 36–41
12.7.7	Integrate and evaluate multiple sources of information presented in diverse formats and media in order to address a question or solve a problem	R7 pp. 42–47
12.8.8	Evaluate an author's premises, claims, and evidence by corroborating or challenging them	R8 pp. 48–53
12.9.9	Integrate information from diverse sources into a coherent understanding of an idea or event	R9 pp. 54–59
12.10.10	Read and comprehend history/social studies texts of appropriate complexity	R10 pp. 60–65
Reading Science/Technical Subjects		
13.1.1	Cite specific textual evidence to support analysis of science and technical texts	R1 pp. 6–11
13.2.2	Determine central ideas or conclusions; summarize complex concepts by paraphrasing into simpler but accurate terms	R2 pp. 12–17
13.3.3	Follow precisely a complex multistep procedure; analyze the results based on explanations in the text	R3 pp. 18–23
13.4.4	Determine the meaning of domain-specific words and phrases as they are used in a special scientific or technical context	R4 pp. 24–29
13.5.5	Analyze how the text structures information into categories or hierarchies, demonstrating understanding	R5 pp. 30–35
13.6.6	Analyze the author's purpose in providing an explanation, describing a procedure, or discussing an experiment	R6 pp. 36–41
13.7.7	Integrate and evaluate multiple sources of information presented in diverse formats and media in order to address a question or solve a problem	R7 pp. 42–47
13.8.8	Evaluate the hypotheses, data, analysis, and conclusions in a science or technical text, corroborating or challenging conclusions	R8 pp. 48–53
13.9.9	Synthesize information from a range of sources into a coherent understanding, resolving conflicting information when possible	R9 pp. 54–59
13.10.10	Read and comprehend science/technical texts of appropriate complexity	R10 pp. 60–65

Minnesota Strand/Standard	Focus of Minnesota Standard	For More Information
Writing History/Social Studies, Science and Technical Subjects		
14.1.1	Write arguments focused on disciple-specific content	W1 pp. 70–77
14.2.2	Write informative/explanatory texts as they apply to each discipline and reporting format, including the narration of historical events, scientific procedures, or technical processes	W2 pp. 78–85
14.3.3	NA	
14.4.4	Produce clear and coherent writing in which the development, organization, and style are appropriate to task, purpose, and audience	W4 pp. 92–97
14.5.5	Use a writing process to develop and strengthen writing as needed by planning, revising, editing, rewriting, or trying a new approach	W5 pp. 98–103
14.6.6	Use technology to produce, publish, and update individual or shared writing projects	W6 pp. 104–109
14.7.7	Conduct research projects to answer a question or solve a problem; synthesize multiple sources, demonstrating understanding of the subject	W7 pp. 110–115
14.8.8	Gather relevant information from multiple print and digital sources; assess the usefulness of each source; integrate information, avoiding plagiarism and overreliance on any one source	W8 pp. 116–121
14.9.9	Draw evidence from informational texts to support analysis, reflection, and research	W9 pp. 122–127
14.10.10	Write routinely for a range of discipline-specific tasks, purposes, and audiences	W10 pp. 128–133

Mississippi, English I/II

Mississippi Strand/Standard	Focus of Mississippi Standard	For More Information
Reading Literature		
RL.1	Cite strong and thorough textual evidence to support analysis of what the text says explicitly and implicitly	R1 pp. 6–11
RL.2	Determine a theme or central idea of a text and analyze its development and how it is shaped by specific details; summarize the text	R2 pp. 12–17
RL.3	Analyze how characters develop, interact, and advance the plot or develop the theme	R3 pp. 18–23
RL.4	Determine the meaning of words and phrases as they are used in a text, including figurative and connotative meanings; analyze the cumulative impact of word choice on meaning and tone	R4 pp. 24–29
RL.5	Analyze how an author's choices regarding structure, the order of events, and manipulating time create such effects as mystery, tension, or surprise	R5 pp. 30–35
RL.6	Analyze a point of view, perspective, or cultural experience reflected in a piece of literature	R6 pp. 36–41
RL.7	Analyze the representation of a subject or scene in two different artistic mediums, including what is emphasized or absent in each treatment	R7 pp. 42–47
RL.8	NA	
RL.9	Analyze how an author draws on and transforms source material	R9 pp. 54–59
RL.10	Read literature of appropriate complexity independently with proficiency	R10 pp. 60–65
Reading Informational Text		
RI.1	Cite strong and thorough textual evidence to support analysis of what the text says explicitly and implicitly	R1 pp. 6–11
RI.2	Determine the central idea of a text and analyze its development; summarize main ideas or events	R2 pp. 12–17
RI.3	Analyze how the author structures an analysis or series of ideas or events, including the order, how they are developed, and the connections between them	R3 pp. 18–23

(Continued)

Mississippi Strand/Standard	Focus of Mississippi Standard	For More Information
Reading Informational Text		
RI.4	Determine the meaning of words and phrases in a text; analyze the cumulative impact of specific word choices	R4 pp. 24–29
RI.5	Analyze in detail how ideas or claims are developed by particular sentences, paragraphs, or larger portions of text	R5 pp. 30–35
RI.6	Analyze how an author uses rhetoric to advance a point of view, perspective, or purpose	R6 pp. 36–41
RI.7	Analyze various accounts of a subject told in different mediums	R7 pp. 42–47
RI.8	Evaluate the argument in a text; assess reasoning and evidence; identify false statements and fallacious reasoning	R8 pp. 48–53
RI.9	Analyze U.S. documents of historical and literary significance, noting how they address related themes and concepts	R9 pp. 54–59
RI.10	Read and comprehend appropriately complex informational texts independently and proficiently	R10 pp. 60–65
Writing		
W.1	Write arguments to support claims, using valid reasoning and relevant and sufficient evidence	W1 pp. 70–77
W.2	Write informative/explanatory texts to effectively examine and convey complex ideas, concepts, and information	W2 pp. 78–85
W.3	Write narratives to develop real or imagined experiences or events using effective technique, well-chosen details, and well-structured event sequences	W3 pp. 86–91
W.4	Produce writing in which the development, organization, style, and features are appropriate to the task, genre, purpose, and audience	W4 pp. 92–97
W.5	Develop and strengthen writing as needed by planning, revising, and editing, rewriting, or trying a new approach	W5 pp. 98–103
W.6	Use technology to produce, publish, and update individual or shared writing projects	W6 pp. 104–109
W.7	Conduct research projects to answer a question or solve a problem; synthesize multiple sources; demonstrate understanding of the subject	W7 pp. 110–115
W.8	Gather information from multiple sources, using advanced searches effectively; assess usefulness of sources; integrate information, avoiding plagiarism	W8 pp. 116–121
W.9	Draw evidence from texts to support analysis, reflection, research, and/or synthesis	W9 pp. 122–127
W.10	Write routinely over short and extended time frames for a range of audiences, tasks, and purposes	W10 pp. 128–133
Speaking and Listening		
SL.1	Engage effectively in a range of collaborative discussions with diverse partners, building on others' ideas and expressing their own clearly and persuasively	SL1 pp. 138–143
SL.2	Integrate multiple sources of information presented in diverse media or formats; evaluate credibility and accuracy of sources and noting discrepancies	SL2 pp. 144–149
SL.3	Evaluate a speaker's point of view, reasoning, and use of evidence and rhetoric; identify fallacious reasoning or exaggerated or distorted evidence	SL3 pp. 150–155
SL.4	Present information clearly, concisely, and logically; ensure organization, development, substance, and style are appropriate to purpose, audience, and task	SL4 pp. 156–161
SL.5	Make strategic use of digital media in presentations to enhance understanding and to add interest	SL5 pp. 162–167
SL.6	Adapt speech to a variety of contexts and tasks; demonstrate a command of formal English when appropriate	SL6 pp. 168–173
Language		
L.1	Demonstrate command of the conventions of standard English grammar and usage when writing or speaking	L1 pp. 178–183
L.2	Demonstrate command of the conventions of standard English capitalization, punctuation, and spelling when writing	L2 pp. 184–189

Mississippi Strand/Standard	Focus of Mississippi Standard	For More Information
Language		
L.3	Apply knowledge of language to make effective choices for meaning or style, and to comprehend more fully when reading or listening	L3 pp. 190–195
L.4	Determine or clarify the meaning of unknown and multiple-meaning words and phrases, choosing flexibly from an array of strategies	L4 pp. 196–201
L.5	Demonstrate understanding of figurative language, word relationships, and nuances in word meanings	L5 pp. 202–207
L.6	Acquire and use accurately general academic and domain-specific words and phrases; demonstrate independence in gathering vocabulary knowledge	L6 pp. 208–213
Reading History/Social Studies		
RH.1	Cite specific textual evidence to support analysis of primary and secondary sources	R1 pp. 6–11
RH.2	Determine central ideas or information of a primary or secondary source; summarize how they develop	R2 pp. 12–17
RH.3	Analyze in detail a series of events; determine whether earlier events caused later ones	R3 pp. 18–23
RH.4	Determine the meaning of words and phrases, including vocabulary describing political, social, or economic aspects of history/social studies	R4 pp. 24–29
RH.5	Analyze how a text uses structure to emphasize key points or advance an explanation or analysis	R5 pp. 30–35
RH.6	Compare the point of view of two or more authors for how they treat the same or similar topics	R6 pp. 36–41
RH.7	Integrate quantitative or technical analysis with qualitative analysis	R7 pp. 42–47
RH.8	Assess the extent to which reasoning and evidence support the author's claim	R8 pp. 48–53
RH.9	Compare and contrast treatment of the same topic in several primary and secondary sources	R9 pp. 54–59
RH.10	Read and comprehend history/social studies texts of appropriate complexity	R10 pp. 60–65
Reading Science/Technical Subjects		
RST.1	Cite specific textual evidence to support analysis of science and technical texts	R1 pp. 6–11
RST.2	Determine central ideas or conclusions; trace the explanation of a complex process; provide an accurate summary	R2 pp. 12–17
RST.3	Follow precisely a complex multistep procedure, attending to special cases or exceptions defined in the text	R3 pp. 18–23
RST.4	Determine the meaning of domain-specific words and phrases as they are used in a special scientific or technical context	R4 pp. 24–29
RST.5	Analyze the structure of relationships among concepts in a text	R5 pp. 30–35
RST.6	Analyze the author's purpose in providing an explanation, describing a procedure, or discussing an experiment	R6 pp. 36–41
RST.7	Translate quantitative or technical information expressed in words into visual form, and translate information expressed visually into words	R7 pp. 42–47
RST.8	Assess the extent to which reasoning and evidence support the author's claim or recommendation for solving a problem	R8 pp. 48–53
RST.9	Compare and contrast findings presented in a text to those from other sources, noting where they support or contradict previous explanations	R9 pp. 54–59
RST.10	Read and comprehend science/technical texts of appropriate complexity	R10 pp. 60–65
Writing History/Social Studies, Science and Technical Subjects		
WHST.1	Write arguments focused on disciple-specific content	W1 pp. 70–77
WHST.2	Write informative/explanatory texts, including the narration of historical events, scientific procedures, or technical processes	W2 pp. 78–85

(Continued)

Mississippi Strand/Standard	Focus of Mississippi Standard	For More Information
Writing History/Social Studies, Science and Technical Subjects		
WHST.3	NA	
WHST.4	Produce clear and coherent writing in which the development, organization, and style are appropriate to task, purpose, and audience	W4 pp. 92–97
WHST.5	Develop and strengthen writing as needed by planning, revising, editing, rewriting, or trying a new approach	W5 pp. 98–103
WHST.6	Use technology to produce, publish, and update individual or shared writing projects	W6 pp. 104–109
WHST.7	Conduct research projects to answer a question or solve a problem; synthesize multiple sources, demonstrating understanding of the subject	W7 pp. 110–115
WHST.8	Gather relevant information from multiple print and digital sources; assess the usefulness of each source; integrate information, avoiding plagiarism	W8 pp. 116–121
WHST.9	Draw evidence from informational texts to support analysis, reflection, and research	W9 pp. 122–127
WHST.10	Write routinely for a range of discipline-specific tasks, purposes, and audiences	W10 pp. 128–133

Mississippi, English III/IV

Mississippi Strand/Standard	Focus of Mississippi Standard	For More Information
Reading Literature		
RL.1	Cite strong and thorough textual evidence to support analysis of what the text says explicitly and implicitly	R1 pp. 6–11
RL.2	Determine two or more themes or central ideas and analyze their development; restate and summarize main ideas or events	R2 pp. 12–17
RL.3	Analyze how characters develop, interact, and advance the plot or develop the theme	R3 pp. 18–23
RL.4	Determine the meaning of words and phrases as they are used in a text, including figurative and connotative meanings; analyze the cumulative impact of word choice on meaning and tone	R4 pp. 24–29
RL.5	Analyze how an author's choices concerning how to structure specific parts of the text contribute to its overall structure and meaning	R5 pp. 30–35
RL.6	Analyze a case in which grasping point of view requires distinguishing what is directly stated from what is really meant	R6 pp. 36–41
RL.7	Analyze multiple representations of a story, drama, or poem, evaluating how each interprets the source text	R7 pp. 42–47
RL.8	NA	
RL.9	Demonstrate knowledge of 18th, 19th, and early 20th century foundational works of American literature	R9 pp. 54–59
RL.10	Read and comprehend a range of literature from a variety of cultures	R10 pp. 60–65
Reading Informational Text		
RI.1	Cite strong and thorough textual evidence to support analysis of what the text says explicitly and implicitly, including where the text leaves matters uncertain	R1 pp. 6–11
RI.2	Determine two or more central ideas of a text and analyze their development; restate or summarize main ideas or events	R2 pp. 12–17
RI.3	Analyze a complex set of ideas or sequence of events and explain how specific individuals, ideas, or events interact and develop	R3 pp. 18–23
RI.4	Determine the meaning of words and phrases in a text; analyze how an author uses and refines the meaning of key terms over the course of a text	R4 pp. 24–29

Mississippi Strand/Standard	Focus of Mississippi Standard	For More Information
Reading Informational Text		
RI.5	Analyze and evaluate the effectiveness of the structure in an exposition or argument	R5 pp. 30–35
RI.6	Analyze how an author's style and content contribute to the power, persuasiveness, or impact of the text	R6 pp. 36–41
RI.7	Integrate and evaluate multiple sources of information presented in different media or formats in order to address a question or solve a problem	R7 pp. 42–47
RI.8	Delineate and evaluate the reasoning in seminal U.S. texts, including the application of constitutional principles and use of legal reasoning, and the premises, purposes, and arguments in works of public policy	R8 pp. 48–53
RI.9	Analyze 17th, 18th, and 19th century foundational U.S. and world documents of literary significance	R9 pp. 54–59
RI.10	Read and comprehend literary nonfiction independently and proficiently	R10 pp. 60–65
Writing		
W.1	Write arguments to support claims, using valid reasoning and relevant and sufficient evidence	W1 pp. 70–77
W.2	Write informative/explanatory texts to examine and convey complex ideas, concepts, and information clearly and accurately	W2 pp. 78–85
W.3	Write narratives to develop real or imagined experiences or events using effective technique, well-chosen details, and well-structured event sequences	W3 pp. 86–91
W.4	Produce writing in which the development, organization, style, and features are appropriate to the task, genre, purpose, and audience	W4 pp. 92–97
W.5	Develop and strengthen writing as needed by planning, revising, and editing, rewriting, or trying a new approach	W5 pp. 98–103
W.6	Use technology to produce, publish, and update individual or shared writing projects	W6 pp. 104–109
W.7	Conduct research projects to answer a question or solve a problem; synthesize multiple sources; demonstrate understanding of the subject	W7 pp. 110–115
W.8	Gather information from multiple sources, using advanced searches effectively; assess strengths and limitations of sources; integrate information, avoiding plagiarism and overreliance on any one source	W8 pp. 116–121
W.9	Draw evidence from texts to support analysis, reflection, and research	W9 pp. 122–127
W.10	Write routinely over shorter and extended time frames for a range of audiences, tasks, and purposes	W10 pp. 128–133
Speaking and Listening		
SL.1	Engage effectively in a range of collaborative discussions with diverse partners, building on others' ideas and expressing their own clearly and persuasively	SL1 pp. 138–143
SL.2	Integrate multiple sources of information presented in diverse media or formats; evaluate credibility and accuracy of sources and note discrepancies	SL2 pp. 144–149
SL.3	Evaluate a speaker's point of view, reasoning, and use of evidence and rhetoric; assess the stance, premises, link among ideas, word choice, emphasis, and tone	SL3 pp. 150–155
SL.4	Present information, conveying a clear and distinct perspective, address alternative viewpoints; presentation is appropriate to purpose, audience, and task	SL4 pp. 156–161
SL.5	Make strategic use of digital media in presentations to enhance understanding and to add interest	SL5 pp. 162–167
SL.6	Adapt speech to a variety of contexts and tasks; demonstrate a command of formal English when appropriate	SL6 pp. 168–173
Language		
L.1	Demonstrate command of the conventions of standard English grammar and usage when writing or speaking	L1 pp. 178–183
L.2	Demonstrate command of the conventions of standard English capitalization, punctuation, and spelling when writing	L2 pp. 184–189

(Continued)

Mississippi Strand/Standard	Focus of Mississippi Standard	For More Information
Language		
L.3	Apply knowledge of language to make effective choices for meaning or style, and to comprehend more fully when reading or listening	L3 pp. 190–195
L.4	Determine or clarify the meaning of unknown and multiple-meaning words and phrases, choosing flexibly from an array of strategies	L4 pp. 196–201
L.5	Demonstrate understanding of figurative language, word relationships, and nuances in word meanings	L5 pp. 202–207
L.6	Acquire and use accurately general academic and domain-specific words and phrases; demonstrate independence in gathering vocabulary knowledge	L6 pp. 208–213
Reading History/Social Studies		
RH.1	Cite specific textual evidence to support analysis of primary and secondary sources	R1 pp. 6–11
RH.2	Determine central ideas or information of a primary or secondary source; summarize how they develop	R2 pp. 12–17
RH.3	Evaluate explanations for actions or events and determine which best accords with textual evidence	R3 pp. 18–23
RH.4	Determine the meaning of words and phrases, including figurative and connotative meanings; analyze the impact of specific word choices	R4 pp. 24–29
RH.5	Analyze in detail how a complex primary source is structured	R5 pp. 30–35
RH.6	Evaluate authors' differing points of view on the same historical event	R6 pp. 36–41
RH.7	Integrate and evaluate multiple sources of information presented in diverse formats and media in order to address a question or solve a problem	R7 pp. 42–47
RH.8	Evaluate an author's premises, claims, and evidence by corroborating or challenging them	R8 pp. 48–53
RH.9	Integrate information from diverse sources into a coherent understanding of an idea or event	R9 pp. 54–59
RH.10	Read and comprehend history/social studies texts of appropriate complexity	R10 pp. 60–65
Reading Science/Technical Subjects		
RST.1	Cite specific textual evidence to support analysis of science and technical texts	R1 pp. 6–11
RST.2	Determine central ideas or conclusions; summarize complex concepts by paraphrasing into simpler but accurate terms	R2 pp. 12–17
RST.3	Follow precisely a complex multistep procedure; analyze the results based on explanations in the text	R3 pp. 18–23
RST.4	Determine the meaning of domain-specific words and phrases as they are used in a special scientific or technical context	R4 pp. 24–29
RST.5	Analyze how the text structures information into categories or hierarchies, demonstrating understanding	R5 pp. 30–35
RST.6	Analyze the author's purpose in providing an explanation, describing a procedure, or discussing an experiment	R6 pp. 36–41
RST.7	Integrate and evaluate multiple sources of information presented in diverse formats and media in order to address a question or solve a problem	R7 pp. 42–47
RST.8	Evaluate the hypotheses, data, analysis, and conclusions in a science or technical text, corroborating or challenging conclusions	R8 pp. 48–53
RST.9	Synthesize information from a range of sources into a coherent understanding, resolving conflicting information when possible	R9 pp. 54–59
RST.10	Read and comprehend science/technical texts of appropriate complexity	R10 pp. 60–65
Writing History/Social Studies, Science and Technical Subjects		
WHST.1	Write arguments focused on disciple-specific content	W1 pp. 70–77
WHST.2	Write informative/explanatory texts, including the narration of historical events, scientific procedures, or technical processes	W2 pp. 78–85

Mississippi Strand/Standard	Focus of Mississippi Standard	For More Information
Writing History/Social Studies, Science and Technical Subjects		
WHST.3	NA	
WHST.4	Produce clear and coherent writing in which the development, organization, and style are appropriate to task, purpose, and audience	W4 pp. 92–97
WHST.5	Develop and strengthen writing as needed by planning, revising, editing, rewriting, or trying a new approach	W5 pp. 98–103
WHST.6	Use technology to produce, publish, and update individual or shared writing projects	W6 pp. 104–109
WHST.7	Conduct research projects to answer a question or solve a problem; synthesize multiple sources, demonstrating understanding of the subject	W7 pp. 110–115
WHST.8	Gather relevant information from multiple print and digital sources; assess the usefulness of each source; integrate information, avoiding plagiarism and overreliance on any one source	W8 pp. 116–121
WHST.9	Draw evidence from informational texts to support analysis, reflection, and research	W9 pp. 122–127
WHST.10	Write routinely for a range of discipline-specific tasks, purposes, and audiences	W10 pp. 128–133

Missouri, Grades 9–10

Missouri Strand/Standard	Focus of Missouri Standard	For More Information
Reading Literary Text		
RL.1	Comprehend and Interpret Texts	
RL.1.A	Evidence/Inference: Draw conclusions, infer and analyze by citing textual evidence	R1 pp. 6–11
RL.1.B	Word Meanings: Determine the meaning of words as they are used in the text	R4 pp. 24–29
RL.1.C	Text Features: Interpret visual elements of text	NA
RL.1.D	Summarize/Theme: Determine two or more themes in a text, analyze their development, and summarize the text	R2 pp. 12–17
RL.2	Analyze Craft and Structure	
RL.2.A	Structure: Analyze how an author's choices about how to structure a text, order events, or manipulate time impact the reader	R5 pp. 30–35
RL.2.B	Point of View: Analyze how point of view is reflected in the characters, setting, and plot	R6 pp. 36–41
RL.2.C	Craft and Meaning: Analyze the cumulative impact of word choice and syntax on meaning and tone	R4 pp. 24–29
RL.2.D	Interaction and Meaning: Analyze how complex characters develop over the course of a text	R3 pp. 18–23
RL.3	Synthesize Ideas From Multiple Texts	
RL.3.A	Texts in Forms: Analyze multiple performances of a story, drama, or poem, evaluating how each version interprets the source text	R7 pp. 42–47
RL.3.B	Relationships in Texts: Explain how and why an author transforms source material within a text	R9 pp. 54–59
RL.3.C	Historical Context: Explain how multiple texts reflect historical and/or cultural contexts	NA
RL.3.D	Comprehension: Read and comprehend literature read independently	R10 pp. 60–65
Reading Informational Text		
RI.1	Comprehend and Interpret Texts	
RI.1.A	Evidence/Inference: Draw conclusions, infer and analyze by citing textual evidence	R1 pp. 6–11

(Continued)

Missouri Strand/Standard	Focus of Missouri Standard	For More Information
Reading Informational Text		
RI.1.B	Word Meanings: Determine the meaning of words as they are used in the text	R4 pp. 24–29
RI.1.C	Text Features: Interpret visual elements of text	NA
RI.1.D	Summarize/Claim: Explain two or more main ideas in a text, analyze their development, and summarize the text	R2 pp. 12–17
RI.2	Analyze Craft and Structure	
RI.2.A	Structure: Analyze how an author's choices about how to structure a text and sequence information impacts the reader	R5 pp. 30–35
RI.2.B	Point of View: Explain how an author uses rhetoric to advance point of view or purpose	R6 pp. 36–41
RI.2.C	Craft and Meaning: Analyze how word choice and syntax impact meaning and tone	R4 pp. 24–29
RI.2.D	Argument/Evidence: Evaluate an author's argument and assess the reasoning and evidence; recognize false statements and fallacious reasoning	R8 pp. 48–53
RI.3	Synthesize Ideas From Multiple Texts	
RI.3.A	Texts/Forms: Analyze how similar topics are presented in different media formats	R7 pp. 42–47
RI.3.B	Relationships/Texts: Evaluate how effectively two or more texts develop similar topics	R9 pp. 54–59
RI.3.C	Historical Context: Explain how the text reflects historical and/or cultural contexts	NA
RI.3.D	Comprehension: Read and comprehend informational texts read independently	R10 pp. 60–65
Writing and Researching		
W.1	Approaching the Task as a Researcher	
W.1.A	Research: Conduct research to answer a question; gather relevant information from multiple resources; assess credibility of sources; integrate information	W7 pp. 110–115 W8 pp. 116–121
W.2	Approaching the Task as a Writer	
W.2.A	Development: Follow a writing process to produce clear and coherent narrative, expository, and argumentative writing appropriate to the task, purpose, and audience	W1 pp. 70–77 W2 pp. 78–85 W3 pp. 86–91 W4 pp. 92–97
W.3	Approaching the Task as a Reader	
W.3.A	Revise and Edit: Review, revise and edit writing (organization and content; word choice, syntax, style; conventions; transitions) with consideration for the task, purpose, and audience; use technology to produce and publish writing	W1 pp. 70–77 W2 pp. 78–85 W3 pp. 86–91 W5 pp. 98–103 W6 pp. 104–109 L1 pp. 178–183 L2 pp. 184–189
Speaking and Listening		
SL.1	Collaborating	
SL.1.A	Conversations: Work with peers to set rules for discussions and decision-making	SL1 pp. 138–143
SL.1.B	Questioning: Delineate a speaker's argument, evaluating point of view, reasoning, and evidence; pose and respond to questions that relate the discussion to broader themes; verify or challenge ideas and conclusions	SL1 pp. 138–143 SL3 pp. 150–155
SL.1.C	Viewpoints of Others: Respond to diverse perspectives; summarize points of agreement and disagreement; resolve contradictions when possible; determine what additional information is needed	SL1 pp. 138–143 SL2 pp. 144–149
SL.2	Presenting	
SL.2.A	Verbal Delivery: Speak audibly, and to the point; use conventions of language appropriate to task, purpose, and audience	SL4 pp. 156–161 SL6 pp. 168–173

Missouri Strand/Standard	Focus of Missouri Standard	For More Information
Speaking and Listening		
SL.2.B	Nonverbal: Make eye contact with listeners and use effective gestures to communicate and engage	SL4 pp. 156–161
SL.2.C	Multimedia: Plan and deliver presentations based on the task, audience, and purpose, making strategic use of multimedia to enhance understanding of claims and evidence, and add interest	SL4 pp. 156–161 SL5 pp. 162–167

Missouri, Grades 11–12

Missouri Strand/Standard	Focus of Missouri Standard	For More Information
Reading Literary Text		
RL.1	Comprehend and Interpret Texts	
RL.1.A	Evidence/Inference: Draw conclusions, infer and analyze by citing textual evidence	R1 pp. 6–11
RL.1.B	Word Meanings: Determine the meaning of words as they are used in the text	R4 pp. 24–29
RL.1.C	Text Features: Interpret visual elements of text	NA
RL.1.D	Summarize/Theme: Determine two or more themes in a text, analyze their development, and relate to the world; summarize the text	R2 pp. 12–17
RL.2	Analyze Craft and Structure	
RL.2.A	Structure: Analyze how an author's choices about how to structure parts of a text contribute to its overall meaning and impact	R5 pp. 30–35
RL.2.B	Point of View: Analyze a case in which recognizing point of view requires distinguishing what is directly stated from what is implied	R6 pp. 36–41
RL.2.C	Craft and Meaning: Analyze how the author's word choice and use of syntax contribute to meaning, tone, and impact	R4 pp. 24–29
RL.2.D	Interaction and Meaning: Evaluate the impact of the author's choices regarding how to develop and relate elements of a text	R3 pp. 18–23
RL.3	Synthesize Ideas From Multiple Texts	
RL.3.A	Texts in Forms: Analyze the representation of a subject in two different artistic mediums	R7 pp. 42–47
RL.3.B	Relationships in Texts: Synthesize ideas from two or more texts about similar topics	R9 pp. 54–59
RL.3.C	Historical Context: Explain how multiple texts reflect historical and/or cultural contexts	NA
RL.3.D	Comprehension: Read and comprehend literature read independently	R10 pp. 60–65
Reading Informational Text		
RI.1	Comprehend and Interpret Texts	
RI.1.A	Evidence/Inference: Draw conclusions, infer and analyze by citing textual evidence	R1 pp. 6–11
RI.1.B	Word Meanings: Determine the meaning of words as they are used in the text	R4 pp. 24–29
RI.1.C	Text Features: Interpret visual elements of text	NA
RI.1.D	Summarize/Claim: Explain two or more main ideas in a text, analyze their development, and relate to the world; summarize the text	R2 pp. 12–17
RI.2	Analyze Craft and Structure	
RI.2.A	Structure: Analyze how an author's choices about how to structure parts of a text contribute to its meaning	R5 pp. 30–35
RI.2.B	Point of View: Analyze a text in which the author's point of view is not obvious	R6 pp. 36–41

(Continued)

Missouri Strand/Standard	Focus of Missouri Standard	For More Information
Reading Informational Text		
RI.2.C	Craft and Meaning: Evaluate how the author's word choice and syntax contribute to meaning and tone	R4 pp. 24–29
RI.2.D	Argument/Evidence: Evaluate an author's argument and reasoning for effectiveness, validity, logic and relevance of the evidence	R8 pp. 48–53
RI.3	Synthesize Ideas From Multiple Texts	
RI.3.A	Texts/Forms: Analyze the representation of a subject in two different mediums	R7 pp. 42–47
RI.3.B	Relationships/Texts: Synthesize information from two or more texts about similar topics	R9 pp. 54–59
RI.3.C	Historical Context: Explain how the text reflects historical and/or cultural contexts	NA
RI.3.D	Comprehension: Read and comprehend informational texts read independently	R10 pp. 60–65
Writing and Researching		
W.1	Approaching the Task as a Researcher	
W.1.A	Research: Conduct research to answer a question; gather relevant information from multiple resources; assess credibility of sources; integrate information	W7 pp. 110–115 W8 pp. 116–121
W.2	Approaching the Task as a Writer	
W.2.A	Development: Follow a writing process to produce clear and coherent narrative, expository, and argumentative writing appropriate to the task, purpose, and audience	W1 pp. 70–77 W2 pp. 78–85 W3 pp. 86–91 W4 pp. 92–97
W.3	Approaching the Task as a Reader	
W.3.A	Revise and Edit: Review, revise and edit writing (organization and content; word choice, syntax, style; conventions; transitions) with consideration for the task, purpose, and audience; use technology to produce and publish writing	W1 pp. 70–77 W2 pp. 78–85 W3 pp. 86–91 W5 pp. 98–103 W6 pp. 104–109 L1 pp. 178–183 L2 pp. 184–189
Speaking and Listening		
SL.1	Collaborating	
SL.1.A	Conversations: Work with peers to set rules for discussions and decision-making; set goals and deadlines; establish individual roles as needed	SL1 pp. 138–143
SL.1.B	Questioning: Delineate a speaker's argument, evaluating point of view, reasoning, and evidence; pose and respond to questions that probe reasoning and evidence; verify or challenge ideas and conclusions; promote divergent and creative perspectives	SL1 pp. 138–143 SL3 pp. 150–155
SL.1.C	Viewpoints of Others: Respond to diverse perspectives; synthesize claims on all sides of an issue; make new connections in light of the evidence and reasoning presented	SL1 pp. 138–143 SL2 pp. 144–149
SL.2	Presenting	
SL.2.A	Verbal Delivery: Speak audibly, and to the point; use conventions of language appropriate to task, purpose, and audience; strategically vary volume, pitch, and pace	SL4 pp. 156–161 SL6 pp. 168–173
SL.2.B	Nonverbal: Make eye contact with listeners and use effective gestures to communicate and engage	SL4 pp. 156–161
SL.2.C	Multimedia: Plan and deliver presentations based on the task, audience, and purpose, making strategic use of multimedia to enhance understanding of findings, reasoning, and evidence, and add to interest	SL4 pp. 156–161 SL5 pp. 162–167

Nebraska, Grades 9–10

Nebraska Strand/Standard	Focus of Nebraska Standard	For More Information
LA10.1	**Reading:** Students will learn and apply reading skills and strategies to comprehend text	
LA10.1.1	Concepts of Print: Students will demonstrate knowledge of the concepts of print	NA
LA10.1.2	Phonological Awareness: Students will demonstrate phonological awareness through oral activities	NA
LA10.1.3	Word Analysis: Students will use phonetic analysis to read and write grade-level text	NA
LA10.1.4	Fluency: Students will develop accuracy, phrasing, and expression while reading a variety of grade-level print/digital text to support comprehension	NA
LA10.1.5	Vocabulary: Students will build and use conversational, academic, and content-specific grade-level vocabulary	L4 pp. 196–201 L5 pp. 202–207 L6 pp. 208–213
LA10.1.6	Comprehension: Students will construct meaning by applying prior knowledge, using text information, and monitoring comprehension while reading increasingly complex grade-level literary and informational text	R1 pp. 6–11 R2 pp. 12–17 R3 pp. 18–23 R4 pp. 24–29 R5 pp. 30–35 R6 pp. 36–41 R8 pp. 48–53 R9 pp. 54–59 R10 pp. 60–65
LA10.2	**Writing:** Students will learn and apply writing skills and strategies to communicate	
LA10.2.1	Writing Process: Students will apply the writing process to plan, draft, revise, edit, and publish writing using correct spelling, grammar, punctuation, and other conventions of standard English appropriate for grade-level	W5 pp. 98–103 W6 pp. 104–109 W10 pp. 128–133 L1 pp. 178–183 L2 pp. 184–189
LA10.2.2	Writing Modes: Students will write in multiple modes for a variety of purposes and audiences across disciplines	W1 pp. 70–77 W2 pp. 78–85 W3 pp. 86–91 W7 pp. 110–115 W8 pp. 116–121 W9 pp. 122–127
LA10.3	**Speaking and Listening:** Students will develop and apply speaking and listening skills and strategies to communicate for a variety of purposes	
LA10.3.1	Speaking: Students will develop, apply, and refine speaking skills and strategies to communicate key ideas in a variety of situations	SL4 pp. 156–161 SL5 pp. 162–167 SL6 pp. 168–173
LA10.3.2	Listening: Students will develop and demonstrate active listening skills across a variety of situations	SL2 pp. 144–149 SL3 pp. 150–155
LA10.3.3	Reciprocal Communication: Students will develop, apply, and adapt reciprocal communication skills	SL1 pp. 138–143 L3 pp. 190–195
LA10.4	**Multiple Literacies:** Students will apply information fluency and practice digital citizenship	
LA10.4.1	Information Fluency: Students will evaluate, create, and communicate information in a variety of media and formats	R7 pp. 42–47 R8 pp. 48–53 W8 pp. 116–121 W9 pp. 122–127
LA10.4.2	Digital Citizenship: Students will practice the norms of appropriate and responsible technology use	W6 pp. 104–109 SL5 pp. 162–167

Nebraska, Grades 11–12

Nebraska Strand/Standard	Focus of Nebraska Standard	For More Information
LA12.1	**Reading:** Students will learn and apply reading skills and strategies to comprehend text	
LA12.1.1	Concepts of Print: Students will demonstrate knowledge of the concepts of print	NA
LA12.1.2	Phonological Awareness: Students will demonstrate phonological awareness through oral activities	NA
LA12.1.3	Word Analysis: Students will use phonetic analysis to read and write grade-level text	NA
LA12.1.4	Fluency: Students will develop accuracy, phrasing, and expression while reading a variety of grade-level print/digital text to support comprehension	NA
LA12.1.5	Vocabulary: Students will build and use conversational, academic, and content-specific grade-level vocabulary	L4 pp. 196–201 L5 pp. 202–207 L6 pp. 208–213
LA12.1.6	Comprehension: Students will construct meaning by applying prior knowledge, using text information, and monitoring comprehension while reading increasingly complex grade-level literary and informational text	R1 pp. 6–11 R2 pp. 12–17 R3 pp. 18–23 R4 pp. 24–29 R5 pp. 30–35 R6 pp. 36–41 R8 pp. 48–53 R9 pp. 54–59 R10 pp. 60–65
LA12.2	**Writing:** Students will learn and apply writing skills and strategies to communicate	
LA12.2.1	Writing Process: Students will apply the writing process to plan, draft, revise, edit, and publish writing using correct spelling, grammar, punctuation, and other conventions of standard English appropriate for grade-level	W5 pp. 98–103 W6 pp. 104–109 W10 pp. 128–133 L1 pp. 178–183 L2 pp. 184–189
LA12.2.2	Writing Modes: Students will write in multiple modes for a variety of purposes and audiences across disciplines	W1 pp. 70–77 W2 pp. 78–85 W3 pp. 86–91 W7 pp. 110–115 W8 pp. 116–121 W9 pp. 122–127
LA12.3	**Speaking and Listening:** Students will develop and apply speaking and listening skills and strategies to communicate for a variety of purposes	
LA12.3.1	Speaking: Students will develop, apply, and refine speaking skills and strategies to communicate key ideas in a variety of situations	SL4 pp. 156–161 SL5 pp. 162–167 SL6 pp. 168–173
LA12.3.2	Listening: Students will develop and demonstrate active listening skills across a variety of situations	SL2 pp. 144–149 SL3 pp. 150–155
LA12.3.3	Reciprocal Communication: Students will develop, apply, and adapt reciprocal communication skills	SL1 pp. 138–143 L3 pp. 190–195
LA12.4	**Multiple Literacies:** Students will apply information fluency and practice digital citizenship	
LA12.4.1	Information Fluency: Students will evaluate, create, and communicate information in a variety of media and formats	R7 pp. 42–47 R8 pp. 48–53 W8 pp. 116–121 W9 pp. 122–127
LA12.4.2	Digital Citizenship: Students will practice the norms of appropriate and responsible technology use	W6 pp. 104–109 SL5 pp. 162–167

New Jersey, Grades 9–10

New Jersey Strand/Standard	Focus of New Jersey Standard	For More Information
Reading Literature		
RL.1	Cite strong and thorough textual evidence and make relevant connections to support analysis of what the text says explicitly and implicitly	R1 pp. 6–11
RL.2	Determine a theme or central idea of a text and analyze its development and how it is shaped by specific details; summarize the text	R2 pp. 12–17
RL.3	Analyze how characters develop, interact, and advance the plot or develop the theme	R3 pp. 18–23
RL.4	Determine the meaning of words and phrases as they are used in a text, including figurative and connotative meanings; analyze the cumulative impact of word choice on meaning and tone	R4 pp. 24–29
RL.5	Analyze how an author's choices regarding structure, the order of events, and manipulating time create such effects as mystery, tension, or surprise	R5 pp. 30–35
RL.6	Analyze a point of view, perspective, or cultural experience reflected in a piece of literature	R6 pp. 36–41
RL.7	Analyze the representation of a subject or scene in two different artistic mediums, including what is emphasized or absent in each treatment	R7 pp. 42–47
RL.8	NA	
RL.9	Analyze and reflect on how an author draws on and transforms source material	R9 pp. 54–59
RL.10	Read literature of appropriate complexity independently with proficiency	R10 pp. 60–65
Reading Informational Text		
RI.1	Accurately cite strong and thorough textual evidence and make relevant connections to support analysis of what the text says explicitly and implicitly	R1 pp. 6–11
RI.2	Determine the central idea of a text and analyze its development; summarize main ideas or events	R2 pp. 12–17
RI.3	Analyze how the author structures an analysis or series of ideas or events, including the order, how they are developed, and the connections between them	R3 pp. 18–23
RI.4	Determine the meaning of words and phrases in a text; analyze the cumulative impact of specific word choices	R4 pp. 24–29
RI.5	Analyze in detail how ideas or claims are developed by particular sentences, paragraphs, or larger portions of text	R5 pp. 30–35
RI.6	Analyze how an author uses rhetoric to advance a point of view, perspective, or purpose	R6 pp. 36–41
RI.7	Analyze various perspectives presented in different mediums	R7 pp. 42–47
RI.8	Describe and evaluate the argument in a text; assess reasoning and evidence; identify false statements and fallacious reasoning	R8 pp. 48–53
RI.9	Analyze and reflect on U.S. documents of historical and literary significance, noting how they address related themes and concepts	R9 pp. 54–59
RI.10	Read and comprehend appropriately complex informational texts independently and proficiently	R10 pp. 60–65
Writing		
W.1	Write arguments to support claims, using valid reasoning and relevant and sufficient evidence	W1 pp. 70–77
W.2	Write informative/explanatory texts to effectively examine and convey complex ideas, concepts, and information	W2 pp. 78–85
W.3	Write narratives to develop real or imagined experiences or events using effective technique, well-chosen details, and well-structured event sequences	W3 pp. 86–91
W.4	Produce writing in which the development, organization, style, and features are appropriate to the task, genre, purpose, and audience	W4 pp. 92–97

(Continued)

New Jersey Strand/Standard	Focus of New Jersey Standard	For More Information
Writing		
W.5	Develop and strengthen writing as needed by planning, revising, and editing, rewriting, or trying a new approach	W5 pp. 98–103
W.6	Use technology to produce, publish, and update individual or shared writing projects	W6 pp. 104–109
W.7	Conduct research projects to answer a question or solve a problem; synthesize multiple sources; demonstrate understanding of the subject	W7 pp. 110–115
W.8	Gather information from multiple sources, using advanced searches effectively; assess usefulness of sources; integrate information, avoiding plagiarism	W8 pp. 116–121
W.9	Draw evidence from texts to support analysis, reflection, research, and/or synthesis	W9 pp. 122–127
W.10	Write routinely over short and extended time frames for a range of audiences, tasks, and purposes	W10 pp. 128–133
Speaking and Listening		
SL.1	Engage effectively in a range of collaborative discussions with diverse partners, building on others' ideas and expressing their own clearly and persuasively	SL1 pp. 138–143
SL.2	Integrate multiple sources of information presented in diverse media or formats; evaluate credibility and accuracy of sources and noting discrepancies	SL2 pp. 144–149
SL.3	Evaluate a speaker's point of view, reasoning, and use of evidence and rhetoric; identify fallacious reasoning or exaggerated or distorted evidence	SL3 pp. 150–155
SL.4	Present information clearly, concisely, and logically; ensure organization, development, substance, and style are appropriate to purpose, audience, and task	SL4 pp. 156–161
SL.5	Make strategic use of digital media in presentations to enhance understanding and to add interest	SL5 pp. 162–167
SL.6	Adapt speech to a variety of contexts and tasks; demonstrate a command of formal English when appropriate	SL6 pp. 168–173
Language		
L.1	Demonstrate command of the conventions of standard English grammar and usage when writing or speaking	L1 pp. 178–183
L.2	Demonstrate command of the conventions of standard English capitalization, punctuation, and spelling when writing	L2 pp. 184–189
L.3	Apply knowledge of language to make effective choices for meaning or style, and to comprehend more fully when reading or listening	L3 pp. 190–195
L.4	Determine or clarify the meaning of unknown and multiple-meaning words and phrases, choosing flexibly from an array of strategies	L4 pp. 196–201
L.5	Demonstrate understanding of figurative language, word relationships, and nuances in word meanings	L5 pp. 202–207
L.6	Acquire and use accurately general academic and domain-specific words and phrases; demonstrate independence in gathering vocabulary knowledge	L6 pp. 208–213
Reading History/Social Studies		
RH.1	Accurately cite specific textual evidence to support analysis of primary and secondary sources	R1 pp. 6–11
RH.2	Determine theme, central ideas, or information of a primary or secondary source; summarize how they develop	R2 pp. 12–17
RH.3	Analyze in detail a series of events; determine whether earlier events caused later ones	R3 pp. 18–23
RH.4	Determine the meaning of words and phrases, including vocabulary describing political, social, or economic aspects of history/social studies	R4 pp. 24–29
RH.5	Analyze how a text uses structure to emphasize key points or advance an explanation or analysis	R5 pp. 30–35

New Jersey Strand/Standard	Focus of New Jersey Standard	For More Information
Reading History/Social Studies		
RH.6	Compare the point of view of two or more authors for how they treat the same or similar topics	R6 pp. 36–41
RH.7	Integrate quantitative or technical analysis with qualitative analysis	R7 pp. 42–47
RH.8	Assess the extent to which reasoning and evidence support the author's claim	R8 pp. 48–53
RH.9	Compare and contrast treatment of the same topic or of various perspectives in several primary and secondary sources	R9 pp. 54–59
RH.10	Read and comprehend history/social studies texts of appropriate complexity	R10 pp. 60–65
Reading Science/Technical Subjects		
RST.1	Accurately cite specific textual evidence to support analysis of science and technical texts	R1 pp. 6–11
RST.2	Determine central ideas, themes, or conclusions; trace the explanation of a complex process; provide an accurate summary	R2 pp. 12–17
RST.3	Follow precisely a complex multistep procedure, attending to special cases or exceptions defined in the text	R3 pp. 18–23
RST.4	Determine the meaning of domain-specific words and phrases as they are used in a special scientific or technical context	R4 pp. 24–29
RST.5	Analyze the structure of relationships among concepts in a text	R5 pp. 30–35
RST.6	Analyze the author's purpose in providing an explanation, describing a procedure, or discussing an experiment	R6 pp. 36–41
RST.7	Translate quantitative or technical information expressed in words into visual form, and translate information expressed visually into words	R7 pp. 42–47
RST.8	Assess the extent to which reasoning and evidence support the author's claim or recommendation for solving a problem	R8 pp. 48–53
RST.9	Compare and contrast findings presented in a text to those from other sources, noting where they support or contradict previous explanations	R9 pp. 54–59
RST.10	Read and comprehend science/technical texts of appropriate complexity	R10 pp. 60–65
Writing History/Social Studies, Science and Technical Subjects		
WHST.1	Write arguments focused on disciple-specific content	W1 pp. 70–77
WHST.2	Write informative/explanatory texts, including the narration of historical events, scientific procedures, or technical processes	W2 pp. 78–85
WHST.3	NA	
WHST.4	Produce clear and coherent writing in which the development, organization, and style are appropriate to task, purpose, and audience	W4 pp. 92–97
WHST.5	Develop and strengthen writing as needed by planning, revising, editing, rewriting, or trying a new approach	W5 pp. 98–103
WHST.6	Use technology to produce, publish, and update individual or shared writing projects	W6 pp. 104–109
WHST.7	Conduct research projects to answer a question or solve a problem; synthesize multiple sources, demonstrating understanding of the subject	W7 pp. 110–115
WHST.8	Gather relevant information from multiple print and digital sources; assess the usefulness of each source; integrate information, avoiding plagiarism	W8 pp. 116–121
WHST.9	Draw evidence from informational texts to support analysis, reflection, and research	W9 pp. 122–127
WHST.10	Write routinely for a range of discipline-specific tasks, purposes, and audiences	W10 pp. 128–133

New Jersey, Grades 11–12

New Jersey Strand/Standard	Focus of New Jersey Standard	For More Information
Reading Literature		
RL.1	Cite strong and thorough textual evidence and make relevant connections to support analysis of what the text says explicitly and implicitly	R1 pp. 6–11
RL.2	Determine two or more themes or central ideas and analyze their development; restate and summarize main ideas or events	R2 pp. 12–17
RL.3	Analyze the impact of the author's choices regarding how to develop and relate elements of a story	R3 pp. 18–23
RL.4	Determine the meaning of words and phrases as they are used in a text, including figurative and connotative meanings; analyze the cumulative impact of word choice on meaning and tone	R4 pp. 24–29
RL.5	Analyze how an author's choices concerning how to structure specific parts of the text contribute to its overall structure and meaning	R5 pp. 30–35
RL.6	Analyze a case in which grasping point of view requires distinguishing what is directly stated from what is really meant	R6 pp. 36–41
RL.7	Analyze multiple representations of a story, drama, or poem, evaluating how each interprets the source text	R7 pp. 42–47
RL.8	NA	
RL.9	Demonstrate knowledge of and reflect on 18th, 19th, and early 20th century foundational works of American literature	R9 pp. 54–59
RL.10	Read and comprehend a range of literature from a variety of cultures	R10 pp. 60–65
Reading Informational Text		
RI.1	Accurately cite strong and thorough textual evidence to support analysis of what the text says explicitly and implicitly, including where the text leaves matters uncertain	R1 pp. 6–11
RI.2	Determine two or more central ideas of a text and analyze their development; restate or summarize main ideas or events	R2 pp. 12–17
RI.3	Analyze a complex set of ideas or sequence of events and explain how specific individuals, ideas, or events interact and develop	R3 pp. 18–23
RI.4	Determine the meaning of words and phrases in a text; analyze how an author uses and refines the meaning of key terms over the course of a text	R4 pp. 24–29
RI.5	Analyze and evaluate the effectiveness of the structure in an exposition or argument	R5 pp. 30–35
RI.6	Analyze how an author's style and content contribute to the power, persuasiveness, or impact of the text	R6 pp. 36–41
RI.7	Integrate and evaluate multiple sources of information presented in different media or formats in order to address a question or solve a problem	R7 pp. 42–47
RI.8	Delineate and evaluate the reasoning in seminal U.S. texts, including the application of constitutional principles and use of legal reasoning, and the premises, purposes, and arguments in works of public policy	R8 pp. 48–53
RI.9	Analyze 17th, 18th, and 19th century foundational U.S. and world documents of literary significance	R9 pp. 54–59
RI.10	Read and comprehend literary nonfiction independently and proficiently	R10 pp. 60–65
Writing		
W.1	Write arguments to support claims, using valid reasoning and relevant and sufficient evidence	W1 pp. 70–77
W.2	Write informative/explanatory texts to examine and convey complex ideas, concepts, and information clearly and accurately	W2 pp. 78–85
W.3	Write narratives to develop real or imagined experiences or events using effective technique, well-chosen details, and well-structured event sequences	W3 pp. 86–91

New Jersey Strand/Standard	Focus of New Jersey Standard	For More Information
Writing		
W.4	Produce writing in which the development, organization, style, and features are appropriate to the task, genre, purpose, and audience	W4 pp. 92–97
W.5	Develop and strengthen writing as needed by planning, revising, and editing, rewriting, or trying a new approach	W5 pp. 98–103
W.6	Use technology to produce, publish, and update individual or shared writing projects	W6 pp. 104–109
W.7	Conduct research projects to answer a question or solve a problem; synthesize multiple sources; demonstrate understanding of the subject	W7 pp. 110–115
W.8	Gather information from multiple sources, using advanced searches effectively; assess strengths and limitations of sources; integrate information, avoiding plagiarism and overreliance on any one source	W8 pp. 116–121
W.9	Draw evidence from texts to support analysis, reflection, and research	W9 pp. 122–127
W.10	Write routinely over shorter and extended time frames for a range of audiences, tasks, and purposes	W10 pp. 128–133
Speaking and Listening		
SL.1	Engage effectively in a range of collaborative discussions with diverse partners, building on others' ideas and expressing their own clearly and persuasively	SL1 pp. 138–143
SL.2	Integrate multiple sources of information presented in diverse media or formats; evaluate credibility and accuracy of sources and note discrepancies	SL2 pp. 144–149
SL.3	Evaluate a speaker's point of view, reasoning, and use of evidence and rhetoric; assess the stance, premises, link among ideas, word choice, emphasis, and tone	SL3 pp. 150–155
SL.4	Present information, conveying a clear and distinct perspective, address alternative viewpoints; presentation is appropriate to purpose, audience, and task	SL4 pp. 156–161
SL.5	Make strategic use of digital media in presentations to enhance understanding and to add interest	SL5 pp. 162–167
SL.6	Adapt speech to a variety of contexts and tasks; demonstrate a command of formal English when appropriate	SL6 pp. 168–173
Language		
L.1	Demonstrate command of the conventions of standard English grammar and usage when writing or speaking	L1 pp. 178–183
L.2	Demonstrate command of the conventions of standard English capitalization, punctuation, and spelling when writing	L2 pp. 184–189
L.3	Apply knowledge of language to make effective choices for meaning or style, and to comprehend more fully when reading or listening	L3 pp. 190–195
L.4	Determine or clarify the meaning of unknown and multiple-meaning words and phrases, choosing flexibly from an array of strategies	L4 pp. 196–201
L.5	Demonstrate understanding of figurative language, word relationships, and nuances in word meanings	L5 pp. 202–207
L.6	Acquire and use accurately general academic and domain-specific words and phrases; demonstrate independence in gathering vocabulary knowledge	L6 pp. 208–213
Reading History/Social Studies		
RH.1	Accurately cite specific textual evidence to support analysis of primary and secondary sources	R1 pp. 6–11
RH.2	Determine theme, central ideas, or information of a primary or secondary source; summarize how they develop	R2 pp. 12–17
RH.3	Evaluate explanations for actions or events and determine which best accords with textual evidence	R3 pp. 18–23
RH.4	Determine the meaning of words and phrases, including figurative and connotative meanings; analyze the impact of specific word choices	R4 pp. 24–29

(Continued)

New Jersey Strand/Standard	Focus of New Jersey Standard	For More Information
Reading History/Social Studies		
RH.5	Analyze in detail how a complex primary source is structured	R5 pp. 30–35
RH.6	Evaluate authors' differing points of view on the same historical event	R6 pp. 36–41
RH.7	Integrate and evaluate multiple sources of information presented in diverse formats and media in order to address a question or solve a problem	R7 pp. 42–47
RH.8	Evaluate an author's premises, claims, and evidence by corroborating or challenging them	R8 pp. 48–53
RH.9	Integrate information from diverse sources into a coherent understanding of an idea or event	R9 pp. 54–59
RH.10	Read and comprehend history/social studies texts of appropriate complexity	R10 pp. 60–65
Reading Science/Technical Subjects		
RST.1	Accurately cite specific textual evidence to support analysis of science and technical texts	R1 pp. 6–11
RST.2	Determine central ideas, themes, or conclusions; summarize complex concepts by paraphrasing into simpler but accurate terms	R2 pp. 12–17
RST.3	Follow precisely a complex multistep procedure; analyze the results based on explanations in the text	R3 pp. 18–23
RST.4	Determine the meaning of domain-specific words and phrases as they are used in a special scientific or technical context	R4 pp. 24–29
RST.5	Analyze how the text structures information into categories or hierarchies, demonstrating understanding	R5 pp. 30–35
RST.6	Analyze the author's purpose in providing an explanation, describing a procedure, or discussing an experiment	R6 pp. 36–41
RST.7	Integrate and evaluate multiple sources of information presented in diverse formats and media in order to address a question or solve a problem	R7 pp. 42–47
RST.8	Evaluate the hypotheses, data, analysis, and conclusions in a science or technical text, corroborating or challenging conclusions	R8 pp. 48–53
RST.9	Synthesize information from a range of sources into a coherent understanding, resolving conflicting information when possible	R9 pp. 54–59
RST.10	Read and comprehend science/technical texts of appropriate complexity	R10 pp. 60–65
Writing History/Social Studies, Science and Technical Subjects		
WHST.1	Write arguments focused on disciple-specific content	W1 pp. 70–77
WHST.2	Write informative/explanatory texts, including the narration of historical events, scientific procedures, or technical processes	W2 pp. 78–85
WHST.3	NA	
WHST.4	Produce clear and coherent writing in which the development, organization, and style are appropriate to task, purpose, and audience	W4 pp. 92–97
WHST.5	Develop and strengthen writing as needed by planning, revising, editing, rewriting, or trying a new approach	W5 pp. 98–103
WHST.6	Use technology to produce, publish, and update individual or shared writing projects	W6 pp. 104–109
WHST.7	Conduct research projects to answer a question or solve a problem; synthesize multiple sources, demonstrating understanding of the subject	W7 pp. 110–115
WHST.8	Gather relevant information from multiple print and digital sources; assess the usefulness of each source; integrate information, avoiding plagiarism and overreliance on any one source	W8 pp. 116–121
WHST.9	Draw evidence from informational texts to support analysis, reflection, and research	W9 pp. 122–127
WHST.10	Write routinely for a range of discipline-specific tasks, purposes, and audiences	W10 pp. 128–133

Oklahoma, Grades 9–10

Oklahoma Strand/Standard	Focus of Oklahoma Standard	For More Information
Speaking and Listening		
1.R.1	Listen actively and speak clearly	SL1 pp. 138–143
1.R.2	Evaluate, analyze, and synthesize a speaker's message	SL2 pp. 144–149
1.R.3	Engage in collaborative discussions	SL1 pp. 138–143
1.W.1	Give formal and informal presentations	SL4 pp. 156–161
1.W.2	Work effectively with diverse groups	SL1 pp. 138–143
Reading and Writing Process		
2.R.1	Summarize, paraphrase, and synthesize ideas	R2 pp. 12–17
2.R.2	Analyze details in texts	R1 pp. 6–11
2.W.1	Apply components of a recursive writing process	W5 pp. 98–103
2.W.2	Plan and prewrite a first draft	W5 pp. 98–103
2.W.3	Choose an organizational structure	W4 pp. 92–97
2.W.4	Edit and revise multiple drafts	W5 pp. 98–103
2.W.5	Use resources to find correct spellings	L2 pp. 184–189
Critical Reading and Writing		
3.R.1	Analyze and compare works written on the same topic. Evaluate historical, cultural, and/or global influences on authors' choices	R9 pp. 54–59
3.R.2	Evaluate points of view and perspectives in more than one text; explain how multiple points of view contribute to meaning	R6 pp. 36–41
3.R.3	Analyze how authors use key literary elements	R3 pp. 18–23 R5 pp. 30–35
3.R.4	Evaluate literary devices to support interpretations of texts	L5 pp. 202–207
3.R.5	Distinguish among different kinds of evidence	R8 pp. 48–53
3.R.6	Comparatively analyze structures of texts	R5 pp. 30–35
3.R.7	Make connections between and across multiple texts	R7 pp. 42–47
3.W.1	Write narratives	W3 pp. 86–91
3.W.2–3	Write informative texts	W2 pp. 78–85
3.W.4–6	Write arguments	W1 pp. 70–77
Vocabulary		
4.R.1	Increase knowledge of academic, domain-specific vocabulary	L6 pp. 208–213
4.R.2	Use word parts to determine the meaning of words	L4 pp. 196–201
4.R.3	Use context clues to determine or clarify the meaning of words	L4 pp. 196–201
4.R.4	Analyze the relationships among multiple-meaning words	L5 pp. 202–207
4.R.5	Use a dictionary, glossary, or thesaurus	L4 pp. 196–201
4.W.1	Use domain-specific vocabulary in writing	L6 pp. 208–213
4.W.2	Select appropriate language to create a specific effect according to purpose in writing	L3 pp. 190–195

(Continued)

Oklahoma Strand/Standard	Focus of Oklahoma Standard	For More Information
Language		
5.R	Apply knowledge of grammar and rhetorical style to analyze and evaluate a variety of texts	L3 pp. 190–195
5.W	Demonstrate command of grammar, mechanics, and usage through writing and other modes of communication	L1 pp. 178–183 L2 pp. 184–189
Research		
6.R.1–3	Use viable research questions to find information about a specific topic; synthesize resources to acquire knowledge; evaluate the relevance, reliability, and validity of the information	W7 pp. 110–115
6.W.1–4	Write research papers; integrate findings from sources; avoid plagiarism and cite sources to create reports, projects, and presentations	W8 pp. 116–121
Multimodal Literacies		
7.R.1–2	Analyze techniques used in written, oral, visual, digital, non-verbal, and interactive texts; analyze the impact of selected media and formats on meaning	R7 pp. 42–47
7.W.1–2	Create visual and/or multimedia presentations using variety of media forms	W6 pp. 104–109
Independent Reading and Writing		
8.R	Read independently for extended periods	R10 pp. 60–65
8.W	Write independently over extended periods	W10 pp. 128–133

Oklahoma, Grades 11–12

Oklahoma Strand/Standard	Focus of Oklahoma Standard	For More Information
Speaking and Listening		
1.R.1	Listen actively and speak clearly	SL1 pp. 138–143
1.R.2	Evaluate, analyze, and synthesize a speaker's message	SL2 pp. 144–149
1.R.3	Engage in collaborative discussions	SL1 pp. 138–143
1.W.1	Give formal and informal presentations	SL4 pp. 156–161
1.W.2	Work effectively with diverse groups	SL1 pp. 138–143
Reading and Writing Process		
2.R.1	Summarize, paraphrase, and synthesize ideas	R2 pp. 12–17
2.R.2	Analyze details in texts	R1 pp. 6–11
2.W.1	Apply components of a recursive writing process	W5 pp. 98–103
2.W.2	Plan and prewrite a first draft	W5 pp. 98–103
2.W.3	Choose an organizational structure	W4 pp. 92–97
2.W.4	Edit and revise multiple drafts	W5 pp. 98–103
2.W.5	Use resources to find correct spellings	L2 pp. 184–189
Critical Reading and Writing		
3.R.1	Analyze and compare works written on the same topic. Evaluate historical, cultural, and/or global influences on authors' choices	R9 pp. 54–59
3.R.2	Evaluate points of view and perspectives in more than one text; explain how multiple points of view contribute to meaning	R6 pp. 36–41

Oklahoma Strand/Standard	Focus of Oklahoma Standard	For More Information
Critical Reading and Writing		
3.R.3	Analyze how authors use key literary elements	R3 pp. 18–23 R5 pp. 30–35
3.R.4	Evaluate literary devices to support interpretations of texts	L5 pp. 202–207
3.R.5	Distinguish among different kinds of evidence	R8 pp. 48–53
3.R.6	Comparatively analyze structures of texts	R5 pp. 30–35
3.R.7	Make connections between and across multiple texts	R7 pp. 42–47
3.W.1	Write narratives	W3 pp. 86–91
3.W.2–3	Write informative texts	W2 pp. 78–85
3.W.4–6	Write arguments	W1 pp. 70–77
Vocabulary		
4.R.1	Increase knowledge of academic, domain-specific vocabulary	L6 pp. 208–213
4.R.2	Use word parts to determine the meaning of words	L4 pp. 196–201
4.R.3	Use context clues to determine or clarify the meaning of words	L4 pp. 196–201
4.R.4	Analyze the relationships among multiple-meaning words	L5 pp. 202–207
4.R.5	Use a dictionary, glossary, or thesaurus	L4 pp. 196–201
4.W.1	Use domain-specific vocabulary in writing	L6 pp. 208–213
4.W.2	Select appropriate language to create a specific effect according to purpose in writing	L3 pp. 190–195
Language		
5.R	Apply knowledge of grammar and rhetorical style to analyze and evaluate a variety of texts	L3 pp. 190–195
5.W	Demonstrate command of grammar, mechanics, and usage through writing and other modes of communication	L1 pp. 178–183 L2 pp. 184–189
Research		
6.R.1–3	Use viable research questions to find information about a specific topic; synthesize resources to acquire knowledge; evaluate the relevance, reliability, and validity of the information	W7 pp. 110–115
6.W.1–4	Write research papers; integrate findings from sources; avoid plagiarism and cite sources to create reports, projects, and presentations	W8 pp. 116–121
Multimodal Literacies		
7.R.1–2	Analyze techniques used in written, oral, visual, digital, non-verbal, and interactive texts; analyze the impact of selected media and formats on meaning	R7 pp. 42–47
7.W.1–2	Create visual and/or multimedia presentations using variety of media forms	W6 pp. 104–109
Independent Reading and Writing		
8.R	Read independently for extended periods	R10 pp. 60–65
8.W	Write independently over extended periods	W10 pp. 128–133

Pennsylvania, Grades 9–10

Pennsylvania Strand/Standard	Focus of Pennsylvania Standard	For More Information
Reading Informational Text		
CC.1.2.A	Determine the central idea of a text and analyze its development; summarize main ideas or events	R2 pp. 12–17
CC.1.2.B	Cite strong and thorough textual evidence to support analysis of what the text says explicitly and implicitly	R1 pp. 6–11
CC.1.2.C	Analyze how the author structures an analysis or series of ideas or events, including the order, how they are developed, and the connections between them	R3 pp. 18–23
CC1.2.D	Analyze how an author uses rhetoric to advance a point of view, perspective, or purpose	R6 pp. 36–41
CC1.2.E	Analyze in detail how ideas or claims are developed by particular sentences, paragraphs, or larger portions of text	R5 pp. 30–35
CC1.2.F	Determine the meaning of words and phrases in a text; analyze the cumulative impact of specific word choices	R4 pp. 24–29
CC1.2.G	Analyze various accounts of a subject told in different mediums	R7 pp. 42–47
CC1.2.H	Evaluate the argument in a text; assess reasoning and evidence; identify false statements and fallacious reasoning	R8 pp. 48–53
CC1.2.I	Analyze U.S. documents of historical and literary significance, noting how they address related themes and concepts	R9 pp. 54–59
CC1.2.J	Acquire and use accurately general academic and domain-specific words and phrases; demonstrate independence in gathering vocabulary knowledge	L6 pp. 208–213
CC1.2.K	Determine or clarify the meaning of unknown and multiple-meaning words and phrases, choosing flexibly from an array of strategies	L4 pp. 196–201
CC1.2.L	Read and comprehend appropriately complex informational texts	R10 pp. 60–65
Reading Literature		
CC1.3.A	Determine a theme or central idea of a text and analyze its development and how it is shaped by specific details; summarize the text	R2 pp. 12–17
CC1.3.B	Cite strong and thorough textual evidence to support analysis of what the text says explicitly and implicitly	R1 pp. 6–11
CC1.3.C	Analyze how characters develop, interact, and advance the plot or develop the theme	R3 pp. 18–23
CC1.3.D	Analyze a point of view, perspective, or cultural experience reflected in a piece of literature	R6 pp. 36–41
CC1.3.E	Analyze the author's choices regarding structure, the order of events, and manipulating time	R5 pp. 30–35
CC1.3.F	Determine the meaning of words and phrases as they are used in a text, including figurative and connotative meanings; analyze the cumulative impact of word choice on meaning and tone	R4 pp. 24–29
CC1.3.G	Analyze the representation of a subject or scene in two different artistic mediums, including what is emphasized or absent in each treatment	R7 pp. 42–47
CC1.3.H	Analyze how an author draws on and transforms source material	R9 pp. 54–59
CC1.3.I	Determine or clarify the meaning of unknown and multiple-meaning words and phrases, choosing flexibly from an array of strategies	L4 pp. 196–201
CC1.3.J	Acquire and use accurately general academic and domain-specific words and phrases; demonstrate independence in gathering vocabulary knowledge	L6 pp. 208–213
CC1.3.K	Read and comprehend a range of fiction	R10 pp. 60–65
Writing		
CC1.4.A-F	Write informative/explanatory texts to effectively examine and convey complex ideas, concepts, and information; demonstrate command of the conventions of standard English capitalization, punctuation, and spelling when writing	W2 pp. 78–85 W4 pp. 92–97 L2 pp. 184–189
CC1.4.G-L	Write arguments to support claims, using valid reasoning and relevant and sufficient evidence; demonstrate command of the conventions of standard English capitalization, punctuation, and spelling when writing	W1 pp. 70–77 W4 pp. 92–97 L2 pp. 184–189

Pennsylvania Strand/Standard	Focus of Pennsylvania Standard	For More Information
Writing		
CC1.4.M-R	Write narratives to develop real or imagined experiences or events using effective technique, well-chosen details, and well-structured event sequences; demonstrate command of the conventions of standard English capitalization, punctuation, and spelling when writing	W3 pp. 86–91 W4 pp. 92–97 L2 pp. 184–189
CC1.4.S	Draw evidence from texts to support analysis, reflection, and research	W9 pp. 122–127
CC1.4.T	Develop and strengthen writing as needed by planning, revising, and editing, rewriting, or trying a new approach	W5 pp. 98–103
CC1.4.U	Use technology to produce, publish, and update individual or shared writing projects	W6 pp. 104–109
CC1.4.V	Conduct research projects to answer a question or solve a problem; synthesize multiple sources; demonstrate understanding of the subject	W7 pp. 110–115
CC1.4.W	Gather information from multiple sources, using advanced searches effectively; assess strengths and limitations of sources; integrate information, avoiding plagiarism	W8 pp. 116–121
CC1.4.X	Write routinely over shorter and extended time frames for a range of audiences, tasks, and purposes	W10 pp. 128–133
CC1.5.A	Engage effectively in a range of collaborative discussions with diverse partners, building on others' ideas and expressing their own clearly and persuasively	SL1 pp. 138–143
CC1.5.B	Evaluate a speaker's point of view, reasoning, and use of evidence and rhetoric; identify fallacious reasoning or exaggerated or distorted evidence	SL3 pp. 150–155
CC1.5.C	Integrate multiple sources of information presented in diverse media or formats; evaluate credibility and accuracy of sources and note discrepancies	SL2 pp. 144–149
CC1.5.D	Present information clearly, concisely, and logically; ensure organization, development, substance, and style are appropriate to purpose, audience, and task	SL4 pp. 156–161
CC1.5.E	Adapt speech to a variety of contexts and tasks; demonstrate a command of formal English when appropriate	SL6 pp. 168–173
CC1.5.F	Make strategic use of digital media in presentations to enhance understanding and to add interest	SL5 pp. 162–167
CC1.5.G	Demonstrate command of the conventions of standard English grammar and usage when speaking	L1 pp. 178–183

Pennsylvania, Grades 11–12

Pennsylvania Strand/Standard	Focus of Pennsylvania Standard	For More Information
Reading Informational Text		
CC.1.2.A	Determine two or more themes or central ideas and analyze their development; restate and summarize main ideas or events	R2 pp. 12–17
CC.1.2.B	Cite strong and thorough textual evidence to support analysis of what the text says explicitly and implicitly	R1 pp. 6–11
CC.1.2.C	Analyze the impact of the author's choices regarding how to develop and relate elements of a story	R3 pp. 18–23
CC.1.2.D	Analyze how an author's point of view shapes the text	R6 pp. 36–41
CC.1.2.E	Analyze and evaluate the effectiveness of the structure in an exposition or argument	R5 pp. 30–35
CC.1.2.F	Evaluate how words and phrases shape meaning and tone in texts	R4 pp. 24–29
CC.1.2.G	Integrate and evaluate multiple sources of information presented in different media or formats in order to address a question or solve a problem	R7 pp. 42–47
CC.1.2.H	Delineate and evaluate the reasoning in seminal U.S. texts, including the application of constitutional principles and use of legal reasoning, and the premises, purposes, and arguments in works of public policy	R8 pp. 48–53
CC.1.2.I	Analyze foundational U.S. and world documents of literary significance	R9 pp. 54–59
CC.1.2.J	Acquire and use accurately general academic and domain-specific words and phrases; demonstrate independence in gathering vocabulary knowledge	L6 pp. 208–213

(Continued)

Pennsylvania Strand/Standard	Focus of Pennsylvania Standard	For More Information
Reading Informational Text		
CC1.2.K	Determine or clarify the meaning of unknown and multiple-meaning words and phrases, choosing flexibly from an array of strategies	L4 pp. 196–201
CC1.2.L	Read and comprehend literary nonfiction independently and proficiently	R10 pp. 60–65
Reading Literature		
CC1.3.A	Determine two or more themes or central ideas and analyze their development; restate and summarize main ideas or events	R2 pp. 12–17
CC1.3.B	Cite strong and thorough textual evidence to support analysis of what the text says explicitly and implicitly	R1 pp. 6–11
CC1.3.C	Analyze the impact of the author's choices regarding how to develop and relate elements of a story	R3 pp. 18–23
CC1.3.D	Analyze how an author's point of view shapes the text	R6 pp. 36–41
CC1.3.E	Evaluate the structure of texts	R5 pp. 30–35
CC1.3.F	Analyze the cumulative impact of word choice on meaning and tone	R4 pp. 24–29
CC1.3.G	Analyze multiple representations of a story, drama, or poem, evaluating how each interprets the source text	R7 pp. 42–47
CC1.3.H	Demonstrate knowledge of foundational works of American literature	R9 pp. 54–59
CC1.3.I	Determine or clarify the meaning of unknown and multiple-meaning words and phrases, choosing flexibly from an array of strategies	L4 pp. 196–201
CC1.3.J	Acquire and use accurately general academic and domain-specific words and phrases; demonstrate independence in gathering vocabulary knowledge	L6 pp. 208–213
CC1.3.K	Read and comprehend a range of fiction	R10 pp. 60–65
Writing		
CC1.4.A-F	Write informative/explanatory texts to examine and convey complex ideas, concepts, and information clearly and accurately; demonstrate command of the conventions of standard English capitalization, punctuation, and spelling when writing	W2 pp. 78–85 W4 pp. 92–97 L2 pp. 184–189
CC1.4.G-L	Write arguments to support claims, using valid reasoning and relevant and sufficient evidence; demonstrate command of the conventions of standard English capitalization, punctuation, and spelling when writing	W1 pp. 70–77 W4 pp. 92–97 L2 pp. 184–189
CC1.4.M-R	Write narratives to develop real or imagined experiences or events using effective technique, well-chosen details, and well-structured event sequences; demonstrate command of the conventions of standard English capitalization, punctuation, and spelling when writing	W3 pp. 86–91 W4 pp. 92–97 L2 pp. 184–189
CC1.4.S	Draw evidence from texts to support analysis, reflection, and research	W9 pp. 122–127
CC1.4.T	Develop and strengthen writing as needed by planning, revising, and editing, rewriting, or trying a new approach	W5 pp. 98–103
CC1.4.U	Use technology to produce, publish, and update individual or shared writing projects	W6 pp. 104–109
CC1.4.V	Conduct research projects to answer a question or solve a problem; synthesize multiple sources; demonstrate understanding of the subject	W7 pp. 110–115
CC1.4.W	Gather information from multiple sources, using advanced searches effectively; assess strengths and limitations of sources; integrate information, avoiding plagiarism and overreliance on any one source	W8 pp. 116–121
CC1.4.X	Write routinely over shorter and extended time frames for a range of audiences, tasks, and purposes	W10 pp. 128–133
CC1.5.A	Engage effectively in a range of collaborative discussions with diverse partners, building on others' ideas and expressing their own clearly and persuasively	SL1 pp. 138–143
CC1.5.B	Evaluate a speaker's point of view, reasoning, and use of evidence and rhetoric; assess the stance, premises, link among ideas, word choice, emphasis, and tone	SL3 pp. 150–155
CC1.5.C	Integrate multiple sources of information presented in diverse media or formats; evaluate credibility and accuracy of sources and note discrepancies	SL2 pp. 144–149
CC1.5.D	Present information, conveying a clear and distinct perspective, address alternative viewpoints; presentation is appropriate to purpose, audience, and task	SL4 pp. 156–161
CC1.5.E	Adapt speech to a variety of contexts and tasks; demonstrate a command of formal English when appropriate	SL6 pp. 168–173
CC1.5.F	Make strategic use of digital media in presentations to enhance understanding and to add interest	SL5 pp. 162–167
CC1.5.G	Demonstrate command of the conventions of standard English grammar and usage when speaking	L1 pp. 178–183

South Carolina, English 1/2

South Carolina Strand/Standard	Focus of South Carolina Standard	For More Information
Reading Literary Text		
5.1	Cite strong and thorough textual evidence to support analysis of what the text says explicitly and implicitly	R1 pp. 6–11
6.1	Determine a theme of a text and analyze its development and how it is shaped by specific details; summarize the text	R2 pp. 12–17
7.1	Analyze the representation of a subject or scene in two different artistic mediums, including what is emphasized or absent in each treatment	R7 pp. 42–47
7.2	Investigate how literary texts allude to themes and archetypes from historical and cultural traditions	R9 pp. 54–59
8.1	Analyze how characters develop, interact, and advance the plot or develop the theme	R3 pp. 18–23
9.1, 10.1	Determine the meaning of words and phrases as they are used in a text, including figurative and connotative meanings; analyze the cumulative impact of word choice on meaning and tone	R4 pp. 24–29
11.1	Analyze how the author's point of view and purpose shape content, meaning, and style	R6 pp. 36–41
12.1–12.2	Analyze how an author's choices regarding structure, the order of events, and manipulating time create such effects as mystery, tension, or surprise	R5 pp. 30–35
13.1–13.3	Read grade-level text independently, with proficiency, for variety of purposes	R10 pp. 60–65
Reading Informational Text		
5.1	Cite strong and thorough textual evidence to support analysis of what the text says explicitly and implicitly	R1 pp. 6–11
6.1	Determine the central idea of a text and analyze its development; summarize main ideas or events	R2 pp. 12–17
7.1	Evaluate how the use of different mediums impacts the reader's understanding of events, topics, and concepts	R7 pp. 42–47
8.1, 9.1	Determine the meaning of words and phrases in a text; analyze the cumulative impact of specific word choices	R4 pp. 24–29
8.2	Analyze how the author uses text structures to shape meaning and tone	R3 pp. 18–23
10.1	Analyze how an author uses rhetoric to advance a point of view, perspective, or purpose	R6 pp. 36–41
11.1	Analyze in detail how ideas or claims are developed by particular sentences, paragraphs, or larger portions of text	R5 pp. 30–35
11.2	Evaluate the argument in a text; assess reasoning and evidence; identify false statements and fallacious reasoning	R8 pp. 48–53
12.1–12.3	Read and comprehend grade-level informational texts independently and proficiently, for a variety of purposes	R10 pp. 60–65
Writing		
1.1	Write arguments to support claims, using valid reasoning and relevant and sufficient evidence; use an appropriate organizational structure; develop and strengthen writing as needed by planning, revising, and editing, rewriting, or trying a new approach; gather information from multiple sources; assess usefulness of sources; integrate information, avoiding plagiarism	W1 pp. 70–77 W4 pp. 92–97 W5 pp. 98–103 W8 pp. 116–121 W9 pp. 122–127
2.1	Write informative/explanatory texts to effectively examine and convey complex ideas, concepts, and information; use appropriate transitions, precise language, and a concluding statement; develop and strengthen writing as needed by planning, revising, and editing, rewriting, or trying a new approach; gather information from multiple sources; assess usefulness of sources; integrate information, avoiding plagiarism	W2 pp. 78–85 W4 pp. 92–97 W5 pp. 98–103 W8 pp. 116–121 W9 pp. 122–127

(Continued)

South Carolina Strand/Standard	Focus of South Carolina Standard	For More Information
Writing		
3.1	Write narratives to develop real or imagined experiences or events using effective technique, well-chosen details, and well-structured event sequences; develop and strengthen writing as needed by planning, revising, and editing, rewriting	W3 pp. 86–91 W4 pp. 92–97 W5 pp. 98–103
4	Demonstrate command of the conventions of standard English grammar and usage when writing or speaking	L1 pp. 178–183
5	Demonstrate command of the conventions of standard English capitalization, punctuation, and spelling when writing	L2 pp. 184–189
6.1	Write routinely over short and extended time frames for a range of audiences, tasks, and purposes	W10 pp. 128–133
Communication		
1.1	Integrate multiple sources of information presented in diverse media or formats; evaluate credibility and accuracy of sources and noting discrepancies	SL2 pp. 144–149
1.2	Engage effectively in a range of collaborative discussions with diverse partners, building on others' ideas and expressing their own clearly and persuasively	SL1 pp. 138–143
2.1	Present information clearly, concisely, and logically; ensure organization, development, substance, and style are appropriate to purpose, audience, and task	SL4 pp. 156–161
2.4	Adapt speech to a variety of contexts and tasks; demonstrate a command of formal English when appropriate	SL6 pp. 168–173
3.2	Make strategic use of media forms in presentations to enhance understanding for diverse audiences	SL5 pp. 162–167
4.1–4.3	Evaluate a speaker's point of view, reasoning, and use of evidence and rhetoric; identify fallacious reasoning or exaggerated or distorted evidence	SL3 pp. 150–155

South Carolina, English 3/4

South Carolina Strand/Standard	Focus of South Carolina Standard	For More Information
Reading Literature		
5.1	Cite strong and thorough textual evidence to support analysis of what the text says explicitly and implicitly	R1 pp. 6–11
6.1	Determine two or more themes or central ideas and analyze their development across multiple texts, citing evidence; provide a summary	R2 pp. 12–17
7.1	Analyze the development of theme across diverse media, modality, and format	R7 pp. 42–47
7.2	Investigate how literary texts allude to themes and archetypes from historical and cultural traditions	R9 pp. 54–59
8.1	Analyze how characters develop, interact, and advance the plot or develop the theme	R3 pp. 18–23
9.1, 10.1	Determine the meaning of words and phrases as they are used in a text, including figurative and connotative meanings; analyze the impact of the author's use of language and word choice on meaning and tone	R4 pp. 24–29
11.1	Analyze how the author's point of view and purpose shape content, meaning, and style	R6 pp. 36–41
12.1–12.2	Analyze and critique how an author's choices concerning how to structure text, order events, and manipulate time contribute to overall structure and meaning	R5 pp. 30–35
13.1–13.3	Read and comprehend a range of literature from a variety of cultures	R10 pp. 60–65
Reading Informational Text		
5.1	Cite significant textual evidence to support synthesis of what the text says explicitly and implicitly, including where the text leaves matters uncertain	R1 pp. 6–11
6.1	Determine two or more central ideas of a text and analyze their development; provide a summary of the text	R2 pp. 12–17

South Carolina Strand/Standard	Focus of South Carolina Standard	For More Information
Reading Informational Text		
7.1	Evaluate how the use of different mediums impacts the reader's understanding of events, topics, and concepts	R7 pp. 42–47
8.1, 9.1	Determine the meaning of words and phrases in a text; analyze how an author uses and refines the meaning of key terms over the course of a text	R4 pp. 24–29
8.2	Analyze and evaluate the effectiveness of the text structures an author uses to shape meaning and tone	R3 pp. 18–23
10.1	Determine the author's point of view and analyze how style and content contribute to the power, persuasiveness, or beauty of the text	R6 pp. 36–41
11.1	Analyze and evaluate the effectiveness of the text features and structure in an exposition or argument	R5 pp. 30–35
11.2	Analyze and critique the reasoning in historical, scientific, technical, and argument writing	R8 pp. 48–53
12.1–12.3	Read and comprehend grade-level text independently and proficiently	R10 pp. 60–65
Writing		
1.1	Write arguments to support claims, using valid reasoning and relevant and sufficient evidence; use an appropriate organizational structure; develop and strengthen writing as needed by planning, revising, and editing, rewriting, or trying a new approach; gather information from multiple sources; assess usefulness of sources; integrate information, avoiding plagiarism	W1 pp. 70–77 W4 pp. 92–97 W5 pp. 98–103 W8 pp. 116–121 W9 pp. 122–127
2.1	Write informative/explanatory texts to effectively examine and convey complex ideas, concepts, and information; use appropriate transitions, precise language, and a concluding statement; develop and strengthen writing as needed by planning, revising, and editing, rewriting, or trying a new approach; gather information from multiple sources; assess usefulness of sources; integrate information, avoiding plagiarism	W2 pp. 78–85 W4 pp. 92–97 W5 pp. 98–103 W8 pp. 116–121 W9 pp. 122–127
3.1	Write narratives to develop real or imagined experiences or events using effective technique, well-chosen details, and well-structured event sequences; develop and strengthen writing as needed by planning, revising, and editing, rewriting	W3 pp. 86–91 W4 pp. 92–97 W5 pp. 98–103
4	Demonstrate command of the conventions of standard English grammar and usage when writing or speaking	L1 pp. 178–183
5	Demonstrate command of the conventions of standard English capitalization, punctuation, and spelling when writing	L2 pp. 184–189
6.1	Write routinely over short and extended time frames for a range of audiences, tasks, and purposes	W10 pp. 128–133
Communication		
1.1	Integrate multiple sources of information presented in diverse media or formats; evaluate credibility and accuracy of sources and note discrepancies	SL2 pp. 144–149
1.2	Engage effectively in a range of collaborative discussions with diverse partners, building on others' ideas and expressing their own clearly and persuasively	SL1 pp. 138–143
2.1	Present information, conveying a clear and distinct perspective, address alternative viewpoints; presentation is appropriate to purpose, audience, and task	SL4 pp. 156–161
2.4	Adapt speech to a variety of contexts and tasks; demonstrate a command of formal English when appropriate	SL6 pp. 168–173
3.2	Make strategic use of media forms in presentations to enhance understanding and to add interest	SL5 pp. 162–167
4.1–4.3	Evaluate a speaker's point of view, reasoning, and use of evidence and rhetoric; assess the stance, premises, link among ideas, word choice, emphasis, and tone	SL3 pp. 150–155

Tennessee, Grades 9–10

Tennessee Strand/Standard	Focus of Tennessee Standard	For More Information
Reading Literature		
RL.1	Cite strong and thorough textual evidence to support analysis of what the text says explicitly and implicitly	R1 pp. 6–11
RL.2	Determine a theme or central idea of a text and analyze its development and how it is shaped by specific details; summarize the text	R2 pp. 12–17
RL.3	Analyze how characters develop, interact, and advance the plot or develop the theme	R3 pp. 18–23
RL.4	Determine the meaning of words and phrases as they are used in a text, including figurative and connotative meanings; analyze the cumulative impact of word choice on meaning and tone	R4 pp. 24–29
RL.5	Analyze how an author's choices regarding structure, the order of events, and manipulating time create such effects as mystery, tension, or surprise	R5 pp. 30–35
RL.6	Analyze a point of view, perspective, or cultural experience reflected in a piece of literature	R6 pp. 36–41
RL.7	Analyze the representation of a subject or scene in two different artistic mediums, including what is emphasized or absent in each treatment	R7 pp. 42–47
RL.8	NA	
RL.9	Analyze how an author draws on and transforms source material	R9 pp. 54–59
RL.10	Read literature of appropriate complexity independently with proficiency	R10 pp. 60–65
Reading Informational Text		
RI.1	Cite strong and thorough textual evidence to support analysis of what the text says explicitly and implicitly	R1 pp. 6–11
RI.2	Determine the central idea of a text and analyze its development; summarize main ideas or events	R2 pp. 12–17
RI.3	Analyze how the author structures an analysis or series of ideas or events, including the order, how they are developed, and the connections between them	R3 pp. 18–23
RI.4	Determine the meaning of words and phrases in a text; analyze the cumulative impact of specific word choices	R4 pp. 24–29
RI.5	Analyze in detail how ideas or claims are developed by particular sentences, paragraphs, or larger portions of text	R5 pp. 30–35
RI.6	Analyze how an author uses rhetoric to advance a point of view, perspective, or purpose	R6 pp. 36–41
RI.7	Analyze various accounts of a subject told in different mediums	R7 pp. 42–47
RI.8	Evaluate the argument in a text; assess reasoning and evidence; identify false statements and fallacious reasoning	R8 pp. 48–53
RI.9	Analyze U.S. documents of historical and literary significance, noting how they address related themes and concepts	R9 pp. 54–59
RI.10	Read and comprehend appropriately complex informational texts independently and proficiently	R10 pp. 60–65
Writing		
W.1	Write arguments to support claims, using valid reasoning and relevant and sufficient evidence	W1 pp. 70–77
W.2	Write informative/explanatory texts to effectively examine and convey complex ideas, concepts, and information	W2 pp. 78–85
W.3	Write narratives to develop real or imagined experiences or events using effective technique, well-chosen details, and well-structured event sequences	W3 pp. 86–91
W.4	Produce writing in which the development, organization, style, and features are appropriate to the task, genre, purpose, and audience	W4 pp. 92–97
W.5	Develop and strengthen writing as needed by planning, revising, and editing, rewriting, or trying a new approach	W5 pp. 98–103

Tennessee Strand/Standard	Focus of Tennessee Standard	For More Information
Writing		
W.6	Use technology to produce, publish, and update individual or shared writing projects	W6 pp. 104–109
W.7	Conduct research projects to answer a question or solve a problem; synthesize multiple sources; demonstrate understanding of the subject	W7 pp. 110–115
W.8	Gather information from multiple sources, using advanced searches effectively; assess usefulness of sources; integrate information, avoiding plagiarism	W8 pp. 116–121
W.9	Draw evidence from texts to support analysis, reflection, research, and/or synthesis	W9 pp. 122–127
W.10	Write routinely over short and extended time frames for a range of audiences, tasks, and purposes	W10 pp. 128–133
Speaking and Listening		
SL.1	Engage effectively in a range of collaborative discussions with diverse partners, building on others' ideas and expressing their own clearly and persuasively	SL1 pp. 138–143
SL.2	Integrate multiple sources of information presented in diverse media or formats; evaluate credibility and accuracy of sources and noting discrepancies	SL2 pp. 144–149
SL.3	Evaluate a speaker's point of view, reasoning, and use of evidence and rhetoric; identify fallacious reasoning or exaggerated or distorted evidence	SL3 pp. 150–155
SL.4	Present information clearly, concisely, and logically; ensure organization, development, substance, and style are appropriate to purpose, audience, and task	SL4 pp. 156–161
SL.5	Make strategic use of digital media in presentations to enhance understanding and to add interest	SL5 pp. 162–167
SL.6	Adapt speech to a variety of contexts and tasks; demonstrate a command of formal English when appropriate	SL6 pp. 168–173
Language		
L.1	Demonstrate command of the conventions of standard English grammar and usage when writing or speaking	L1 pp. 178–183
L.2	Demonstrate command of the conventions of standard English capitalization, punctuation, and spelling when writing	L2 pp. 184–189
L.3	Apply knowledge of language to make effective choices for meaning or style, and to comprehend more fully when reading or listening	L3 pp. 190–195
L.4	Determine or clarify the meaning of unknown and multiple-meaning words and phrases, choosing flexibly from an array of strategies	L4 pp. 196–201
L.5	Demonstrate understanding of figurative language, word relationships, and nuances in word meanings	L5 pp. 202–207
L.6	Acquire and use accurately general academic and domain-specific words and phrases; demonstrate independence in gathering vocabulary knowledge	L6 pp. 208–213

Tennessee, Grades 11–12

Tennessee Strand/Standard	Focus of Tennessee Standard	For More Information
Reading Literature		
RL.1	Cite strong and thorough textual evidence to support analysis of what the text says explicitly and implicitly	R1 pp. 6–11
RL.2	Determine two or more themes or central ideas and analyze their development; restate and summarize main ideas or events	R2 pp. 12–17

(Continued)

Tennessee Strand/Standard	Focus of Tennessee Standard	For More Information
Reading Literature		
RL.3	Analyze the impact of the author's choices regarding how to develop and relate elements of a story	R3 pp. 18–23
RL.4	Determine the meaning of words and phrases as they are used in a text, including figurative and connotative meanings; analyze the cumulative impact of word choice on meaning and tone	R4 pp. 24–29
RL.5	Analyze how an author's choices concerning how to structure specific parts of the text contribute to its overall structure and meaning	R5 pp. 30–35
RL.6	Analyze a case in which grasping point of view requires distinguishing what is directly stated from what is really meant	R6 pp. 36–41
RL.7	Analyze multiple representations of a story, drama, or poem, evaluating how each interprets the source text	R7 pp. 42–47
RL.8	NA	
RL.9	Demonstrate knowledge of 18th, 19th, and early 20th century foundational works of American literature	R9 pp. 54–59
RL.10	Read and comprehend a range of literature from a variety of cultures	R10 pp. 60–65
Reading Informational Text		
RI.1	Cite strong and thorough textual evidence to support analysis of what the text says explicitly and implicitly, including where the text leaves matters uncertain	R1 pp. 6–11
RI.2	Determine two or more central ideas of a text and analyze their development; restate or summarize main ideas or events	R2 pp. 12–17
RI.3	Analyze a complex set of ideas or sequence of events and explain how specific individuals, ideas, or events interact and develop	R3 pp. 18–23
RI.4	Determine the meaning of words and phrases in a text; analyze how an author uses and refines the meaning of key terms over the course of a text	R4 pp. 24–29
RI.5	Analyze and evaluate the effectiveness of the structure in an exposition or argument	R5 pp. 30–35
RI.6	Analyze how an author's style and content contribute to the power, persuasiveness, or impact of the text	R6 pp. 36–41
RI.7	Integrate and evaluate multiple sources of information presented in different media or formats in order to address a question or solve a problem	R7 pp. 42–47
RI.8	Delineate and evaluate the reasoning in seminal U.S. texts, including the application of constitutional principles and use of legal reasoning, and the premises, purposes, and arguments in works of public policy	R8 pp. 48–53
RI.9	Analyze 17th, 18th, and 19th century foundational U.S. and world documents of literary significance	R9 pp. 54–59
RI.10	Read and comprehend literary nonfiction independently and proficiently	R10 pp. 60–65
Writing		
W.1	Write arguments to support claims, using valid reasoning and relevant and sufficient evidence	W1 pp. 70–77
W.2	Write informative/explanatory texts to examine and convey complex ideas, concepts, and information clearly and accurately	W2 pp. 78–85
W.3	Write narratives to develop real or imagined experiences or events using effective technique, well-chosen details, and well-structured event sequences	W3 pp. 86–91
W.4	Produce writing in which the development, organization, style, and features are appropriate to the task, genre, purpose, and audience	W4 pp. 92–97

Tennessee Strand/Standard	Focus of Tennessee Standard	For More Information
Writing		
W.5	Develop and strengthen writing as needed by planning, revising, and editing, rewriting, or trying a new approach	W5 pp. 98–103
W.6	Use technology to produce, publish, and update individual or shared writing projects	W6 pp. 104–109
W.7	Conduct research projects to answer a question or solve a problem; synthesize multiple sources; demonstrate understanding of the subject	W7 pp. 110–115
W.8	Gather information from multiple sources, using advanced searches effectively; assess strengths and limitations of sources; integrate information, avoiding plagiarism and overreliance on any one source	W8 pp. 116–121
W.9	Draw evidence from texts to support analysis, reflection, and research	W9 pp. 122–127
W.10	Write routinely over shorter and extended time frames for a range of audiences, tasks, and purposes	W10 pp. 128–133
Speaking and Listening		
SL.1	Engage effectively in a range of collaborative discussions with diverse partners, building on others' ideas and expressing their own clearly and persuasively	SL1 pp. 138–143
SL.2	Integrate multiple sources of information presented in diverse media or formats; evaluate credibility and accuracy of sources and note discrepancies	SL2 pp. 144–149
SL.3	Evaluate a speaker's point of view, reasoning, and use of evidence and rhetoric; assess the stance, premises, link among ideas, word choice, emphasis, and tone	SL3 pp. 150–155
SL.4	Present information, conveying a clear and distinct perspective, address alternative viewpoints; presentation is appropriate to purpose, audience, and task	SL4 pp. 156–161
SL.5	Make strategic use of digital media in presentations to enhance understanding and to add interest	SL5 pp. 162–167
SL.6	Adapt speech to a variety of contexts and tasks; demonstrate a command of formal English when appropriate	SL6 pp. 168–173
Language		
L.1	Demonstrate command of the conventions of standard English grammar and usage when writing or speaking	L1 pp. 178–183
L.2	Demonstrate command of the conventions of standard English capitalization, punctuation, and spelling when writing	L2 pp. 184–189
L.3	Apply knowledge of language to make effective choices for meaning or style, and to comprehend more fully when reading or listening	L3 pp. 190–195
L.4	Determine or clarify the meaning of unknown and multiple-meaning words and phrases, choosing flexibly from an array of strategies	L4 pp. 196–201
L.5	Demonstrate understanding of figurative language, word relationships, and nuances in word meanings	L5 pp. 202–207
L.6	Acquire and use accurately general academic and domain-specific words and phrases; demonstrate independence in gathering vocabulary knowledge	L6 pp. 208–213

Utah, Grades 9–10

Utah Strand/Standard	Focus of Utah Standard	For More Information
Reading Literature		
RL.1	Cite strong and thorough textual evidence to support analysis of what the text says explicitly and implicitly	R1 pp. 6–11
RL.2	Determine a theme or central idea of a text and analyze its development and how it is shaped by specific details; summarize the text	R2 pp. 12–17
RL.3	Analyze how characters develop, interact, and advance the plot or develop the theme	R3 pp. 18–23
RL.4	Determine the meaning of words and phrases as they are used in a text, including figurative and connotative meanings; analyze the cumulative impact of word choice on meaning and tone	R4 pp. 24–29
RL.5	Analyze how an author's choices regarding structure, the order of events, and manipulating time create such effects as mystery, tension, or surprise	R5 pp. 30–35
RL.6	Analyze a point of view, perspective, or cultural experience reflected in a piece of literature	R6 pp. 36–41
RL.7	Analyze the representation of a subject or scene in two different artistic mediums, including what is emphasized or absent in each treatment	R7 pp. 42–47
RL.8	NA	
RL.9	Analyze how an author draws on and transforms source material	R9 pp. 54–59
RL.10	Read literature of appropriate complexity independently with proficiency	R10 pp. 60–65
Reading Informational Text		
RI.1	Cite strong and thorough textual evidence to support analysis of what the text says explicitly and implicitly	R1 pp. 6–11
RI.2	Determine the central idea of a text and analyze its development; summarize main ideas or events	R2 pp. 12–17
RI.3	Analyze how the author structures an analysis or series of ideas or events, including the order, how they are developed, and the connections between them	R3 pp. 18–23
RI.4	Determine the meaning of words and phrases in a text; analyze the cumulative impact of specific word choices	R4 pp. 24–29
RI.5	Analyze in detail how ideas or claims are developed by particular sentences, paragraphs, or larger portions of text	R5 pp. 30–35
RI.6	Analyze how an author uses rhetoric to advance a point of view, perspective, or purpose	R6 pp. 36–41
RI.7	Analyze various accounts of a subject told in different mediums	R7 pp. 42–47
RI.8	Evaluate the argument in a text; assess reasoning and evidence; identify false statements and fallacious reasoning	R8 pp. 48–53
RI.9	Analyze U.S. documents of historical and literary significance, noting how they address related themes and concepts	R9 pp. 54–59
RI.10	Read and comprehend appropriately complex informational texts independently and proficiently	R10 pp. 60–65
Writing		
W.1	Write arguments to support claims, using valid reasoning and relevant and sufficient evidence	W1 pp. 70–77
W.2	Write informative/explanatory texts to effectively examine and convey complex ideas, concepts, and information	W2 pp. 78–85
W.3	Write narratives to develop real or imagined experiences or events using effective technique, well-chosen details, and well-structured event sequences	W3 pp. 86–91
W.4	Produce writing in which the development, organization, style, and features are appropriate to the task, genre, purpose, and audience	W4 pp. 92–97

Utah Strand/Standard	Focus of Utah Standard	For More Information
Writing		
W.5	Develop and strengthen writing as needed by planning, revising, and editing, rewriting, or trying a new approach	W5 pp. 98–103
W.6	Use technology to produce, publish, and update individual or shared writing projects	W6 pp. 104–109
W.7	Conduct research projects to answer a question or solve a problem; synthesize multiple sources; demonstrate understanding of the subject	W7 pp. 110–115
W.8	Gather information from multiple sources, using advanced searches effectively; assess usefulness of sources; integrate information, avoiding plagiarism	W8 pp. 116–121
W.9	Draw evidence from texts to support analysis, reflection, research, and/or synthesis	W9 pp. 122–127
W.10	Write routinely over short and extended time frames for a range of audiences, tasks, and purposes	W10 pp. 128–133
Speaking and Listening		
SL.1	Engage effectively in a range of collaborative discussions with diverse partners, building on others' ideas and expressing their own clearly and persuasively	SL1 pp. 138–143
SL.2	Integrate multiple sources of information presented in diverse media or formats; evaluate credibility and accuracy of sources and noting discrepancies	SL2 pp. 144–149
SL.3	Evaluate a speaker's point of view, reasoning, and use of evidence and rhetoric; identify fallacious reasoning or exaggerated or distorted evidence	SL3 pp. 150–155
SL.4	Present information clearly, concisely, and logically; ensure organization, development, substance, and style are appropriate to purpose, audience, and task	SL4 pp. 156–161
SL.5	Make strategic use of digital media in presentations to enhance understanding and to add interest	SL5 pp. 162–167
SL.6	Adapt speech to a variety of contexts and tasks; demonstrate a command of formal English when appropriate	SL6 pp. 168–173
Language		
L.1	Demonstrate command of the conventions of standard English grammar and usage when writing or speaking	L1 pp. 178–183
L.2	Demonstrate command of the conventions of standard English capitalization, punctuation, and spelling when writing	L2 pp. 184–189
L.3	Apply knowledge of language to make effective choices for meaning or style, and to comprehend more fully when reading or listening	L3 pp. 190–195
L.4	Determine or clarify the meaning of unknown and multiple-meaning words and phrases, choosing flexibly from an array of strategies	L4 pp. 196–201
L.5	Demonstrate understanding of figurative language, word relationships, and nuances in word meanings	L5 pp. 202–207
L.6	Acquire and use accurately general academic and domain-specific words and phrases; demonstrate independence in gathering vocabulary knowledge	L6 pp. 208–213
Reading History/Social Studies		
RH.1	Cite specific textual evidence to support analysis of primary and secondary sources	R1 pp. 6–11
RH.2	Determine central ideas or information of a primary or secondary source; summarize how they develop	R2 pp. 12–17
RH.3	Analyze in detail a series of events; determine whether earlier events caused later ones	R3 pp. 18–23
RH.4	Determine the meaning of words and phrases, including vocabulary describing political, social, or economic aspects of history/social studies	R4 pp. 24–29
RH.5	Analyze how a text uses structure to emphasize key points or advance an explanation or analysis	R5 pp. 30–35
RH.6	Compare the point of view of two or more authors for how they treat the same or similar topics	R6 pp. 36–41

(Continued)

Utah Strand/Standard	Focus of Utah Standard	For More Information
Reading History/Social Studies		
RH.7	Integrate quantitative or technical analysis with qualitative analysis	R7 pp. 42–47
RH.8	Assess the extent to which reasoning and evidence support the author's claim	R8 pp. 48–53
RH.9	Compare and contrast treatment of the same topic in several primary and secondary sources	R9 pp. 54–59
RH.10	Read and comprehend history/social studies texts of appropriate complexity	R10 pp. 60–65
Reading Science/Technical Subjects		
RST.1	Cite specific textual evidence to support analysis of science and technical texts	R1 pp. 6–11
RST.2	Determine central ideas or conclusions; trace the explanation of a complex process; provide an accurate summary	R2 pp. 12–17
RST.3	Follow precisely a complex multistep procedure, attending to special cases or exceptions defined in the text	R3 pp. 18–23
RST.4	Determine the meaning of domain-specific words and phrases as they are used in a special scientific or technical context	R4 pp. 24–29
RST.5	Analyze the structure of relationships among concepts in a text	R5 pp. 30–35
RST.6	Analyze the author's purpose in providing an explanation, describing a procedure, or discussing an experiment	R6 pp. 36–41
RST.7	Translate quantitative or technical information expressed in words into visual form, and translate information expressed visually into words	R7 pp. 42–47
RST.8	Assess the extent to which reasoning and evidence support the author's claim or recommendation for solving a problem	R8 pp. 48–53
RST.9	Compare and contrast findings presented in a text to those from other sources, noting where they support or contradict previous explanations	R9 pp. 54–59
RST.10	Read and comprehend science/technical texts of appropriate complexity	R10 pp. 60–65
Writing History/Social Studies, Science and Technical Subjects		
WHST.1	Write arguments focused on disciple-specific content	W1 pp. 70–77
WHST.2	Write informative/explanatory texts, including the narration of historical events, scientific procedures, or technical processes	W2 pp. 78–85
WHST.3	NA	
WHST.4	Produce clear and coherent writing in which the development, organization, and style are appropriate to task, purpose, and audience	W4 pp. 92–97
WHST.5	Develop and strengthen writing as needed by planning, revising, editing, rewriting, or trying a new approach	W5 pp. 98–103
WHST.6	Use technology to produce, publish, and update individual or shared writing projects	W6 pp. 104–109
WHST.7	Conduct research projects to answer a question or solve a problem; synthesize multiple sources, demonstrating understanding of the subject	W7 pp. 110–115
WHST.8	Gather relevant information from multiple print and digital sources; assess the usefulness of each source; integrate information, avoiding plagiarism	W8 pp. 116–121
WHST.9	Draw evidence from informational texts to support analysis, reflection, and research	W9 pp. 122–127
WHST.10	Write routinely for a range of discipline-specific tasks, purposes, and audiences	W10 pp. 128–133

Utah, Grades 11–12

Utah Strand/Standard	Focus of Utah Standard	For More Information
Reading Literature		
RL.1	Cite strong and thorough textual evidence to support analysis of what the text says explicitly and implicitly	R1 pp. 6–11
RL.2	Determine two or more themes or central ideas and analyze their development; restate and summarize main ideas or events	R2 pp. 12–17
RL.3	Analyze how characters develop, interact, and advance the plot or develop the theme	R3 pp. 18–23
RL.4	Determine the meaning of words and phrases as they are used in a text, including figurative and connotative meanings; analyze the cumulative impact of word choice on meaning and tone	R4 pp. 24–29
RL.5	Analyze how an author's choices concerning how to structure specific parts of the text contribute to its overall structure and meaning	R5 pp. 30–35
RL.6	Analyze a case in which grasping point of view requires distinguishing what is directly stated from what is really meant	R6 pp. 36–41
RL.7	Analyze multiple representations of a story, drama, or poem, evaluating how each interprets the source text	R7 pp. 42–47
RL.8	NA	
RL.9	Demonstrate knowledge of 18th, 19th, and early 20th century foundational works of American literature	R9 pp. 54–59
RL.10	Read and comprehend a range of literature from a variety of cultures	R10 pp. 60–65
Reading Informational Text		
RI.1	Cite strong and thorough textual evidence to support analysis of what the text says explicitly and implicitly, including where the text leaves matters uncertain	R1 pp. 6–11
RI.2	Determine two or more central ideas of a text and analyze their development; restate or summarize main ideas or events	R2 pp. 12–17
RI.3	Analyze a complex set of ideas or sequence of events and explain how specific individuals, ideas, or events interact and develop	R3 pp. 18–23
RI.4	Determine the meaning of words and phrases in a text; analyze how an author uses and refines the meaning of key terms over the course of a text	R4 pp. 24–29
RI.5	Analyze and evaluate the effectiveness of the structure in an exposition or argument	R5 pp. 30–35
RI.6	Analyze how an author's style and content contribute to the power, persuasiveness, or impact of the text	R6 pp. 36–41
RI.7	Integrate and evaluate multiple sources of information presented in different media or formats in order to address a question or solve a problem	R7 pp. 42–47
RI.8	Delineate and evaluate the reasoning in seminal U.S. texts, including the application of constitutional principles and use of legal reasoning, and the premises, purposes, and arguments in works of public policy	R8 pp. 48–53
RI.9	Analyze 17th, 18th, and 19th century foundational U.S. and world documents of literary significance	R9 pp. 54–59
RI.10	Read and comprehend literary nonfiction independently and proficiently	R10 pp. 60–65
Writing		
W.1	Write arguments to support claims, using valid reasoning and relevant and sufficient evidence	W1 pp. 70–77
W.2	Write informative/explanatory texts to examine and convey complex ideas, concepts, and information clearly and accurately	W2 pp. 78–85
W.3	Write narratives to develop real or imagined experiences or events using effective technique, well-chosen details, and well-structured event sequences	W3 pp. 86–91

(Continued)

Utah Strand/Standard	Focus of Utah Standard	For More Information
Writing		
W.4	Produce writing in which the development, organization, style, and features are appropriate to the task, genre, purpose, and audience	W4 pp. 92–97
W.5	Develop and strengthen writing as needed by planning, revising, and editing, rewriting, or trying a new approach	W5 pp. 98–103
W.6	Use technology to produce, publish, and update individual or shared writing projects	W6 pp. 104–109
W.7	Conduct research projects to answer a question or solve a problem; synthesize multiple sources; demonstrate understanding of the subject	W7 pp. 110–115
W.8	Gather information from multiple sources, using advanced searches effectively; assess strengths and limitations of sources; integrate information, avoiding plagiarism and overreliance on any one source	W8 pp. 116–121
W.9	Draw evidence from texts to support analysis, reflection, and research	W9 pp. 122–127
W.10	Write routinely over shorter and extended time frames for a range of audiences, tasks, and purposes	W10 pp. 128–133
Speaking and Listening		
SL.1	Engage effectively in a range of collaborative discussions with diverse partners, building on others' ideas and expressing their own clearly and persuasively	SL1 pp. 138–143
SL.2	Integrate multiple sources of information presented in diverse media or formats; evaluate credibility and accuracy of sources and note discrepancies	SL2 pp. 144–149
SL.3	Evaluate a speaker's point of view, reasoning, and use of evidence and rhetoric; assess the stance, premises, link among ideas, word choice, emphasis, and tone	SL3 pp. 150–155
SL.4	Present information, conveying a clear and distinct perspective, address alternative viewpoints; presentation is appropriate to purpose, audience, and task	SL4 pp. 156–161
SL.5	Make strategic use of digital media in presentations to enhance understanding and to add interest	SL5 pp. 162–167
SL.6	Adapt speech to a variety of contexts and tasks; demonstrate a command of formal English when appropriate	SL6 pp. 168–173
Language		
L.1	Demonstrate command of the conventions of standard English grammar and usage when writing or speaking	L1 pp. 178–183
L.2	Demonstrate command of the conventions of standard English capitalization, punctuation, and spelling when writing	L2 pp. 184–189
L.3	Apply knowledge of language to make effective choices for meaning or style, and to comprehend more fully when reading or listening	L3 pp. 190–195
L.4	Determine or clarify the meaning of unknown and multiple-meaning words and phrases, choosing flexibly from an array of strategies	L4 pp. 196–201
L.5	Demonstrate understanding of figurative language, word relationships, and nuances in word meanings	L5 pp. 202–207
L.6	Acquire and use accurately general academic and domain-specific words and phrases; demonstrate independence in gathering vocabulary knowledge	L6 pp. 208–213
Reading History/Social Studies		
RH.1	Cite specific textual evidence to support analysis of primary and secondary sources	R1 pp. 6–11
RH.2	Determine central ideas or information of a primary or secondary source; summarize how they develop	R2 pp. 12–17
RH.3	Evaluate explanations for actions or events and determine which best accords with textual evidence	R3 pp. 18–23
RH.4	Determine the meaning of words and phrases, including figurative and connotative meanings; analyze the impact of specific word choices	R4 pp. 24–29

Utah Strand/Standard	Focus of Utah Standard	For More Information
Reading History/Social Studies		
RH.5	Analyze in detail how a complex primary source is structured	R5 pp. 30–35
RH.6	Evaluate authors' differing points of view on the same historical event	R6 pp. 36–41
RH.7	Integrate and evaluate multiple sources of information presented in diverse formats and media in order to address a question or solve a problem	R7 pp. 42–47
RH.8	Evaluate an author's premises, claims, and evidence by corroborating or challenging them	R8 pp. 48–53
RH.9	Integrate information from diverse sources into a coherent understanding of an idea or event	R9 pp. 54–59
RH.10	Read and comprehend history/social studies texts of appropriate complexity	R10 pp. 60–65
Reading Science/Technical Subjects		
RST.1	Cite specific textual evidence to support analysis of science and technical texts	R1 pp. 6–11
RST.2	Determine central ideas or conclusions; summarize complex concepts by paraphrasing into simpler but accurate terms	R2 pp. 12–17
RST.3	Follow precisely a complex multistep procedure; analyze the results based on explanations in the text	R3 pp. 18–23
RST.4	Determine the meaning of domain-specific words and phrases as they are used in a special scientific or technical context	R4 pp. 24–29
RST.5	Analyze how the text structures information into categories or hierarchies, demonstrating understanding	R5 pp. 30–35
RST.6	Analyze the author's purpose in providing an explanation, describing a procedure, or discussing an experiment	R6 pp. 36–41
RST.7	Integrate and evaluate multiple sources of information presented in diverse formats and media in order to address a question or solve a problem	R7 pp. 42–47
RST.8	Evaluate the hypotheses, data, analysis, and conclusions in a science or technical text, corroborating or challenging conclusions	R8 pp. 48–53
RST.9	Synthesize information from a range of sources into a coherent understanding, resolving conflicting information when possible	R9 pp. 54–59
RST.10	Read and comprehend science/technical texts of appropriate complexity	R10 pp. 60–65
Writing History/Social Studies, Science and Technical Subjects		
WHST.1	Write arguments focused on disciple-specific content	W1 pp. 70–77
WHST.2	Write informative/explanatory texts, including the narration of historical events, scientific procedures, or technical processes	W2 pp. 78–85
WHST.3	NA	
WHST.4	Produce clear and coherent writing in which the development, organization, and style are appropriate to task, purpose, and audience	W4 pp. 92–97
WHST.5	Develop and strengthen writing as needed by planning, revising, editing, rewriting, or trying a new approach	W5 pp. 98–103
WHST.6	Use technology to produce, publish, and update individual or shared writing projects	W6 pp. 104–109
WHST.7	Conduct research projects to answer a question or solve a problem; synthesize multiple sources, demonstrating understanding of the subject	W7 pp. 110–115
WHST.8	Gather relevant information from multiple print and digital sources; assess the usefulness of each source; integrate information, avoiding plagiarism and overreliance on any one source	W8 pp. 116–121
WHST.9	Draw evidence from informational texts to support analysis, reflection, and research	W9 pp. 122–127
WHST.10	Write routinely for a range of discipline-specific tasks, purposes, and audiences	W10 pp. 128–133

Virginia, Grade 9

Virginia Strand/Standard	Focus of Virginia Standard	For More Information
Communication		
9.1	Make planned oral presentations independently and in small groups	SL1 pp. 138–143 SL4 pp. 156–161 SL6 pp. 168–173
9.2	Produce, analyze, and evaluate auditory, visual, and written messages	SL2 pp. 144–149 SL3 pp. 150–155 SL5 pp. 162–167
Reading		
9.3	Apply knowledge of word origins, derivations, and figurative language to extend vocabulary development in authentic texts	L4 pp. 196–201 L5 pp. 202–207 L6 pp. 208–213
9.4	Read, comprehend, and analyze a variety of literary texts including narratives, narrative nonfiction, poetry, and drama	
	• Identify main idea and purpose; summarize text	R2 pp. 12–17
	• Explain relationships between elements of literature	R3 pp. 18–23
	• Compare and contrast the use of literary devices	R4 pp. 24–29
	• Explain the relationship between the author's style and literary effect; analyze how specific word choices and syntax achieve special effects and support author's purpose	R5 pp. 30–35
	• Explain the influence of historical context on a written work	R6 pp. 36–41 R9 pp. 54–59
	• Make predictions, inferences, draw conclusions	R1 pp. 6–11
9.5	Read and analyze a variety of nonfiction texts	
	• Recognize author's purpose and identify main idea; summarize the text	R2 pp. 12–17
	• Identify a position/argument to be confirmed, disproved, or modified; evaluate clarity and accuracy of information	R5 pp. 30–35 R8 pp. 48–53
	• Draw conclusions and make inferences on explicit and implied information using textual support as evidence	R1 pp. 6–11
	• Organize and synthesize information from sources for use in written and oral presentations	W8 pp. 116–121
Writing		
9.6	Develop narrative, expository, and persuasive writings for a variety of audiences and purposes	
	• Generate, gather, organize ideas; plan and organize writing	W4 pp. 92–97
	• Write clear, varied sentences; elaborate ideas; arrange paragraphs logically; use transitions; revise for clarity	W5 pp. 98–103
	• Use technology to plan, draft, revise, edit, and publish writing	W6 pp. 104–109
9.7	Self- and peer-edit writing to correct grammar, capitalization, punctuation, spelling, sentence structure, and paragraphing	L1 pp. 178–183 L2 pp. 184–189
Research		
9.8	Use a variety of resources to access information to create a research product	
	Use technology as a tool to organize, evaluate, and communicate information	W6 pp. 104–109
	Narrow the focus of a search	W7 pp. 110–115
	Find, evaluate, and select sources; make sense of information gathered from diverse sources, identifying misconceptions, conflicting information, point of view or bias; credit sources; avoid plagiarism	W8 pp. 116–121 SL2 pp. 144–149

Virginia, Grade 10

Virginia Strand/Standard	Focus of Virginia Standard	For More Information
Communication		
10.1	Participate in, collaborate in, and report on small-group learning activities	SL1 pp. 138–143 SL4 pp. 156–161 SL6 pp. 168–173
10.2	Analyze, produce, and examine similarities and differences between visual and verbal media messages	SL2 pp. 144–149 SL3 pp. 150–155 SL5 pp. 162–167
Reading		
10.3	Apply knowledge of word origins, derivations, and figurative language to extend vocabulary development in authentic texts	L4 pp. 196–201 L5 pp. 202–207 L6 pp. 208–213
10.4	Read, comprehend, and analyze literary texts of different cultures and eras	
	• Identify main and supporting ideas	R2 pp. 12–17
	• Make predictions and draw inferences	R1 pp. 6–11
	• Explain techniques and literary forms represented in the literature of different cultures and eras; analyze the cultural function of literature; identify universal themes	R6 pp. 36–41
	• Explain the influence of historical context on the form, style, and point of view of a text	R9 pp. 54–59
	• Evaluate how word choices, syntax, tone, and voice shape the meaning of a text, achieve special effects, and support author's purpose	R4 pp. 24–29 R5 pp. 30–35
	• Compare and contrast character development in a play to characterization in other literary forms	R7 pp. 42–47
10.5	Read, interpret, analyze, and evaluate nonfiction texts	
	• Recognize author's intended audience and purpose; identify text organization and structure	R2 pp. 12–17 R3 pp. 18–23
	• Compare and contrast informational texts	R7 pp. 42–47
	• Draw conclusions and make inferences on explicit and implied information using textual support as evidence	R1 pp. 6–11
	• Analyze and synthesize information in order to solve problems, answer questions, and generate new knowledge	SL2 pp. 144–149 W8 pp. 116–121 W9 pp. 122–127
Writing		
10.6	Develop a variety of writing with an emphasis on exposition and analysis	
	• Generate, gather, organize ideas; plan and organize writing	W4 pp. 92–97
	• Write clear, varied sentences; elaborate ideas; arrange paragraphs logically; use transitions; revise for clarity	W5 pp. 98–103
	• Use technology to plan, draft, revise, edit, and publish writing	W6 pp. 104–109
10.7	Self- and peer-edit writing to correct grammar, capitalization, punctuation, spelling, sentence structure, and paragraphing	L1 pp. 178–183 L2 pp. 184–189
Research		
9.8	Collect, evaluate, organize, and present information to create a research project	
	• Use technology as a tool to organize, evaluate, and communicate information	W6 pp. 104–109
	• Develop the central idea or focus	W7 pp. 110–115
	• Find, evaluate, and select sources; make sense of information gathered from diverse sources, identifying misconceptions, conflicting information, point of view or bias; credit sources; avoid plagiarism	W8 pp. 116–121 SL2 pp. 144–149

Virginia, Grade 11

Virginia Strand/Standard	Focus of Virginia Standard	For More Information
Communication		
11.1	Make informative and persuasive presentations	
	• Gather and organize evidence to support a position; present evidence clearly and convincingly	SL4 pp. 156–161
	• Use grammatically correct language appropriate to the audience and purpose	SL6 pp. 168–173
	• Use presentation technology	SL5 pp. 162–167
	• Collaborate and report on group learning activities	SL1 pp. 138–143
11.2	Examine how media influences beliefs and behaviors	
	• Use technology and other information tools to organize and display knowledge	SL5 pp. 162–167
	• Evaluate sources for relationships between intent, factual content, and opinion; determine author's purpose and intended effect on the audience	SL2 pp. 144–149
Reading		
11.3	Apply knowledge of word origins, derivations, and figurative language to extend vocabulary development	
	• Use structural analysis to understand complex words	L3 pp. 190–195
	• Use context, structure, and connotations to determine word meaning	L4 pp. 196–201
	• Discriminate between connotative and denotative meanings; identify the meaning of idioms; identify allusions and figurative language	L5 pp. 202–207
	• Expand general and specialized vocabulary through speaking, reading, and writing	L6 pp. 208–213
11.4	Read, comprehend, and analyze relationships among American literature, history, and culture	
	• Describe contributions of different cultures to American literature; discuss American literature as it reflects traditional and contemporary themes	R9 pp. 54–59
	• Explain how an author's specific word choices, syntax, tone, and voice support the author's purpose	R4 pp. 24–29 R5 pp. 30–35
	• Generate and respond to questions before, during, and after reading texts	R1 pp. 6–11 R2 pp. 12–17
11.5	Read and analyze a variety of nonfiction texts	
	• Draw conclusions and make inferences on explicit and implied information using textual support	R1 pp. 6–11
	• Generate and respond to questions before, during, and after reading texts	R1 pp. 6–11 R2 pp. 12–17
	• Analyze two or more texts addressing the same topic to identify authors' purpose and determine how authors reach similar or different conclusions	R6 pp. 36–41
Writing		
11.6	Write in a variety of forms with an emphasis on persuasion	
	• Generate, gather, organize ideas; plan and organize writing; adapt content, vocabulary, voice, and tone to audience, purpose, and situation	W4 pp. 92–97
	• Produce arguments in writing developing a thesis that demonstrates knowledgeable judgments, addresses counterclaims, and provides effective conclusions	W1 pp. 70–77
	• Revise writing for clarity of content, accuracy, and depth of information	W5 pp. 98–103
	• Use technology to plan, draft, revise, edit, and publish writing	W6 pp. 104–109
11.7	Self- and peer-edit writing to correct grammar, capitalization, punctuation, spelling, sentence structure, and paragraphing	L1 pp. 178–183 L2 pp. 184–189

Virginia Strand/Standard	Focus of Virginia Standard	For More Information
Research		
9.8	Analyze, evaluate, synthesize, and organize information to produce a research project	
	• Use technology as a tool to organize, evaluate, and communicate information	W6 pp. 104–109
	• Present information in a logical sequence	W4 pp. 92–97
	• Find, evaluate, and select sources; make sense of information gathered from diverse sources, identifying misconceptions, conflicting information, point of view or bias; credit sources; avoid plagiarism	W8 pp. 116–121 SL2 pp. 144–149
	• Revise writing for clarity of content, accuracy, and depth	W5 pp. 98–103
	• Edit writing for grammar, spelling, punctuation, capitalization, and sentence structure	L1 pp. 178–183 L2 pp. 184–189

Virginia, Grade 12

Virginia Strand/Standard	Focus of Virginia Standard	For More Information
Communication		
12.1	Make a formal oral presentation	
	• Choose the purpose; choose vocabulary, language, and tone appropriate to audience, topic, and purpose	SL4 pp. 156–161
	• Use grammatically correct language appropriate to the audience and purpose	SL6 pp. 168–173
	• Use media, visual literacy, and technology skills to support the presentation	SL5 pp. 162–167
	• Collaborate and report on group learning activities	SL1 pp. 138–143
12.2	Examine how media influences beliefs and behaviors	
	• Evaluate media sources for relationships between intent, factual content, and opinion; determine author's purpose and intended effect on the audience	SL2 pp. 144–149
	• Determine the author's purpose and intended effect on the audience for media message	SL3 pp. 150–155
Reading		
12.3	Apply knowledge of word origins, derivations, and figurative language to extend vocabulary development	
	• Use structural analysis to understand complex words	L3 pp. 190–195
	• Use context, structure, and connotations to determine word meaning	L4 pp. 196–201
	• Discriminate between connotative and denotative meanings; identify the meaning of idioms; identify allusions and figurative language	L5 pp. 202–207
	• Expand general and specialized vocabulary through speaking, reading, and writing	L6 pp. 208–213
12.4	Read, comprehend, and analyze the development of British literature and literature of other cultures	
	• Explain how the sound of a poem supports the subject, mood, and theme	R4 pp. 24–29

(Continued)

Virginia Strand/Standard	Focus of Virginia Standard	For More Information
Reading		
	• Analyze how dramatic conventions contribute to theme and effect	R5 pp. 30–35
	• Compare and contrast dramatic elements of plays from British, American, and other cultures	R7 pp. 42–47
12.5	Read and analyze a variety of nonfiction texts	
	• Draw conclusions and make inferences on explicit and implied information using textual support	R1 pp. 6–11
	• Generate and respond to questions before, during, and after reading texts	R1 pp. 6–11 R2 pp. 12–17
	• Analyze two or more texts addressing the same topic to identify authors' purpose and determine how authors reach similar or different conclusions	R6 pp. 36–41
	• Identify false premises in persuasive writing	SL2 pp. 144–149
Writing		
12.6	Develop expository and informational, analyses, and persuasive/argumentative writings	
	• Generate, gather, organize ideas; plan and organize writing; adapt content, vocabulary, voice, and tone to audience, purpose, and situation	W4 pp. 92–97
	• Produce arguments in writing developing a thesis that demonstrates knowledgeable judgments, addresses counterclaims, and provides effective conclusions	W1 pp. 70–77
	• Revise writing for clarity of content, accuracy, and depth of information	W5 pp. 98–103
	• Use technology to plan, draft, revise, edit, and publish writing	W6 pp. 104–109
12.7	Revise and edit writing to correct grammar, capitalization, punctuation, spelling, sentence structure, and paragraphing	L1 pp. 178–183 L2 pp. 184–189
Research		
9.8	Write documented research papers	
	• Use technology as a tool to organize, evaluate, and communicate information	W6 pp. 104–109
	• Frame, analyze, and synthesize information to solve problems, answer questions, and generate new knowledge	W7 pp. 110–115
	• Critically evaluate the accuracy, quality, and validity of information; synthesize information to support the thesis and present information in a logical manner; credit sources; avoid plagiarism	W8 pp. 116–121 SL2 pp. 144–149
	• Revise writing for clarity of content, accuracy, and depth	W5 pp. 98–103
	• Edit writing for grammar, spelling, punctuation, capitalization, and sentence structure	L1 pp. 178–183 L2 pp. 184–189

West Virginia, Grades 9–10

West Virginia Strand/Standard	Focus of West Virginia Standard	For More Information
Reading Literature		
R.C1.1	Cite strong and thorough textual evidence to support analysis of what the text says explicitly and implicitly	R1 pp. 6–11
R.C1.2	Determine a theme or central idea of a text and analyze its development and how it is shaped by specific details; summarize the text	R2 pp. 12–17
R.C1.3	Analyze how characters develop, interact, and advance the plot or develop the theme	R3 pp. 18–23
R.C2.1	Determine the meaning of words and phrases as they are used in a text, including figurative and connotative meanings; analyze the cumulative impact of word choice on meaning and tone	R4 pp. 24–29
R.C2.2	Analyze how an author's choices regarding structure, the order of events, and manipulating time create such effects as mystery, tension, or surprise	R5 pp. 30–35
R.C2.3	Analyze a point of view, perspective, or cultural experience reflected in a piece of literature	R6 pp. 36–41
R.C3.1	Analyze the representation of a subject or scene in two different artistic mediums, including what is emphasized or absent in each treatment	R7 pp. 42–47
R.C3.2	Analyze how an author draws on and transforms source material	R9 pp. 54–59
R.C4.1	Read literature of appropriate complexity independently with proficiency	R10 pp. 60–65
Reading Informational Text		
R.C1.4	Cite strong and thorough textual evidence to support analysis of what the text says explicitly and implicitly	R1 pp. 6–11
R.C1.5	Determine the central idea of a text and analyze its development; summarize main ideas or events	R2 pp. 12–17
R.C1.6	Analyze how the author structures an analysis or series of ideas or events, including the order, how they are developed, and the connections between them	R3 pp. 18–23
R.C2.4	Determine the meaning of words and phrases in a text; analyze the cumulative impact of specific word choices	R4 pp. 24–29
R.C2.5	Analyze in detail how ideas or claims are developed by particular sentences, paragraphs, or larger portions of text	R5 pp. 30–35
R.C2.6	Analyze how an author uses rhetoric to advance a point of view, perspective, or purpose	R6 pp. 36–41
R.C3.3	Analyze various accounts of a subject told in different mediums	R7 pp. 42–47
R.C3.4	Evaluate the argument in a text; assess reasoning and evidence; identify false statements and fallacious reasoning	R8 pp. 48–53
R.C3.5	Analyze U.S. documents of historical and literary significance, noting how they address related themes and concepts	R9 pp. 54–59
R.C4.2	Read and comprehend appropriately complex informational texts independently and proficiently	R10 pp. 60–65
Writing		
W.C9.1	Write arguments to support claims, using valid reasoning and relevant and sufficient evidence	W1 pp. 70–77
W.C9.2	Write informative/explanatory texts to effectively examine and convey complex ideas, concepts, and information	W2 pp. 78–85
W.C9.3	Write narratives to develop real or imagined experiences or events using effective technique, well-chosen details, and well-structured event sequences	W3 pp. 86–91
W.C10.1	Produce writing in which the development, organization, style, and features are appropriate to the task, genre, purpose, and audience	W4 pp. 92–97

(Continued)

West Virginia Strand/Standard	Focus of West Virginia Standard	For More Information
Writing		
W.C10.2	Develop and strengthen writing as needed by planning, revising, and editing, rewriting, or trying a new approach	W5 pp. 98–103
W.C10.3	Use technology to produce, publish, and update individual or shared writing projects	W6 pp. 104–109
W.C11.1	Conduct research projects to answer a question or solve a problem; synthesize multiple sources; demonstrate understanding of the subject	W7 pp. 110–115
W.C11.2	Gather information from multiple sources, using advanced searches effectively; assess usefulness of sources; integrate information, avoiding plagiarism	W8 pp. 116–121
W.C11.3	Draw evidence from texts to support analysis, reflection, research, and/or synthesis	W9 pp. 122–127
W.C12.1	Write routinely over shorter and extended time frames for a range of audiences, tasks, and purposes	W10 pp. 128–133
Speaking and Listening		
SL.C13.1	Engage effectively in a range of collaborative discussions with diverse partners, building on others' ideas and expressing their own clearly and persuasively	SL1 pp. 138–143
SL.C13.2	Integrate multiple sources of information presented in diverse media or formats; evaluate credibility and accuracy of sources and noting discrepancies	SL2 pp. 144–149
SL.C13.3	Evaluate a speaker's point of view, reasoning, and use of evidence and rhetoric; identify fallacious reasoning or exaggerated or distorted evidence	SL3 pp. 150–155
SL.C14.1	Present information clearly, concisely, and logically; ensure organization, development, substance, and style are appropriate to purpose, audience, and task	SL4 pp. 156–161
SL.C14.2	Make strategic use of digital media in presentations to enhance understanding and to add interest	SL5 pp. 162–167
SL.C14.3	Adapt speech to a variety of contexts and tasks; demonstrate a command of formal English when appropriate	SL6 pp. 168–173
Language		
L.C15.1	Demonstrate command of the conventions of standard English grammar and usage when writing or speaking	L1 pp. 178–183
L.C15.2	Demonstrate command of the conventions of standard English capitalization, punctuation, and spelling when writing	L2 pp. 184–189
L.C16.1	Apply knowledge of language to make effective choices for meaning or style, to comprehend more fully when reading or listening, and to write and edit so that it conforms to the guidelines in a style manual appropriate for the writing type	L3 pp. 190–195
L.C17.1	Determine or clarify the meaning of unknown and multiple-meaning words and phrases, choosing flexibly from an array of strategies	L4 pp. 196–201
L.C17.2	Demonstrate understanding of figurative language, word relationships, and nuances in word meanings	L5 pp. 202–207
L.C17.3	Acquire and use accurately general academic and domain-specific words and phrases; demonstrate independence in gathering vocabulary knowledge	L6 pp. 208–213

West Virginia, Grades 11–12

West Virginia Strand/Standard	Focus of West Virginia Standard	For More Information
Reading Literature		
R.C1.1	Cite strong and thorough textual evidence to support analysis of what the text says explicitly and implicitly	R1 pp. 6–11
R.C1.2	Determine two or more themes or central ideas and analyze their development; restate and summarize main ideas or events	R2 pp. 12–17

West Virginia Strand/Standard	Focus of West Virginia Standard	For More Information
Reading Literature		
R.C1.3	Analyze the impact of the author's choices regarding how to develop and relate elements of a story	R3 pp. 18–23
R.C2.1	Determine the meaning of words and phrases as they are used in a text, including figurative and connotative meanings; analyze the cumulative impact of word choice on meaning and tone	R4 pp. 24–29
R.C2.2	Analyze how an author's choices concerning how to structure specific parts of the text contribute to its overall structure and meaning	R5 pp. 30–35
R.C2.3	Analyze a case in which grasping point of view requires distinguishing what is directly stated from what is really meant	R6 pp. 36–41
R.C3.1	Analyze multiple representations of a story, drama, or poem, evaluating how each interprets the source text	R7 pp. 42–47
R.C3.2	Demonstrate knowledge of 18th, 19th, and early 20th century foundational works of American literature	R9 pp. 54–59
R.C4.1	Read and comprehend a range of literature from a variety of cultures	R10 pp. 60–65
Reading Informational Text		
R.C1.4	Cite strong and thorough textual evidence to support analysis of what the text says explicitly and implicitly, including where the text leaves matters uncertain	R1 pp. 6–11
R.C1.5	Determine two or more central ideas of a text and analyze their development; restate or summarize main ideas or events	R2 pp. 12–17
R.C1.6	Analyze a complex set of ideas or sequence of events and explain how specific individuals, ideas, or events interact and develop	R3 pp. 18–23
R.C2.4	Determine the meaning of words and phrases in a text; analyze how an author uses and refines the meaning of key terms over the course of a text	R4 pp. 24–29
R.C2.5	Analyze and evaluate the effectiveness of the structure in an exposition or argument	R5 pp. 30–35
R.C2.6	Analyze how an author's style and content contribute to the power, persuasiveness, or impact of the text	R6 pp. 36–41
R.C3.3	Integrate and evaluate multiple sources of information presented in different media or formats in order to address a question or solve a problem	R7 pp. 42–47
R.C3.4	Delineate and evaluate the reasoning in seminal U.S. texts, including the application of constitutional principles and use of legal reasoning, and the premises, purposes, and arguments in works of public policy	R8 pp. 48–53
R.C3.5	Analyze 17th, 18th, and 19th century foundational U.S. and world documents of literary significance	R9 pp. 54–59
R.C4.2	Read and comprehend literary nonfiction independently and proficiently	R10 pp. 60–65
Writing		
W.C9.1	Write arguments to support claims, using valid reasoning and relevant and sufficient evidence	W1 pp. 70–77
W.C9.2	Write informative/explanatory texts to examine and convey complex ideas, concepts, and information clearly and accurately	W2 pp. 78–85
W.C9.3	Write narratives to develop real or imagined experiences or events using effective technique, well-chosen details, and well-structured event sequences	W3 pp. 86–91
W.C10.1	Produce writing in which the development, organization, style, and features are appropriate to the task, genre, purpose, and audience	W4 pp. 92–97
W.C10.2	Develop and strengthen writing as needed by planning, revising, and editing, rewriting, or trying a new approach	W5 pp. 98–103

(Continued)

West Virginia Strand/Standard	Focus of West Virginia Standard	For More Information
Writing		
W.C10.3	Use technology to produce, publish, and update individual or shared writing projects	W6 pp. 104–109
W.C11.1	Conduct research projects to answer a question or solve a problem; synthesize multiple sources; demonstrate understanding of the subject	W7 pp. 110–115
W.C11.2	Gather information from multiple sources, using advanced searches effectively; assess strengths and limitations of sources; integrate information, avoiding plagiarism and overreliance on any one source	W8 pp. 116–121
W.C11.3	Draw evidence from texts to support analysis, reflection, and research	W9 pp. 122–127
W.C12.1	Write routinely over shorter and extended time frames for a range of audiences, tasks, and purposes	W10 pp. 128–133
Speaking and Listening		
SL.C13.1	Engage effectively in a range of collaborative discussions with diverse partners, building on others' ideas and expressing their own clearly and persuasively	SL1 pp. 138–143
SL.C13.2	Integrate multiple sources of information presented in diverse media or formats; evaluate credibility and accuracy of sources and note discrepancies	SL2 pp. 144–149
SL.C13.3	Evaluate a speaker's point of view, reasoning, and use of evidence and rhetoric; assess the stance, premises, link among ideas, word choice, emphasis, and tone	SL3 pp. 150–155
SL.C14.1	Present information, conveying a clear and distinct perspective, address alternative viewpoints; presentation is appropriate to purpose, audience, and task	SL4 pp. 156–161
SL.C14.2	Make strategic use of digital media in presentations to enhance understanding and to add interest	SL5 pp. 162–167
SL.C14.3	Adapt speech to a variety of contexts and tasks; demonstrate a command of formal English when appropriate	SL6 pp. 168–173
Language		
L.C15.1	Demonstrate command of the conventions of standard English grammar and usage when writing or speaking	L1 pp. 178–183
L.C15.2	Demonstrate command of the conventions of standard English capitalization, punctuation, and spelling when writing	L2 pp. 184–189
L.C16.1	Apply knowledge of language to make effective choices for meaning or style, and to comprehend more fully when reading or listening	L3 pp. 190–195
L.C17.1	Determine or clarify the meaning of unknown and multiple-meaning words and phrases, choosing flexibly from an array of strategies	L4 pp. 196–201
L.C17.2	Demonstrate understanding of figurative language, word relationships, and nuances in word meanings	L5 pp. 202–207
L.C17.3	Acquire and use accurately general academic and domain-specific words and phrases; demonstrate independence in gathering vocabulary knowledge	L6 pp. 208–213

The Complete Common Core
State Standards: Decoded

Part 1

The Common Core State Standards

Reading

College and Career Readiness Anchor Standards for

Reading 9–12

Source: Common Core State Standards

The grades 6–12 standards on the following pages define what students should understand and be able to do by the end of each grade. They correspond to the College and Career Readiness (CCR) anchor standards by number. The CCR and grade-specific standards are necessary complements— the former providing broad standards, the latter providing additional specificity—that together define the skills and understandings that all students must demonstrate.

Key Ideas and Details

1. Read closely to determine what the text says explicitly and to make logical inferences from it; cite specific textual evidence when writing or speaking to support conclusions drawn from the text.
2. Determine central ideas or themes of a text and analyze their development; summarize the key supporting details and ideas.
3. Analyze how and why individuals, events, and ideas develop and interact over the course of a text.

Craft and Structure

4. Interpret words and phrases as they are used in a text, including determining technical, connotative, and figurative meanings, and analyze how specific word choices shape meaning or tone.
5. Analyze the structure of texts, including how specific sentences, paragraphs, and larger portions of the text (e.g., a section, chapter, scene, or stanza) relate to one another and the whole.
6. Assess how point of view or purpose shapes the content and style of a text.

Integration of Knowledge and Ideas

7. Integrate and evaluate content presented in diverse formats and media, including visually and quantitatively, as well as in words.*
8. Delineate and evaluate the argument and specific claims in a text, including the validity of the reasoning as well as the relevance and sufficiency of the evidence.
9. Analyze how two or more texts address similar themes or topics to build knowledge or to compare the approaches the authors take.

Range of Reading and Level of Text Complexity

10. Read and comprehend complex literary and informational texts independently and proficiently.

Note on Range and Content of Student Reading

To become college and career ready, students must grapple with works of exceptional craft and thought whose range extends across genres, cultures, and centuries. Such works offer profound insights into the human condition and serve as models for students' thinking and writing. Along with high-quality contemporary works, these texts should be chosen from among seminal U.S. documents, the classics of American literature, and the timeless dramas of Shakespeare. Through wide and deep reading of literature and literary nonfiction of steadily increasing sophistication, students gain a reservoir of literary and cultural knowledge, references, and images; the ability to evaluate intricate arguments; and the capacity to surmount the challenges posed by complex texts.

* Please consult the full Common Core State Standards document (and all updates and appendices) at http://www.corestandards.org/ELA-Literacy. See "Research to Build Knowledge" in the Writing section and "Comprehension and Collaboration" in the Speaking and Listening section for additional standards relevant to gathering, assessing, and applying information from print and digital sources.

Source: Copyright © 2010. National Governors Association Center for Best Practices and Council of Chief State School Officers. All rights reserved.

College and Career Readiness Anchor Standards for

Reading

The College and Career Readiness (CCR) anchor standards are the same for all middle and high school students, regardless of subject area or grade level. What varies is the specific content at each grade level, most notably the level of complexity of the texts, skills, and knowledge at each subsequent grade level in each disciplinary domain. The guiding principle here is that the core reading skills should not change as students advance; rather, the level at which they learn and can perform those skills should increase in complexity as students move from one grade to the next.

Key Ideas and Details

This first strand of reading standards emphasizes students' ability to identify key ideas and themes in a text, whether literary, informational, primary, or foundational and whether in print, graphic, quantitative, or mixed media formats. The focus of this first set of standards is on *reading to understand*, during which students focus on *what* the text says. The premise is that students cannot delve into the deeper (implicit) meaning of any text if they cannot first grasp the surface (explicit) meaning of that text. Beyond merely identifying these ideas, readers must learn to see how these ideas and themes, or the story's characters and events, develop and evolve over the course of a text. Such reading demands that students know how to identify, evaluate, assess, and analyze the elements of a text for their importance, function, and meaning within the text.

Craft and Structure

The second set of standards builds on the first, focusing not on *what* the text says but *how* it says it, the emphasis here being on analyzing how texts are made to serve a function or achieve a purpose. These standards ask readers to examine the choices the author makes in terms of words and sentence and paragraph structure and how these choices contribute to the meaning of the text and the author's larger purpose. Inherent in the study of craft and structure is how these elements interact with and influence the ideas and details outlined in the first three standards.

Integration of Knowledge and Ideas

This third strand might be summed up as *reading to extend or deepen one's knowledge* of a subject by comparing what a range of sources have said about it over time and across different media. In addition, these standards emphasize the importance of being able to read the arguments; that is, they look at how to identify the claims the texts make and evaluate the evidence used to support those claims regardless of the media. Finally, these standards ask students to analyze the choice of means and medium the author chooses and the effect those choices have on ideas and details. Thus, if a writer integrates words, images, and video in a mixed media text, readers should be able to examine how and why the author did that for stylistic and rhetorical purposes.

Range of Reading and Level of Text Complexity

The Common Core State Standards document itself offers the most useful explanation of what this last standard means in a footnote titled "Note on range and content of student reading," which accompanies the reading standards:

> To become college and career ready, students must grapple with works of exceptional craft and thought whose range extends across genres, cultures, and centuries. Such works offer profound insights into the human condition and serve as models for students' own thinking and writing. Along with high-quality contemporary works, these texts should be chosen from among seminal U.S. documents, the classics of American literature, and the timeless dramas of Shakespeare. Through wide and deep reading of literature and literary nonfiction of steadily increasing sophistication, students gain a reservoir of literary and cultural knowledge, references, and images; the ability to evaluate intricate arguments; and the capacity to surmount the challenges posed by complex texts. (CCSS 2010, p. 35)

Reading 1: Read closely to determine what the text says explicitly and to make logical inferences from it; cite specific textual evidence when writing or speaking to support conclusions drawn from the text.

9–10 Literature

Cite strong and thorough textual evidence to support analysis of what the text says explicitly as well as inferences drawn from the text.

11–12 Literature

Cite strong and thorough textual evidence to support analysis of what the text says explicitly as well as inferences drawn from the text, **including determining where the text leaves matters uncertain**.

9–10 Informational Text

Cite strong and thorough textual evidence to support analysis of what the text says explicitly as well as inferences drawn from the text.

11–12 Informational Text

Cite strong and thorough textual evidence to support analysis of what the text says explicitly as well as inferences drawn from the text, **including determining where the text leaves matters uncertain**.

9–10 History/Social Studies

Cite specific textual evidence to support analysis of primary and secondary sources, attending to such features as the date and origin of information.

11–12 History/Social Studies

Cite specific textual evidence to support analysis of primary and secondary sources, **connecting insights gained from specific details to an understanding of the text as a whole**.

9–10 Science/Technical Subjects

Cite specific textual evidence to support analysis of science and technical texts, attending to the precise details of explanations or descriptions.

11–12 Science/Technical Subjects

Cite specific textual evidence to support analysis of science and technical texts, attending to **important distinctions the author makes and to any gaps or inconsistencies in the account**.

Source: Copyright © 2010. National Governors Association Center for Best Practices and Council of Chief State School Officers. All rights reserved.

What the **Student** Does

9–10 Literature

Gist: Literal comprehension accompanied by evidence from the text. Say what happens in the story or what the poem says based on evidence from the text, without making personal connections or commentary.

• What happens in this story, play, or poem?
• Which specific details are most important to mention?
• What is the setting (time, place, atmosphere)?
• Who is involved? What do they say, do, think, and feel?
• How specific and detailed is the evidence drawn from the text?

11–12 Literature

Gist: Literal comprehension supported with evidence. Report the events of the story or what the poem says based on details from the text, without explaining what the text means or why it is important; note those places where the text is ambiguous or unclear.

• What happens in this story, play, or poem?
• Which specific details are most important to cite?
• What is the setting (time, place, atmosphere)?
• Who is involved? What do they say, do, think, and feel?
• Which parts of the text are ambiguous or vague?

9–10 Informational Text

Gist: Literal comprehension accompanied by evidence from the text. Say what happens in the text or what it says based on evidence from the text, without making personal connections or commentary.

• What is the subject—and what does it say about that?
• Which specific details are most important to mention?
• What is the setting (time, place, atmosphere)?
• Who is involved? What do they say, do, think, and feel?
• How specific and detailed is the evidence drawn from the text?

11–12 Informational Text

Gist: Literal comprehension supported with evidence. Report the events of the story or what the poem says based on details from the text, without explaining what the text means or why it is important; note those places where the text is ambiguous or unclear.

• What is the subject—and what does it say about that?
• Which specific details are most important to cite?
• What is the setting (time, place, atmosphere)?
• Who is involved? What do they say, do, think, and feel?
• Which parts of the text are ambiguous or vague?

9–10 History/Social Studies

Gist: Literal comprehension supported with evidence. Say what the primary source says about its subject and what secondary sources say about that same subject and/or the primary source, using evidence from the texts to support your statements.

• What type of text is this: primary or secondary?
• What are the subject and the source of information of the text?
• What does the text say or suggest about this subject?
• Who is the author or speaker of the text?
• How specific, detailed, and accurate is my textual evidence?

11–12 History/Social Studies

Gist: Literal comprehension supported with evidence. Report in precise detail what the primary source and secondary sources say about their subject (or the texts the secondary sources may discuss), using evidence from these texts to support your assertions. Include in your retelling of the text any insights about the text and how these contribute to your understanding of these texts when considered together.

• What type of text is this: primary or secondary?
• What are the subject and the source of information of the text?
• What does the text say or suggest about this subject?
• How specific, detailed, and accurate is my textual evidence?
• How do my revelations about the text and its contents add to my understanding of the text itself?

9–10 Science/Technical Subjects

Gist: Literal comprehension supported with precise details from the text. Sum up what the text says in precise detail and language, using evidence from the text to support your statements. Look closely at the words used to describe or explain when analyzing the text.

• What type of text is this?
• What is the subject of this text?
• What does the text say about this subject?
• Which precise details/data are important to mention?
• How precise, accurate, and detailed is my textual evidence?

11–12 Science/Technical Subjects

Gist: Literal comprehension backed up with precise details from the texts. Report in detail what the text says, indicating those areas where the author emphasizes the difference between key elements or causes inconsistencies by leaving out key information when describing what they did or discovered.

• What is the subject of this text?
• What does the text say about this subject?
• Which precise details/data are important to mention?
• How precise, accurate, and detailed is my textual evidence?
• What key distinctions or inconsistencies should I report?

What the **Teacher** Does

To teach students how to "read closely," do the following:

- Provide students access to the text—via tablet or photocopy—so they can annotate it as directed.
- Model close reading for students by thinking aloud as you go through the text with them or displaying your annotations on a tablet via an LCD projector; show them how to examine a text by scrutinizing its words, sentence structures, or any other details needed to understand its explicit meaning.
- Display the text via tablet or computer as you direct students' attention—by highlighting, circling, or otherwise drawing their attention—to specific words, sentences, or paragraphs that are essential to the meaning of the text; as you do this, ask them to explain what a word means or how it is used in that sentence or how a specific sentence contributes to the meaning of the larger text.
- Pose questions—about words, actions, details—that require students to look closely at the text for answers.

To get students to determine "what the text says explicitly," do the following:

- Ask students to "say what it *says*"—not what it means, since the emphasis here is on its literal meaning.
- Offer students an example of what it means to read explicitly and support your inferences with evidence; then tell them what a passage explicitly says, asking them to find evidence inside the text to support their statement about its meaning.
- Give students several pieces of evidence and ask them to determine what explicit idea in the text the evidence supports.

To develop students' ability to "cite specific textual evidence," do the following:

- Offer them a set of samples of evidence of different degrees of specificity and quality to evaluate, requiring them to choose the one that is best and provide a rationale for their choice.
- Show students how you would choose evidence from the text to support your inference; discuss with them the questions you would ask to arrive at that selection.

To "make logical inferences," ask students to do the following:

- Add what they *learned* (from the text about this subject) compared to what they already *know* (about that subject); then, have students *confirm* that their reasoning is sound by finding evidence for their inferences.
- Think aloud (with your guidance) about the process and how they make such inferences, and then have students find and use evidence to support their inferences.

To identify "uncertainties," "gaps," or "inconsistencies," students can try the following:

- Read—or *reread*—key sections that focus on reasoning or evidence, and ask, "So what?" or any of the reporter's questions (who, what, when, where, why, how) that seem appropriate to the text or topic, looking for those spots that cannot answer these basic questions logically or fully.

To help your English Language Learners, try this strategy:

- Repeat the process used to make such inferences, verbally labeling each step as you demonstrate it; then ask them to demonstrate their ability to do it on their own or with your prompting. Post the steps (e.g., "Inferences = What You Know + What You Learned") with an example on a poster or handout they can reference on their own as needed.

Notes

Academic Vocabulary: Key Words and Phrases

Analysis of primary and secondary sources: Primary sources are those accounts recorded from people who witnessed or participated in the event themselves; these sources include journals, letters, oral history recordings; secondary sources are those written by others *based on* primary sources and the opinions of scholars past and present.

Attending to such features: Close reading demands paying attention to any features, such as format, source, or date published, that might add subtle but noteworthy meaning to the document.

Cite specific textual evidence: All claims, assertions, or arguments about what a text means or says require evidence from within the text itself, not the reader's opinion or experience; students should be able to quote or refer to a specific passage from the text to support their idea.

Conclusions drawn from the text: Readers take a group of details (different findings, series of events, related examples) and draw from them an insight or understanding about their meaning or importance within the passage or the text as a whole.

Connecting insights gained from specific details to an understanding of the text as a whole: It is not enough to discern the meaning of a small detail; close reading demands connecting all the dots to reveal how these small details contribute to the meaning of the larger text.

Explicitly: Clearly stated in great or precise detail; may suggest factual information or literal meaning, though not necessarily the case.

Gaps or inconsistencies in the account: Some gaps are intentional, meant to leave room for interpretation or allow for some ambiguity that adds depth and complexity to a text; unintended gaps or inconsistencies undermine the credibility of the work or author by raising questions about the accuracy or reliability of the information.

Important distinctions the author makes: Authors draw a line at times between ideas, categories, or certain elements, attributing more meaning or importance to one than another.

Informational text: These include nonfiction texts from a range of sources and written for a variety of purposes; everything from essays to advertisements, historical documents to op-ed pieces. Informational texts include written arguments as well as infographics.

Literature: This text can include not only fiction, poetry, drama, and graphic stories but also artworks, such as master paintings or works by preeminent photographers.

Logical inferences: To infer, readers add what they *learned* from the text to what they already *know* about the subject; however, for the inference to be logical, it must be based on evidence *from the text*.

Read closely (or close reading): Reading that emphasizes not only surface details but the deeper meaning and larger connections between words, sentences, and the full text; this also demands scrutiny of craft, including arguments and style used by the author.

Strong and thorough textual evidence: Not all evidence is created equal; students need to choose those examples or quotations that provide the best example of what they are saying or most compelling quotation to support their assertion.

Support conclusions: Related to citing textual evidence, this phrase requires readers to back up their claims about what a text says with evidence, such as examples, details, or quotations.

Text: In its broadest meaning, a text is whatever one is trying to read: a poem, essay, essay, or article; in its more modern sense, a text can also be an image, an artwork, speech, or multimedia format such as a website, film, or social media message, such as a Tweet.

Where the text leaves matters uncertain: The writer may intend to be ambiguous or unclear to imply a lack of clarity or resolution about this subject; it can also mean the writer did not tie up loose ends, thus, creating a weak link in an argument or narrative.

Reading 2: Determine central ideas or themes of a text and analyze their development; summarize the key supporting details and ideas.

9–10 Literature

Determine a theme or central idea of a text and analyze in detail its development over the course of the text, including how it emerges and is shaped and refined by specific details; provide an objective summary of the text.

11–12 Literature

Determine **two or more** themes or central **ideas** of a text and analyze their development over the course of the text, including how **they interact** and **build on one another to produce a complex account**; provide an objective summary of the text.

9–10 Informational Text

Determine a central idea of a text and analyze its development over the course of the text, including how it emerges and is shaped and refined by specific details; provide an objective summary of the text.

11–12 Informational Text

Determine **two or more central ideas of a text** and analyze **their** development over the course of the text, including how **they interact and build on one another to provide a complex analysis;** provide an objective summary of the text.

9–10 History/Social Studies

Determine the central ideas or information of a primary or secondary source; provide an accurate summary of how key events or ideas develop over the course of the text.

11–12 History/Social Studies

Determine the central ideas or information of a primary or secondary source; provide an accurate summary **that makes clear the relationships among the key details and ideas.**

9–10 Science/Technical Subjects

Determine the central ideas or conclusions of a text; trace the text's explanation or depiction of a complex process, phenomenon, or concept; provide an accurate summary of the text.

11–12 Science/Technical Subjects

Determine the central ideas or conclusions of a text; summarize **complex concepts, processes, or information presented in a text by paraphrasing them in simpler but still accurate terms.**

Source: Copyright © 2010. National Governors Association Center for Best Practices and Council of Chief State School Officers. All rights reserved.

What the **Student** Does

9–10 Literature

Gist: Read to discover the main idea or theme, examining. how the author introduces and treats this idea or theme as the text unfolds; then summarize the text without analyzing it.

- What key idea does the author introduce that may matter later?
- What does the author say about this idea over the course of the text?
- What details contribute most to the major theme at different junctures?
- What details are so integral they must be included in a summary?

9–10 Informational Text

Gist: Read to discover the main idea, examining how the author introduces and develops this idea from beginning to end; then summarize but do not analyze the text.

- What key idea plays an important role throughout the text?
- What does the author say (or suggest) about this idea throughout the text?
- What events or details contribute most at different junctures in the text?
- What details are so integral to the text they must be included the summary?

9–10 History/Social Studies

Gist: Read like a historian, economist, or social scientist, focusing on the dominant ideas and facts in both primary and secondary sources and providing a summary of how those key ideas and major events evolve over time in the text.

- What ideas, details, and events does the author explore throughout the text?
- Is this a primary or secondary source?
- How do those events and ideas interact with each other to shape the meaning of the text?
- How do these ideas and facts change in terms of their meaning, importance, or effect over the course of the text?

9–10 Science/Technical Subjects

Gist: Read like a scientist or engineer who must explain a complex processes, an event or idea, identifying the main ideas or conclusions. Summarize the content using precise, objective language.

- What key ideas or conclusions does this text emphasize?
- How does that process, phenomenon, or idea evolve over the course of the text?
- What ideas or details are most essential to include in any summary of this text?

11–12 Literature

Gist: Read for central ideas or multiple themes, noting how the different themes or ideas connect and complement each other to add complexity; then without analysis, summarize the text.

- What big ideas or themes does the author include in the text?
- How does the author's treatment of these main ideas and themes add to their meaning throughout the text?
- What details are so integral they must be included in the summary of it?

11–12 Informational Text

Gist: Read to discover the main ideas, examining how the author treats these idea from beginning to end; then summarizing, without analysis, what the text says.

- What key ideas play an important role throughout the text?
- How does the author treat or develop these ideas throughout the text?
- What events or details contribute most at different junctures throughout the text?
- What details are so integral to the text they must be included the summary?

11–12 History/Social Studies

Gist: Read like a historian, economist, or social scientist, focusing on the dominant ideas and facts in both primary and secondary sources, and examining with precision how those facts and ideas relate to each other. Summarize these relationships, ideas, and events with accuracy.

- What ideas, details, or events does the author explore—and how does the meaning or importance of these facts and ideas change from start to finish?
- Is this a primary or secondary source?
- What facts, events, or relationships must any summary be sure to include?

11–12 Science/Technical Subjects

Gist: Read like a scientist or engineer who must explain a complex process, events, or ideas, then identify the main ideas or conclusions. Using language that is concise and precise, write a paraphrase of those complex ideas and processes.

- What key ideas or conclusions does this text emphasize?
- What is the text saying about those ideas or conclusions?
- What ideas or details must be included in any paraphrase of this text?

What the **Teacher** Does

To have students "determine the central ideas and themes of a text," do the following:

- Ask students to generate all possible ideas and themes after skimming and scanning the text, then determine which of them the text most fully develops.
- Tell students to figure out which words, phrases, or images recur throughout the text that might signal they are the central idea?
- Have students consider what hints the title, subheadings, bold words, graphics, images, or captions offer as to the central ideas.
- Complete a think-aloud with students when working with new or complex texts to model the questions you ask and mental moves you make as an experienced reader of this type of text to make sense of it.

To have students analyze the development of central ideas or themes, do the following:

- Direct students to underline, label, or somehow code all the words, images, or other details related to the central ideas or themes throughout the text; then examine how their use evolves over the course of the text.
- Provide students with sentence frames ("Early on the author says X about _____, then suggests Y, finally arguing Z about _____ by the end.") or graphic organizers that help them map an idea from the beginning to the end of the text to better see how it develops (through word choice, imagery, figurative speech).

To have students provide an objective summary of the text, do the following:

- Try having students summarize using different formats and modes: presentation slide, Tweets, lists, index cards, limits of 25 or 50 words, or an outline.
- Develop with students a *continuum of importance* to help them learn to evaluate which details are most important to include in a summary.
- Clarify the difference between *objective* and *subjective* by giving examples of each about a different but similar text before they attempt to write an objective summary of other texts.

- Allow students to study models of effective summaries.
- Provide sentence stems typical of those used to summarize this type of text (In_____, Author X argues that _____).

To have students trace the text's explanation or depiction of a complex process, do the following:

- Request that students use a structured note-taking format—outline, storyboard, or some visual explanation using shapes and arrows—to capture and illustrate whatever complex process they are reading about; to these more visual notes, they should add captions or other written notes to describe what is happening, why, and what it means or how it relates to the larger subject of the text.
- Code the text with colors or labels in the margin as students read to indicate the different stages, making special note of what causes the process to begin or change throughout.
- Demonstrate how *you* trace such development of ideas over time.

To have students analyze central themes interacting and building on one another, do the following:

- Ask how one set of images, allusions, or ideas builds on or is otherwise related to those that come before it.
- Have students use a graphic organizer (e.g., one with two or more columns) to jot down the details related to each key theme, looking for patterns across the columns as they go.

To have students paraphrase complex information by paraphrasing them, do the following:

- Model and explain for students the difference between a summary, a paraphrase, a abstract, and a précis.

To help your English Language Learners, try this:

- Make a point of checking that they know and can apply the related concepts—themes, analyze, summarize, and supporting details.

Academic Vocabulary: Key Words and Phrases

Accurate summary: Identifies the key ideas, details, or events in the text and reports them with an emphasis on who did what to whom and when; in other words, the emphasis is on retelling what happened or what the text says with utmost fidelity to the text itself, thus requiring students to check what they say against what the text says happened.

Analyze: This refers to the careful and close examination of the parts or elements from which something is made and how those parts affect or function within the whole to create meaning.

Build on one another: Specifically refers to the notion of how different ideas build on one another within the text in general and over time in particular. This might mean how an idea or a theme, such as the resiliency of the human spirit, is explored through different examples or stories, all of which complement and build on one another as a way of developing that idea over the course of the text.

Complex account: Literary texts often weave several major ideas throughout any given text; when authors cause ideas to interact with one another, it often creates a sense of "things were not as [simple] as they appeared to be" when students scrutinize the text. Everything will seem connected in some complex way.

Complex analysis: Informational texts examine ideas within arguments and explanations of these complex concepts or processes.

Determine central ideas: Some ideas are more important to a work than are others; these are the ideas you could not cut out without fundamentally changing the meaning or quality of the text. Think of the central ideas of a text as you would the beams in a building: They are the main elements that make up the text and that all the supporting details help develop.

Development: Think of a grain of rice added to others one at a time to form a pile; this is how writers develop their ideas—by adding imagery, details, examples, and other information over the course of the text. Thus, when people analyze the development of an idea or theme, for example, they look at how the author does this and what effect such development has on the meaning of the text.

Emerges: This refers to the process of an idea unfolding, slowly coming to the fore as the author develops the idea over time.

Key supporting details and ideas: Important details and ideas support the larger ideas the text develops over time. These details and ideas appear as examples, quotations, or other information used to advance the author's claim(s). Not all details and ideas are equally important, however; so students must learn to identify those that matter the most in the context of the text.

Objective summary: This describes key ideas, details, or events in the text and reports them without adding any commentary or outside description; it is similar to an evening recap of the news that attempts to answer the essential reporter's questions—who, what, where, when, why, and how—*without* commentary.

Paraphrasing: While a summary is much shorter than the text it describes, a paraphrase is nearly as long since it is a form of translating a text into a more accessible language. It is best to paraphrase only short passages, for example, a complex theory or findings from a study to make it accessible to others with less knowledge about this subject or field.

Themes: The ideas the text explains, develops, and explores; there can be more than one, but themes are what the text is actually *about*.

Trace the text's explanation or depiction: To "trace" is to follow something you can already see: Readers follow the stages in a process, noting how it unfolds or relates to the author's argument.

Notes

Reading 3: Analyze how and why individuals, events, and ideas develop and interact over the course of a text.

9–10 Literature

Analyze how complex characters (e.g., those with multiple or conflicting motivations) develop over the course of a text, interact with other characters, and advance the plot or develop the theme.

11–12 Literature

Analyze **the impact of the author's choices regarding how to develop and relate elements of a story or drama (e.g., where a story is set, how the action is ordered, how the characters are introduced and developed).**

9–10 Informational Text

Analyze how the author unfolds an analysis or series of ideas or events, including the order in which the points are made, how they are introduced and developed, and the connections that are drawn between them.

11–12 Informational Text

Analyze **a complex set of ideas or sequence of events and explain how specific individuals, ideas, or events interact and develop over the course of the text.**

9–10 History/Social Studies

Analyze in detail a series of events described in a text; determine whether earlier events caused later ones or simply preceded them.

11–12 History/Social Studies

Evaluate various explanations for actions or events and determine which explanation best accords with textual evidence, acknowledging where the text leaves matters uncertain.

9–10 Science/Technical Subjects

Follow precisely a complex multistep procedure when carrying out experiments, taking measurements, or performing technical tasks attending to special cases or exceptions defined in the text.

11–12 Science/Technical Subjects

Follow precisely a complex multistep procedure when carrying out experiments, taking measurements, or performing technical tasks; **analyze the specific results based on explanations in the text.**

Source: Copyright © 2010. National Governors Association Center for Best Practices and Council of Chief State School Officers. All rights reserved.

What the **Student** Does

9–10 Literature

Gist: Examine how characters interact with others and affect the plot or theme, looking, for example, at motivation and how it adds to the complexity of characters. Also, readers should examine how characters evolve, noting how different, often conflicting motives, advance the plot and contribute to the theme.

- Which characters are most important (and complex)?
- What do the main characters want and why do they want it? What do these desires tell us about them?
- How do the characters evolve over the course of the story?
- What effect does a character's actions or changes have on other key characters?

9–10 Informational Text

Gist: Read to grasp the connections between actions and events as the text unfolds, focusing on how these elements are arranged and what the author says about them. Pay special attention to how, when, and why the author introduces and develops these ideas and events.

- What ideas or events does the author introduce at the beginning of the text?
- What new information, evidence, or details does the author provide?
- How do these additions affect the text?
- What evidence from the text supports and illustrates your claims about the meaning and importance of ideas, people, and events—and the evolving relationship between them?

9–10 History/Social Studies

Gist: Identify those events which matter most in a text, then break down the relationship between these elements, focusing on how each event—a war, discovery, movement, signing of key legislation, declaration, or proclamation—relates to those which precede or follow it.

- Which events are most important in this text?
- How does a given event or moment relate to those which come before or follow that moment?
- How and why did the author choose to arrange events as they did: cause–effect, problem–solution, chronological, or other?

9–10 Science/Technical Subjects

Gist: Identify the steps in a complicated multistep procedure, following the directions with precision when measuring, experimenting, or performing specialized tasks; also, use criteria from the text to determine if a situation is exceptional.

- What are the specific steps—and the proper order—for this procedure?
- What order should those steps go in? How do you know?
- What criteria suggest the current situation is an exception?

11–12 Literature

Gist: Identify the author's key decisions about about setting, characterization, and plot, focusing on how these choices affect the development and meaning of these elements throughout the story or play. Note also the interplay between the different elements (e.g., between the action and the setting).

- Which of the author's decisions most affect the elements of the story and how they develop or connect to each other over time?
- Of these decisions, which most affect the story's meaning?
- How do the author's decisions about setting, plot design, or character development affect the story's meaning or impact?
- How are events in the story arranged—and to what end?

11–12 Informational Text

Gist: Look for sets of ideas or sequences of events that interact with each other throughout the text. Note how various elements—specific individuals, ideas, or events—interact and enhance their own meaning or importance within the larger text.

- What is the subject, content, or focus of this text—people, events, ideas, processes, or experiences?
- How are these elements connected—categories, stages, or other?
- How do these connections affect meaning over the course of the text?
- How do these elements or connections evolve and interact and contribute to the meaning of the text?

11–12 History/Social Studies

Gist: Identify key decisions or acts in a major historical or social movement, process, era, or event about which historians or social scientists disagree, examining those competing explanations and arguments and drawing conclusions about which explanation or argument is best supported by evidence from the texts they read and where the text suggests a lack of evidence or knowledge.

- What is the event, action, or idea about which the texts offer competing positions or explanations?
- What evidence do the most credible, objective texts provide?
- Where and why is the text unclear, ambiguous, or ambivalent?

11–12 Science/Technical Subjects

Gist: Identify the steps in a complicated multistep procedure, following the directions with precision when measuring, experimenting, or performing technical tasks; then use criteria from the text to analyze the results.

- What are the specific steps to follow for this procedure?
- What order should those steps go in? How do you know?
- What criteria does the text offer for analyzing the results?

What the **Teacher** Does

To have students analyze how complex characters develop and interact, do the following:

- Have students generate a list of all the characters, and then determine, according to the criteria they create, which ones are complex and the nature of that complexity.
- Have students build a plot map—individually, in groups, or as a class—noting each time certain key characters interact; analyze who does or says what, in each situation, and its effect on the text.
- Identify the motivations of key characters and those points where their motivations conflict with other characters'; then examine what those conflicts reveal about the characters and how they affect the text as a whole.

To have students analyze how key characters advance or develop plots or themes, do the following:

- Ask students to locate specific passages or key moments in the text where complex characters do or say something that affects the plot or develops a theme; have them make a claim about how the character affects the text, providing examples and textual evidence.
- Create a graphic chart or plot diagram with students and ask them to analyze the plot for moments when characters do something that affects the plot—increase tension, cause change—in a measurable, discernible way. This is sometimes called a "fever chart" to represent the rising and falling action of events in the story.

To have students analyze the impact of the author's choices regarding story elements, do the following:

- Have students list the key choices the author makes about setting, plot sequence, and character development; evaluate all of those within one such category to identify those that impact the story the most, and then examine how and why they do.
- Identify key elements in a story and have students change, remove, or otherwise alter some of these elements to understand how they function within or affect the story.

To have students analyze how complex ideas or events interact and develop over time, do the following:

- Have students determine which ideas are central to the text and then examine how the words, tone, or imagery used shift over the course of the text to affect the meaning or content of the text.

To have students analyze a series of events where earlier ones caused later ones, do the following:

- Have students create a timeline for the text—a list or a more graphic timeline—that shows all the events in sequence, evaluated or ranked by their importance or effect on later events.
- Have students highlight or use sticky notes to identify all references to an event so students can retrace the events after reading the document to evaluate how one led to or impacted another.

To have students evaluate various explanations for events in light of textual evidence, do the following:

- Provide students a sample that shows the event, its explanations and textual evidence, which students must learn to evaluate by identifying the most fitting explanations and evidence. Then have them find the next event, its explanation, and evidence so they show they can do this independently.
- Give students the event or action *without* the explanations or evidence; then tell them to read the text to find the best explanations and textual evidence; to extend the lesson, have them explain why their explanations and evidence are the best.

To have students analyze the specific results based on explanations in the text, do the following:

- Show students how to find and analyze results from their inquiries based on the criteria, legends, or other explanations
- Demonstrate for students how you do this with results from a similar or previous experiment.

To help your English Language Learners, try this:

- Evaluate the language used in the text, any directions for the assignment, and when discussing the assignment in class, find ways you could make the assignment more accessible.

Academic Vocabulary: Key Words and Phrases

Actions or events: To understand "actions" think of the verbs your students study: rebel, discover, invent; events are those landmark moments in history or any other field when things change in ways that merit time spent studying them (war, social movement).

Advance the plot: A story is a bit like a football or basketball game in that every move should be toward the goal; so with a story, every event or detail should advance the story in some useful or meaningful way toward its ultimate purpose or resolution.

Complex characters: Characters can be simple (flat, static) or complex (round, dynamic); only characters who change, who have a rich inner life that interacts with people and their environment could be considered "complex." This is often represented as an arc: what they are like or where they are when the story begins and when it *ends*.

Complex set of ideas or sequence of events: Consider the Industrial Revolution during which a range of ideas and events created the conditions for a new era, or think of a specific sequence of events that led to the Civil Rights Act or Emancipation Proclamation.

Connections that are drawn: Often it is the unexpected connection the author makes between ideas, events, or characters that leads to the greatest insight for us when reading. We could not anticipate that two elements that seemed so separate could be so linked; this is the epiphany that comes from attention to detail.

Determine: This act requires the reader to recognize the different possibilities, choices, and elements available to the author, then decide what effect the author's choice had on the text.

Develop and interact: As stories unfold, characters change in response to events and experiences—interactions with people and ideas. Through these interactions characters evolve.

Develop the theme: A theme is best understood as a phrase that expresses an idea (e.g., the hope for

things unseen, being "a brother's keeper") the text, in whatever form, examines. The author "develops the theme" by adding details, examples, events, or commentary related to this theme; in more complex texts, there is often more than one theme.

Evaluate various explanations: In examining historical events and their interpretation, students should learn that there are inevitably competing views about the meaning, importance, or rationale of an event or action (e.g., dropping the atomic bombs on Japan in WWII). Students must learn to determine, by criteria they create or receive from others, which explanation is the most viable.

Impact of author's choices: A text is a created or *woven* construction: Every choice—of time sequence, words, setting, characters, their names, the grammar and imagery—affects the reader, the meaning of the story, and the characters' development.

Motivations: This refers to what characters want most of all; such desires are often complicated by other, often competing, motives that complicate the character whose desires may conflict with his ideals.

Performing technical tasks attending to special cases: In a science or technical subjects class, one performs "technical tasks" when they experiment in a lab or with models; those tasks attending to (i.e., dealing with or done as a result of) special cases would be the more complex tasks because of their unique conditions that invite exceptions or innovative approaches to solving the problem.

Unfolds an analysis: This refers to the author's approach or how she proceeds when laying out and developing an argument, its reasons, supporting evidence, and other related details.

Where the text leaves matters uncertain: "Leaving matters uncertain" implies a lack of understanding or resolution in some area about what is true, what it means, why it happened, or whether it matters.

Reading 4: Interpret words and phrases as they are used in a text, including determining technical, connotative, and figurative meanings, and analyze how specific word choices shape meaning or tone.

9–10 | Literature

Determine the meaning of words and phrases as they are used in the text, including figurative and connotative meanings; analyze the cumulative impact of specific word choices on meaning and tone (e.g., how the language evokes a sense of time and place; how it sets a formal or informal tone).

11–12 | Literature

Determine the meaning of words and phrases as they are used in the text, including figurative and connotative meanings; **analyze the impact** of specific word choices on meaning and tone, **including words with multiple meanings of language that is particularly fresh, engaging, or beautiful. (Include Shakespeare as well as others.)**

9–10 | Informational Text

Determine the meaning of words and phrases as they are used in a text, including figurative, connotative, and technical meanings; analyze the cumulative impact of specific word choices on meaning and tone (e.g., how the language of a court opinion differs from that of a newspaper).

11–12 | Informational Text

Determine the meaning of words and phrases as they are used in a text, including figurative, connotative, and technical meanings; analyze **how an author uses and refines the meaning of a key term or terms over the course of a text (e.g., how Madison defines *faction* in *Federalist* No. 10).**

9–10 | History/Social Studies

Determine the meaning of words and phrases as they are used in a text, including vocabulary describing political, social, or economic aspects of history/social science.

11–12 | History/Social Studies

Determine the meaning of words and phrases as they are used in a text, including **analyzing how an author uses and refines the meaning of a key term over the course of a text (e.g., how Madison defines *faction* in *Federalist* No. 10).**

9–10 | Science/Technical Subjects

Determine the meaning of symbols, key terms, and other domain-specific words and phrases as they are used in a specific scientific or technical context relevant to *grades 9–10 texts and topics.*

11–12 | Science/Technical Subjects

Determine the meaning of symbols, key terms, and other domain-specific words and phrases as they are used in a specific scientific or technical context relevant to *grades 11–12 texts and topics.*

Source: Copyright © 2010. National Governors Association Center for Best Practices and Council of Chief State School Officers. All rights reserved.

Common Core Reading Standard 4

What the **Student** Does

9–10 Literature

Gist: Determine what words mean and how context affects the meaning of these words and phrases, (i.e., is the author using a word in a literal or a more figurative, connotative way to suggest something else). Consider how the repeated use of words and phrases work together to achieve some cumulative effect (e.g., a series of words and phrases evoking images or notions of conflict might contribute to meaning or tone).

- Which words or phrases contribute the most to the meaning in the text?
- Does the author use these words literally or figuratively?
- How do the different words contribute to the author's tone?
- How does the author's choice of words affect the meaning of the text?

11–12 Literature

Gist: Examine what words mean and how context affects the meaning of these words and phrases, analyzing whether the author is choosing to use a specific word in a literal or more figurative way to suggest something else. Readers study how specific words and phrases make the text beautiful, powerful, or otherwise engaging. Such language is common in Shakespeare and writers such as Hopkins, Morrison, and Conrad.

- Which specific words most affect the meaning in the text?
- What does the dictionary say about the different meanings and etymology of these key words?
- How does this author use words to evoke a sense of wonder in the reader?
- Which key words have multiple meanings in this context?

9–10 Informational Text

Gist: Examine what words mean and how context affects their meaning, assessing whether the author is using words literally or figuratively and how the repeated use of words achieves some cumulative effect. For example, an article reporting a court opinion about gun rights would differ from an op-ed responding to the opinion the next day.

- What are the different possible meanings of this word or phrase as it is used in this text?
- How do the words chosen reflect or respond to the original setting, occasion, or audience?
- How would this subject be described in a newspaper or a blog, for example?
- What is the cumulative effect of the author's chosen words on the purpose, setting, meaning, or tone?

11–12 Informational Text

Gist: Examine how the author uses specific words in relation to context and the author's purpose, determining whether the author uses the words literally or figuratively and analyzing how their meaning affects the text. For example, students might track how Madison uses the word *faction* over the course of *Federalist* No. 10.

- What are the different possible meanings of this word or phrase as it is used in this text?
- How do the author's words reflect or respond to the original setting, occasion, or audience?
- How would this subject be described in a newspaper or blog, for example?
- How do the author's words and phrases contribute to the meaning of the text?

9–10 History/Social Studies

Gist: Focus on words and phrases that describe ideas, movements, or eras discussed in articles, textbooks, primary source documents, and other text types. Such words often express concepts and abstractions such as *liberty*.

- What are the key words in this document? How are they used?
- Why does the author use this word or phrase in this context?
- How has the meaning of this word changed over time?

11–12 History/Social Studies

Gist: Analyze words and phrases in context as used in articles textbooks, primary source documents, and other texts, noting the author's use of key words in the text to refine their meaning and impact through repeated use.

- What are the key words in this document? How are they used?
- Why does the author use this word or phrase in this context?
- How does the meaning or effect of repeated words change over time?

9–10 Science/Technical Subjects

Gist: Concentrate on how the author uses key symbols and words in different contexts to direct, explain, inform, or persuade readers of texts and topics appropriate to grades 9 and 10.

- When, where, how, and why are symbols used here?
- What specialized terms are used that are necessary to know in order to understand key concepts?
- How do the words and symbols contribute to or affect the text?

11–12 Science/Technical Subjects

Gist: Concentrate on how the author uses key symbols and words in different contexts to direct, explain, inform, or persuade readers of texts and topics appropriate to grades 10 and 11.

- When, where, how, and why are symbols used here?
- What specialized terms are used that are necessary to know in order to understand key concepts?
- How do the words and symbols contribute to or effect the text?

What the **Teacher** Does

To have students interpret words and phrases as they are used in a text, do the following:

- Direct students' attention to the words, phrases, and other details (captions, diagrams, images) in a sentence and those around it. Point out the ways authors add details to clarify the meaning of words: definition clues such as explanations, synonyms, phrases, and clauses; restatement of the word or phrase (e.g., *In other words*); contrast or antonym clues that help define what a word means by using words that mean the exact opposite; other clues such as typography, proximity to images, and the author's general tone.
- Tell students that not all words can be understood through context clues; help them see where context clues can confuse.
- Complete a think-aloud while reading to the class to show how you puzzle out a word or phrase using syntactic, semantic, typographic, etymological, and other types of information to decipher words.

To have students determine the figurative and connotative meaning of words, do the following:

- Identify with students figurative language or words with other connotative meanings; then have them determine the literal or denotative meaning of those words; then ask them to determine, in light of how the words are used in this context, the figurative or connotative meaning.
- Direct students' attention to words used figuratively (simile, metaphor, analogy, euphemism, and pun) and ask them to determine a word's meaning and explain how its use affects the meaning of other words around it or contributes to the meaning of the larger text.
- Have them assess whether a set or series of words used figuratively has a unifying theme (e.g., they are all related to gardens, sports, the law) and, if they do, what it is and how that set of thematic words adds meaning to the text.

To have students analyze the cumulative impact of word choice on meaning and tone, do the following:

- Complete a think-aloud as you read through a text, noting the author's use of certain words that combine with others (through sound, imagery, meaning, or stylistic or rhetorical effect) to add meaning or serve some other purpose (e.g., to reinforce a theme).
- Direct students to highlight, code, or otherwise indicate (by alternately circling, underlining, or putting dotted lines under words) those words or phrases that are connected; ask them then what conclusions they can draw from the patterns, connections, or general use of words about their meaning.
- Provide students a list of words or phrases with a common theme left unstated; ask them what the words have in common and how that relates to the text from which they come.

To have students determine the meaning of discipline-specific words, symbols, terms, do the following:

- Show students how to make use of any textual features—sidebars, captions, typography (is the word in **bold** and thus in the glossary), diagrams, footers, or glossaries in the chapter or in the appendix—available in the textbook.
- Teach students, when appropriate, the root words or etymology of certain subject-specific words (bio = life, ology = study of) as part of the study of any discipline.

To have students analyze how authors use and refine the meaning of key terms, have students do the following:

- Cut and paste the whole text into www.wordle.net to see which words are used most frequently in the text; then choose those which are most important to the text or topic and see how they are used over time and how their meaning shifts.
- Access a text, if possible, in a digital form so you can use the search feature to find all the instances of a word; then you can examine with students its use in those different contexts and trace how its meaning changes from beginning to the end of the text.

To help your English Language Learners, try this:

- Use these words as often as possible, speaking them aloud so students hear them used in context and pronounced correctly.

Academic Vocabulary: Key Words and Phrases

Connotative meanings: Words have a primary or literal meaning; some also have a secondary or connotative meaning, which implies an additional idea or feeling related to the word or phrase.

Cumulative impact: When a specific word (*fair* in *Lord of the Flies*) or phrase ("an honorable man" in *Julius Caesar*) is repeated throughout a text or an important passage, it has a cumulative effect, a bit like a snowball gathering mass and speed.

Domain-specific words and phrases: Within each discipline or branch of that discipline, certain words (*cell, division*) have a domain-specific use in, for example, biology; other words, however, are unique to that discipline and are, thus, essential for students to know to read, discuss, and write about complex texts in that subject.

Evokes a sense of time and place: Language brings to life a time or place through its rhythms, phrases, words, and their syntax; antiquated phrases spoken by a contemporary character suggest one thing. Language, such as Mark Twain and Zora Neal Hurston, used evokes a time, a culture, a place, and one's character.

Figurative meanings: Figures of speech (or figurative language) are those often colorful ways we develop of saying something; they include euphemism, hyperbole, irony, understatement, metaphor, simile, and paradox, among others. Some of them are specific to an era, region, or social group and, thus, can confuse readers.

Interpret: Best understood as a way of explaining what someone said or wrote using more accessible, familiar language for those who lack experience with or knowledge of the subject or this type of text.

Key terms: In highly technical or scientific subjects, certain terms are an essential part of the precision and accuracy that discipline demands. In some subjects, a certain term (e.g., *evolution, uncertainty,* or *entropy*) represents a specific idea or applies to a very precise process.

Court opinion: A statement announcing a decision after a case is tried. The judge summarizes the facts, reads the applicable law, explains how it relates to the case, provides the rationale behind the decision, and states the judgment, which is usually written.

Shape meaning or tone: Certain words carry added, often implied meanings; we describe these as "loaded words," for they have the power to affect the meaning of the words around them or to influence the speaker's tone (e.g., turning it from sincere to ironic).

Symbols: In humanities classes, a symbol suggests some greater meaning when it is attached to an idea; thus, the bald eagle symbolizes the American spirit; in science and math, however, symbols represent operations, procedures, and concepts such as change (Δ) or pi (π).

Technical meanings: These would be words with specialized meanings specific to the subject being investigated, explained, or argued about; one example might be the distinctions made between political philosophies, such as libertarian and republican.

Tone—informal and formal: When thinking of tone, think about tone *of voice*. The formal tone of the Constitution matches its importance and subject; the informal tone of a literary text signals the relationship between the individuals and reveals the character of the speaker.

Words and phrases as they are used in a text: The point of close reading is to understand what the text really says; to do this, students must scrutinize the words and phrases used by the author as they are the key to determining what the author really means or what the text says; also, they are an essential source of evidence.

Uses and refines the meaning of a key term over the course of a text: When first introduced, certain words establish a general idea that the author, through repeated and careful use, refines in an attempt to invest in it more meaning and importance each time it is used.

Reading 5: Analyze the structure of texts, including how specific sentences, paragraphs, and larger portions of the text (e.g., a section, chapter, scene, or stanza) relate to one another and the whole.

9–10   Literature

Analyze how an author's choices concerning how to structure a text, order events within it (e.g., parallel plots), and manipulate time (e.g., pacing, flashbacks) create such effects as mystery, tension, or surprise.

11–12   Literature

Analyze how an author's choices concerning how to structure **specific parts of** a text (e.g., **the choice of where to begin or end a story, the choice to provide a comedic or tragic resolution) contribute to its overall structure and meaning as well as its aesthetic impact.**

9–10   Informational Text

Analyze in detail how an author's ideas or claims are developed and refined by particular sentences, paragraphs, or larger portions of a text (e.g., a section or chapter).

11–12   Informational Text

Analyze **and evaluate the effectiveness of the structure an author uses in his or her exposition or argument, including whether the structure makes points clear, convincing, and engaging.**

9–10   History/Social Studies

Analyze how a text uses structure to emphasize key points or advance an explanation or analysis.

11–12   History/Social Studies

Analyze **in detail how a complex primary source is structured, including how key sentences, paragraphs, and larger portions of the text contribute to the whole.**

9–10   Science/Technical Subjects

Analyze the structure of the relationships among concepts in a text, including relationships among key terms (e.g., *force, friction, reaction force, energy*).

11–12   Science/Technical Subjects

Analyze **how the text structures information or ideas into categories or hierarchies, demonstrating understanding of the information or ideas.**

Source: Copyright © 2010. National Governors Association Center for Best Practices and Council of Chief State School Officers. All rights reserved.

What the **Student** Does

9–10 | Literature

Gist: Examine how an author's choices about structure and narrative design affect the plot, pacing, and perceptions of the reader, focusing on how techniques such as flashbacks, parallel plots, or nonlinear-episodic narratives, create a sense of wonder, anxiety, or awe in readers.

- Why did the author use or put that sentence or larger section in that place?
- How is time, location, mood, or purpose affected by the author's arrangement of events, details, or time?
- How does the author structure the story, poem, or play—and to what end?

9–10 | Informational Text

Gist: Concentrate on how the author arranges details, evidence, or events to support and develop a claim or idea, analyzing how the writer begins and then refines the idea by connecting sentences, paragraphs, and larger chunks (sections, chapters) as they explore and advance their idea(s) and claim(s).

- What idea or claim does the writer examine or advance?
- How does the author develop or refine these ideas or claims at the sentence, paragraph, section, and chapter level?
- How do these structural elements add meaning, clarity, or coherence?

9–10 | History/Social Studies

Gist: Concentrate on how the author organizes crucial ideas, details, or events to emphasize a point or support a claim, noting, for example, how he or she uses chronological, cause–effect, or problem–solution structure to stress how a sequence led to a certain outcome or provided the argument for a course of action.

- What key point(s) does this author attempt to emphasize?
- How does the author organize the information, examples, or evidence within the text to stress these key ideas or advance the argument?
- How effective is the structure the author uses to emphasize or advance his or her key points or claims?

9–10 | Science/Technical Subjects

Gist: Focus on how the author organizes ideas and information using organizational patterns, strategies, or graphic formats to reveal and emphasize the relationship between details, ideas, and key terms such as *force*, *division*, and *evolution*.

- What big ideas and key terms does the author try to explain?
- How and why does the author structure the ideas and information within the text in this way?
- How effective is the approach the author takes for organizing these details, processes, or terms?

11–12 | Literature

Gist: Analyze how an author uses and places specific elements of a text such as where and how the story begins or ends, examining why the author chose a nonlinear structure such as *in media res*, for example, and how that choice impacts the story and the reader's experience of it.

- Why does this author begin the story in this way?
- How would you describe the overall structure of the story in terms of its impression or effect on the reader?
- Which choices regarding structure most contribute to the story's meaning and aesthetic impact?

11–12 | Informational Text

Gist: Assess how an author's choices about structure affect clarity, cogency, and coherence, analyzing the degree to which choices about how to organize sentences, paragraphs, and larger units (sections, chapters) enhance the clarity and quality of the text, or strengthen the writer's claims.

- What idea or claim does the writer examine or advance?
- Why does the author use these organizational structures?
- How do the writer's choices about structure make the text more clear, convincing, or engaging?

11–12 | History/Social Studies

Gist: Identify the precise words, phrases, techniques, or structures used to give structure to the content of a primary source document, noting how certain transitions and spatial or other formatting techniques indicate a shift in time, emphasis, or focus within a sentence, a paragraph, or a section of the text as a whole.

- What techniques does this author use to organize information?
- How does the author use these structures to emphasize or advance key ideas in the document?
- Which elements make this text "complex," and how does that complexity contribute to the text as a whole?

11–12 | Science/Technical Subjects

Gist: Examine how the author uses hierarchies, categories, or sequences to illustrate the relationship between information and ideas and the degree of understanding the author's approach demonstrates about that topic or term.

- How does the author structure the ideas and information within the text—and to what end?
- What does this particular organizational approach allow the author to reveal or emphasize?
- What does the author's approach to organizing information suggest about their knowledge of the content?

What the **Teacher** Does

To have students analyze the structure of texts, do the following:

- Direct students to determine the author's purpose, audience, and occasion for this text; then ask them to identify how these factors influence the choices the author makes about the structure of the text.
- Ask them to examine the macrostructure of the text—its layout, format, design on the page or screen, and its features and elements—as part of their analysis of how the text functions to create meaning or achieve the author's intended result(s).
- Have students identify the organizational pattern or rhetorical mode of this text—compare–contrast, problem–solution, cause–effect, chronological, and so on—and then examine what additional choices the author makes—about tone, style, the use of images, narrative, examples, and embedding of other media—join with the organizational pattern to create a sense of surprise, tension, or mystery when reading the text.
- Model for students how you determine the structure of a complex text and use that knowledge to better understand and analyze the text through close reading.
- Have students locate all structural elements—transitions, subheadings, parallel plots, shifts in time—and analyze how they affect the reader's response and text's meaning.

To have students analyze how specific sentences and larger portions relate, do the following:

- Ask students to annotate a text specifically to identify those sentences that create structure or cause significant moments within the text at the paragraph level. These might be sentences that shift the focus of the text to new topics or to other perspectives on the same subject; they might be sentences that create a point of emphasis on a certain idea, event, or other aspect of the text.

To have students analyze the author's choices about structure and order within, do the following:

- Work with students to determine the organizational pattern of the text (e.g., sequential or chronological)

and its rhetorical mode (to define, compare, or explain); then, first together, and then, on their own, have students assess how each sentence and the different elements within the text create order and meaning while also helping the author achieve his or her purpose.

To have students analyze how an author's ideas or claims are developed through sentences, paragraphs, and larger sections, do the following:

- Model your process of determining an author's claim or main ideas and how each subsequent sentence, paragraph, and larger section (chapter, subsection, or extended passage) supports, advances, or otherwise relates to that claim or idea.
- Have students create what some call a "backward outline" of the text (to analyze instead of compose such a text) to show how it is organized around a main idea or claim and the relationship of each section to the larger structure of the text.

To have students analyze how the text structure is used to emphasize and advance, do the following:

- Model for students how authors use certain words and phrases, as well as syntactic, grammatical, and typographic (bold, italics, case) elements, to emphasize key ideas and advance plots, explanations, or analyses.

To help your English Language Learners, try this:

- Display the text using an LCD projector with different versions of the same text that show it unchanged, formatted to reveal, for example, all the transitions (in one highlighted color) in another version, and, in a different slide, certain key sentences within the paragraph or text that are particularly important (highlighted in a different version) to help these students better grasp the abstract and, for some, foreign concept of structure, transitions, and effect on the larger text.

Academic Vocabulary: Key Words and Phrases

Advance an explanation or analysis: Authors use devices such as transitions, organizational patterns (compare–contrast, cause–effect), and strategies (chronological order or order of importance) that allow them to emphasize certain ideas to advance their analysis or explanation of these ideas.

Aesthetic impact: A work of literature read at this level in this way should be an aesthetic encounter and, thus, make on students the sort of impact any great work of art should. The question here is not only what effect does it have on the reader but also *how* does the author arrange things to achieve that aesthetic impact?

Argument: Academic arguments are those designed to explain a position or idea; persuade readers to change what they think, believe, or feel about an issue; alter how they act; or resolve disagreements between different parties about an issue. Writers attempt to accomplish these objectives by presenting a series of claims that they then support with reasons, evidence, and various appeals. Arguments are not the same as claims, propositions, thesis statements, or assertions.

Complex primary source: An example of such a resource might be the notebooks of Lewis and Clark, which are complex because of the range of content—images, diagrams, scientific tables, observation notes, individual commentary on what they did, saw, realized. A primary source is one that reports what happened from one who was there and saw it firsthand; what makes it complex is the diversity of purposes texts, elements, objectives, and possible biases.

Emphasize key points: Authors arrange details, examples, or other contents to emphasize the key ideas the writer is exploring. Thus, by using such strategies as organizing contents from least to most important or cause and effect, the writer is able to use the structure of the piece to emphasize key points.

Exposition: This is detailed explanation of the background information needed to understand what the writer will discuss in the text; in fiction, it is often found more at the beginning of the story, prior to the rising action; in nonfiction, it can occur throughout.

Flashbacks: This is a narrative device that refers back to and emphasizes earlier events or details from the story that would add dramatic tension or insight to the story.

Hierarchies: One of many possible organizational strategies, this is an approach that ranks its ideas from the top or most important to bottom or least important.

Mystery (tension and surprise): It is the fundamental tension of wondering *what will happen next* that draws readers forward in a narrative.

Pacing: Authors, primarily through their narrators, control how quickly a story unfolds, creating sections (or whole books) that we call "page-turners" because the story moves quickly; other sections are more deliberative, interrupted by commentary or reflection, which has the effect of slowing the pace of the story down.

Relationships among key terms: Reading closely requires looking at the individual words authors choose.

Particular sentences, paragraphs, or larger portions of a text: This refers to the levels at which authors treat and develop ideas throughout the text; some authors work at the microlevel (sentence) and others emphasize the macrolevel (section/chapter).

Structure of texts: How authors organize their ideas and the text as a whole. Through structural patterns—at the sentence-, the paragraph-, and the whole-text level—authors emphasize certain ideas and create such effects as tension, mystery, and humor.

Notes

Reading 6: Assess how point of view or purpose shapes the content and style of a text.

9–10   Literature

Analyze a particular point of view or cultural experience reflected in a work of literature from outside the United States, drawing on a wide reading of world literature.

11–12   Literature

Analyze **a case in which grasping** point of view **requires distinguishing what is directly stated in a text from what is really meant (e.g., satire, sarcasm, irony, or understatement).**

9–10   Informational Text

Determine an author's point of view or purpose in a text and analyze how an author uses rhetoric to advance that point of view or purpose.

11–12   Informational Text

Determine an author's point of view or purpose in a text **in which the rhetoric is particularly effective, analyzing how style and content contribute to the power, persuasiveness, or beauty of the text.**

9–10   History/Social Studies

Compare the point of view of two or more authors for how they treat the same or similar topics, including which details they include and emphasize in their respective accounts.

11–12   History/Social Studies

Evaluate authors' different points of view on the same historical event or issue by assessing the authors' claims, reasons, and evidence.

9–10   Science/Technical Subjects

Analyze the author's purpose in providing an explanation, describing a procedure, or discussing an experiment in a text, defining the question the author seeks to address.

11–12   Science/Technical Subjects

Analyze the author's purpose in providing an explanation, describing a procedure, or discussing an experiment in a text, **identifying important issues that remain unsolved.**

Source: Copyright © 2010. National Governors Association Center for Best Practices and Council of Chief State School Officers. All rights reserved.

What the **Student** Does

9–10 Literature

Gist: Examine how authors from outside the United States treat a particular culture, experience, or perspective in a wide range of literary works.

- Who is telling the story, and how does culture, experience, or status affect his or her persepctive?
- Why does the author tell the story from this point of view or in this way?
- How does the author's or character's perspective or experience shape their attitude toward the subject of this text?

9–10 Informational Text

Gist: Draw conclusions about the author's perspective, analyzing the author's purpose and the rhetorical choices the author uses to achieve that purpose or promote a certain perspective.

- What does the author's language and point of view tell us about their attitude or purpose?
- What are the possible sources of bias to look for when reading this text?
- How credible and logical are this author's ideas and argument?

9–10 History/Social Studies

Gist: Examine the similarities and differences between multiple perspectives on the same event, idea, or experience, drawing conclusions about the perspective and purpose of each author based on what they omit, downplay, or emphasize to advance his or her claim or achieve his or her purpose.

- What is the subject of these texts or documents you are comparing?
- What are the authors' stated or implied point of view and purpose in relation to this subject?
- Which aspects of this subject do the different the authors emphasize?

9–10 Science/Technical Subjects

Gist: Examine the author's purpose, taking into consideration the questions he or she attempts to address, or any procedures and experiments he or she may discuss.

- Why does the author attempt to explain, describe, discuss, or define this subject?
- What is the question the author seeks to answer or at least address in this text?
- What does the author try to do: explain, describe, discuss, or define?

11–12 Literature

Gist: Determine a character's point of view by examining what is and is *not* said, what is not stated but implied through techniques such as satire, sarcasm, irony, or understatement.

- Who is the narrator in this text?
- How does this narrator view and speak about the events, ideas, and people in the story—with sincerity? Irony? Sarcasm? Other?
- Where and when does the author distinguish between what the characters say and what they think?

11–12 Informational Text

Gist: Determine the author's point of view and purpose (to persuade, inform, inspire, or entertain), noting those strategies the author uses to achieve these stated or implied objectives and to make the text more compelling, persuasive, or elegant.

- What is the subject—and the author's perspective about it?
- What is the author's objective?
- What language or rhetorical devices does the author use to achieve their purpose?

11–12 History/Social Studies

Gist: Examine competing claims about the meaning, importance, or causes of the same historical event or issue, evaluating the claims and evidence the author uses to support those claims.

- What event or issue is the subject of these different texts?
- How would you characterize and compare the authors' different perspectives on this subject?
- What criteria would you use to assess the authors' claims, reasons, or evidence?

11–12 Science/Technical Subjects

Gist: Examine the author's purpose, taking into consideration the questions he or she attempts to address, or any procedures and experiments he or she may discuss, noting those issues the author fails to resolve or address.

- How and why does the author provide this information?
- What question is the author trying to answer or address here?
- What questions or issues remain unanswered or unresolved?

What the **Teacher** Does

To have students assess how point of view or purpose shapes content and style, do the following:

- Define and discuss with students just what point of view (POV) means and entails, providing not just written and spoken definitions but also visual illustrations with drawings, images, artworks, or film clips.
- Extend the lesson to include the different types of POV—omniscient, unreliable, first, second, third person—and how this notion of point of view relates to the narrator, especially when that narrator is an unreliable narrator. To clarify these elements of POV, students could apply the ideas to previously read stories to show they know before moving into new ones.
- Have students first determine what the POV in the text is; then ask students to determine why the author chose *that* POV as a means to achieve his purpose.
- Direct students to generate words that characterize the style of the writing; then ask them to explain how these words are shaped by the POV (i.e., how the POV guided the writer to make certain choices about diction, tone, setting).

To have students analyze a particular point of view or cultural experience, do the following:

- Lead a discussion or ask students to work together to generate all the different aspects that shape the POV of a person from another culture (e.g., education, experience, status, family, and so on); then ask them to determine which of these is most important when analyzing the POV of a character.
- Have students identify those cultural experiences (reflected in a work from outside the United States) that most influence how a character views themselves and the world and how those experiences apply specifically to the work they are currently studying.

To have students determine how an author uses rhetoric to advance the POV, do the following:

- Ask students to identify the author's POV or purpose; then consider the choice of words, the arrangement of details, and the use of imagery or figurative speech in light of the occasion, audience, and purpose.

To have students compare the POV of two or more authors, do the following:

- Begin by modeling for students what it looks like to compare two authors in this way, discussing aloud with the class what you are doing and why and how you would, for example, use these details in your written analysis of the two sources.
- Create a three-column organizer with key topics common to both listed in the middle column; as students go through the text, have them gather examples and observations about the two authors' treatment of the topic, listing these under the respective titles for later use.
- Repeat the same process when students are examining different POVs on historical events (e.g., Korean War) by listing the claims, reasons, and evidence for those acts or events under the appropriate columns.

To have students analyze an author's purpose in providing an explanation, do the following:

- With students, generate different reasons *why* an author would explain, describe, or discuss scientific procedures and how such explanations relate to questions the author tries to answer.

To help your English Language Learners, try this:

- Make connections to students' cultures or experience to help explain their different POV about some subjects so they get a more personal, concrete grasp of subject.

Notes

Academic Vocabulary: Key Words and Phrases

Assess: In this instance, *assess* means not to test but to determine what the point of view is and how it shapes the story.

Case: This means a text or scene within a larger text in which the author employs a tone, such as satire, sarcasm, irony, or understatement.

Claims: An assertion you want readers to accept as true or act on; your thesis is the *primary* claim you will develop and support with evidence throughout your paper. A claim is debatable: It requires supporting evidence to counter inevitable challenges.

Content and style of a text: The perspective from which you tell a story limits what content you can include and the style you use when you write about it. Point of view determines what the narrator sees, knows, hears, and can say—and how she can say it.

Cultural experience: Would allow for a wide range of literature about the experience of living in or immigrating to the United States but would also include literature about the perspective and experiences of those from other parts of the world as a way of increasing students' understanding of those people and places.

Directly stated: This is what is literally written on the page and taken at face value, as opposed to what is implied, suggested, or inferred.

Evidence: This includes, when taken from reliable sources, facts, examples, data in the form of statistics, findings, or results (from surveys, observations, experiments, reports), expert opinions, interviews (of experts or firsthand witnesses), and quotations from the text.

Irony: A tone or technique that adds subtle humor, typically at a character's expense, as a result of a meaningful difference between what is said and what is really meant; what a character/narrator thinks is true and what actually is; what the audience knows and the character knows about a person or situation. Irony can be comedic, dramatic, or tragic, depending on the context.

Point of view (POV): The place, vantage point, or consciousness through which we hear or see someone describe a situation, tell a story, or make an argument. Different POVs are distinguished by how much the narrator or reporter knows: first person (I/me), third person (she/they); an *omniscient* POV knows what everyone thinks and feels; a *limited* POV knows only so much about a character or knows only what one character (out of many) thinks; an *unreliable* narrator is not trustworthy. In some cases, multiple POVs can be used or represented within one text.

Purpose: People want to accomplish one of four purposes when they write or speak: to persuade, inform, express, or entertain. One could add others—to explain or inspire, for example—but these four account for most situations.

Rhetoric: This is language used to achieve certain outcomes, most often through arguments intended to change beliefs, actions, or values. The purpose and approach depend on the rhetorical situation: One speaks differently at a funeral than at a wedding, during a trial than to their constituents. Some would argue that we are always using language to achieve some outcome.

Sarcasm: This is a crude form of irony used to humiliate or wound another.

Satire: This is a style of writing through which authors ridicule or mock the failings of others, often those who think they are superior.

Treat: Best understood as a synonym for "handle" or "address" or "examine," as in compare "how [two authors] treat [i.e., address, examine, handle] the subject of childhood in these poems."

Understatement: One makes a statement in much less forceful or emphatic language than might be expected for the purpose of highlighting some aspect of the subject or creating an ironic tone.

Reading 7: Integrate and evaluate content presented in diverse formats and media, including visually and quantitatively, as well as in words.*

9–10 | Literature

Analyze the representation of a subject or a key scene in two different artistic mediums, including what is emphasized or absent in each treatment (e.g., Auden's "Musée des Beaux Arts" and Breughel's "Landscape with the Fall of Icarus").

11–12 | Literature

Analyze **multiple interpretations of a story, drama, or poem** (e.g., recorded or live production of a play or recorded novel or poetry), **evaluating how each version interprets the source text. (Include at least one play by Shakespeare and one play by an American dramatist.)**

9–10 | Informational Text

Analyze various accounts of a subject told in different mediums (e.g., a person's life story in both print and multimedia), determining which details are emphasized in each account.

11–12 | Informational Text

Integrate and evaluate multiple sources of information presented in different media or formats (e.g., visually, quantitatively) as well as in words in order to address a question or solve a problem.

9–10 | History/Social Studies

Integrate quantitative or technical analysis (e.g., charts, research data) with qualitative analysis in print or digital text.

11–12 | History/Social Studies

Integrate **and evaluate multiple sources of information presented in diverse formats and media (e.g., visually, quantitatively, as well as in words)** in order to address a question or solve a problem.

9–10 | Science/Technical Subjects

Translate quantitative or technical information expressed in words in a text into visual form (e.g., table or chart) and translate information expressed visually or mathematically (e.g., in an equation) into words.

11–12 | Science/Technical Subjects

Integrate and evaluate multiple sources of information presented in diverse formats and media (e.g., quantitative data, video, multimedia) in order to address a question or solve a problem.

---

*Please consult the full Common Core State Standards document (and all updates and appendices) at http://www.corestandards.org/ELA-Literacy. See "Research to Build Knowledge" in the Writing section and "Comprehension and Collaboration" in the Speaking and Listening section for additional standards relevant to gathering, assessing, and applying information from print and digital sources.

Source: Copyright © 2010. National Governors Association Center for Best Practices and Council of Chief State School Officers. All rights reserved.

What the **Student** Does

9–10 Literature

Gist: Study the same subject (or scene) in two different artistic mediums (e.g., writing and painting), analyzing how one medium emphasizes a detail the other may leave out or downplay.

- What is the story or scene being represented in these different artistic media?
- How does the painter's or photographer's treatment of the subject or scene compare with the writer's?
- Which elements—words, color, texture, video, or mixed media—does the author or artist use to emphasize some aspect of the story or character portrayed? What is not included?

11–12 Literature

Gist: Examine different performances of a literary text (e.g., stage, film, audio), assessing the quality and result of various interpretations of the same play by Shakespeare or an American playwright.

- What story, drama, or poem is being interpreted in these different performances?
- How do these interpretations compare in their treatment of the same source text?
- Which of these different interpretations of Shakespeare's (or an American playwright's) play is most interesting, compelling, or insightful?

9–10 Informational Text

Gist: Examine how alternative reports of the same subject (e.g., event, a person's life) differ according to the medium used (print, film, other), comparing and discussing the importance of those details each treatment emphasizes—or ignores.

- What is the subject of these competing reports?
- Which details are emphasized in one or another of these stories, but perhaps not all the reports?
- Which details does one medium or account of the subject emphasize over another—and to what effect?

11–12 Informational Text

Gist: Examine a range of sources in different media or formats, all focused on how to solve a problem or address a question, choosing those details which, when considered together, offer the best response to the question or problem.

- What is the question these different sources are trying to answer or problem they want to solve?
- Which details from these different sources are most relevant to the question or problem being considered?
- What criteria are most appropriate for evaluating these sources?

9–10 History/Social Studies

Gist: Examine both quantitative and qualitative analyses in print or digital media, drawing conclusions based on the data and analysis of that data as presented in the different sources.

- What are you investigating?
- What conclusions can you draw about this topic from these different sources?
- What information in each source best relates to or addresses the topic?

11–12 History/Social Studies

Gist: Compare various sources in different media and formats (e.g., graphs, charts, infographics, words), choosing the sources your evaluation indicates will address a question or solve a problem.

- What question or problem are you attempting to answer or address?
- What criteria are you using to evaluate information in the different sources?
- What information can you combine from these different sources to best address the question or problem?

9–10 Science/Technical Subjects

Gist: Recast words into numerical or visual explanations and visa versa, expressing quantitative information such as charts, tables, or equations in words.

- What are the key ideas in this text which might be expressed in a different format?
- Which format would best express the ideas the writer conveys in writing?
- What factors make one format more effective than another as a means revealing the different aspects of your idea?

11–12 Science/Technical Subjects

Gist: Compare various sources of data in different media and formats (e.g., quantitative, data, video, multimedia), choosing those sources you conclude will best address a question or solve a problem.

- What question or problem are you addressing?
- What criteria are you using to evaluate information in the different sources?
- What information can you combine from these different sources to best address the question or problem?

What the **Teacher** Does

To have students integrate and evaluate content in diverse formats and media, do the following:

- Have students start with what the different sources—regardless of format or media—are saying about the subject and how it differs from what other sources are saying about the same subject.
- Have students create or locate the criteria by which the content in these different formats and media will be evaluated; then apply those criteria to these sources.
- Generate questions students should use to guide their reading of different texts across formats and media, including visual and quantitative documents on their own or embedded into a larger written document.

To have students analyze a subject in two different artistic mediums, do the following:

- Demonstrate for students how you read such artistic texts, thinking aloud about the questions you ask, what you ask them about, and how you use them to understand and note what is emphasized in artworks, including paintings and photographs such as those by Dorothea Lange that achieve the level of artistic and thematic complexity.
- Ask students to first list, then use, the questions they generate or learn to ask when analyzing artworks.
- View with students the artistic works online through, for example, Google Art Project, in pairs in the lab where they view and discuss the works in depth and take notes for use in subsequent papers.
- Have students study examples of established art critics evaluating the same or similar works through sources such as the *Wall Street Journal* column "A Masterpiece," in which a critic shows not only how to read such artworks but also how to write about them.

To integrate and evaluate multiple sources of information, do the following:

- Develop a focus question students then seek to answer with evidence or examples from different sources, including quantitative, visual, or multimedia sources.

- Model for the class how you integrate ideas from these different sources and formats into one coherent view about a subject, then use examples, details, or quotations from those sources when writing or speaking about them to support your claims about what they mean or why they are important.

To have students analyze multiple interpretations of a literary text, do the following:

- Set up some sort of note-taking format for students—several columns, one for each version of the work you are studying—and identify key points of emphasis across the interpretations worth comparing (e.g., how each version of *Hamlet* interprets Claudius's opening address to the assembled guests).
- Have students gather different artists' renderings of a character, story, or scene from a literary work, then compare them with the source text (e.g., view different paintings of Ophelia and compare these with the lines from *Hamlet* that describe her).

To have students integrate quantitative or technical with qualitative analysis, do the following:

- Think aloud as you model this for students, describing what you do, how you do it, and why; use the appropriate terms for the types of charts or data you refer to, and discuss the questions you use to evaluate these different analytical forms to answer a question or solve a problem.

To help your English Language Learners, try this:

- Prepare these students with information about each format (charts, graphs) or type of media needed to understand what they hear, see, or read since these may be new forms or concepts to some.

Academic Vocabulary: Key Words and Phrases

Account: This is a report or a story one tells about an experience, era, or event about which people can tell conflicting stories about what happened or what they think is, according to their account, true.

Analysis (technical vs. quantitative): To analyze, one breaks something into its components, the parts from which it is made, thereby attempting to understand how it works or what effect it has. Here, the author analyzes something by either technical/quantitative means (charts, diagrams, or numerical or statistical representations) or qualitative methods (written narrative).

Artistic mediums: *Medium* refers to the form one uses to express an idea; options include words, images, or sounds; it can also mean a painting, movie, photograph, mixed media work, or printed page.

Digital text: Any document of any sort created or reformatted to be read, viewed, or experienced on a computer, tablet, smartphone, or other digital technology that is interactive, multiple-media, or web-enabled, or otherwise incorporates digital technology.

Diverse formats: Consider the same information presented in numbers, narrative, and images; graphic, written, mixed media, or spoken not only to allow the reader to consider a subject from multiple perspectives but also to see how and why others communicate this information differently through these diverse formats.

Information expressed visually or mathematically: See "Analysis." The emphasis here is on how the same ideas are expressed in different ways or to different effect in one form or another.

Integrate: Readers must combine different perspectives from various media into a coherent understanding or position about the subject.

Interpretations: The standard says *multiple* interpretations, suggesting the same text can often allow for different ideas about what it says or means; readers analyze these different readings of the same

text to reconcile the competing claims about what the text means or says.

Representation of a subject or key scene: As it is used here, this refers to a subject or key scene that appears in different mediums; so one would examine, for example, the moment Cain killed Abel as it was interpreted by authors, poets, painters, filmmakers, and so on to see what insights one medium offers that another cannot.

Source text: This standard distinguishes between "sources" and "source texts," which are best understood as primary texts (i.e., the one being read, studied). Otherwise, "source" refers to a website, book, interview, or any other type of source of information.

Translate: Students explain information in one form (quantitative or narrative) using another, showing they are able to read and can understand the ideas and claims represented with visuals (charts, graphs) equally well in words (or vice versa).

Treatment: This is used as one would use the words *response to*, *adaptation of*, or *version of* the same story (e.g., *The Odyssey*) or character (e.g., Odysseus) in different mediums (fiction and painting).

Version: One could compare Coppola's treatment of Conrad's *Heart of Darkness* in his movie *Apocalypse Now*, or one could contrast different films of *Hamlet* available, from the most modern adaptation to the more classical performances.

Visual form/visually: Visual explanations, often called infographics, may include the traditional pie chart or bar graph but may also incorporate many other features that make these visual or graphic forms much more complex than the previous generation of such texts. Thus, to read these visuals, students must be able to read them as arguments, explanations, or even narratives expressed through numbers and signs or patterns and shapes that they must learn to restate in words.

Reading 8: Delineate and evaluate the argument and specific claims in a text, including the validity of the reasoning as well as the relevance and sufficiency of the evidence.

9–10 Literature

(Not applicable to literature)

11–12 Literature

(Not applicable to literature)

9–10 Informational Text

Delineate and evaluate the argument and specific claims in a text, assessing whether the reasoning is valid and the evidence is relevant and sufficient; identify false statements and fallacious reasoning.

11–12 Informational Text

Delineate and evaluate the **reasoning in seminal U.S. texts, including the application of constitutional principles and use of legal reasoning (e.g., in U.S. Supreme Court majority opinions and dissents) and the premises, purposes, and arguments in works of public advocacy (e.g.,** *The Federalist,* **presidential addresses).**

9–10 History/Social Studies

Assess the extent to which the reasoning and evidence in a text support the author's claims.

11–12 History/Social Studies

Evaluate the author's premises, claims, and evidence by corroborating or challenging them with other information.

9–10 Science/Technical Subjects

Assess the extent to which the reasoning and evidence in a text support the author's claim or a recommendation for solving a scientific or technical problem.

11–12 Science/Technical Subjects

Evaluate the hypotheses, data, analysis, and conclusions in a science or technical text, verifying the data when possible and corroborating or challenging conclusions with other sources of information.

Source: Copyright © 2010. National Governors Association Center for Best Practices and Council of Chief State School Officers. All rights reserved.

What the **Student** Does

9–10 Literature

Gist: The 9–10 Common Core Standards state that this standard is "not applicable to literature."

11–12 Literature

Gist: As in grades 9–10, the 11–12 Common Core Standards declare this standard does "not [apply] to literature."

9–10 Informational Text

Gist: Examine specific claims or arguments of the text, paying special attention to the rationale, credibility, and adequacy of the evidence presented throughout by the author. In addition to assessing the integrity and quality of the argument, readers also assess claims and reasoning for their veracity and logic, identifying those which are simply not true or are weakened by flaws in their logic.

- What argument or claims does this text make—to what end?
- What evidence does the author provide to support an argument or claim?
- How valid and detailed is the evidence provided by the author?
- Where are the flaws in the author's argument?

11–12 Informational Text

Gist: Assess the logic or rationale informing key foundational American documents, such as how the constitutional principles apply to or inform the legal reasoning behind major Supreme Court opinions and dissents. Further, students evaluate and analyze the premises, purposes, and arguments used or outlined in many major policy or advocacy documents such as presidential addresses, constitutional amendments, or texts such as *The Federalist*.

- What argument or claims does this text make—to what end?
- What evidence is used to support a major argument or claim?
- How valid and detailed is the evidence provided?
- Where are the flaws in the author's argument?

9–10 History/Social Studies

Gist: Evaluate how effective and adequate the author's logic and support are for the argument or claims made. This means evaluating not only the relationship between the claims and evidence to ensure they align with each other but also determining the quality of the evidence and logic on which those claims depend so much.

- What arguments or claims does this text make?
- What evidence does the author provide to support any claims made in the text?
- What criteria do you or the author use to assess the quality of the reasoning and evidence behind the claims?

11–12 History/Social Studies

Gist: Evaluate how effective and logical the author's premises and claims are by testing them against established data or reliable authorities on this subject. Students can also consult other sources on the same subject in order to evaluate the strength and quality of the author's evidence and reasoning.

- What arguments or claims does this text make?
- What evidence does the author provide to support any claims made in the text?
- What criteria do you or the author use to assess the quality of additional sources you use to check the reasoning and evidence behind the claims?

9–10 Science/Technical Subjects

Gist: Measure how effective and adequate the reasoning and evidence are and the degree to which they support any proposed solutions to scientific or technical problems, not only evaluating the relationship between the claims and the evidence to ensure they align, but also determining the quality of the evidence and logic on which those claims are based.

- What claim or recommendation does the author make here?
- What evidence does the author provide to support any claims or recommendations for solving scientific or technical problems?
- What criteria do you or the author use to determine the quality of the reasoning and evidence behind the claims?

11–12 Science/Technical Subjects

Gist: Identify the hypotheses, key data sets, analysis of that data, and any conclusions drawn about its meaning and importance, confirming the reliability and validity of the data and further testing their own and the author's conclusions about the subject by consulting other reliable sources of information on this subject.

- What are the subject and the objective of this text?
- What do the hypotheses and data say about this subject?
- How well does the available data on this subject corroborate what you concluded based on your own reading of the text and related data?

What the **Teacher** Does

To have students delineate the argument, do the following:

- Tell students first how to identify what the argument *is* and how you figured that out so they know where to direct their critical attention.
- Ask students to label, list, or otherwise identify the following elements related to the argument: the claims made in the text, the reasons stated or implied for those claims, any evidence cited, and how that evidence relates to and supports the claims.
- List on the board three primary goals of argument in academic writing: *to explain ideas or positions* to others, *to persuade people* to change what they think, or *to mediate or reconcile conflicts* between parties about the truth, meaning, or importance of something. Provide students examples, when first introducing them to reading arguments, of different types of arguments, asking them to sort them into the appropriate categories listed previously.
- Assign the class arguments from foundational texts (e.g., U.S. Constitution) and seminal U.S. documents (e.g., presidential addresses, major Supreme Court opinions), which they must study to determine what type of argument it is.

To have students evaluate the specific claims made in these different texts, do the following:

- Have students first determine what type of claims they encounter: claims of fact (X is—or is *not*—true), claims of value (X is valid or not, right or wrong, important or not), and claims of policy (X must—or must *not*—be changed).
- Together, go through a complex text that makes such claims and identify the precise claim and its type.

To have students delineate and evaluate the reasoning in seminal U.S. texts, do the following:

- Model for the class as you read, evaluate, and locate the premises, purposes, and arguments within such seminal U.S. texts as a speech by Martin Luther King, Jr. or an opinion by the Supreme Court.
- Ask students to tape the source text on a larger sheet of paper and, working in groups, annotate its claims as they discuss them and the premises, purposes, and evidence that inform those arguments.

- Provide students with more contemporary arguments that both support and challenge older arguments, such as the Second Amendment, requiring them to evaluate the reasoning and evidence behind them all as students assess the arguments or evidence today.

To have students evaluate a study's hypotheses, data, analysis, and conclusions, do the following:

- Evaluate with students the reliability and validity of the sources they cite and ways they use the data to defend their findings; students can research the sources or data as part of their assessment, reporting what they find and whether it supports or refutes the study's conclusions.
- Parse out with students the reasoning behind a scientific claim and its evidence: Does their reasoning add up to a logical conclusion based on the evidence? And is that evidence relevant and sufficient?

To have students evaluate the reasoning, premises, purposes, and claims, do the following:

- Teach students which questions to ask to determine if the evidence is relevant, accurate, and sufficient to support their claim.
- Provide students with a range of models for them to practice evaluating, each one positioned to be just a little more complex than the previous one to help them refine their application of criteria for an effective claim or piece of evidence.

To have students corroborate or check an author's position with other information, do the following:

- Identify with students those elements—premises, claims, evidence, or reasoning—which merit scrutiny and have students research these points for information that supports or refutes the author's position.

To help your English Language Learners, try this:

- Try using different colored highlighters or an LCD projector to allow you to better identify and represent the role of the different elements of argument. Remember also that argument may raise cultural issues with those from cultures where it is disrespectful to argue.

Academic Vocabulary: Key Words and Phrases

Advocacy (public): In this case specifically, it refers to works of public advocacy, which means the student would read this document as a call for action or support for another's call to act.

Application: This refers to one's ability to read, understand, and apply principles outlined in the U.S. Constitution and the reasoning behind the Constitution as it relates to established and contested laws.

Argument: The writer or speaker adopts a position about which he or she attempts to persuade others to think or feel differently about an issue, to change how they act, or to resolve disagreements between themselves and other parties about an issue. Writers and speakers accomplish these ends by presenting claims supported with reasons, evidence, and appeals. Arguments are related to but different from claims, propositions, thesis statements, or assertions.

Assess: Assessment in this context is all about the logic of one's claims. Such assessment asks one to examine the reliability, credibility, and timeliness of all sources used to support one's claims.

Challenging: The reader questions any suspect claims, assumptions, evidence, or reasoning, looking for the holes, flaws, or inconsistencies; the reader then provides evidence or counterarguments intended to undermine the author's argument.

Claims: A specific assertion that authors want readers to accept as true and act on; the author's thesis is the *primary* claim he or she will make, develop, and support with evidence throughout the paper. Because a claim is debatable, it requires supporting evidence to counter inevitable challenges critical readers will make as they assess the validity of the claims, logic, and evidence.

Conclusions: When reading scientific reports or findings, readers must zero in on the conclusions and the reasoning and evidence behind those conclusions to determine if they are valid and well supported with evidence from the experiment or other reliable source.

Corroborating: When reading their own or others' conclusions, students need to also gather the appropriate evidence that supports and defends their findings or conclusions.

Data: When reading any scientific or technical text, students examine the results used to support their claims about the meaning or importance of the data to determine if it is valid and reliable.

Delineate: The reader must be able to describe or represent in precise detail the author's argument, as well as her claims, reasoning, and evidence; to delineate is to draw a line between what is and is *not* the exact argument, claim, reasoning, or evidence.

Evidence (relevance and sufficiency of): It is the reader's job to determine if the evidence is, in fact, related to the claim and does, indeed, provide adequate support. If the evidence is from an unreliable source (personal experience) or is limited to a few details, the reader should consider the evidence irrelevant and insufficient.

False statements: Different from fallacies, these statements are simply not true; whether they are deliberate lies is up to the reader.

Hypotheses: The author's proposed explanation of some idea based on limited evidence provided from his or her investigations that require further evidence to prove.

Premise: This is an assertion on which subsequent theories or investigations are based; thus, the reader examines those premises the author accepts as true or uses as support for any claims.

Reasoning: Readers are looking to determine if the student's logic is based on valid, reliable evidence from current and credible sources or on one or more fallacies that are false or misleading, connected as they are by dubious links between the claim and evidence.

Notes

Reading 9: Analyze how two or more texts address similar themes or topics to build knowledge or to compare the approaches the authors take.

9–10 Literature	**11–12** Literature
Analyze how an author draws on and transforms source material in a specific work (e.g., how Shakespeare treats a theme or topic from Ovid or the Bible or how a later author draws on a play by Shakespeare).	Demonstrate knowledge of eighteenth-, nineteenth, and early-twentieth-century foundational works of American literature, including how two or more texts from the same period treat similar themes or topics.

9–10 Informational Text	**11–12** Informational Text
Analyze seminal U.S. documents of historical and literary significance (e.g., Washington's Farewell Address, the Gettysburg Address, Roosevelt's Four Freedom's speech, King's "Letter from Birmingham Jail"), including how they address related themes and concepts.	Analyze **seventeenth-, eighteenth-, and nineteenth-century foundational** U.S. documents of historical and literary significance (**including The Declaration of Independence, the Preamble to the Constitution, the Bill of Rights, and Lincoln's Second Inaugural Address**) for their themes, purposes, and rhetorical features.

9–10 History/Social Studies	**11–12** History/Social Studies
Compare and contrast treatments of the same topic in several primary and secondary sources.	Integrate information from diverse sources, both primary and secondary, into a coherent understanding of an idea or event, noting discrepancies among sources.

9–10 Science/Technical Subjects	**11–12** Science/Technical Subjects
Compare and contrast findings presented in a text to those from other sources (including their own experiments), noting when the findings support or contradict previous explanations or accounts.	Synthesize information from a range of sources (e.g., texts, experiments, simulations) into a coherent understanding of a process phenomenon, or concept, resolving conflicting information when possible.

Source: Copyright © 2010. National Governors Association Center for Best Practices and Council of Chief State School Officers. All rights reserved.

What the **Student** Does

9–10 Literature

Gist: Identify the original source such as a myth, a folktale, or a Bible story the author adopts or adapts in the work being studied, examining how and why the author changes the original source to meet the needs of the current text.

- Which early or original sources does the author draw on?
- Why did the author choose that story from Ovid, the Bible, or some other established source?
- How are the source story and its modern adaptation similar or different?

9–10 Informational Text

Gist: Analyze how specific landmark United States documents of great historical and literary importance treat certain common themes and ideas (e.g., liberty, justice, independence), including those choices authors made in light of their purpose, the occasion, and the audience at that time.

- What type of document is this and why was it written?
- What are the subject and themes of this text?
- How do these different documents address or respond to the same event, concept, or theme?

9–10 History/Social Studies

Gist: Examine how different primary and secondary sources address the same topic or event, noting where, when, and why the different texts and their authors agree and disagree with each other about major events and ideas.

- What is the topic the authors of these various sources examine?
- What are the key differences and similarities between the different documents in their treatment of the subject?
- Are there noticeable differences between the primary and secondary sources in terms of perspective, interpretation, or facts?

9–10 Science/Technical Subjects

Gist: Examine the similarities and differences between various texts and the findings they report, comparing published results, previous reports, and their own findings from experiments they conduct themselves.

- What are the latest findings on this topic?
- What other sources report findings that may challenge, support, or clarify those reported here?
- What are the points about which different sources on this subject agree—and disagree?

11–12 Literature

Gist: Know and read a range of earlier (18th–20th century) major works in American literature, comparing how two or more of these texts from the same period, though not necessarily from the same genre, treat the same theme or topic.

- What are some topics commonly explored in early works of American literature?
- Which writers or literary works from the 18th through the early 20th century should students study for this unit?
- How do these two (or more) works from the same historical period treat the same topic?

11–12 Informational Text

Gist: Examine the themes, purpose, and rhetorical features that make specific foundational documents from the United States so important historically and stylistically. Students should know those 17th- through 19th-century foundational American texts such as the Declaration of Independence, the Constitution, and Bill of Rights, noting those themes, purposes, and rhetorical techniques used in them to achieve such great ends.

- Who wrote this specific foundational document—and in what context, for what audience, for what purpose?
- What is the subject or theme of this text?
- What specific element(s) lend this particular document its enduring meaning, importance, or power?

11–12 History/Social Studies

Gist: Gather together information from a range of primary and secondary sources, each one about the same idea or event, to comprehend it more fully, taking time to consider those important details or facts that were missing from these sources or ways in which they did not agree even though they are about the same idea or event.

- What is the subject of these different primary and secondary sources?
- What ideas or evidence in each source is essential to connect with the other sources for a coherent or full understanding?
- Are there noticeable differences between the primary and secondary sources in terms of perspective, interpretation, or the facts? If so, in what way or areas do the sources disagree?

11–12 Science/Technical Subjects

Gist: Gather information from various sources such as texts, experiments, and simulations to create a new and fuller sense of how a process works, or what a concept means, resolving those points where the data conflicts as needed.

- What sources are you consulting for this information?
- Where, when, and how do the different sources conflict?
- Which details from the different sources are essential to include in your synthesis of all these sources about this topic?

What the **Teacher** Does

To have students analyze how two or more texts address similar themes or topics, do the following:

- Use colors (as you display the text or a passage via LCD projector) to code the two themes or topics as they appear or develop and refer to each other; narrate your thinking aloud as you do this so students see what you are doing and understand how the colors that represent each theme or topic connect with the others throughout the text.
- Have students use highlighters or digital color tools (if they are working on-screen) to examine the development of ideas into a larger fabric of knowledge about an idea over time or examine how each author approaches the treatment of these ideas in their texts compared with the others being studied. Let students' reading be guided by the question, What patterns emerge over the course of the text in each author's approach to the topic and theme?

To have students analyze how an author draws on and transforms source material, do the following:

- Think aloud for the students to show them how you notice any clues *in the text* that signal it derives from a given myth, Bible story, or theme from one such as Dante or Ovid. Indicate for students the signal words, phrases, images, or patterns that alert you to the presence of the source story in this modern poem, play, or story.
- Give students the original source story (the story of Job, the relevant Grimms' tale, the passage from Dante's *Inferno*) before—or after—they read the modern text that makes use of the source story, asking them to look closely to note the similarities or echoes between them and how the inclusion of that source material contributes to the meaning of the more modern text.

To have students analyze how two or more texts from early America are related, do the following:

- Set up students on computers with the documents open in a word processor; have them skim the document to glean the ideas and related key words used to express those ideas; then use the search function of the word processor to locate all the instances of a particular word, phrase, or image. Have students discuss with partners or neighbors what they notice about the patterns and what it might mean.
- Provide students with a printed version of a foundational U.S. document formatted with extra-wide margins for space; ask students to label all the different themes that recur throughout the document(s) and how those are used to reinforce the argument or achieve the purpose of the document's author. Or have students label various rhetorical features—repetition, figurative language, and parallel structure, for example—used in the document and make notes in the wider margins about how these affect the meaning of the text and its impact on the intended audience.

To have students examine the treatment or use of primary and secondary sources:

- Offer students several clear examples of primary and secondary sources, first, so they know what these terms mean and how they differ so they will know them when they see or read them.
- Have students use a graphic organizer with multiple columns for each source; have students jot down key ideas or quotations that represent how each source treats that idea, drawing conclusions about how they compare when you are finished and citing examples to support and illustrate your claims.

To have students note discrepancies or resolve conflicting information, do the following:

- Format a document to create parallel (side-by-side) texts so students can read across texts, noting where the two texts differ in a discernible way from each other, and then draw conclusions about the meaning of those discrepancies.

To help your English Language Learners, try this:

- Read aloud from these texts as you display them or as students follow along on copies of their own so they see and hear the more antiquated language of these often older or more complex texts.

Academic Vocabulary: Key Words and Phrases

Approaches: *The approaches the authors take* could refer to the choices the author makes about stylistic elements such as voice, imagery, or format; it could also refer to the author's choice to approach the subject through a particular point of view or genre.

Build knowledge: Stresses the author's efforts to build the reader's knowledge about the subject of the text; given the reference to several foundational or canonical texts, this would mean looking at how the author draws on and provides for the reader the necessary information to read and understand those stories alluded to or embedded within the story.

Coherent understanding of an idea or event: Readers should "Integrate information from diverse sources, both primary and secondary, into a coherent understanding." As the readers consider multiple sources, they create an understanding of the text that holds together and is logical based on the evidence from the supporting texts.

Demonstrate knowledge of: The standard is saying it expects students to know and be able to read and understand not just contemporary texts but those written in the 18th century through the early 20th century, often in different styles, using antiquated language, and often assuming a familiarity with the Bible or certain classical themes or works.

Diverse sources: The standard specifies primary and secondary sources (as opposed to diverse *types*, which would imply various media). Primary sources are those recorded by people who were present at and noted their thoughts about an event; secondary sources, such as articles or books, draw on those primary sources to make their claims about the meaning or importance of a person or event.

Draws on and transforms source material: The tendency in many authors is to adapt those stories we already know—Grimms' fairy tales, biblical stories, myths—for our modern tastes, transforming them in the process so they seem new but add depth to the text through the resonant echoes of older, familiar stories.

Findings: This refers to the results from a scientific study: That is, it refers to what the scientist *found* as a result of her experiment. The reader's job is to evaluate how credible these findings are in light of what we know to be true and the evidence the writer provides.

Foundational works: Those documents such as the Declaration of Independence and Constitution that provide the foundation for the country and its principles. They are, in other words, the *foundation* on which the country and its ideas and culture are built. A primary source document, however, would be a letter Thomas Jefferson wrote about the debate over the Constitution while sitting in the room observing and participating in it.

Process phenomenon: The student in a science or technical subject reads a variety of opinions about the meaning and importance, the causes and effects, or the findings and conclusions from a process; it becomes the reader's job to determine which details are valid and reliable and, thus, support the conclusions about this process.

Rhetorical features: These are rhetorical devices such as repetition, metaphor, alliteration, paradox, or metonymy (to name a few) used to achieve the intended effect of the authors.

Seminal U.S. documents: These are culturally important documents; unlike "foundational documents," which establish the laws and principles by which the country governs itself, seminal texts define the culture, coming as they often do at crucial moments in the country's history when the writer or speaker attempts to clarify certain core ideals.

Synthesize: Often mistaken for summarizing, this calls for the reader to take the details from different sources and create some new, deeper understanding of the original material.

Reading 10: Read and comprehend complex literary and informational texts independently and proficiently.

9–10 Literature

By the end of grade 9, read and comprehend literature, including stories, dramas, and poems, in the grades 9–10 text complexity band proficiently, with scaffolding as needed at the high end of the range.

By the end of grade 10, read and comprehend literature, including stories, dramas, and poems, at the high end of the grades 9–10 text complexity band independently and proficiently.

11–12 Literature

By the end of **grade 11**, read and comprehend literature, including stories, dramas, and poems, in the grades **11–CCR** text complexity band proficiently, with scaffolding as needed at the high end of the range.

By the end of **grade 12**, read and comprehend literature, including stories, dramas, and poems, in the grades **11–CCR** text complexity band independently and proficiently.

9–10 Informational Text

By the end of grade 9, read and comprehend literary nonfiction in the grades 9–10 text complexity band proficiently, with scaffolding as needed at the high end of the range.

By the end of grade 10, read and comprehend literary nonfiction at the high end of grades 9–10 text complexity band independently and proficiently.

11–12 Informational Text

By the end of **grade 11**, read and comprehend literary nonfiction in the grades **11–CCR** text complexity band proficiently, with scaffolding as needed at the high end of the range.

By the end of **grade 12**, read and comprehend literary nonfiction at the high end of grades **11–CCR** text complexity band independently and proficiently.

9–10 History/Social Studies

By the end of grade 10, read and comprehend history/social studies texts in the grades 9–10 text complexity band independently and proficiently.

11–12 History/Social Studies

By the end of **grade 12**, read and comprehend history/social studies texts in the grades 11–12 text complexity band independently and proficiently.

9–10 Science/Technical Subjects

By the end of grade 10, read and comprehend science/technical texts in the grades 9–10 text complexity band independently and proficiently.

11–12 Science/Technical Subjects

By the end of **grade 12**, read and comprehend science/technical texts in the grades 11–12 text complexity band independently and proficiently.

Source: Copyright © 2010. National Governors Association Center for Best Practices and Council of Chief State School Officers. All rights reserved.

What the **Student** Does

9–10 Literature

Gist: Read the full range of literary texts—fiction, poetry, and drama—appropriate for grades 9–10, receiving help only when needed as they reach the high end of the 9–10 complexity band for literary texts.

- What type of text is this—and is it more or less complex than the last text you read?
- What do you need to know to read and understand this text independently at the 9th- or 10th-grade level?
- What sort of techniques or strategies might help you read this text if you find it more difficult than previous readings?

9–10 Informational Text

Gist: Read the full range of literary nonfiction texts appropriate for grades 9–10, receiving help only when needed as they reach the high end of the 9–10 complexity band for nonfiction literary texts.

- What type of text is this—and is it more or less complex than the last text you read?
- What do you need to know to read and understand this text independently at the 9th- or 10th-grade level?
- What sort of techniques or strategies might help you read this text if you find it more difficult than previous readings?

9–10 History/Social Studies

Gist: Read a range of history/social studies texts appropriate for grades 9–10, receiving help only when needed as they reach the high end of the 9–10 complexity band.

- What type of text is this—and is it more or less complex than the last text you read?
- What do you need to know to read and understand this text independently at the 9th- or 10th-grade level?
- What sort of techniques or strategies might help you read this text if you find it more difficult than previous readings?

9–10 Science/Technical Subjects

Gist: Read a range of science/technical texts appropriate for grades 9–10, receiving help only when needed as they reach the high end of the 9–10 complexity band.

- What type of text is this—and is it more or less complex than the last text you read?
- What do you need to know to read and understand this text independently at the 9th- or 10th-grade level?
- What sort of techniques or strategies might help you read this text if you find it more difficult than previous readings?

11–12 Literature

Gist: Read the full range of literary texts—fiction, poetry, and drama—appropriate for grades 11–12, receiving help only when needed as they reach the high end of the 11–12 complexity band for literary texts.

- What type of text is this—and is it more or less complex than the last text you read?
- What do you need to know to read and understand this text independently at the 11th- or 12th-grade level?
- What sort of techniques or strategies might help you read this text if you find it more difficult than previous readings?

11–12 Informational Text

Gist: Read the full range of nonfiction literary texts—fiction, poetry, and drama—appropriate for grades 11–12, receiving help only when needed as they reach the high end of the 11–12 complexity band for nonfiction literary texts.

- What type of text is this—and is it more or less complex than the last text you read?
- What do you need to know to read and understand this text independently at the 11th- or 12th-grade level?
- What sort of techniques or strategies might help you read this text if you find it more difficult than previous readings?

11–12 History/Social Studies

Gist: Read a range of history/social studies texts appropriate for grades 11–12, receiving help only when needed as they reach the high end of the 11–12 complexity band.

- What type of text is this—and is it more or less complex than the last text you read?
- What do you need to know to read and understand this text independently at the 11th- or 12th-grade level?
- What sort of techniques or strategies might help you read this text if you find it more difficult than previous readings?

11–12 Science/Technical Subjects

Gist: Read a range of science/technical texts appropriate for grades 11–12, receiving help only when needed as they reach the high end of the 11–12 complexity band.

- What type of text is this—and is it more or less complex than the last text you read?
- What do you need to know to read and understand this text independently at the 11th- or 12th-grade level?
- What sort of techniques or strategies might help you read this text if you find it more difficult than previous readings?

What the **Teacher** Does

To have students read and comprehend complex texts independently and proficiently, do the following:

- Assign an array of literary (novels, plays, and poems) and informational texts (literary nonfiction, essays, biographies, historical accounts) to be read in class and outside so students can build their stamina, speed, and confidence with longer and more complex texts.

- Organize students into groups (inquiry circles, literature circles, book clubs); each group reads a different book or the same as the others, using the discussion within the group to help them work through the challenges the book presents and engage in more independent discussions about the book.

- Engage in a full-class close reading on occasion, modeling for the class what such close reading looks like and discussing how you do it as you go; then let students take on more of the responsibility for reading and discussing, which teachers first facilitate, then relinquish.

- Teach students a range of questions to ask when they read different types of texts and techniques they can use throughout their reading process as needed with different types of texts before, during, and after they read each text.

- Assign a series of readings, both informational and literary, about the same subject (e.g., survival, transformation, the environment) to understand it in depth from different perspectives.

- Evaluate the texts you assign using the Common Core complexity criteria and arrange them, when possible, in order of complexity so students are consistently reading texts that challenge them (not merely with their length but also in their complexity) more than those they previously read.

To have students provide scaffolding as needed at the high end of the range, do the following:

- Provide targeted questions or directions students can use to guide them when engaging in close reading of any type of text; such questions might direct their attention to stylistic elements or rhetorical features, nuances of plot or character, or how these elements interact with one another and the setting in the story.

- Encourage students to consult annotated versions of the texts they are studying in their textbooks or that you provide (or find available online) as students develop their capacity to read closely, gradually phasing out such support as they develop their own independence.

To have students develop students' ability to read complex history and science texts, do the following:

- Expose them to an array of texts written by experts in the fields in popular journals (e.g., *Discovery*, *Scientific American*) and other sources (blogs, reports, news articles) where the quality of the writing will challenge them, and, because of the often shorter nature of the articles, require students to consider the subject from a range of perspectives, sources, or fields.

- Include in the history, social science, science, or technical subjects longer texts, including books or long-form journalism about scientific, technical, economic, or historical events and processes written by leading authors and journalists in those fields. Students might read these longer works as part of an ongoing inquiry into the environment, historical events, or cultures, giving a presentation or writing a report when they finish.

To help your English Language Learners, try this:

- Help them find books and other texts appropriate to their current reading level but which challenge them with ideas, language, and other elements that are new or more complex than previous texts they have read.

Academic Vocabulary: Key Words and Phrases

11–CCR text complexity band: The individual text complexity bands correspond with associated grade levels (6–8, 9–10, 11–12). The levels themselves are determined by the three-part model of text complexity discussed in Appendix A of the complete CCSS document. The three factors in text complexity are *qualitative dimensions* (levels of meaning, language complexity as determined by attentive reader), *quantitative dimensions* (word length and frequency, sentence length, and cohesion), and *reader and task considerations* (factors related to a specific reader such as motivation, background knowledge, persistence; others associated with the task itself such as the purpose or demands of the task itself).

CCR: College and Career Readiness standards in reading, writing, speaking, and listening are the foundation on which the Common Core State Standards are built. They first appeared, in draft form, in documents developed by the Council of Chief State School Officers (CCSSO) and the National Governors Association (NGA) in 2009.

Complex literary and informational texts: *Complex* is not the same as *difficult*; literary and informational texts are complex for different reasons as they are written for mostly different purposes. In the context of the standards, complexity is one measure of a work's quality but is at the heart of the CCSS when it comes to reading.

High end of the range: If they are seniors, this means the high end of the 12th grade in terms of complexity or performance; students reading at this level at the end of a year should be able to read independently, with little, less, or no teachers' guidance.

History/social studies texts: Those texts commonly studied in history and social studies classes, including graphs, maps, primary source documents, foundational and seminal documents, and a range of informational texts that explain the importance of key individuals and the cause and effect of various historical events and eras.

Independently: One is able to read whatever texts are assigned without the aid of the teacher or, when challenged by the teacher with a complex text, is able to do the work as assigned without the aid of scaffolding or guided instruction.

Informational: Texts designed to inform, though this can include argument, a range of expository texts, and also a range of media and formats, including infographics and videos.

Literary nonfiction: These include informational texts, often books or essays, that use novelistic and other literary techniques to engage readers, and then use the story to convey the information. Examples would include *Band of Brothers*, *Unbroken*, and *In the Garden of the Beasts*.

Proficiently: This describes the way and the level at which the individual student is able to read complex texts; proficiency is equated with skill, though not mastery.

Scaffolding: This is support from teachers, aids, or other students who help a student read a text or complete a task; examples include providing background knowledge, reading aloud, or any other strategy designed to help students become independent readers or writers.

Science/technical texts: These texts include many types and formats, all of which fall into the informational text category, but which may include infographic or quantitative texts, as well as narratives of lab procedures that explain how they arrived at a result. Such highly technical texts stress clarity through objective, structured prose.

Text complexity band: This indicates the text difficulty associated with the grade levels around which the Common Core standards are organized: grades 2–3, 4–5, 6–8, 9–10, and 11–CCR.

The Common Core State Standards

Writing

College and Career Readiness Anchor Standards for
Writing 9–12

Source: Common Core State Standards

The grades 6–12 standards on the following pages define what students should understand and be able to do by the end of each grade. They correspond to the CCR anchor standards by number. The CCR and grade-specific standards are necessary complements—the former providing broad standards, the latter providing additional specificity—that together define the skills and understandings that all students must demonstrate.

Text Types and Purposes*

1. Write arguments to support claims in an analysis of substantive topics or texts, using valid reasoning and relevant and sufficient evidence.
2. Write informative/explanatory texts to examine and convey complex ideas and information clearly and accurately through the elective selection, organization, and analysis of content.
3. Write narratives to develop real or imagined experiences or events using elective technique, well-chosen details, and well-structured event sequences.

Production and Distribution of Writing

4. Produce clear and coherent writing in which the development, organization, and style are appropriate to task, purpose, and audience.
5. Develop and strengthen writing as needed by planning, revising, editing, rewriting, or trying a new approach.
6. Use technology, including the Internet, to produce and publish writing and to interact and collaborate with others.

Research to Build and Present Knowledge

7. Conduct short as well as more sustained research projects based on focused questions, demonstrating understanding of the subject under investigation.
8. Gather relevant information from multiple print and digital sources, assess the credibility and accuracy of each source, and integrate the information while avoiding plagiarism.
9. Draw evidence from literary or informational texts to support analysis, reflection, and research.

Range of Writing

10. Write routinely over extended time frames (time for research, reflection, and revision) and shorter time frames (a single sitting or a day or two) for a range of tasks, purposes, and audiences.

Note on Range and Content of Student Writing

For students, writing is a key means of asserting and defending claims, showing what they know about a subject, and conveying what they have experienced, imagined, thought, and felt. To be CCR writers, students must take task, purpose, and audience into careful consideration, choosing words, information, structures, and formats deliberately. They need to know how to combine elements of different kinds of writing—for example, to use narrative strategies within argument and explanation within narrative—to produce complex and nuanced writing. They need to be able to use technology strategically when creating, refining, and collaborating on writing. They have to become adept at gathering information, evaluating sources, and citing material accurately and reporting findings from their research and analysis of sources in a clear and cogent manner. They must have the flexibility, concentration, and fluency to produce high-quality, first-draft text under a tight deadline as well as the capacity to revisit and make improvements to a piece of writing over multiple drafts when circumstances encourage or require it.

* These broad types of writing include many subgenres. See Appendix A for definitions of key writing types.

Source: Copyright © 2010. National Governors Association Center for Best Practices and Council of Chief State School Officers. All rights reserved.

College and Career Readiness Anchor Standards for

Writing

The College and Career Readiness (CCR) anchor standards are the same for all middle and high school students, regardless of subject area or grade level. What varies is the sophistication of the writing of the three types—argument, informative/explanatory, and narrative—stressed at each subsequent grade level in each disciplinary domain. The core writing skills should not change as students advance; rather, the level at which they learn and can perform those skills should increase in complexity as students move from one grade to the next.

Text Types and Purposes*

Argument appears first as it is essential to success in college and develops the critical faculties needed in the adult world. Crafting arguments requires students to analyze texts or topics, and determine which evidence best supports their arguments. Informational/explanatory writing conveys ideas, events, and findings by choosing and explaining the behavior, meaning, or importance of key details.

Students draw from a range of sources, including primary and secondary sources. Narrative writing includes not just stories but accounts of historical events and lab procedures. Students write to change minds, hearts, and actions (argument); to extend readers' knowledge or acceptance of ideas and procedures (informational/explanatory); and to inform, inspire, persuade, or entertain (narrative).

Production and Distribution of Writing

This set of anchor standards involves the stages of the writing process. These standards also highlight the importance of knowing who the audience is and the style and format the writer should use to achieve a purpose. Students also learn the skills needed throughout the writing process: generating ideas, trying other styles,

structures, perspectives, or processes as they bring their ideas into focus and some final form. Finally, these standards call for writers to use technology not only to publish but to collaborate throughout the writing process with others.

Research to Build and Present Knowledge

These standards focus on inquiry processes of varying lengths, all of which should develop students' knowledge of the subject they are investigating and the skills needed to conduct that investigation. Students acquire and refine the ability to find, evaluate, and

use a range of sources during these research projects, which can take as long as a period to as much as a month. Such inquiries demand students correctly cite the source of all information to ensure they learn what plagiarism is and how to avoid it.

Range of Writing

This standard emphasizes not only what students write but how often and for what purposes they write over the course of the school year. Writing, as this standard makes clear, is something students should be doing constantly and for

substantial lengths of time. Also, they should write for an array of reasons and audiences and in response to a mix of topics and tasks.

---

* These broad types of writing include many subgenres. See Appendix A for definitions of key writing types.

Writing 1: Write arguments to support claims in an analysis of substantive topics or texts, using valid reasoning and relevant and sufficient evidence.

9–10 English Language Arts	**11–12** English Language Arts
Write arguments to support claims in an analysis of substantive topics or texts, using valid reasoning and relevant and sufficient evidence.	Write arguments to support claims in an analysis of substantive topics or texts, using valid reasoning and relevant and sufficient evidence.

9–10 English Language Arts

Write arguments to support claims in an analysis of substantive topics or texts, using valid reasoning and relevant and sufficient evidence.

a. Introduce precise claim(s), distinguish the claim(s) from alternate or opposing claims, and create an organization that establishes clear relationships among claim(s), counterclaims, reasons, and evidence.
b. Develop claim(s) and counterclaims fairly, supplying evidence for each while pointing out the strengths and limitations of both in a manner that anticipates the audience's knowledge level and concerns.
c. Use words, phrases, and clauses to link the major sections of the text, create cohesion, and clarify the relationships between claim(s) and reasons, between reasons and evidence, and between claim(s) and counterclaims.
d. Establish and maintain a formal style and objective tone while attending to the norms and conventions of the discipline in which they are writing.
e. Provide a concluding statement or section that follows from and supports the argument presented.

11–12 English Language Arts

Write arguments to support claims in an analysis of substantive topics or texts, using valid reasoning and relevant and sufficient evidence.

a. Introduce precise, **knowledgeable** claim(s), **establish the significance of the claim(s)**, distinguish the claim(s) from alternate or opposing claims, and create an organization **that logically sequences** claim(s), counterclaims, reasons, and evidence.
b. Develop claim(s) and counterclaims fairly **and thoroughly**, supplying **the most relevant** evidence for each while pointing out the strengths and limitations of both in a manner that anticipates the audience's knowledge level, concerns, **values, and possible biases**.
c. Use words, phrases, and clauses **as well as varied syntax** to link the major sections of the text, create cohesion, and clarify the relationships between claim(s) and reasons, between reasons and evidence, and between claim(s) and counterclaims.
d. Establish and maintain a formal style and objective tone while attending to the norms and conventions of the discipline in which they are writing.
e. Provide a concluding statement or section that follows from and supports the argument presented.

* These broad types of writing include many subgenres. See Appendix A for definitions of key writing types.

Source: Copyright © 2010. National Governors Association Center for Best Practices and Council of Chief State School Officers. All rights reserved.

What the **Student** Does

9–10 English Language Arts

Gist: Craft arguments to support claims, analyzing complex texts or topics, all of which students support with sound reasoning and evidence that is both appropriate and adequate. Students begin by introducing a specific claim(s), which should be precise and distinct from other competing claim(s), establishing an organizing structure that clarifies the relationship between various claim(s), counterclaims, reasons, and evidence. Students then examine the claim(s) and counterclaims without bias, pointing out the strengths and flaws of both sides in response to readers' forthcoming objections. Students choose words, phrases, and clauses that connect ideas, improve cohesion, and explain the relationships between claim(s) and reasons, reasons and evidence, and claim(s) and counterclaims. Students accomplish all the preceding through writing that is formal and objective in style and tone, and follows those rules established for different types of writing in each discipline. Finally, students create for the reader a conclusion that states their key ideas and supports their argument in a way that logically follows from all they said prior to the conclusion.

- What argument are you making about this topic or text?
- What alternate or counter claims do you include? And do you treat these fairly and develop them fully?
- What evidence do you provide to support your claim(s)?
- How would you describe the tone and style of your writing in this piece? Objective? Formal?
- How do the ideas in your concluding statement or section logically follow from all that you said prior to the conclusion?

11–12 English Language Arts

Gist: Craft arguments to support claims, analyzing complex texts or topics, all of which students support with sound reasoning and evidence that is both appropriate and adequate. Students begin by introducing a specific, insightful claim(s), which should be precise and distinct from other competing claim(s), establishing their importance and an organizing structure that imposes a logical sequence on and clarifies the relationship between various claim(s), counterclaims, reasons, and evidence. Students then examine the claim(s) and counterclaims in depth, providing only the most pertinent evidence for both sides while pointing out the strengths and flaws of each in anticipation of readers' knowledge, objections, opinions, and biases. Students vary their syntax and choose words, phrases, and clauses that connect ideas, improve cohesion, and reveal the relationships between claim(s) and reasons, reasons and evidence, and claim(s) and counterclaims. Students accomplish all the preceding through writing that is formal and objective in style and tone, following those rules established for different types of writing in each discipline. Finally, students create for the reader a conclusion that states their key ideas and supports their argument in a way that logically follows from all they said prior to the conclusion.

- What argument are you making about this topic or text?
- What alternate or counter claims do you include? And are your claims knowledgeable, precise, and substantive?
- What evidence do you provide to support your claim(s)—and is it the most relevant?
- How would you describe the tone and style of your writing in this piece? Objective? Formal?
- How do the ideas in your concluding statement or section logically follow from all that you said prior to the conclusion?

Writing 1: Write arguments to support claims in an analysis of substantive topics or texts, using valid reasoning and relevant and sufficient evidence.

9–10	Social Studies, Science, and Technical Subjects

Write arguments focused on *discipline-specific content.*

a. Introduce precise claim(s), distinguish the claim(s) from alternate or opposing claims, and create an organization that establishes clear relationships among the claim(s), counterclaims, reasons, and evidence.

b. Develop claim(s) and counterclaims fairly, supplying data and evidence for each while pointing out the strengths and limitations of both claim(s) and counterclaims in a discipline-appropriate form and in a manner that anticipates the audience's knowledge level and concerns.

c. Use words, phrases, and clauses to link the major sections of the text, create cohesion, and clarify the relationships between claim(s) and reasons, between reasons and evidence, and between claim(s) and counterclaims.

d. Establish and maintain a formal style and objective tone while attending to the norms and conventions of the discipline in which they are writing.

e. Provide a concluding statement or section that follows from or supports the argument presented.

11–12	Social Studies, Science, and Technical Subjects

Write arguments focused on *discipline-specific content.*

a. Introduce precise, **knowledgeable** claim(s), **establish the significance of the claim(s),** distinguish the claim(s) from alternate or opposing claims, and create an organization that **logically sequences** the claim(s), counterclaims, reasons, and evidence.

b. Develop claim(s) and counterclaims fairly **and thoroughly,** supplying **the most relevant** data and evidence for each while pointing out the strengths and limitations of both claim(s) and counterclaims in a discipline-appropriate form that anticipates the audience's knowledge level, concerns, **values, and possible biases**.

c. Use words, phrases, and clauses **as well as varied syntax** to link the major sections of the text, create cohesion, and clarify the relationships between claim(s) and reasons, between reasons and evidence, and between claim(s) and counterclaims.

d. Establish and maintain a formal style and objective tone while attending to the norms and conventions of the discipline in which they are writing.

e. Provide a concluding statement or section that follows from or supports the argument presented.

---

* These broad types of writing include many subgenres. See Appendix A for definitions of key writing types.

Source: Copyright © 2010. National Governors Association Center for Best Practices and Council of Chief State School Officers. All rights reserved.

What the **Student** Does

Social Studies, Science, and Technical Subjects

Gist: Craft arguments about discipline-specific content, which students support with sound reasoning and evidence that is both appropriate and adequate. Students begin by introducing a specific claim(s), which should be precise and distinct from other competing claim(s), establishing an organizing structure that clarifies the relationship between various claim(s), counterclaims, reasons, and evidence. Students then examine the claim(s) and counterclaims without bias, pointing out the strengths and flaws of both sides in response to readers' forthcoming objections. Students choose words, phrases, and clauses that connect ideas, improve cohesion, and explain the relationships between claim(s) and reasons, reasons and evidence, and claim(s) and counterclaims. Students accomplish all the preceding through writing that is formal and objective in style and tone, and follows those rules established for different types of writing in each discipline. Finally, students create for the reader a conclusion that states their key ideas and supports their argument in a way that logically follows from all they said prior to the conclusion.

- What argument are you making about this topic or text?
- What alternate or counter claims do you include? And do you treat these fairly and develop them fully?
- What evidence do you provide to support your claim(s)?
- How would you describe the tone and style of your writing in this piece? Objective? Formal?
- How do the ideas in your concluding statement or section logically follow from all that you said prior to the conclusion?

Social Studies, Science, and Technical Subjects

Gist: Craft arguments about discipline-specific content, which students support with sound reasoning and evidence that is both appropriate and adequate. Students begin by introducing a specific, insightful claim(s), which should be precise and distinct from other competing claim(s), establishing their importance and an organizing structure that imposes a logical sequence on and clarifies the relationship between various claim(s), counterclaims, reasons, and evidence. Students then examine the claim(s) and counterclaims in depth, providing only the most pertinent evidence for both sides while pointing out the strengths and flaws of each in anticipation of readers' knowledge, objections, opinions, and biases. Students vary their syntax and choose words, phrases, and clauses that connect ideas, improve cohesion, and reveal the relationships between claim(s) and reasons, reasons and evidence, and claim(s) and counterclaims. Students accomplish all the preceding through writing that is formal and objective in style and tone, following those rules established for different types of writing in each discipline. Finally, students create for the reader a conclusion that states their key ideas and supports their argument in a way that logically follows from all they said prior to the conclusion.

- What argument are you making about this topic or text?
- What alternate or counter claims do you include? And are your claims knowledgeable, precise, and substantive?
- What evidence do you provide to support your claim(s)—and is it the most relevant?
- How would you describe the tone and style of your writing in this piece? Objective? Formal?
- How do the ideas in your concluding statement or section logically follow from all that you said prior to the conclusion?

What the **Teacher** Does

To develop students' ability to write arguments in their discipline, do the following:

- Provide students with a range of sample arguments so they learn to distinguish between effective and ineffective arguments.
- Have students read whole papers to see how writers use claims and evidence over the course of the whole text.
- Use structured note-taking formats (e.g., columns with headers such as claim, reason, evidence) in the early stages to help students understand the elements and see how they work together to support the argument.
- Give students sets of claims with varying degrees of specificity and insight; ask them to evaluate each by some criteria or arrange them all on a continuum of quality.
- Require students to label the elements of their argument (e.g., claim, evidence, reason), and evaluate the quality of each in light of whatever criteria are most appropriate on that occasion.
- Ask students to provide a list of possible counterclaims, alternative positions, values, or biases to consider when writing their claims or evaluating/responding to those of others.
- Generate questions to help students analyze texts and topics, evidence and reasoning, and claims and counterclaims when developing their claims or supporting them.
- Examine sentences for a variety of style and syntax, especially as these help clarify and emphasize the relationships and general cohesion between the different elements.
- Help students establish and apply criteria for determining the quality of topics and texts, claims and counterclaims, and evidence and reasons.
- Generate words that are appropriate to the tone, topic, and type of argument, as well as the audience, occasion, and purpose; this can be done as a class, in groups, or independently.
- Invite students to use such techniques as backward outlining to assess the logic of their arguments within a paragraph or the whole text.
- Have students investigate how they might use data—statistics, surveys, or other quantitative information—to support their claims; include in this discussion why they should or should not do so.
- Keep and use both professional and student models for subsequent study of what to do—and what *not* to do.
- Develop a guide or scoring rubric based on the Common Core writing standard description for argument.
- Instruct students in how to gather and evaluate evidence when preparing to write (e.g., during the research or prewriting phase).
- Discuss with students the formats and styles used by different disciplines or on special occasions.
- Think aloud about an effective and ineffective model or some portion (e.g., introducing the claims) of the paper; you might display it on a big screen as you walk through it and point out what is and is not effective and why that is.
- Distribute highlighters or crayons, and then ask students to indicate those words that create cohesion by linking or serving as transitions between claims and reasons, reasons and evidence, and claims and counterclaims.

To help your English Language Learners, try this:

- Discuss the *idea* of argument, as it may be a foreign and even troubling concept for many students, given their culture's emphasis on respect for authorities and elders.

Notes

Academic Vocabulary: Key Words and Phrases

Analysis: Dividing ideas, content, or processes into separate elements to examine what it is, how it works, and what it is made from.

Anticipate the audience: Writers must consider how readers will respond and what they will find offensive, confusing, or important.

Argument: Arguments have three objectives: to explain, to persuade, and to mediate conflicts between positions, readers, or ideas. Writers make logical claims—supported with reasons, evidence, and different appeals—to advance their argument(s).

Biases: Writers or readers favor one position over another; such prejudices and values are important for writers to consider or readers to be aware of (in themselves or writers).

Claim: This is a word with many apparent, sometimes confusing iterations: *proposition, assertion, thesis;* sometimes mistaken for same as *argument*. It is not the same as the subject or topic: A claim must be able to be argued and must require defense through evidence. Alternate or opposing claims suggest other, sometimes contradictory, claims one should consider. Effective claims are precise, clear, properly qualified, and affirmative. A thesis statement is the writer's main claim.

Clarify the relationships between claim(s) and reasons: Writers should have a reason for the claim(s) they make. They think X *(the claim) is true because of* Y *(a reason)*. This relationship between claims and reasons should be based on evidence, not opinions or preferences.

Cohesion: One idea or sentence connects to another to create a sense of flow; reasons, claims, evidence, and ideas all work together.

Concluding statement or section: Writers provide some statement or section that connects all the claims and evidence, and then shows how they support the argument presented in the paper or speech.

Distinguish: This means to perceive something as, to explain how something is, or to argue that it is different or distinct from others that seem, on the surface, similar.

Establish the significance of the claim: *Significance* is also sometimes replaced with *substantive;* however, both mean the claim should be important, based on real and thorough knowledge about the subject.

Evidence: Each discipline has its own standards for evidence, but most lists would include quotations, observations, interviews, examples, facts, data, results from surveys and experiments, and, when appropriate, personal experience.

Formal style: Writers use words and tone appropriate for occasion and audience; this includes a more objective tone to suggest some critical distance from the subject or claim.

Norms and conventions of the discipline: Disciplines have their own conventions for style, format, and presentation; this applies to which words and information writers use, to how the writer uses them, and to what tone is used when discussing them.

Organization: This applies to how information and ideas are arranged within the document in general and the paragraphs and sentences in particular. All should be organized to best support the claims made.

Reasons/reasoning: Writers must base their claims and ideas on more than personal preferences or opinions when constructing arguments; reasons demand evidence, information, and logic.

Substantive topics or texts: Writers are expected to be writing about compelling, important ideas or texts that examine big questions meant to challenge the reader.

Syntax: Varied syntax refers to how a writer arranges words, phrases, clauses, and sentences in length, patterns, and word order; such arrangements have both stylistic and rhetorical effects.

Writing 2: Write informative/explanatory texts to examine and convey complex ideas and information clearly and accurately through the effective selection, organization, and analysis of content.

9–10 English Language Arts	*11–12* English Language Arts
Write informative/explanatory texts to examine and convey complex ideas, concepts, and information clearly and accurately through the effective selection, organization, and analysis of content.	Write informative/explanatory texts to examine and convey complex ideas, concepts, and information clearly and accurately through the effective selection, organization, and analysis of content.

9–10 English Language Arts

Write informative/explanatory texts to examine and convey complex ideas, concepts, and information clearly and accurately through the effective selection, organization, and analysis of content.

a. Introduce a topic; organize complex ideas, concepts, and information to make important connections and distinctions; include formatting (e.g., headings), graphics (e.g., figures, tables), and multimedia when useful to aiding comprehension.

b. Develop the topic with well-chosen, relevant, and sufficient facts, extended definitions, concrete details, quotations, or other information and examples appropriate to the audience's knowledge of the topic.

c. Use appropriate and varied transitions to link the major sections of the text, create cohesion, and clarify the relationships among complex ideas and concepts.

d. Use precise language and domain-specific vocabulary to manage the complexity of the topic.

e. Establish and maintain a formal style and objective tone while attending to the norms and conventions of the discipline in which they are writing.

f. Provide a concluding statement or section that follows from and supports the information or explanation presented (e.g., articulating implications or the significance of the topic).

11–12 English Language Arts

Write informative/explanatory texts to examine and convey complex ideas, concepts, and information clearly and accurately through the effective selection, organization, and analysis of content.

a. Introduce a topic; organize complex ideas, concepts, and information **so that each new element builds on that which precedes it to create a unified whole**; include formatting (e.g., headings), graphics (e.g., figures, tables), and multimedia when useful to aiding comprehension.

b. Develop the topic **thoroughly by selecting the most significant and** relevant facts, extended definitions, concrete details, quotations, or other information and examples appropriate to the audience's knowledge of the topic.

c. Use appropriate and varied transitions **and syntax** to link the major sections of the text, create cohesion, and clarify the relationships among complex ideas and concepts.

d. Use precise language, domain-specific vocabulary, **and techniques such as metaphor, simile, and analogy** to manage the complexity of the topic.

e. Establish and maintain a formal style and objective tone while attending to the norms and conventions of the discipline in which they are writing.

f. Provide a concluding statement or section that follows from and supports the information or explanation presented (e.g., articulating implications or the significance of the topic).

* These broad types of writing include many subgenres. See Appendix A for definitions of key writing types.

Source: Copyright © 2010. National Governors Association Center for Best Practices and Council of Chief State School Officers. All rights reserved.

What the **Student** Does

9–10 English Language Arts

Gist: Inform readers about or explain complex ideas, processes, or events in language that is clear, precise, and formal, incorporating and organizing only the essential details, facts, examples, and quotations needed to provide a thorough analysis of the content. Students begin by introducing the topic, organizing any major ideas and information in ways that connect and distinguish between different ideas, using formatting (e.g., headings, sidebars), graphics (e.g., figures and tables), and multimedia to enhance clarity and comprehension. Students then build and refine their topic by selecting those facts that are salient and well suited to the their purpose, while making use, as needed, of other techniques such as extended definitions, concrete details, quotations, and other information or data that may be relevant. Next, students insert a variety of transitions where appropriate to connect ideas and details and improve cohesion and clarity. In addition, students write in the language specific to that discipline, using words with precision to resolve any confusion or make clear what to some is complex. Students accomplish all the preceding through writing that is formal and objective in style and tone, and follows those rules established for different types of writing in each discipline. Finally, students end their paper with a conclusion that logically follows from all that precedes it, discussing the meaning or importance of the topic and their ideas about it.

- What is your subject—and what are you saying about it?
- What ideas, details, or sources are most important to include?
- What are the purpose, audience, and situation for this writing?
- What organizational techniques and supporting transitions do you use to clarify and emphasize your ideas?
- How would you describe the tone and style of your writing? Objective? Formal?
- What are the main ideas you discuss or emphasize in the conclusion—and how do those relate with all that preceded them?

11–12 English Language Arts

Gist: Inform readers about or explain complex ideas, processes, or events in language that is clear, precise, and formal, incorporating and organizing only the essential details, facts, examples, and quotations needed to provide a thorough analysis of the content. Students begin by introducing the topic, organizing any major ideas and information in ways that allow new elements to complement what precedes them and achieve a cohesive whole; they also connect and distinguish between different ideas, using formatting (e.g., headings, sidebars), graphics (e.g., figures and tables), and multimedia to enhance clarity and comprehension. Students then build and refine their topic in depth by choosing only those facts that are most salient and well suited to the their purpose, while making use, as needed, of other techniques such as extended definitions, concrete details, quotations, and other information or data that may be relevant. Next, students insert a variety of transitions and syntax where appropriate to join important sections of the text and improve cohesion and clarity among significant ideas. In addition, students write in the language specific to that discipline, using such devices as metaphor, simile, and analogy to resolve any confusion or make clear what to some is complex. Students accomplish all the preceding through writing that is formal and objective in style and tone, and follows those rules established for different types of writing in each discipline. Finally, students end their paper with a conclusion that logically follows from all that precedes it, discussing the meaning or importance of the topic and their ideas about it.

- What is your subject—and what are you saying about it?
- What ideas, details, or sources are most important to include—and how do those you include build on each other to create a unified whole?
- What criteria should you apply when choosing which facts, details, or other information to include?
- How do you vary the syntax and use transitions to clarify and emphasize your ideas?
- What domain-specific language or figurative speech do you use to manage the complexity of this topic?
- How would you describe the tone and style of your writing? Objective? Formal?
- What are the main ideas you discuss or emphasize in the conclusion—and how do those relate with all that preceded them?

Writing 2: Write informative/explanatory texts to examine and convey complex ideas and information clearly and accurately through the effective selection, organization, and analysis of content.

9–10 Social Studies, Science, and Technical Subjects	11–12 Social Studies, Science, and Technical Subjects
Write informative/explanatory texts, including the narration of historical events, scientific procedures/experiments, or technical processes.	Write informative/explanatory texts, including the narration of historical events, scientific procedures/experiments, or technical processes.
a. Introduce a topic and organize ideas, concepts, and information to make important connections and distinctions; include formatting (e.g., headings), graphics (e.g., figures, tables), and multimedia when useful to aiding comprehension.	a. Introduce a topic and organize complex ideas, concepts, and information **so that each new element builds on that which precedes it to create a unified whole**; include formatting (e.g., headings), graphics (e.g., figures, tables), and multimedia when useful to aiding comprehension.
b. Develop the topic with well-chosen, relevant, and sufficient facts, extended definitions, concrete details, quotations, or other information and examples appropriate to the audience's knowledge of the topic.	b. Develop the topic **thoroughly by selecting the most significant and** relevant facts, extended definitions, concrete details, quotations, or other information and examples appropriate to the audience's knowledge of the topic.
c. Use varied transitions and sentence structures to link the major sections of the text, create cohesion, and clarify the relationships among ideas and concepts.	c. Use varied transitions and sentence structures to link the major sections of the text, create cohesion, and clarify the relationships among **complex** ideas and concepts.
d. Use precise language and domain-specific vocabulary to manage the complexity of the topic and convey a style appropriate to the discipline and context as well as to the expertise of likely readers.	d. Use precise language, domain-specific vocabulary **and techniques such as metaphor, simile, and analogy** to manage the complexity of the topic; convey a knowledgeable stance in a style that responds to the discipline and context as well as to the expertise of likely readers.
e. Establish and maintain a formal style and objective tone while attending to the norms and conventions of the discipline in which they are writing.	e. Provide a concluding statement or section that follows from and supports the information or explanation provided (e.g., articulating implications or the significance of the topic).
f. Provide a concluding statement or section that follows from and supports the information or explanation presented (e.g., articulating implications or the significance of the topic).	

* These broad types of writing include many subgenres. See Appendix A for definitions of key writing types.

Source: Copyright © 2010. National Governors Association Center for Best Practices and Council of Chief State School Officers. All rights reserved.

What the **Student** Does

9–10 Social Studies, Science, and Technical Subjects

Gist: Inform readers about, explain, or narrate complex ideas, historical events, scientific procedures/experiments, or technical processes. Students begin by introducing the topic, organizing any major ideas and information in ways that connect and distinguish between different ideas, using formatting (e.g., headings, sidebars), graphics (e.g., figures and tables), and multimedia to enhance clarity and comprehension. Students then build and refine their topic by selecting those facts that are most salient and well suited to the their purpose, while making use, as needed, of other techniques such as extended definitions, concrete details, quotations, and other information or data that may be relevant. Next, students insert a variety of transitions where appropriate to connect ideas and details and improve cohesion and clarity. In addition, students write in the language specific to that discipline, using words with precision to resolve any confusion or make clear what to some is complex. Students accomplish all the preceding through writing that is formal and objective in style and tone, and follows those rules established for different types of writing in each discipline. Finally, students end their paper with a conclusion that logically follows from all that precedes it, discussing the meaning or importance of the topic and their ideas about it.

- What is your subject—and what are you saying about it?
- What ideas, details, or sources are most important to include?
- What are the purpose, audience, and situation for this writing?
- What organizational techniques and supporting transitions do you use to clarify and emphasize your ideas?
- How would you describe the tone and style of your writing? Objective? Formal?
- What are the main ideas you discuss or emphasize in the conclusion—and how do those relate with all that preceded them?

11–12 Social Studies, Science, and Technical Subjects

Gist: Inform readers about, explain, or narrate complex ideas, historical events, scientific procedures/experiments, or technical processes. Students begin by introducing the topic, organizing any major ideas and information in ways that allow new elements to complement what precedes them and achieve a cohesive whole; they also connect and distinguish between different ideas, using formatting (e.g., headings, sidebars), graphics (e.g., figures and tables), and multimedia to enhance clarity and comprehension. Students then build and refine their topic in depth by choosing only those facts that are most salient and well suited to the their purpose, while making use, as needed, of other techniques such as extended definitions, concrete details, quotations, and other information or data that may be relevant. Next, students insert a variety of transitions and syntax where appropriate to join important sections of the text and improve cohesion and clarity among complex ideas. In addition, students write in the language specific to that discipline, using such devices as metaphor, simile, and analogy to resolve any confusion or make clear what to some is complex. Students accomplish all the preceding through writing that is formal and objective in style and tone, and follows those rules established for different types of writing in each discipline. Finally, students end their paper with a conclusion that logically follows from all that precedes it, discussing the meaning or importance of the topic and their ideas about it.

- What is your subject—and what are you saying about it?
- What ideas, details, or sources are most important to include—and how do those you include build on each other to create a unified whole?
- What criteria should you apply when choosing which facts, details, or other information to include?
- How do you vary the syntax and use transitions to clarify and emphasize your ideas?
- What domain-specific language or figurative speech do you use to manage the complexity of this topic?
- How would you describe the tone and style of your writing? Objective? Formal?
- What are the main ideas you discuss or emphasize in the conclusion—and how do those relate with all that preceded them?

What the **Teacher** Does

To introduce students to informative/explanatory texts, do the following:

- Show them a range of examples—from students, professional writers, or even yourself—so they see what it is that you want them to do and get a sense of what they should include.
- Discuss the contents, conventions, and other elements of the type of informational/explanatory text you want them to write.
- Give students a copy of a sample text and, if possible, display it on a screen so you can annotate portions of it while discussing the writer's decisions and the text's relevant features.

To format and integrate graphics and multimedia into the text, have students do the following:

- Offer direct instruction to the whole class or a smaller group of students who need to learn how to use those features of the word processor or other software applications.
- Give students step-by-step directions or create a link to a web tutorial they can watch if they do not know how.
- Give them samples that show them different types of graphs, tables, and other options they might consider when incorporating information or data into their papers.

To develop their topic with details, examples, and information, have students do the following:

- Work directly with them to generate ideas and gather evidence, data, examples, or other content; then develop with them criteria for how to evaluate and choose the best of the bunch to work into their writing.
- Use sentence stems or templates from a book like *They Say/I Say* (by Graff and Birkenstein) to teach students how to introduce or frame the quotation and then comment on the meaning or importance of that quotation.

To have students use varied transitions to link ideas and create cohesion, do the following:

- Generate with students or provide them a list of transition words and phrases specific to the

type of writing they are doing (e.g., cause–effect, compare–contrast).
- Have students go through their papers once they have a complete draft and highlight the first six words of each sentence; then they can evaluate existing transitions and add others where they would improve clarity and cohesion.

To help students use precise language and academic vocabulary, do the following:

- Direct them to go circle any words in their papers that are abstract, too general, or otherwise ineffective; then have them generate words that could replace weaker words or phrases.
- Generate with the class words they might or should use when writing about a specific subject, procedure, event, or person; this might include specific verbs, nouns, and adjectives for use when, for example, explaining a process or procedure.
- Provide examples of or demonstrate for them how to use other techniques such as metaphors, similes, and analogies.

To establish and maintain the conventions for a discipline, have students do the following:

- Establish for the class the proper tone, format, and other genre conventions for the type of discipline-specific writing assigned.
- Give students a checklist or annotated sample that illustrates all the discipline-specific conventions they must include.

To prepare them to write about historical events, procedures, processes, or complex ideas, have students do the following:

- Discuss the ideas, details, or other contents that they should include to help them generate new ideas about what to say and how to organize it when they begin to write.

To help your English Language Learners, try this one thing:

- Break the process down into stages, providing students with examples and instruction at each stage before moving on to the next to ensure they understand and are doing the work correctly.

Academic Vocabulary: Key Words and Phrases

Analogy: Writers show how two things are similar to explain a foreign or complex idea to a reader. Analogies are a form of argument: The writer attempts to convince others the connection is true.

Audience's knowledge of the topic: This phrase emphasizes clarity in writing; thus, if a writer ignores the audience's lack or excess of knowledge about a topic, he or she risks confusing or insulting them.

Cohesion: This refers to how well things stick together to create a clear flow from one idea to the next. Generally, the beginning of a sentence should clearly connect to the words at the end of the previous sentence as the writing unfolds.

Complex ideas: Since students will be writing about an idea from multiple perspectives or drawing evidence from multiple sources to support their claims about a text or subject, writing about such complex ideas, which are often abstract, poses unique challenges.

Concrete details: This refers to specific details that refer to actual objects or places; it is the difference between Thomas Jefferson declaring the British guilty of "repeated injuries and usurpations" and listing the crimes committed by the British under its "absolute Tyranny" against the American colonies in the Declaration of Independence.

Distinctions: Writers distinguish between different ideas, characters, plot developments, or any other details to reveal those that contribute most to the work's meaning.

Domain-specific vocabulary: When writing about any topic or text in a specific subject, writers must explain or describe it using the language of that discipline if they are to be accurate and precise.

Explanatory texts: Such texts are defined by their objective: to explain to or to inform the audience about a topic using facts and an objective tone; the writer's role here is to report what he or she sees.

Extended definitions: Transcend basic definitions by discussing the qualities, history, value, and purpose of whatever they are defining; also, often assign synonyms for the subject being defined.

Formatting: Today's technology allows writers to emphasize ideas, connections, or other details through headers, fonts (style, size, and typeface), color, graphics, and spatial arrangement on the page.

Graphics: This includes tables and graphs, charts and images, and infographics, which incorporate many graphic elements to represent the complexity of a process, an idea, or an event.

Metaphor: This is one thing used to mean or represent another by comparing them in ways that are imaginative.

Norms and conventions of the discipline: Each discipline supplies requirements about how to write about and format documents in that particular subject. Literary analysis papers are written in the present tense; scientific papers have prescribed sections that must all be included and indicated with proper subheadings.

Objective tone: The purpose of informational writing is to inform or explain but not persuade. An objective tone maintains a distance from its subject, interjecting no emotions about the subject.

Selection, organization, and analysis of content: Writers choose the most important facts and details about the subject, organizing them to achieve a clear objective, then analyzing how those elements relate to one another and the larger idea of the paper in general, while also analyzing what each detail contributes to the meaning of that text.

Simile: The writer creates a new meaning by comparing one thing explicitly to another using *like*, *as*, or *as though*. Similes are less emphatic as a consequence of using *like* or *as*, which are indirect.

Transitions: They connect one sentence or idea to another, allowing writers to express the nature or importance of the relationship between those two ideas.

Writing 3: Write narratives to develop real or imagined experiences or events using effective technique, well-chosen details, and well-structured event sequences.

9–10 English Language Arts

Write narratives to develop real or imagined experiences or events using effective technique, well-chosen details, and well-structured event sequences.

a. Engage and orient the reader by setting out a problem, situation, or observation, establishing one or multiple point(s) of view, and introducing a narrator and/or characters; create a smooth progression of experiences or events.

b. Use narrative techniques, such as dialogue, pacing, description, reflection, and multiple plot lines, to develop experiences, events, and/or characters.

c. Use a variety of techniques to sequence events so that they build on one another to create a coherent whole.

d. Use precise words and phrases, telling details, and sensory language to convey a vivid picture of the experiences, events, setting, and/or characters.

e. Provide a conclusion that follows from and reflects on what is experienced, observed, or resolved over the course of the narrative.

11–12 English Language Arts

Write narratives to develop real or imagined experiences or events using effective technique, well-chosen details, and well-structured event sequences.

a. Engage and orient the reader by setting out a problem, situation, or observation **and its significance**, establishing one or multiple point(s) of view, and introducing a narrator and/or characters; create a smooth progression of experiences or events.

b. Use narrative techniques, such as dialogue, pacing, description, reflection, and multiple plot lines, to develop experiences, events, and/or characters.

c. Use a variety of techniques to sequence events so that they build on one another **to create a coherent whole and build toward a particular tone and outcome (e.g., a sense of mystery, suspense, growth, or resolution).**

d. Use precise words and phrases, telling details, and sensory language to convey a vivid picture of the experiences, events, setting, and/or characters.

e. Provide a conclusion that follows from and reflects on what is experienced, observed, or resolved over the course of the narrative.

9–10 Social Studies, Science, and Technical Subjects

(Not applicable)

11–12 Social Studies, Science, and Technical Subjects

(Not applicable)

* These broad types of writing include many subgenres. See Appendix A for definitions of key writing types.

Source: Copyright © 2010. National Governors Association Center for Best Practices and Council of Chief State School Officers. All rights reserved.

What the **Student** Does

9–10 English Language Arts

Gist: Construct narratives—fictional, biographical, and autobiographical—that describe real or imagined experiences or events from the student's own or others' lives. Students first report a problem, situation, or observation, establishing the different perspectives the story will examine through the narrator(s) and/or character(s), in a logical progression from one event or experience to the next. Students then develop these experiences, events, or characters through techniques such as dialogue, setting, plots (sometimes multiple plot lines), sensory details, flashbacks, and characterization. Students also arrange details and events into a logical sequence that allows ideas and events to complement each other as the story unfolds to create a coherent whole. Students choose words and phrases carefully, selecting words that evoke the experience or the sense of place and people involved. Students end the narrative in a satisfying logical way that connects all its elements, while allowing the writer to reflect on the events, experiences, or observations described in the narrative.

- What problem, situation, or observation do you report—and from what point of view?
- How do you arrange the elements of the story—and to what end?
- What language is most appropriate for this story, occasion, audience, and purpose?
- What precise details or other aspects of this experience are important to include in the story?
- How should you end this story so you provide readers with insight and a satisfying conclusion?

11–12 English Language Arts

Gist: Construct narratives—fictional, biographical, and autobiographical—that describe real or imagined experiences or events from the student's own or others' lives. Students first report a problem, situation, or observation, establishing its importance and the different perspectives the story will examine through the narrator(s) and/or character(s), in a logical progression from one event or experience to the next. Students then develop these experiences, events, or characters through techniques such as dialogue, setting, plots (sometimes multiple plot lines), sensory details, flashbacks, and characterization, all of which combine to create a distinct tone and effect, such as mystery or surprise. Students also arrange details and events into a logical sequence that allows ideas and events to complement each other as the story unfolds to create a coherent whole. Students choose words and phrases carefully, selecting words that evoke the experience or the sense of place and people involved. Students end the narrative in a satisfying logical way that connects all its elements, while allowing the writer to reflect on the events, experiences, or observations described in the narrative.

- What problem, situation, or observation do you report—and from what point of view?
- How do you arrange the elements of the story—and to what end?
- What language is most appropriate for this story, occasion, audience, and purpose?
- How do the elements of this story combine to create a tone or outcome such as surprise, growth, or resolution?
- How should you end this story so you provide readers with insight and a satisfying conclusion?

9–10 Social Studies, Science, and Technical Subjects

The Common Core State Standards states that "writ[ing] narratives to develop real or imagined experiences or events" is "not applicable."

11–12 Social Studies, Science, and Technical Subjects

The Common Core State Standards states that "writ[ing] narratives to develop real or imagined experiences or events" is "not applicable."

What the **Teacher** Does

To have students write narratives about real or imagined experiences, do the following:

- Have students read a diverse sampling of narratives similar to and slightly different from the sort you want them to write.
- Guide students through the process of creating a story map, storyboard, or other graphic form that allows them to identify, discuss, and arrange the different events or scenes in the story.
- Generate with students or provide a list of the elements of an effective narrative of the story you are assigning.
- Consider allowing students to incorporate images in their narrative if they are appropriate and complement the narrative.

To have students set out a problem or create a situation in a narrative, do the following:

- Have students establish a problem up front that the story will examine and the protagonist will solve after a series of scenarios richly imagined.
- Ask students to imagine a situation in rich detail (perhaps one inspired by another book they have read or a subject or era they studied), and then describe how characters (or they, if it is a personal narrative) responded and changed over the course of the story.
- Lead students through the creation of a detailed observation about an event, process, or experience, guiding them by examples and questions that prompt them to add sensory details; then generate with them questions they should ask and apply to their narrative as they write the second part, which comments on the meaning or importance of what they observed.
- Have students describe the same event or experience from multiple perspectives to explore how point of view affects one's perception of an idea, event, or era or the people involved.

To have students introduce or develop a narrator or characters in a narrative, do the following:

- Help students develop questions that not only portray the character's physical persona but also reveal the character's personality and motivations within the context of the story.
- Provide students with a list of archetypal characters as a starting place to help them imagine their own.
- Ask students, when writing personal narratives that involve people they know, to fill in a graphic organizer with boxes like what the person says, does, thinks, and feels prior to writing.

To have students use a range of narrative techniques to engage the reader, do the following:

- Introduce students to different plot lines and story structures, including the traditional linear format (exposition, rising action, conflict, falling action, and resolution) as well as more episodic or lyric narrative formats that string a series of impressions together as a way of telling story about a person, an event, or an experience.
- Have students analyze the dialogue and other techniques used in the stories they study for ideas they can use in their own.

To have students sequence events in a coherent way throughout a narrative, do the following:

- Have students write on sticky notes or index cards key events or scenes in the narrative they are creating; then ask them to arrange them in different ways, stopping to explain to others what they are thinking, until they find the sequence that best works with the story they are trying to tell.
- Have students use a presentation software program to create the story as a series of slides, with notes and images on the slides so they can manipulate and better understand the elements of their story.

To help your English Language Learners, try this one thing:

- Give students the opportunity to draw the story first as a cartoon strip with notes and captions and dialogue, in their own language if they prefer, before asking them to write the story; if possible, give them the chance to tell their story before writing it.

Academic Vocabulary: Key Words and Phrases

Coherent whole: This refers to the degree to which all the parts of the story hold together to create a complete picture of the events reported.

Conclusion: One always looks for some *point* or ideas one can draw from a story; otherwise, why tell it? Conclusions in narrative tales are often more subtle than other forms, which have more specific structure about where and how to conclude the story.

Description: Stories rely on precise, detailed descriptions of people, places, and events to bring them alive in vivid ways that convey the emotions and capture the reader's imagination.

Develop (experiences, events, or characters): When one develops, for example, characters in a story, one describes them in detail, adding specific details that bring the character alive; such development must also reflect the person, place, or events moving through time and, as a result, changing if they are to seem real.

Event sequences: How the writer arranges the events in a story directly affects how the story affects readers; some events create tension, mystery, and surprise; others create humor, nostalgia, and wonder.

Growth: Characters evolve over the course of a story in response to events; dynamic or round characters are fully developed and grow in response to the people and events in the story.

Mystery: Narratives about people reveal aspects of our human nature—the good and bad elements of it—that often cause readers to feel a sense of wonder or dismay about the mysterious nature of humans.

Narrative: This is a story one tells, whether in prose or verse, a novel or a play, or even an epic poem. A narrative can be fictional or grounded in facts, such as an autobiographical or historical narrative.

Pacing: This is the speed at which the action unfolds or the story is told; pacing affects the tone, mood, and atmosphere of the story, instilling in readers a feeling of anxiety, nostalgia, despair, or excitement.

Plot line: This is the sequence of events that makeup the story; complex narratives often have several plot lines, some intersecting to create tension in or otherwise help to develop the main plot line.

Points of view: From whose perspective do we experience the story? Do we get the first-person point of view (I, me, my), second-person point of view (you, your), or third-person (he, his, them) point of view? How does the point of view affect our response to or the meaning of the story?

Real or imagined experience: Narratives that are imagined are fictional (novels, plays, poems, and fairy tales); those that are real are based on personal or historical records (memoirs or autobiographies).

Resolution: Also known as the falling action or dénouement, the resolution falls near the end of the story and involves all the conflicts and problems explored throughout the story. Complex literary narratives involve multiple conflicts or plot lines that culminate in often surprising, unpredictable resolutions.

Sensory language: This evokes a place, person, or situation through its use of smells, sounds, textures, and other such rich details.

Setting out a problem, situation, or observation: This appears near the front where it can establish a problem or situation that the story then traces to show how the characters solve or respond to over the course of the story. Some narrative genres, such as fairy tales, state the problem as one of the conventions of that genre.

Technique: This reminds us that literary narratives are carefully crafted to create certain emotional impacts on the reader; to study the writer's technique is to study how his or her work affects the reader.

Tone: This is tone of voice; another word for this is *attitude*, as in one's tone of voice reveals his or her personality or feelings about certain events, details, or characters in the story.

Writing 4: Produce clear and coherent writing in which the development, organization, and style are appropriate to task, purpose, and audience.

9–10 | English Language Arts

Produce clear and coherent writing in which the development, organization, and style are appropriate to task, purpose, and audience. (Grade-specific expectations for writing types are defined in writing standards 1–3.)

11–12 | English Language Arts

Produce clear and coherent writing in which the development, organization, and style are appropriate to task, purpose, and audience. (Grade-specific expectations for writing types are defined in writing standards 1–3 above.)

9–10 | Social Studies, Science, and Technical Subjects

Produce clear and coherent writing in which the development, organization, and style are appropriate to task, purpose, and audience.

11–12 | Social Studies, Science, and Technical Subjects

Produce clear and coherent writing in which the development, organization, and style are appropriate to task, purpose, and audience.

Source: Copyright © 2010. National Governors Association Center for Best Practices and Council of Chief State School Officers. All rights reserved.

What the **Student** Does

9–10 English Language Arts

Gist: Write with clarity and coherence in a style that is appropriate to the assignment, objective, and audience, arranging and developing their ideas with that end in mind. Grade 9–10 students strive to achieve these qualities with all the different types of writing—argument, information/explanatory, and narrative—discussed in writing standards 1–3.

- What are the topic and the task of this writing assignment?
- What is your purpose: to inform, explain, argue, or entertain?
- How best to organize details to achieve clarity and coherence so as to fully address the task, purpose, and audience?
- Which words, transitions, and sentence styles offer the greatest clarity and coherence as related to your purpose?
- Which examples, details, quotations, or evidence are most appropriate to your task, topic, and purpose?

11–12 English Language Arts

Gist: Write with clarity and coherence in a style that is appropriate to the assignment, objective, and audience, arranging and developing their ideas with that end in mind. Grade 11–12 students strive to achieve these qualities with all the different types of writing—argument, information/explanatory, and narrative—discussed in writing standards 1–3.

- What are the topic and the task of this writing assignment?
- What is your purpose: to inform, explain, argue, or entertain?
- How best to organize details to achieve clarity and coherence so as to fully address the task, purpose, and audience?
- Which words, transitions, and sentence styles offer the greatest clarity and coherence as related to your purpose?
- Which examples, details, quotations, or evidence are most appropriate to your task, topic, and purpose?

9–10 Social Studies, Science, and Technical Subjects

Gist: Write with clarity and coherence in a style that is appropriate to the assignment, objective, and audience, arranging and developing their ideas with that end in mind.

- What are the topic and the task of this writing assignment?
- What is your purpose: to inform, explain, argue, or entertain?
- How best to organize details to achieve clarity and coherence so as to fully address the task, purpose, and audience?
- Which words, transitions, and sentence styles offer the greatest clarity and coherence as related to your purpose?
- Which examples, details, quotations, or evidence are most appropriate to your task, topic, and purpose?

11–12 Social Studies, Science, and Technical Subjects

Gist: Write with clarity and coherence in a style that is appropriate to the assignment, objective, and audience, arranging and developing their ideas with that end in mind.

- What are the topic and the task of this writing assignment?
- What is your purpose: to inform, explain, argue, or entertain?
- How best to organize details to achieve clarity and coherence so as to fully address the task, purpose, and audience?
- Which words, transitions, and sentence styles offer the greatest clarity and coherence as related to your purpose?
- Which examples, details, quotations, or evidence are most appropriate to your task, topic, and purpose?

What the **Teacher** Does

To have students produce writing that is clear and coherent, do the following:

- Establish for students first what these terms mean and why they are important to good writing by showing them models from different writers.
- Direct students to highlight or underline the subject of each sentence in their narrative; once they have done this, ask them to find all abstract subjects or long compound subjects and replace these with concrete subjects that fit the actions of the sentence.
- Determine the extent to which all the sentences in a paragraph and the larger piece itself work together to make one coherent whole; think of each sentence as a piece in a larger puzzle that should, when assembled, make sense.

To have students ensure that their writing is effectively organized, do the following:

- Make clear—or ask students to do the same—the task, purpose, and occasion for this writing; then have students assess these to determine the best way to organize, present, and develop the topic in the paper.
- Provide students with a variety of organizational structures to choose from, helping them to evaluate each in light of their purpose, the task, the audience, and the occasion.
- Have students create some sort of map, outline, or plan before writing to improve the organization of the writing; if students already have a draft, ask them to create a reverse outline that is based on the draft of the text they already wrote.

To develop students' ideas to the fullest effect, have students do the following:

- Gather and incorporate into the writing examples, details, data, information, or quotations that illustrate or support their ideas.
- Explain what the examples, details, data, information, or quotations mean and why they are important in relation to the main idea or claim they are developing.

- Consider integrating graphs, tables, charts, images, or infographics of some other sort to illustrate and reinforce some point students are trying to make.

To have students produce clear and coherent writing, have students do the following:

- Determine who the audience for the piece of writing will be, including their biases, current knowledge, expectations, and assumptions so they can anticipate and respond appropriately to the audience's concerns and questions about your topic.
- Have students evaluate the task and all related directions to be sure students know what they must do, include, or avoid in this piece of writing.
- Establish purpose—to convey ideas, events, and findings by choosing and explaining the behavior, meaning, or importance of key details. Draw from a range of sources, including primary and secondary sources; write to extend readers' knowledge or acceptance of ideas and procedures.

To have students determine what style is most appropriate to the occasion, do the following:

- Show students samples from different authors or agencies so they see what real language and formats look like in this discipline for this type of text, purpose, and audience.
- Talk with students about beginning with the end in mind—the impression you hope to make or end you hope to achieve—and ask what choices they need to make about style and organization in light of their purpose.

To help your English Language Learners, try this one thing:

- Meet individually with your ELL students to ensure they have time and opportunity to talk about the assignment and their needs as they try to write it.

Academic Vocabulary: Key Words and Phrases

Audience: This is considered an essential part of the rhetorical situation when writing. Key considerations include who the audience is, what they already know or need to learn to understand the writer's message, and how the audience is likely to respond to what you write. What biases do they have that you must anticipate and address if you are to effectively advance your argument?

Clear: Clarity is a fundamental quality of good writing. Writers achieve such clarity by choosing precise words and joining them in logical ways through grammar that further enhances the clarity of the ideas expressed. They achieve this clarity by using concrete or specific nouns or subjects instead of abstractions; also, they include verbs that express actions and avoid unnecessary use of passive voice, which often undermines clarity in writing.

Coherent: Think of your words and sentences as building blocks in a larger structure, such as a wall or fort; all work together to form a strong, stable structure that serves a purpose; coherent writing, where each word and sentence adds to the larger whole of the text, creates a sense of clarity.

Development: Includes everything from examples and quotations, to details and other forms of evidence used to support and illustrate whatever the writer is saying about the subject. All such forms of development should extend, clarify, or otherwise enhance the writer's claims. Development can also come in the form of figures, tables, or images that add more information or further illustration.

Organization: No one approach or strategy is appropriate for organizing ideas in academic writing; what matters is that there is a clear, appropriate, logical, and effective structure to the ideas. One can arrange information from new to old, least to most important, areas of agreement to areas of disagreement, or more traditional forms such as spatial, sequential, and solution among others. Also important are the transitional phrases or words used to signal organizational shifts.

Purpose: This generally means that a writer simply has *something* she is trying to accomplish through this piece; the writer's purpose also intersects with and is shaped by the rhetorical situation (occasion, topic, and audience). The most common purposes are to persuade, to inform/explain, to entertain, or to inspire.

Style: To speak of style is to discuss how the writing sounds, how it moves, and how it feels when one reads or hears it read; it involves the words and how those words are joined to others to form patterns of sound and meaning in the service of some larger idea or purpose, so that the style complements and helps the writer to achieve their purpose.

Task: Whatever the directions tell the writer to do is the "task." Directions might ask the student to read one or more texts, drawing from them the details and examples necessary to support their argument about a subject, or the task might ask students to write a letter to the editor in which they take a position for or against a certain controversial subject, such as banning sodas in school or changing the age at which one can apply for a driver's license.

Notes

Writing 5: Develop and strengthen writing as needed by planning, revising, editing, rewriting, or trying a new approach.

9–10 English Language Arts

Develop and strengthen writing as needed by planning, revising, editing, rewriting, or trying a new approach, focusing on addressing what is most significant for a specific purpose and audience. (Editing for conventions should demonstrate command of Language Standards 1–3 up to and including grades 9–10 on page 54 of the full CCSS document.)

11–12 English Language Arts

Develop and strengthen writing as needed by planning, revising, editing, rewriting, or trying a new approach, focusing on addressing what is most significant for a specific purpose and audience. (Editing for conventions should demonstrate command of Language Standards 1–3 up to and including grades 11–12 on page 54 of the full CCSS document.)

9–10 Social Studies, Science, and Technical Subjects

Develop and strengthen writing as needed by planning, revising, editing, rewriting, or trying a new approach, focusing on addressing what is most significant for a specific purpose and audience.

11–12 Social Studies, Science, and Technical Subjects

Develop and strengthen writing as needed by planning, revising, editing, rewriting, or trying a new approach, focusing on addressing what is most significant for a specific purpose and audience.

Source: Copyright © 2010. National Governors Association Center for Best Practices and Council of Chief State School Officers. All rights reserved.

What the **Student** Does

9–10 English Language Arts

Gist: Plan, revise, edit (for clarity, concision, correctness), rewrite portions or all of a paper as needed, or try a new method, technique, or strategy, addressing those aspects of a given piece which matter most to your purpose and audience in the context of this writing task. Students know their command of Language Standards 1–3 up through grades 9–10 as spelled out on page 54 of the original CCSS document.

* What are your subject, purpose, audience, and task for this piece of writing?
* Which planning methods will help you most for this paper: outlining, chunking, brainstorming, using index cards or sticky notes (so you can play with arrangement of ideas?
* What are the most pressing editing needs for this paper: content, clarity, concision, cohesion, coherence, or correctness?
* What other approaches will satisfy the needs of your audience and achieve your purpose?

11–12 English Language Arts

Gist: Plan, revise, edit (for clarity, concision, correctness), rewrite portions or all of a paper as needed, or try a new method, technique, or strategy, addressing those aspects of a given piece which matter most to your purpose and audience in the context of this writing task. Students know their command of Language Standards 1–3 up through grades 11–12 as spelled out on page 54 of the original CCSS document.

* What are your subject, purpose, audience, and task for this piece of writing?
* Which planning methods will help you most for this paper: outlining, chunking, brainstorming, using index cards or sticky notes (so you can play with arrangement of ideas?
* What are the most pressing editing needs for this paper: content, clarity, concision, cohesion, coherence, or correctness?
* What other approaches will satisfy the needs of your audience and achieve your purpose?

9–10 Social Studies, Science, and Technical Subjects

Gist: Plan, revise, edit (for clarity, concision, correctness), rewrite portions or all of a paper as needed, or try a new method, technique, or strategy, addressing those aspects of a given piece that matter most to your purpose and audience in the context of this writing task.

* What are your subject, purpose, audience, and task for this piece of writing?
* Which planning methods will help you most for this paper: outlining, chunking, brainstorming, using index cards or sticky notes (so you can play with arrangement of ideas?
* What are the most pressing editing needs for this paper: content, clarity, concision, cohesion, coherence, or correctness?
* What other approaches will satisfy the needs of your audience and achieve your purpose?

11–12 Social Studies, Science, and Technical Subjects

Gist: Plan, revise, edit (for clarity, concision, correctness), rewrite portions or all of a paper as needed, or try a new method, technique, or strategy, addressing those aspects of a given piece that matter most to your purpose and audience in the context of this writing task.

* What are your subject, purpose, audience, and task for this piece of writing?
* Which planning methods will help you most for this paper: outlining, chunking, brainstorming, using index cards or sticky notes (so you can play with arrangement of ideas?
* What are the most pressing editing needs for this paper: content, clarity, concision, cohesion, coherence, or correctness?
* What other approaches will satisfy the needs of your audience and achieve your purpose?

What the **Teacher** Does

To improve students' ability to plan prior to beginning to write, do the following:

- Provide opportunities for generative conversations about the text, topic, or task *before* they begin to write about it; if possible, have them capture all ideas on posters, whiteboards, sticky notes, or other means, and then post them to an online site they can access later for further reference or even addition.
- Show students how you or professional writers prepare to write by either demonstrating live in front of them or providing examples of such notes and plans by major writers, many of which are available through the *Paris Review*.
- Expose them to a range of planning strategies—mapping, outlining, sticky notes or index cards, apps or features of Microsoft Word you use—and then let them choose the one or ones that suit their ways of working best.

To improve students' capacity to revise, edit, or rewrite, do the following:

- Require them to focus on one specific aspect of the writing that would lead to improved clarity and comprehension by the audience; for example, students could revise the structure of the paper to improve the reader's ability to navigate and understand your complex ideas that are now brought into greater focus through the use of subheadings.
- Teach students specific aspect of editing—concision, for example—and then, after modeling for students (perhaps by using a portion of a student's paper); ask them to apply the techniques by cutting 50, 100, or more words (depending on the length).
- Ask them to go through their paper and, after reading each sentence, ask of that sentence (and their ideas), "So what?" If the next sentence does not answer that question, look for ways to rewrite the sentence or paragraph so that it does explain why any idea, quotation, or claim matters or what it means.
- After first modeling for the class, have students read one another's papers, stopping at any point to jot

a question in the margin about some aspect of the writing that they do not understand (e.g., "How does this relate to the previous sentence?").

To help students develop and try new approaches to a writing task, do the following:

- Show them what it means to rewrite the same story, event, or process by either modeling it for them live, bringing in several different versions of a paper about the same topic, or sharing samples from writers who tried the same method.
- Provide students with, for example, a list of different approaches to writing an introduction; then direct them to choose two or three of these techniques and write as many different introductions, each one in a style or voice very different from the others; these they should share with peers for feedback on which is most effective.

To develop students' ability to focus on what is most significant, do the following:

- Give them a graphic organizer of some sort (e.g., one shaped like a target) that is designed to establish a focus to which all parts of the essay should connect in some substantial way.
- Have students write a reverse outline based on the essay's current content and organization.
- Ask students to determine what question their essay seeks to answer; then go through their draft and ask what question each paragraph attempts to answer and how that question relates to the overarching question they are trying to answer in the paper.

To help your English Language Learners, try this one thing:

- Have them turn their entire paper into a sentence outline in the word processing program to examine the relationship between each sentence or paragraph and those that precede them, revising as necessary to improve the focus and flow of the paper.

Notes

Academic Vocabulary: Key Words and Phrases

Audience: Whether the audience is known (the teacher, the class, the school, or the local community) or unknown (a prospective employer, anyone who visits the class blog, or a wiki), students must consider who that audience is and what they do and do not know before writing.

Conventions: These are rules that apply to and govern the genre, format, grammar, and other aspects of writing this paper, including spelling.

Develop: Refers to the process one follows to improve a piece of writing before one even sets words down on paper, that is, such steps as gathering and generating ideas for the writing, taking time to outline, brainstorm, or map one's ideas. Once those ideas are down in a rough draft, development means seeking for better words, editing out unnecessary words, or improving clarity and cohesion by tightening the sentences.

Editing: When students rewrite the paper to make it more concise, coherent, or cohesive, they are editing; when one looks for and fixes spelling and mechanics, they are proofreading. Editing can and, with more fluent writers, does take place throughout the composing process, not just at the end, as with proofreading.

New approach: At some point, the writer may feel the current approach—the voice, the style, the perspective, or the stance—is not effective, at which point it makes sense to write the whole piece over in some new style, different format, or alternate perspective to better convey one's ideas to the audience on this occasion.

Planning: Students can do many things to plan: outline ideas, gather and generate ideas, and block off the main ideas before refining them into an outline or making concept maps, mind maps, brainstorms to generate and make connections between ideas. Some make lists of what they need to do, read, or include; all should review the assignment requirements repeatedly throughout the planning process to make sure they include all they should.

Purpose: We always have some purpose when we write, whether it is to persuade, inform, entertain, or inspire. It is essential that they know what it is they are trying to achieve (and for whom and under what circumstances) before they even begin to write as their purpose influences everything from the words and structures they choose to the media and formats they use. Even when the writing task is assigned or outlined on a timed writing exam, it is crucial that students learn to identify the purpose and approach the writing with that in mind as they plan, draft, edit, and revise their papers.

Revising: This does not mean, as some think, merely correcting or proofreading a paper. To *revise* is to re*see*, to consider the paper or idea from a whole new angle or hear a different way to express an idea or emotion. Revising the paper should improve not just the clarity and cohesion but also the content as the writer strives to strengthen the arguments, the logic, and the style.

Rewriting: Student writers sometimes need to take a whole paper or some portion of it and rewrite it in light of what they learn after getting that first draft down. Sometimes used interchangeably with *revising*, this phase of the writing process involves not tweaking or polishing up what is there but replacing it with new ideas or language better suited to the audience, the purpose, or the occasion.

Strengthen: This is what revising for concision, clarity, and coherence does to the writing: It strengthens it by tightening the wording, refining the argument, removing what is unnecessary so you can emphasize key ideas, reasoning, or evidence.

Notes

Writing 6: Use technology, including the Internet, to produce and publish writing and to interact and collaborate with others.

9–10 English Language Arts	**11–12** English Language Arts
Use technology, including the Internet, to produce, publish, and update individual or shared writing products, taking advantage of technology's capacity to link to other information and to display information flexibly and dynamically.	Use technology, including the Internet, to produce, publish, and update individual or shared writing products **in response to ongoing feedback, including new arguments or information.**
9–10 Social Studies, Science, and Technical Subjects	**11–12** Social Studies, Science, and Technical Subjects
Use technology, including the Internet, to produce, publish, and update individual or shared writing products, taking advantage of technology's capacity to link to other information and to display information flexibly and dynamically.	Use technology, including the Internet, to produce, publish, and update individual or shared writing products **in response to ongoing feedback, including new arguments or information.**

Source: Copyright © 2010. National Governors Association Center for Best Practices and Council of Chief State School Officers. All rights reserved.

What the **Student** Does

9–10 English Language Arts

Gist: Use technology to compose, investigate, generate, and organize ideas, as well as to format and add functions or features that aid and engage readers by making the written work interactive and readable. Students incorporate into these texts digital features such as hotlinks, embedded video, visual explanations (e.g., graphs, diagrams, charts), and elements of design (e.g., fonts, colors, layouts) that add not only style but also substance, using either document design software or web-based applications to compose papers, blogs, wikis, and social media, while also allowing students to collaborate on, provide feedback about, and publish their compositions.

- What is your topic? Purpose? Audience? Occasion?
- What application, device, or other digital tools would enhance your efforts to inform, explain, entertain, or argue?
- Which features—links, video, graphics, other media or design features—should you use in this document to improve its clarity and effectiveness?
- How can you use technology to collaborate with or respond to others?
- Where, when, and how should you consider publishing or sharing this digital composition?

11–12 English Language Arts

Gist: Use technology to compose, investigate, generate, and organize ideas, as well as to format and add functions or features that aid and engage readers. Students include digital features such as hotlinks, embedded video, visual explanations (e.g., graphs, diagrams, charts), and elements of design (e.g., fonts, colors, layouts) that add not only style but also substance. Students incorporate new ideas, arguments, or perspectives into their writing, applying digital tools that allow them to collaborate on, provide and respond to feedback about, and publish their papers, blogs, or other digital compositions through social media.

- What application, device, or other digital tools would enhance your efforts to inform, explain, entertain, or argue?
- What new arguments, information, or viewpoints should you consider adding to this composition?
- Which features—links, video, graphics, other media or design features—should you use in this document to improve its clarity and effectiveness?
- How can you use technology to collaborate with or respond to others?
- Where, when, and how should you consider publishing or sharing this digital composition?

9–10 Social Studies, Science, and Technical Subjects

Gist: Use technology to compose, investigate, generate, and organize ideas, as well as to format and add functions or features that aid and engage readers by making the written work interactive and readable. Students incorporate into these texts digital features such as hotlinks, embedded video, visual explanations (e.g., graphs, diagrams, charts), and elements of design (e.g., fonts, colors, layouts) that add not only style but also substance, using either document design software or web-based applications to compose papers, blogs, wikis, and social media, while also allowing students to collaborate on, provide feedback about, and publish their compositions.

- What is your topic? Purpose? Audience? Occasion?
- What application, device, or other digital tools would enhance your efforts to inform, explain, entertain, or argue?
- Which features—links, video, graphics, other media or design features—should you use in this document to improve its clarity and effectiveness?
- How can you use technology to collaborate with or respond to others?
- Where, when, and how should you consider publishing or sharing this digital composition?

11–12 Social Studies, Science, and Technical Subjects

Gist: Use technology to compose, investigate, generate, and organize ideas, as well as to format and add functions or features that aid and engage readers. Students include digital features such as hotlinks, embedded video, visual explanations (e.g., graphs, diagrams, charts), and elements of design (e.g., fonts, colors, layouts) that add not only style but also substance. Students incorporate new ideas, arguments, or perspectives into their writing, applying digital tools that allow them to collaborate on, provide and respond to feedback about, and publish their papers, blogs, or other digital compositions through social media.

- What application, device, or other digital tools would enhance your efforts to inform, explain, entertain, or argue?
- What new arguments, information, or viewpoints should you consider adding to this composition?
- Which features—links, video, graphics, other media or design features—should you use in this document to improve its clarity and effectiveness?
- How can you use technology to collaborate with or respond to others?
- Where, when, and how should you consider publishing or sharing this digital composition?

What the **Teacher** Does

To have students use technology to produce, publish, and collaborate, do the following:

- Provide direct instruction as needed in the use of any devices, platforms, applications, or software for a given assignment.
- Ensure that students can access and use the technology as you intend or expect (e.g., if you say they must collaborate through an online discussion group, do all have access and know-how?).
- Display, when possible, the contents of your own screen via a projector so they can follow along or check their work against yours if you are guiding them through a sequence of steps.
- Prepare ahead of time as needed (e.g., checking to see that the lab printer is working and loaded with paper) so that you will not lose instructional time.

To have students use the Internet to produce writing, do the following:

- Explore different online applications designed to help students generate, organize, and develop their ideas.
- Create links to specific resources you want students to visit for content to incorporate into their paper; such content might include primary source documents, images, or applications students can use to create infographics for their papers.
- Instruct students in the use of free programs such as Google Docs or various graphics applications that they can use to produce their texts or develop content to embed in those texts.

To have students use technology to produce writing, do the following:

- Look for ways for students to use technology— computers, tablets, displays, interactive whiteboards, document cameras—that are efficient, effective, and appropriate to the writing task.
- Evaluate the writing assignment for small but worthwhile opportunities that allow you to teach students additional features of word processing (e.g.,

how to embed images, how to design the page so text flows around images, how to insert headers), graphic design (e.g., infographics, images, layout), or even multimedia formatting (e.g., how to embed a slide show or a video clip in a written document that would be read on a screen).

To have students use the Internet to publish writing, do the following:

- Consider carefully the options and implications of publishing student work (especially if it contains images or any copyrighted material) online.
- Try setting up a class blog to which all can contribute in one place to make it easier to maintain, monitor, and model how to use.
- Take those extra steps, when publishing for all the world to see, to ensure that the writing is correct, appropriate, and formatted according to the platform to which they are publishing.

To have students use technology, including the Internet, to interact or collaborate, do the following:

- Set up a group or collaborative space online (via Google Docs, a wiki site, or any other platform that allows users to create a password-protected space) where they can meet to discuss and respond to one another's ideas and writing in or outside of class.
- Gather useful links—to applications, primary source sites, exhibits, or other rich resources related to a paper they are writing—which they explore together in class or at home during the process of gathering and generating ideas for writing.

To help your English Language Learners, try this one thing:

- Make sure they have access to and know how to use the platform, application, software, computer, or tablet you are assuming all students have at home and know how to use in the ways you have assigned.

Notes

Academic Vocabulary: Key Words and Phrases

Capacity to link to other information: This is done by embedding hotlinks that connect a word or image, when clicked, to content within or outside the website one is currently viewing.

Collaborate: Students work together to come up with ideas for their writing or respond to one another's papers using features like Comments (Google Docs) or Track Changes (Microsoft Word).

Display information flexibly and dynamically: Information written for digital displays—computers, smartphones, tablets, computers, and televisions—affords the writer an array of formats and features. Flexibly and dynamically suggest that writers embed images and graphics as alternatives or supplements to words and incorporate more dynamic forms, such as embedded video, slide shows, or other interactive visuals available to those writing on and for computers.

Feedback: This includes comments from the teacher or classmates about writing provided through recorded voice memos, features such as Microsoft Word's Track Changes, or annotations of any sort offered through tablet applications that allow the reader to offer feedback via voice, digital highlighters, digital sticky notes, or annotations written on the digital document itself.

Interact: Students collaborate in a written dialogue online through chat groups, social media, e-mail, and other such interactive platforms to generate ideas about a text they are analyzing, a paper they are writing, or a topic they are exploring (prior to writing). Thus, they are using technology to facilitate and extend discussions, generate ideas, provide feedback to peers' papers, or write and share their writing with others for feedback or publication.

New arguments: These new arguments would come in response to either critical readers who suggest other perspectives and ideas or the writer's continued research online about the subject during which new ideas, evidence, or arguments surface that merit being included in the paper or other document the student is writing.

Ongoing feedback: *Throughout the entire composing process* students receive—from one or more sources—ideas about how they can improve some aspect of whatever they are writing.

Produce: This means using a range of technology tools—computers, applications, digital cameras to capture images or make videos, instruments for scientific data gathering, software, and advanced calculators for mathematics—to generate the content and help students write.

Publish: Use computers to publish and distribute quality materials around school, the community, or online.

Technology: This refers to using computers to compose, revise, and correct any papers; also, this implies using applications to gather or generate data, evidence, or content (in the form of quantitative information, examples, graphic displays, and still and video images) to incorporate into the paper itself. Technology is also an essential research tool for writers: the Internet in general, as well as specialized databases and other online resources. Using technology also means writing with and for a range of forms, formats, and features: essays, blogs, wikis, websites, multimedia presentations, or digital essays using the full spectrum of available digital features (color, size, hotlinks, and embedded media) to communicate or publish the work for audiences to read on smartphones, tablets, computers, presentation screens—and, of course, paper.

Writing products: Given the emphasis here on the use of technology, such products would include not only the traditional papers students write, but also such new and emerging forms as blogs, wikis, websites, Tweets, presentations, and multimedia or hybrid texts.

Notes

_____

_____

_____

_____

Research to Build and Present Knowledge

Writing 7: Conduct short as well as more sustained research projects to answer a question (including a self-generated question) or solve a problem; narrow or broaden the inquiry when appropriate; synthesize multiple sources on the subject, demonstrating understanding of the subject under investigation.

9–10 English Language Arts

Conduct short as well as more sustained research projects to answer a question (including a self-generated question) or solve a problem; narrow or broaden the inquiry when appropriate; synthesize multiple sources on the subject, demonstrating understanding of the subject under investigation.

11–12 English Language Arts

Conduct short as well as more sustained research projects to answer a question (including a self-generated question) or solve a problem; narrow or broaden the inquiry when appropriate; synthesize multiple sources on the subject, demonstrating understanding of the subject under investigation.

9–10 Social Studies, Science, and Technical Subjects

Conduct short as well as more sustained research projects to answer a question (including a self-generated question) or solve a problem; narrow or broaden the inquiry when appropriate; synthesize multiple sources on the subject, demonstrating understanding of the subject under investigation.

11–12 Social Studies, Science, and Technical Subjects

Conduct short as well as more sustained research projects to answer a question (including a self-generated question) or solve a problem; narrow or broaden the inquiry when appropriate; synthesize multiple sources on the subject, demonstrating understanding of the subject under investigation.

Source: Copyright © 2010. National Governors Association Center for Best Practices and Council of Chief State School Officers. All rights reserved.

Common Core Writing Standard 7

What the **Student** Does

9-10 English Language Arts

Gist: Investigate topics, problems, or questions posed by others or generated themselves as part of a short or a more extended research project, limiting or extending the scope of their inquiry as needed. Students examine different sources or perspectives on the subject, first showing they understand, then synthesizing those different sources about the topic they are investigating.

- What is the subject of your inquiry—and what are you trying to discover about it?
- What questions should you ask when researching this topic?
- How might you refine or narrow your search for information or sources related to this topic?
- What new ideas or connections can you derive from the different sources you have read, viewed, or examined?

11-12 English Language Arts

Gist: Investigate topics, problems, or questions posed by others or generated themselves as part of a short or a more extended research project, limiting or extending the scope of their inquiry as needed. Students examine different sources or perspectives on the subject, first showing they understand, then synthesizing those different sources about the topic they are investigating.

- What is the subject of your inquiry—and what are you trying to discover about it?
- What questions should you ask when researching this topic?
- How might you refine or narrow your search for information or sources related to this topic?
- What new ideas or connections can you derive from the different sources you have read, viewed, or examined?

9-10 Social Studies, Science, and Technical Subjects

Gist: Investigate topics, problems, or questions posed by others or generated themselves as part of a short or a more extended research project, limiting or extending the scope of their inquiry as needed. Students examine different sources or perspectives on the subject, first showing they understand, then synthesizing those different sources about the topic they are investigating.

- What is the subject of your inquiry—and what are you trying to discover about it?
- What questions should you ask when researching this topic?
- How might you refine or narrow your search for information or sources related to this topic?
- What new ideas or connections can you derive from the different sources you have read, viewed, or examined?

11-12 Social Studies, Science, and Technical Subjects

Gist: Investigate topics, problems, or questions posed by others or generated themselves as part of a short or a more extended research project, limiting or extending the scope of their inquiry as needed. Students examine different sources or perspectives on the subject, first showing they understand, then synthesizing those different sources about the topic they are investigating.

- What is the subject of your inquiry—and what are you trying to discover about it?
- What questions should you ask when researching this topic?
- How might you refine or narrow your search for information or sources related to this topic?
- What new ideas or connections can you derive from the different sources you have read, viewed, or examined?

Part 2 | Writing **111**

What the **Teacher** Does

To have students conduct short as well as more sustained research projects, do the following:

- Organize units of study around a big idea, an essential question, or a cultural conflict; these might be framed as inquiries into long-standing arguments that provide students opportunities to formulate a response to or take a stand on the subject, which they then gather evidence to support.
- Identify key questions or problems students can investigate in some depth within the constraints of a class period, using their findings when writing, speaking, or interviewing someone about that subject. Students might, for example, investigate a specific aspect of the Holocaust to generate questions for a speaker coming the following day and about whom they will write a subsequent paper combining biographical and historical content.

To have students answer questions (including self-generated questions) or solve problems, do the following:

- Discuss with students the process you or respected writers, scientists, historians, economists, and others go through to discover a subject, and then ask questions or identify problems related to that subject for their inquiry.
- Pass out sticky notes to all in the class; then ask them to list a subject on the top of the note that relates to the text or topic the class is studying; then tell them to write a question about that text or topic that could be developed into a compelling paper. Finally, have them stick all the notes on the front board and let the whole class examine them as part of the process of learning to ask questions and solve problems in the papers they write.

To have students narrow or broaden an inquiry into a subject, have students do the following:

- Begin by restating their topic, task, inquiry, or problem as a question, making it as specific as they can (i.e.,

What is the question their paper is trying to answer?).
- Narrow their inquiry (into a question or problem) by adding words and phrases that specifically relate to actions and relationships: *contribution, definition, cause, conflict, evolution,* and *interaction.*
- Extend or broaden their inquiry by investigating what others have found in the past and how that changed the understanding of that subject in the field, or ask questions about the internal history of the subject (e.g., how has our perception or attitude toward ____ changed over the last decade—and why?) to connect it to the larger questions within the field.
- Broaden or narrow their topic or problem by making room in students' inquiry for alternative or opposing perspectives on your topic or text; some might call this exploring the dialectic nature of any topic or text students might study.

To have students synthesize multiple sources on a subject, do the following:

- Ask students to identify key ideas, terms, perspectives, or arguments across sources; then guide them through the process, providing models as needed, of analyzing these connections to find some idea, question, or problem that links them all and is worth investigating.
- Have students note a set of quotations or specific examples about an idea or problem that is examined by all these texts; then draw from those quotations some conclusion about the "real problem" or the "question no one is asking" about this subject.

To help your English Language Learners, try this one thing:

- Clarify what *synthesis* means and how to do it; but also, take time to make sure they first comprehend the texts since students cannot synthesize different texts if they do not first understand them.

Notes

Academic Vocabulary: Key Words and Phrases

Demonstrating understanding of the subject: Students show the depth of their knowledge and their research skills by gathering a range of quality information, data, evidence, and examples related to the problem, question, or topic they are investigating; they then demonstrate what they have learned by choosing the most salient details and examples and using those to support their claims in a coherent, logical manner throughout the paper.

Narrow or broaden the inquiry: As students begin to investigate a question, problem, or topic, they often encounter information that suggests they open up the inquiry a bit to allow for more perspectives or possible ideas to explore; at other times, they feel overwhelmed by all the information they find on a topic and would be better served by narrowing an inquiry to a more refined or specific question or topic about which they can make a reasonable claim.

Questions (includes self-generated questions): Researchers generate their own or investigate others' questions about a topic of substance; such questions are often the driving purpose of the research: *We are investigating X to determine how X leads to Y.*

Research (short and more sustained): Students and teachers are engaged in research any time they seek information about a question or subject, or ask themselves or others questions about causes, types, effects, meaning, and importance of anything they find themselves studying for class or their interests. Short or brief inquiries might involve getting some background knowledge on an author, a book, or a period; in science, search for and consider previous findings for certain experiments; in social studies, digging up primary sources to see how people thought about an event at that time or opinion pieces in different newspapers to measure the response to

an event (e.g., dropping of the atomic bomb) from different parts of the country or the world. Longer, more sustained research projects demand far more depth and many more sources from different perspectives. It is a fundamental skill for success in college, one's career, and at home as a consumer who must increasingly take responsibility for researching the best health care program, insurance policy, or cell phone provider.

Solve a problem: This is fundamental to the research task or process to answering some question—as a scientist, a historian, an economist, a consumer, or just a curious person. Embedded within this process are such skills as generating questions (to help frame or refine the problem), gathering data and possible solutions, and evaluating and choosing those solutions for which one finds the greatest support and evidence during one's research.

Subject under investigation: This refers to the topic, the research question, or the problem the student seeks to understand and develop an argument about after completing the research. This subject can come from students themselves or from a teacher or institution (e.g., college board or the students' state or district) who requires students to study in depth a sustained or a brief research project.

Synthesize multiple sources: Any genuine research project of any substance must consider the subject from different and competing angles if it is to arrive at any meaningful or significant insight. Also, one must consider multiple sources, some of which offer counterarguments or alternative perspectives if their claims and arguments are to be considered reliable, valid, and substantial. Of course, these sources must all come from established, trustworthy sources if they are to be cited or used to support one's claims.

Notes

Writing 8: Gather relevant information from multiple print and digital sources, assess the credibility and accuracy of each source, and integrate the information while avoiding plagiarism.

9–10 English Language Arts

Gather relevant information from multiple authoritative print and digital sources, using advanced searches effectively; assess the usefulness of each source in answering the research question; integrate information into the text selectively to maintain the flow of ideas, avoiding plagiarism and following a standard format for citation.

11–12 English Language Arts

Gather relevant information from multiple authoritative print and digital sources, using advanced searches effectively; assess the **strengths and limitations** of each source **in terms of the task, purpose, and audience**; integrate information into the text selectively to maintain the flow of ideas, avoiding plagiarism **and overreliance on any one source** and following a standard format for citation.

9–10 Social Studies, Science, and Technical Subjects

Gather relevant information from multiple print and digital sources, using search terms effectively; assess the credibility and accuracy of each source; and quote or paraphrase the data and conclusions of others while avoiding plagiarism and following a standard format for citation.

11–12 Social Studies, Science, and Technical Subjects

Gather relevant information from multiple authoritative print and digital sources, using advanced searches effectively; assess the **usefulness of each source in answering the research question; integrate information into the text selectively to maintain the flow of ideas**, avoiding plagiarism and following a standard format for citation.

Source: Copyright © 2010. National Governors Association Center for Best Practices and Council of Chief State School Officers. All rights reserved.

What the **Student** Does

9–10 English Language Arts

Gist: Search for and collect credible, useful information from a range of established sources, including print and digital, observations and interviews, evaluating a source's value based on its authority and relevance to the question students are trying to answer or the problem they are trying to solve. Students then incorporate the information from their sources into their paper or report, selecting and arranging this information to maintain the flow of the text and its ideas and citing all their sources correctly according to the established format so they avoid plagiarism.

- What is the research question or the problem you will investigate?
- What types of sources will you use and what are the criteria for choosing and evaluating the quality of those sources?
- What alternative or advanced search techniques should you consider using for this research question?
- Where and how can you most effectively and seamlessly integrate information, evidence, or quotations into the text without hampering the flow of ideas or your writing style?
- What passages should be cited so as to avoid any possible allegations of plagiarism?

11–12 English Language Arts

Gist: Search for and collect credible, useful information from a range of established sources, including print and digital, evaluating each source's strengths and flaws in relation to the task, purpose, and audience, as well as the source's value based on its authority and relevance to the question students are trying to answer or the problem they are trying to solve. Students then incorporate the information from their sources into their paper or report, taking care not to depend too much on a single source while selecting and arranging this information to maintain the flow of the text and its ideas and citing all their sources correctly according to the established format so they avoid plagiarism.

- What is the research question or the problem you will investigate?
- What types of sources will you use and what are the criteria for choosing and evaluating the quality of those sources?
- What are the strengths and limitations of the different sources you used—and how do these relate to the task, the purpose, or the audience?
- Where and how can you most effectively and seamlessly integrate information, evidence, or quotations into the text without hampering the flow of ideas or your writing style?
- What passages should be cited so as to avoid any possible allegations of plagiarism?

9–10 Social Studies, Science, and Technical Subjects

Gist: Search for and collect credible, useful information from a range of established sources, including print and digital, observations and interviews, evaluating a source's value based on its authority and relevance to the question students are trying to answer or the problem they are trying to solve. Students then incorporate the information from their sources into their paper or report, selecting and arranging this information to maintain the flow of the text and its ideas and citing all their sources correctly according to the established format so they avoid plagiarism.

- What is the research question or the problem you will investigate?
- What types of sources will you use and what are the criteria for choosing and evaluating the quality of those sources?
- What alternative or advanced search techniques should you consider using for this research question?
- Where and how can you most effectively and seamlessly integrate information, evidence, or quotations into the text without hampering the flow of ideas or your writing style?
- What passages should be cited so as to avoid any possible allegations of plagiarism?

11–12 Social Studies, Science, and Technical Subjects

Gist: Search for and collect credible, useful information from a range of established sources, including print and digital, evaluating each source's ability help answer the research question in relation to the task, purpose, and audience, as well as the source's value based on its authority and relevance to the question students are trying to answer or the problem they are trying to solve. Students then incorporate the information from their sources into their paper or report, taking care not to depend too much on a single source while selecting and arranging this information to maintain the flow of the text and its ideas and citing all their sources correctly according to the established format so they avoid plagiarism.

- What is the research question or the problem you will investigate?
- What types of sources will you use and what are the criteria for choosing and evaluating the quality of those sources?
- How can you determine the value of the sources—and how do these relate to the research question?
- Where and how can you most effectively and seamlessly integrate information, evidence, or quotations into the text without hampering the flow of ideas or your writing style?
- What passages should be cited so as to avoid any possible allegations of plagiarism?

What the **Teacher** Does

To have students gather relevant information, do the following:

- Begin by first asking students to define the problem they are trying to solve or the question they are investigating.
- Present students with criteria you develop for—or with—them, or that are provided by other audiences for this assignment.
- Give or create with your students an effective means of collecting information, details, examples, data, and all other content for subsequent integration into their paper.

To have students find relevant information from multiple print and digital sources, do the following:

- Expose students to all the available sources—both print and multimedia—they can or must use for this paper, presentation, or project; then explain to them which one they should use for different purposes or content related to their inquiry.
- Collaborate with your school librarian to visit the library for an orientation session focusing on what print and digital resources are available for a specific project; such content might include primary source documents, images, or databases.
- Provide students with a print edition of an article about a topic; then set them up to trace the same story across media to see how each treats it differently, taking time throughout that process to teach them how to read and synthesize the meaning from these different sources and integrate that content into their papers.

To have students assess the credibility and accuracy of each source, do the following:

- Instruct students in the questions they should ask to determine the credibility of any content but especially sources found online.
- Create a structured note-taking handout students can use to determine the credibility of any sources they are evaluating; this note-taking sheet could double as a way of gathering citation information for future works cited on paper.

To have students integrate information without impeding the flow of the writing, do the following:

- Demonstrate for students how to take only the relevant portion of any quotation and incorporate it into their sentences as evidence to support their ideas.
- Distinguish between direct and indirect quotations so they have the option of choosing the one that interferes least with the flow of their writing.
- Provide students with a range of samples illustrating the different ways one can integrate quotations of different lengths using punctuation (e.g., ellipses and brackets), formatting (e.g., block quotations), paraphrasing, or indirect quotations.

To have students avoid plagiarism when choosing and integrating sources, do the following:

- Illustrate for your students the difference between the proper integration and citation of sources in a paper and the improper use (i.e., plagiarism) of such sources.
- Direct students, once they have a complete or even final draft, to highlight *all* content, in whatever form or from whatever source that comes from a source other than themselves; then guide them through the process of determining whether it is properly cited to avoid any allegations of plagiarism.
- Encourage students to submit papers to such services as turnitin.com *before* submitting their final papers for further screening to be sure they identify all sources they should cite.

To help your English Language Learners, try this one thing:

- Talk with them about and take extra pains to ensure they understand the concept of plagiarism and its consequences as some English Language Learners come from countries where it is not considered plagiarism (or an offense) to use the words of others, often well-known writers and scholars, as their own.

Notes

Academic Vocabulary: Key Words and Phrases

Accuracy: The information is true, current, and precise whenever it is used as evidence for a claim or support for a hypothesis; the measurements use the appropriate terms for that subject or discipline to ensure maximum clarity and accuracy of reference.

Assess: Of all the information your search yields or all the quotations and data points you *could* include in your paper, which should you use based on your criteria or research question?

Authoritative sources: These are established sources affiliated with recognized publishers, reputable universities, or respected authors.

Citation: These come in two formats and locations within the paper: in-text parenthetical citations (where the student quotes another's work) and at the end of the paper, in the works cited section that lists all works referred to in the paper. Which format you use (e.g., APA, MLA) depends on the field and the teacher's preferences.

Credibility: This is a measure of the believability of the writer or source of information, based on how current, established, and relevant the source is, as well as the *ethos* of the writer and any source cited.

Flow of ideas: Using such devices as transitional phrases and conjunctions, the writer links one idea to those that precede or follow it to ensure the ideas and logic of the text hold together and complement each other in ways that do not impede the argument the writer is developing. When tables, graphs, or other figures are embedded in the text, writers use captions or other techniques.

Gather relevant information: Information is only relevant to the degree that it answers the research question or supports an argument the writer makes; all else should be left out or dismissed as irrelevant. This is why it is so important to have a carefully conceived, clear, and narrow research question or problem one is reading to answer or solve: Then you know which information is most useful or relevant.

Integrate information into the text selectively to maintain flow: To weave the quotations, examples, details, or evidence into the paper through paraphrase or indirect or direct quotation, students need not include every word of a source when quoting it directly; instead, they embed it in their own sentence in a way (through the use of ellipses to indicate omissions and brackets to signal additions) that maintains or enhances the flow of the text and ideas.

Multiple print and digital sources: Legitimate researchers consider a wide array of sources from different perspectives and in different media to be as thorough as possible in their analysis of the subject.

Overreliance on any one source: When researching a subject, students cannot rely on a few select sources that conveniently offer them a wealth of quotations or evidence. They need to reference (and make use of) a variety of sources that represent different perspectives and stances on the issue or question they are researching if their observations, conclusions, and arguments are to be credible.

Plagiarism: Most often this means including another's words as your own (without using quotation marks); those words can be copied from a famous writer, website, or a fellow student. It is *not* plagiarism to use an author's words so long as you cite them and put quotation marks around those words being quoted.

Standard format for citation: This means MLA style for humanities citations, APA format for others, and various specialized formats for specific scientific papers and disciplines.

Strengths and limitations of each source: Some sources may have particularly good data about one issue but not another; when assessing or quoting sources, it is vital to be aware of the quality and reputation of that source on this subject. A source may, for example, offer quality data about technology and teens but not be weak when it comes to looking at technology and different cultural groups.

Writing 9: Draw evidence from literary or informational texts to support analysis, reflection, and research.

9–10 English Language Arts

Draw evidence from literary or informational texts to support analysis, reflection, and research.

   a. Apply grades 9–10 Reading standards to literature (e.g., "Analyze how an author draws on and transforms source material in a specific work [e.g., how Shakespeare treats a theme or topic from Ovid or the Bible or how a later author draws on a play by Shakespeare]").

   b. Apply grades 9–10 Reading standards to literary nonfiction (e.g., "Delineate and evaluate the argument and specific claims in a text, assessing whether the reasoning is valid and the evidence is relevant and sufficient; identify false statements and fallacious reasoning").

11–12 English Language Arts

Draw evidence from literary or informational texts to support analysis, reflection, and research.

   a. Apply grades **11–12** Reading standards to literature (e.g., **"Demonstrate knowledge of eighteenth-, nineteenth- and early-twentieth-century foundational works of American literature, including how two or more texts from the same period treat similar themes or topics"**).

   b. Apply grades **11–12** Reading standards to literary nonfiction (e.g., "Delineate and evaluate the **reasoning in seminal U.S. texts, including the application of constitutional principles and use of legal reasoning [e.g., in U.S. Supreme Court Case majority opinions and dissents] and the premises, purposes, and arguments in works of public advocacy [e.g.,** *The Federalist,* **presidential addresses]").**

9–10 Social Studies, Science, and Technical Subjects

Draw evidence from informational texts to support analysis, reflection, and research.

11–12 Social Studies, Science, and Technical Subjects

Draw evidence from informational texts to support analysis, reflection, and research.

Source: Copyright © 2010. National Governors Association Center for Best Practices and Council of Chief State School Officers. All rights reserved.

What the **Student** Does

9–10 English Language Arts

Gist: Gather evidence—quotations, examples, information—from literary or informational texts to back up students' claims or explanations when analyzing, reflecting on, or researching a topic or text. Students draw such evidence for their claims by applying grades 9–10 Reading Standards to literature so they can, for example, show how an author such as Shakespeare adapts or adopts stories and ideas from Ovid, the Bible, or certain myths. In addition, students collect evidence for their ideas by applying grades 9–10 Reading Standards to literary nonfiction such as Malcolm Gladwell's *Outliers* in order to analyze and assess the arguments and specific claims the author makes, evaluating the validity and relevance of the author's reasoning and evidence to determine if any of the claims are false or the reasoning is fallacious.

- What are the appropriate sources to consider for evidence to support any analysis, reflection, or research related to your purpose or claim?
- Which literary sources (e.g., Bible, Shakespeare, myths) does the author use, in what way, and to what end in this literary text?
- What is the author's argument or specific claim in this literary nonfiction text?
- What evidence, from which sources, does the author use—and how reliable, logical, and persuasive is it?

11–12 English Language Arts

Gist: Gather evidence—quotations, examples, information—from literary or informational texts to back up students' claims or explanations when analyzing, reflecting on, or researching a topic or text. Students draw such evidence for their claims by applying grades 11–12 Reading Standards to literature, for example, comparing how several 18th- to early-20th-century foundational American literary works handle related ideas or questions. In addition, students collect evidence for their ideas by applying grades 11–12 Reading Standards to literary nonfiction, examining the reasoning of seminal U.S. texts, and majority and dissenting opinions in Supreme Court cases which apply constitutional principles and legal reasoning. In addition, students similarly scrutinize the premises, purposes, and arguments used by authors to advocate for the public interest like *The Federalist* or presidential addresses.

- What are the appropriate sources to consider for evidence to support any analysis, reflection, or research related to your purpose or claim?
- Which foundational works of American literature from the 18th through early 20th century does the author use to examine a topic or theme from different perspectives?
- What constitutional principles or legal reasoning do these authors apply to these seminal U.S. texts or Supreme Court cases?
- What are the various premises, purposes, and arguments the authors use in the service of their argument?

9–10 Social Studies, Science, and Technical Subjects

Gist: Gather evidence—quotations, examples, information—from informational texts to back up students' claims or explanations when analyzing, reflecting on, or researching a topic or text. Students draw such evidence for their claims from different informational sources, analyzing and assessing the arguments and specific claims the authors make, evaluating the validity and relevance of the authors' reasoning and evidence to determine if any of the claims are false or the reasoning is fallacious.

- What are the appropriate sources to consider for evidence to support any analysis, reflection, or research related to your purpose or claim?
- What is the author's argument or specific claim in this informational text?
- What evidence, from which sources, does the author use—and how reliable, logical, and persuasive is it?
- What criteria are you applying when selecting your evidence?
- How are you using this evidence to support any analysis, reflection, or research related to this topic?

11–12 Social Studies, Science, and Technical Subjects

Gist: Gather evidence—quotations, examples, information—from informational texts to back up students' claims or explanations when analyzing, reflecting on, or researching a topic or text. Students draw such evidence for their claims from different informational sources, analyzing and assessing the arguments and specific claims the authors make, evaluating the validity and relevance of the authors' reasoning and evidence to determine if any of the claims are false or the reasoning is fallacious.

- What are the appropriate sources to consider for evidence to support any analysis, reflection, or research related to your purpose or claim?
- What is the author's argument or specific claim in this informational text?
- What evidence, from which sources, does the author use—and how reliable, logical, and persuasive is it?
- What criteria are you applying when selecting your evidence?
- How are you using this evidence to support any analysis, reflection, or research related to this topic?

What the **Teacher** Does

To have students draw evidence from literary or informational texts, do the following:

- Require students to develop a working thesis or guiding question that gives them some means of evaluating the content of any text they read for useful evidence; without any such question or claim to guide them, readers will have no basis on which to evaluate the examples, findings, data, or quotations for possible use.
- Define and illustrate for students what *counts* as evidence so they know what it looks like and, thus, what to search for; this is particularly important for students learning to assess primary sources and other text types such as multimedia and infographics.
- Require students to annotate or code the texts they read with an eye toward using different elements as evidence in a subsequent paper; thus, for example, the teacher might show them how to put a Q in the margin to indicate, upon rereading later, the location of a possible quotation worth using; those using tablets can teach students how to use digital tools to annotate, search texts for specific words, and capture images for future use.

To have students draw evidence from literary texts to support analysis and more, do the following:

- Help students first learn what and how much of a passage to quote by illustrating the difference between using a full quotation (too long) and one that only uses the relevant portion (just right) and is written in the literary present tense.
- Clarify and illustrate for your students when, how, and why to use direct, indirect, and block quotations to support their thesis.
- Teach students how to use ellipses and brackets to edit quotations for concision and grammatical consistency; also, teach how to punctuate the quotation so that it blends in with the rest of the sentence without undermining their voice or style.

- Show students an exemplary sentence of literary analysis; then give students a claim and quotation from the text, asking them to write their analysis of how the evidence supports their claim; then direct them to make their claim and find their evidence from the text they are analyzing, bringing it all together in one sentence.

To have students draw evidence from informational texts for analysis and more, do the following:

- Introduce them to a wide range of sources of evidence, including examples, statistics, expert opinions, interviews, surveys, observations, experiments, primary source documents, and quotations.
- Establish with students—or apply from another source—specific criteria for selecting evidence, demonstrating how to assess the degree to which all evidence is valid, reliable, relevant, and sufficient.
- Permit and show students how to find and use evidence in different forms—graphs, images, charts, tables, even videos—and then integrate and comment on it to support their claims.

To have students use evidence to support analysis, reflection, and research, do the following:

- Display (on a projection screen and/or a handout) contrasting examples of evidence used to support the writer's ideas, ensuring a continuum of quality; have students evaluate, rank, and discuss.
- Analyze together representative examples of how writers on the opinion page of major newspapers use evidence to support their analysis.

To help your English Language Learners, try this one thing:

- Ensure that these students know and can use the different technical terms related to evidence; then use a color-coding system on the computer to display your own, a student's, or a professional writer's sample so your ELL students see the relationship between the writer's claims, evidence, and reasoning.

Notes

Academic Vocabulary: Key Words and Phrases

Analysis: This is the breaking down of the subject, text, event, or process into its component parts to understand what it means or how it works.

Delineate and evaluate the reasoning: This means to separate out the different reasons and associated evidence behind any claims and to evaluate each claim apart from the others so you can determine, when writing about others' ideas, just how sound they are.

Draw evidence: The word *draw* here means to extract, as in *draw water from a well*; thus, people draw out from all that they read, view, hear, or see about a subject the evidence that best supports their claims.

Evidence: This comes in a variety of forms: quantitative data, observation, quotation, example, and findings from surveys and such queries.

Evidence is relevant and sufficient: The data or examples you draw from the sources must be appropriate and useful for the claim you are making; it must also be adequate (e.g., high quality, complete, or thorough) if it is to be effective, reliable, and credible.

Fallacious reasoning: The reasoning behind your arguments must be based on sound premises; the connection between the claim and evidence used to support that claim should match up, agree; otherwise, you offer fallacies such as the *hasty generalization*.

Foundational works: This includes documents such as the Declaration of Independence or the U.S. Constitution, which were written to define the country and the principles on which it was founded.

Identify: This means to point out, indicate, or otherwise single out; to comment on or analyze, for example, false statements.

Legal reasoning: This is how a particular law or constitutional amendment does or does not apply to a crime or case a student might be studying in history, economics, or government.

Literary and informational texts: Literary text includes fiction, drama, poetry, literary nonfiction, art, and graphic novels; informational texts include essays, articles, infographics, mixed media texts, primary source documents, and seminal and foundational documents.

Literary nonfiction (or creative nonfiction): This includes essays, books, or other nonfiction texts such as biographies, memoirs, histories, or narrative accounts of events that use literary or novelistic techniques such as plot, characterization, and point of view in ways that bring the story, its events, and its characters alive.

Public advocacy: These are texts—often speeches or opinion pieces—that appeared in the newspaper, in which leading figures called for action on an issue or in response to an event.

Seminal U.S. texts: These are texts such as the Gettysburg Address or FDR's Four Freedoms speech that are not policy nor specific calls to action, though they may advocate a position; they are part of the cultural canon of our country and represent our values and past.

Support analysis, reflection, and research: In short, it is urging you to provide evidence or examples to support and illustrate whatever analysis you offer, statement you make while reflecting, or finding you make from your research. The key habit of mind for this standard is to support what you say with sound and relevant evidence.

Transforms source material: When writing a literary analysis, students might claim that an author is alluding to or adapting a biblical story or fairy tale in a particular story or poem; the student needs to provide the evidence from, in such a case, the Bible or fairy tale to support their claim.

Treats a theme or topic: This examines how a writer might take a theme or topic from, for example, a Grimms' fairy tale and adapt it for his or her novel, play, or poem.

Notes

Writing 10: Write routinely over extended times (time for research, reflection, and revision) and shorter time (a single sitting or a day or two) for a range of tasks, purposes, and audiences.

9–10 English Language Arts

Write routinely over extended time frames (time for research, reflection, and revision) and shorter time frames (a single sitting or a day or two) for a range of tasks, purposes, and audiences.

11–12 English Language Arts

Write routinely over extended time frames (time for research, reflection, and revision) and shorter time frames (a single sitting or a day or two) for a range of tasks, purposes, and audiences.

9–10 Social Studies, Science, and Technical Subjects

Write routinely over extended time frames (time for reflection and revision) and shorter time frames (a single sitting or a day or two) for a range of discipline-specific tasks, purposes, and audiences.

11–12 Social Studies, Science, and Technical Subjects

Write routinely over extended time frames (time for reflection and revision) and shorter time frames (a single sitting or a day or two) for a range of discipline-specific tasks, purposes, and audiences.

Source: Copyright © 2010. National Governors Association Center for Best Practices and Council of Chief State School Officers. All rights reserved.

What the **Student** Does

9–10 English Language Arts

Gist: Write regularly for a range of reasons, in different contexts, for different lengths of time, including more sustained efforts that allow students time to research, reflect on, and revise what they write about the topic. Students also write shorter assignments, practicing for or writing actual timed writing assessments. In addition, students summarize, describe, compare, contrast, argue, or narrate, using writing to learn, think, and reflect on their process and performance when they write essays, arguments, opinion pieces, analyses, reports, critiques, and more personal responses and reflections about the ideas they study and the texts they read.

- What are the subject, purpose, audience, and occasion for writing?
- What do you want to say about this topic or text?
- What techniques, tools, or strategies would help you prepare for and write this assignment?
- What questions can help you think and write about this topic, text, or task?

11–12 English Language Arts

Gist: Write regularly for a range of reasons, in different contexts, for different lengths of time, including more sustained efforts that allow students time to research, reflect on, and revise what they write about the topic. Students also write shorter assignments, practicing for or writing actual timed writing assessments. In addition, students summarize, describe, compare, contrast, argue, or narrate, using writing to learn, think, and reflect on their process and performance when they write essays, arguments, opinion pieces, analyses, reports, critiques, and more personal responses and reflections about the ideas they study and the texts they read.

- What are the subject, purpose, audience, and occasion for writing?
- What do you want to say about this topic or text?
- What techniques, tools, or strategies would help you prepare for and write this assignment?
- What questions can help you think and write about this topic, text, or task?

9–10 Social Studies, Science, and Technical Subjects

Gist: Write regularly for a range of reasons, in different contexts, for different lengths of time, including more sustained efforts that allow students time to research, reflect on, and revise what they write about the topic. Students also write shorter assignments, practicing for or writing actual timed writing assessments. In addition, students summarize, describe, compare, contrast, argue, or narrate, using writing to learn, think, and reflect on their process and performance when they write essays, arguments, opinion pieces, analyses, reports, critiques, and more personal responses and reflections about the ideas they study and the texts they read.

- What are the subject, purpose, audience, and occasion for writing?
- What do you want to say about this topic or text?
- What techniques, tools, or strategies would help you prepare for and write this assignment?
- What questions can help you think and write about this topic, text, or task?

11–12 Social Studies, Science, and Technical Subjects

Gist: Write regularly for a range of reasons, in different contexts, for different lengths of time, including more sustained efforts that allow students time to research, reflect on, and revise what they write about the topic. Students also write shorter assignments, practicing for or writing actual timed writing assessments. In addition, students summarize, describe, compare, contrast, argue, or narrate, using writing to learn, think, and reflect on their process and performance when they write essays, arguments, opinion pieces, analyses, reports, critiques, and more personal responses and reflections about the ideas they study and the texts they read.

- What are the subject, purpose, audience, and occasion for writing?
- What do you want to say about this topic or text?
- What techniques, tools, or strategies would help you prepare for and write this assignment?
- What questions can help you think and write about this topic, text, or task?

What the **Teacher** Does

To have students write routinely over extended times, do the following:

- Provide regular opportunities for your students to research and then write about the big ideas, questions, and problems that are central to your class and subject area; such investigations might be major research papers or shorter inquiries into a specific topic related to a unit, a book, or a subject they are studying in class.
- Ask students to reflect on what they learn from a process or experience, how they learn it, and why it matters, or have them reflect on their evolving understanding of ideas, drawing examples and connections from the different units or texts they have studied over the semester.
- Make room in the schedule of any paper for time to revise, thereby fostering a culture of revision, a class where students feel they can try ideas and approaches, knowing they can revise.

To have students write routinely over shorter times, do the following:

- Have students write for a single sitting; such writing includes beginning the period by analyzing a text or writing about a topic the class will examine during that period; pausing *during* class to write about or respond to a text, topic, or procedure the class has been studying for the period up to that point; or wrapping up the period by having students write a summary, synthesis, or response to what they have learned about a topic that day.
- Create opportunities for students to write as a way of building on what they read, viewed, or learned that day in class or the previous night for homework; thus, they might come in having read several chapters or short pieces about a topic, which they then synthesize in a paragraph that draws on the previous night's texts for evidence.

- Allow writing opportunities to extend over several days, each day, for example, culminating in a paragraph of a larger paper the students write over the course of the week, then spend the following week revising.

To have students write for various discipline-specific tasks, do the following:

- Create opportunities for students to produce those forms of writing common to the discipline you teach—reviews in an art class; opinion pieces in a government class; Supreme Court briefs in a history class; and poems, essays, and speeches in English classes—in the context of studying those forms.
- Incorporate the sort of writing practiced by people in your discipline as a way of thinking within the discipline; examples would include having students keep field notes like Lewis and Clark, lab notes such as all scientists use to record their thoughts and procedures, and jots, scribbles, and sketches by everyone from writers and scientists to designers and programmers.

To have students write for various purposes, do the following:

- Require students to write regularly to argue, inform/explain, inspire, and entertain and to deepen and extend their learning, to reflect on their processes or progress, to make connections across texts or ideas the class has studied lately.

To help your English Language Learners, try this one thing:

- Reinforce the lessons and techniques from your class by giving all students—but especially your ELL students—the chance to keep practicing the different types of writing you teach them so the forms and features of these different types can become familiar and these students become fluent, confident academic writers.

Notes

Academic Vocabulary: Key Words and Phrases

Audiences: Students need to write for more than just their teachers; other audiences include classmates, other classes, parents, and local businesses and organizations, as well as those found online through blogs, wikis, social media, and other venues appropriate to students.

Discipline-specific tasks, purposes, and audiences: Each subject area has its own traditional forms as well as those types of writing specific to the academic work of those subjects (e.g., timed essays, summaries, analysis, and more). The emphasis here is on the idea that not all writing in all disciplines is written in the same way for the same reasons. The word *tasks* alludes not only the types of writing but also the ways of thinking when one writes; these are best understood through the verbs: *summarize, synthesize, analyze, narrate, compare, contrast, evaluate, describe*, and so on.

Extended times: These are process papers or otherwise long-term assignments that might take anywhere from one week to more than a month in the event that students are writing major research projects over such an extended period as research papers that draw from a wide array of sources, some of which might be book length and, thus, require such longer times. The reference to "research, reflection, and revision" suggests that students should have time to research a topic, reflect on their process, and revise their work, all of which demand substantial time and instruction.

Purposes: This includes such purposes as to inform, explain, persuade, entertain, and inspire.

Range of tasks, purposes, and audiences: See *Discipline-specific* entry above.

Reflection: This is writing that looks back on events or experiences as well as within one's mind to consider what something means, what one learned, how things changed, or why something is important.

Research: This is a question one seeks to answer or a problem one aspires to solve because of investigating a subject in depth from a range of perspectives using different media.

Revision: This includes changes made to a piece of writing not so much for correction or clarity, but to improve the content and ideas, which may evolve as the student learns more through additional research and reflection.

Routinely: Literally to write as part of a routine in the class, for many reasons, not all of which are graded or even collected; writing is a dominant mode of the class as a performance in itself and as a means of preparing to write about a text or topic.

Shorter times: These might begin in class, finish for homework, and then get collected the next day; or it might be timed, in-class assignments used to assess or extend learning. It is not the same as in-class writing; writing of this sort can also be done at home.

Single sitting or a day or two: This is writing that takes place in class, possibly but not necessarily under timed conditions.

Tasks: These are the things students are asked to write or do when they write; examples might include asking students to *read* and *summarize* a text, or asking students to *read* a collection of texts about a topic, and then *draw conclusions* about what the authors say about it; or they might be directed to *contrast* these competing views on the subject, then *construct* an argument that *cites* evidence from those texts.

Notes

Part 3

The Common Core State Standards

Speaking and Listening

College and Career Readiness Anchor Standards for

Speaking and Listening 9–12

Source: Common Core State Standards

The grades 6–12 standards on the following pages define what students should understand and be able to do by the end of each grade. They correspond to the CCR anchor standards by number. The CCR and grade-specific standards are necessary complements—the former providing broad standards, the latter providing additional specificity—that together define the skills and understandings that all students must demonstrate.

Comprehension and Collaboration

1. Prepare for and participate effectively in a range of conversations and collaborations with diverse partners, building on others' ideas and expressing their own clearly and persuasively.
2. Integrate and evaluate information presented in diverse media and formats, including visually, quantitatively, and orally.
3. Evaluate a speaker's point of view, reasoning, and use of evidence and rhetoric.

Presentation of Knowledge and Ideas

4. Present information, findings, and supporting evidence such that listeners can follow the line of reasoning and the organization, development, and style are appropriate to task, purpose, and audience.
5. Make strategic use of digital media and visual displays of data to express information and enhance understanding of presentations.
6. Adapt speech to a variety of contexts and communicative tasks, demonstrating command of formal English when indicated or appropriate.

Note on Range and Content of Student Speaking and Listening

To become college and career ready, students must have ample opportunities to take part in a variety of rich, structured conversations—as part of a whole class, in small groups, and with a partner—built around important content in various domains. They must be able to contribute appropriately to these conversations, to make comparisons and contrasts, and to analyze and synthesize a multitude of ideas in accordance with the standards of evidence appropriate to a particular discipline. Whatever their intended major or profession, high school graduates will depend heavily on their ability to listen attentively to others so that they are able to build on others' meritorious ideas while expressing their own clearly and persuasively. New technologies have broadened and expanded the role that speaking and listening play in acquiring and sharing knowledge and have tightened their link to other forms of communication. The Internet has accelerated the speed at which connections between speaking, listening, reading, and writing can be made, requiring that students be ready to use these modalities nearly simultaneously. Technology itself is changing quickly, creating a new urgency for students to be adaptable in response to change.

Source: Copyright © 2010. National Governors Association Center for Best Practices and Council of Chief State School Officers. All rights reserved.

College and Career Readiness Anchor Standards for

Speaking and Listening

The College and Career Readiness (CCR) anchor standards are the same for all middle and high school students, regardless of subject area or grade level. What varies is the sophistication of the speaking and listening they must do at subsequent grade levels in each disciplinary domain. The fundamental speaking skills should not change as students advance; rather, the level at which they learn and can perform those skills should increase in complexity as students move from one grade to the next.

Comprehension and Collaboration

Discussion in one form or another is a vital, integral part of learning and classroom culture. To ensure students contribute substance, they are expected to read, write, or investigate as directed so they come to class ready to engage in the discussion of that topic or text with peers or the whole class. During these discussions, they learn to acknowledge and respond to others' ideas and incorporate those ideas, as well as others they discover through their research, as evidence to support their conclusions or claims. Details and evidence in various forms and from different sources is first evaluated, then selected as needed by the students to use in their presentations. When listening to others speak, students learn to listen for key details and qualities to evaluate the perspective, logic, evidence, and use of rhetoric in their presentation or speech.

Presentation of Knowledge and Ideas

When giving a presentation, students carefully select which details and evidence to use when supporting their ideas or findings, organizing this information in a clear, concise manner that ensures the audience understands. To that end, students focus on how to best organize and develop their ideas and supporting evidence according to their purpose, audience, occasion, and appointed task. When appropriate, they use digital media to enhance, amplify, or otherwise improve their presentation, adapting their language and delivery as needed to the different contexts, tasks, or audiences.

Speaking and Listening 1: Prepare for and participate effectively in a range of conversations and collaborations with diverse partners, building on others' ideas and expressing their own clearly and persuasively.

9–10	English Language Arts and Social Studies, Science, and Technical Subjects	11–12	English Language Arts and Social Studies, Science, and Technical Subjects

Initiate and participate effectively in a range of collaborative discussions (one-on-one, in groups, and teacher-led) with diverse partners on grades 9–10 topics, texts, and issues, building on others' ideas and expressing their own clearly and persuasively.

a. Come to discussions prepared, having read and researched material under study; explicitly draw on that preparation by referring to evidence from texts and other research on the topic or issue to stimulate a thoughtful, well-reasoned exchange of ideas.

b. Work with peers to set rules for collegial discussions and decision-making (e.g., informal consensus, taking votes on key issues, presentation of alternate views), clear goals and deadlines, and individual roles as needed.

c. Propel conversations by posing and responding to questions that relate the current discussion to broader themes or larger ideas; actively incorporate others into the discussion; and clarify, verify, or challenge ideas and conclusions.

d. Respond thoughtfully to diverse perspectives, summarize points of agreement and disagreement, and, when warranted, qualify or justify their own views and understanding and make new connections in light of the evidence and reasoning presented.

Initiate and participate effectively in a range of collaborative discussions (one-on-one, in groups, and teacher-led) with diverse partners on grades **11–12** topics, texts, and issues, building on others' ideas and expressing their own clearly and persuasively.

a. Come to discussions prepared, having read and researched material under study; explicitly draw on that preparation by referring to evidence from texts and other research on the topic or issue to stimulate a thoughtful, well-reasoned exchange of ideas.

b. Work with peers to **promote civil, democratic** discussions and decision-making, set clear goals and deadlines, and establish individual roles as needed.

c. Propel conversations by posing and responding to questions that **probe reasoning and evidence; ensure a hearing for a full range of positions on a topic or issue;** clarify, verify, or challenge ideas and conclusions; **and promote divergent and creative perspectives.**

d. Respond thoughtfully to diverse perspectives; **synthesize comments, claims, and evidence made on all sides of an issue; resolve contradictions when possible; and determine what additional information or research is required to deepen the investigation or complete the task.**

Note that no distinction is made between the speaking and listening standards for English Language Arts, Social Studies, History, Science, and other technical subjects.

Source: Copyright © 2010. National Governors Association Center for Best Practices and Council of Chief State School Officers. All rights reserved.

What the **Student** Does

9–10 English Language Arts and Social Studies, Science, and Technical Subjects

Gist: Start and contribute to the full spectrum of academic discussions (pairs, groups, full class) with a range of students about those texts and topics appropriate to grades 9–10, complementing classmates' observations and ideas with your own, which you convey in discipline-specific or otherwise academic language. Students bring to any discussion ideas and questions, as well as evidence and examples from their readings or research, using specific passages or details to defend, advance, or build on their own or others' ideas. Students negotiate, as needed, with classmates to set guidelines and protocols for discussions (e.g., consensus model), designating roles and responsibilities as well as timelines and objectives. Participants sustain and extend the discussion by connecting the immediate exchange to previous studies, other classes, or world events. Also, students incorporate others' ideas into the discussion, responding with questions meant to validate, clarify, or refine another's ideas and conclusions. Throughout such class discussions, students listen to and engage with alternative views, culling the key ideas from others' remarks and summarizing them as they present or respond to others' questions about their own ideas, basing their own claims or challenges to others' on evidence and logical reasoning.

- What is the topic, text, or task—and what questions might you ask to help you contribute to the discussion?
- How can you prepare for the discussion so you know what you want to say and have evidence or information to offer during the discussion?
- What questions can you jot down before and throughout the discussion to help you participate in this conversation?
- What is your assigned role in this group discussion?

11–12 English Language Arts and Social Studies, Science, and Technical Subjects

Gist: Start and contribute to the full spectrum of academic discussions (pairs, groups, full class) with a range of students about those texts and topics appropriate to grades 11–12, complementing classmates' observations and ideas with your own, which you convey in discipline-specific or otherwise academic language. Students bring to any discussion ideas and questions, as well as evidence and examples from their readings or research, using specific passages or details to defend, advance, or build on their own or others' ideas. Students, working with their peers, establish clear guidelines and processes for appropriate, inclusive discussions in order to make effective decisions, designate roles and responsibilities, and establish timelines and objectives. Students advance the dialogue by asking and responding to questions that explore the logic and evidence behind the questions and ideas discussed, as well as other perspectives on the topic or text so as to ensure a rich mix of opinions and viewpoints. Students engage with these different views, shaping observations, ideas, claims, and evidence into a new angle or idea which may require them to resolve certain contradictions or identify those areas which merit further study in order to answer the question more fully or complete the assignment.

- What is the topic, text, or task—and what questions might you ask to help you contribute to the discussion?
- How can you prepare for the discussion so you know what you want to say and have evidence or information to offer during the discussion?
- What are the different perspectives (people, other texts, sources) you need to include in your discussion?
- How would you assess the evidence or reasoning used by others in the discussion or the texts you are examining?

What the **Teacher** Does

To prepare and help students to participate in conversations, do the following:

- Send them home with specific questions to investigate—through research, reading, or just reflection—prior to a subsequent discussion the following day about that text or topic.
- Model for the students how to participate in the specific conversation for which you want to prepare them; this may involve sitting with one or more students and demonstrating how, for example, to discuss or respond to their classmates' writing.
- Take them to the library or the computer lab to investigate online resources prior to a guest speaker; the goal of such inquiry should be specific questions they can pose to the guest the next day.
- Provide students with sentence templates that provide them with the language needed to enter the discussion (e.g., *I agree with what Maria said about ___, but disagree that ___*), or generate with them the sorts of questions they should ask when discussing a particular text or topic.
- Review the conventions, rules, roles, or responsibilities that apply to a specialized discussion strategy (e.g., Harkness Method, Literature Circles, Socratic Dialogue, or Great Books Discussion).
- Track participation by keeping a record of the exchange using visual codes that indicate who initiates, responds, or extends; use this to assess and provide feedback for students.

To have students participate in a range of collaborations with diverse partners, do the following:

- Create the culture of respect for other views and ideas within the class that is necessary for students to collaborate with others, articulating for the class (verbally or on handouts and on posters) the norms when working with or responding to others.
- Investigate alternative venues such as videoconferencing or chat for such collaboration with classmates, community members, or people from other countries.

- Use various strategies that require students to work with different people in various contexts and configurations to solve problems, develop ideas, or improve one another's work.

To have students build on others' ideas and effectively express their own, do the following:

- Try, periodically or early on in the year when establishing norms for class discussion, requiring that students first respond to another student's comment before they can offer a new one of their own.
- Direct students to synthesize the different perspectives so far by first writing and then sharing these synthesis statements about what everyone is actually saying.
- Post a list of follow-up questions they can use when asking classmates (or the teacher) to say more about an idea or comment they made in the course of the discussion; as the year passes, these can become more specific, such as challenging another speaker's reasoning or the validity of this evidence.

To teach students how to initiate conversations or respond, do the following:

- Ask them all to write a list of questions about a topic, text, procedure, or result; then ask them to identify one that they think is especially useful for starting a discussion and use that with a neighbor to initiate an exchange.
- Assign students different roles prior to a discussion, one of them being to initiate new strands in the group or class discussion, another being to listen to others' comments and jot down other possible questions or prompts the discussion initiator can use.

To help your English Language Learners, try this one thing:

- Have the full class first write about a text or topic they will subsequently discuss together or in small groups; allow students to read what they wrote if they are not comfortable speaking extemporaneously in class or small groups.

Academic Vocabulary: Key Words and Phrases

Alternate views: This refers to creating guidelines for working with and speaking to those who present different, even opposing views, to promote and help students participate in collegial discussions.

Broader themes: This refers to extending the conversation beyond its current, narrower focus to address related big-picture ideas. Also related to the idea of knowing how to connect what someone, including oneself, is saying to other related topics.

Building on others' ideas: When one student makes a comment or observation, students build on it by adding connections and other insights that often begin with phrases such as "Picking up on what Martha just said, I noticed _____" or "Marco made a good point about _____."

Clearly: This refers to using the language appropriate to the discipline, topic, or text to ensure precision, clarity, and accuracy.

Collegial discussions: This refers to discussing ideas, some of them contentious, with mutual respect for your colleagues even if you do not agree.

Deepen the investigation: At these higher levels the challenge is to explore the deeper levels of the topic as one goes further into it through additional research.

Diverse partners (and perspectives): This refers to people and ideas from different backgrounds, cultures, and perspectives than that of the student; the idea is that one must know how and be able to converse with all people.

Ensure a hearing for a full range of positions: Make a deliberate effort to allow a range of opinions to be heard before any discussion is concluded or ideas summed up.

Explicitly draw on that preparation: Make use of the notes, ideas, or any materials the student prepared specifically for the discussion; this shows how thoroughly the student prepared and how well they anticipated the demands and directions of the discussion.

Expressing: This means articulating, conveying students' ideas instead of merely parroting back classmates' or the author's ideas.

Incorporate: This is used here to mean drawing others, perhaps those least inclined to enter the discussion, into the conversation to hear their views.

Individual roles: These are the specific roles students play or cultivate for themselves in academic discussions.

Initiate: Invite others to join in or start a conversation; in a full-class setting, it can mean initiating a discussion within the class.

Make new connections: Conversations are meant to be generative, to allow room for new and additional ideas as a way of deepening the dialogue about the text or topic; to make such new connections, however, requires that students get the time needed.

Posing questions: Students ask one another or the teacher questions about the text, task, or topic during a class discussion.

Probe reasoning and evidence: Students inquire about why one student says something, questioning the logic or support for ideas.

Promote civil, democratic discussions and decision-making: This is the essential agenda for teaching students to speak and listen well as students because they will become adults who must live and work together to solve problems.

Propel conversations: This means to move or advance conversations along to engage others.

Summarize points of agreement and disagreement: During discussions that grow heated or involve multiple perspectives, participants pause to clarify positions by reiterating them to the speaker and the group.

Synthesize comments, claims, and evidence: Students use all the comments, claims, and evidence provided by others to form their own idea that they might then put forward to the group.

Verify: This means to establish or otherwise confirm the truth of any statements, evidence, or claims made during a small-group or class discussion.

Warranted: This refers to when something is needed, appropriate, or otherwise called for—different from *warrant*, which is a rhetorical term that alerts readers to your assumptions.

　　　　　　　　　　　　　　　Comprehension and Collaboration

Speaking and Listening 2: Integrate and evaluate information presented in diverse media and formats, including visually, quantitatively, and orally.

9–10 English Language Arts and Social Studies, Science, and Technical Subjects	**11–12** English Language Arts and Social Studies, Science, and Technical Subjects
Integrate multiple sources of information presented in diverse media or formats (e.g., visually, quantitatively, orally) evaluating the credibility and accuracy of each source.	Integrate multiple sources of information presented in diverse formats and media (e.g., visually, quantitatively, orally) **in order to make informed decisions and solve problems**, evaluating the credibility and accuracy of each source **and noting any discrepancies among the data.**

Note that no distinction is made between the speaking and listening standards for English Language Arts, Social Studies, History, Science, and other technical subjects.

Source: Copyright © 2010. National Governors Association Center for Best Practices and Council of Chief State School Officers. All rights reserved.

Common Core Speaking and Listening Standard 2

What the **Student** Does

9-10 **English Language Arts and Social Studies, Science, and Technical Subjects**

Gist: Examine a variety of visual, quantitative, oral, and mixed media sources in various formats, determining in the process how credible and accurate each source is. Students then integrate the information from these different sources and various media formats into a presentation, composition, or class discussion about the topic they are studying.

- What are you researching, writing about, presenting, or discussing in class?
- What sources—and in what media or format—should you consider when investigating this topic?
- What criteria will you use to evaluate the credibility, accuracy, and overall quality of each source?
- Are there significant and meaningful differences between certain types of sources (e.g., quantitative) and others (e.g., visual, mixed media, or oral)?
- How can you best capture and integrate sources in different media (e.g., visual, mixed media, or audio)?

11-12 **English Language Arts and Social Studies, Science, and Technical Subjects**

Gist: In order to make informed decisions and solve problems, students consider information from a range of sources in different media or formats. Thus, students examine different sources in visual, quantitative, oral, and mixed media formats, selecting the details, information, or evidence that best suits their needs; they then integrate this information, from these different sources and media formats, into their presentation, composition, or a class discussion about the topic they are studying. Before integrating these different sources, however, students determine the credibility and accuracy of those sources to establish the quality of the contents and their suitability for use in the intended context; in addition, they examine these sources for any gaps or inconsistencies among the data.

- What sources—and in what media or format—should you consider when investigating this topic?
- What criteria will you use to evaluate the credibility, accuracy, and overall quality of each source?
- What significant and meaningful differences exist between certain types (e.g., quantitative) and others (e.g., visual, mixed media, or oral)?
- How can you best capture and integrate sources in different media (e.g., visual, mixed media, or audio)?
- What discrepancies appear in the data provided from different sources? What are the source, nature, and significance of the discrepancies found between sources or within a single source?

What the **Teacher** Does

To have students integrate information presented in different formats and media, do the following:

- Train students to look and listen for information presented through discussions, formal presentations, and online forms, such as TED Talks; instruct students in how to best capture—by recording, taking notes, or deciding they would be better off just listening—the key information from the presentation.
- Play a recorded presentation (e.g., a TED Talk) twice, the first time to get the gist and the second time, now that they know what to look and listen for, to take notes as they watch.
- Demystify this procedure for students by thinking aloud as you demonstrate what you do, how you do it, what questions you ask, and when and why you ask them to determine what information you wish to integrate and how to do so.

To have students evaluate information presented in diverse formats and media, do the following:

- Determine the criteria the students will use to evaluate the information they are presented; in the event that there are no predetermined criteria—from the college board, standards documents, or district programs—the teacher should develop them.
- Demonstrate for students how to evaluate information as it comes in real time during presentations or lectures; keep your own notes along with your students, pausing (if possible) to debrief on what they and you have noted.
- Ask students to compare their notes from a presentation, discussing what they captured and ignored, as well as the criteria by which they evaluated the information from the presentation.

To have students evaluate the credibility and accuracy of each source, do the following:

- Provide or, over time, have students themselves develop questions and criteria used to evaluate the quality of all sources; these questions would focus on the source, timeliness, relevancy, and ethos of the person delivering the information presented.

- Calibrate students' ability to evaluate the information presented by first priming their sensibilities to those details that matter and those that do not; to this end, you might guide students through some samples, asking them to determine the credibility and accuracy of the information based on all they know.

To have students identify discrepancies among the data from different sources, do the following:

- Require students to consult other, perhaps more established, sources, to determine whether the presenter's information aligns with established understandings or should be reevaluated in light of apparent discrepancies.
- Demonstrate for students how to read this information critically to identify alleged or proven discrepancies; then ask them to do as you did, explaining their process; finally, have them apply the techniques themselves independently over time.

To have students solve problems and make decisions based on information, do the following:

- Direct students to first identify the problems they must solve or the decisions they must make so they know what to listen and look for during the presentation, speech, or discussion.
- Develop for (or with) students a cost/benefit or a pro/con organizer into which they can sort information as it comes in during the presentation for later use in determining what to do.

To help your English Language Learners, try this one thing:

- Create a graphic organizer with spaces labeled (or that they can label themselves as needed) for the different sources or criteria so they can process what they hear more efficiently, since listening, analyzing, and gathering will otherwise likely overwhelm English Learners. The organizer reduces the number of tasks they must do simultaneously.

Academic Vocabulary: Key Words and Phrases

Accuracy: This refers to how close the data, information, or other forms of information are to the fact(s) or to whatever the speaker is representing.

Credibility: This is the degree to which the audience can believe what the speaker is saying; related to the Greek notion of ethos, which is where we get the term *ethics*. If you are credible, we believe what you say.

Data: This is typically used to refer to numbers and statistics, quantifiable information from research or experiments that can be gathered, sorted, analyzed, presented, and used as evidence to support conclusions or hypotheses.

Discrepancies among the data: Differences between what one study or scientist found and another that suggest a result or experiment is invalid, due to data contamination or incorrect reporting of results. Discrepancies can skew the results, allowing one to misrepresent a set of findings as true or significant when they are not.

Evaluate: This means to determine the quality, value, use, or importance of data, details, or other forms of information one might include in one's presentation as evidence to support a position.

Format: This includes parts of a speech or presentation charts, slides, graphics, or images, as well as multiple media, all of which allow the speaker to represent their ideas more fully and effectively.

Information presented in diverse media and formats: The content of presentations and speeches these days comes in many different modes, including still and video images, colors, and shapes, as well as more quantitative techniques such as charts, tables, and graphs.

Informed decision: When speaking, they gather such supporting details and when listening, they consider the evidence offered when deciding what is best or correct regarding the speaker's position.

Integrate: This means to join the different sources or data from them into one cohesive body of evidence used to support one's claims about what a speaker or author said or meant about a topic.

Media: This refers to all the different forms your ideas, information, evidence, and data come in, including print, audio, video, photograph, and mixed media, such as websites or presentation slides with embedded digital imagery (still photographs, videos, animations) and audio.

Multiple sources: This refers not to the media so much as the content, the primary emphasis being to base whatever you are saying on a range of sources to support and illustrate your claims or observations.

Visually, quantitatively, orally: This refers to images, video, art, and graphics of any other sort intended to convey the ideas the speaker wants to communicate; This is measureable, numerical, quantifiable data that is displayed or formatted to suit the speaker's purpose; it is also spoken, whether in front of a live audience or for an anonymous listener viewing a slide show online with a voice-over instead.

Notes

Speaking and Listening 3: Evaluate a speaker's point of view, reasoning, and use of evidence and rhetoric.

9–10 English Language Arts and Social Studies, Science, and Technical Subjects	11–12 English Language Arts and Social Studies, Science, and Technical Subjects
Evaluate a speaker's point of view, reasoning, and use of evidence and rhetoric, identifying any fallacious reasoning or exaggerated or distorted evidence.	Evaluate a speaker's point of view, reasoning, and use of evidence and rhetoric, **assessing the stance, premises, links among ideas, word choice, points of emphasis, and tone used.**

Note that no distinction is made between the speaking and listening standards for English Language Arts, Social Studies, History, Science, and other technical subjects.

Source: Copyright © 2010. National Governors Association Center for Best Practices and Council of Chief State School Officers. All rights reserved.

What the **Student** Does

9–10 | English Language Arts and Social Studies, Science, and Technical Subjects

Gist: Scrutinize the speaker's message and the point of view from which that message is conveyed, taking into consideration what biases, values, or assumptions shape the speaker's message and the logic behind the speaker's ideas and claims. In addition, students examine the speaker's logic, analyzing his or her evidence and how that evidence is used to support or advance a position, while also looking for logical fallacies and evidence that is somehow flawed (e.g., exaggerated, distorted, "cherry-picked"). It is in this context, while determining the reliability, accuracy, and timeliness of all evidence that students also examine how the speaker uses rhetoric in the service of any arguments or ideas.

- What do you know—and what is important to consider—about the speaker, subject, occasion, audience, and purpose?
- What are the speaker's claim, stance, and point of view about this subject?
- What evidence and reasoning does the speaker offer—and how is it used to support or advance the speaker's claims or ideas?
- Which rhetorical strategies or devices does the speaker use to achieve his or her purpose or advance his or her idea?
- What criteria guide the author's choice of evidence—and do these criteria lead to any evidence that would be considered flawed, exaggerated, or otherwise inaccurate?

11–12 | English Language Arts and Social Studies, Science, and Technical Subjects

Gist: Scrutinize the speaker's viewpoint, taking into consideration what biases, premises, or points of emphasis reveal the speaker's point of view most accurately. In addition, students examine the speaker's logic, analyzing any evidence used to support or advance a position, while also looking for details about the speaker's stance and attitude as revealed by his or her tone, word choice, or connections between ideas. It is in this context, while determining the reliability, accuracy, and timeliness of all evidence that students also examine how the speaker uses rhetoric in the service of any arguments or ideas, and those premises on which the speaker's arguments are based.

- What do you know—and what is important to consider—about the the speaker, the subject, the occasion, the audience, and the purpose?
- How would you describe the speaker's stance or attitude toward this subject—and its effect on the content of his speech?
- What ideas does this speaker link to in order to establish or advance his or her position or convey his or her attitude toward it?
- What are the ideas or other points the speaker seeks to emphasize—and the means by which he or she seeks to achieve that emphasis?
- Which words used by the speaker most effectively emphasize ideas, convey tone, or advance the his or her claims?

What the **Teacher** Does

To have students evaluate a speaker's point of view (POV), do the following:

- Teach or extend students' existing knowledge of the concept of point of view as it relates to evaluating a speaker.
- Develop the habit in students of asking the fundamental questions when examining their point of view when speaking; this is most easily remembered by teaching them to evaluate the speaker's POV using the acronym SOAPS: subject, occasion, audience, purpose, and speaker.
- Have students generate additional questions they can use to evaluate a speaker's point of view, including questions related to ethics, commitment, motive, originality, implications, and credibility.

To have students evaluate a speaker's reasoning and use of evidence and rhetoric, do the following:

- Clarify first what "reasoning" means and how it applies by providing examples of sound and unsound reasoning.
- Direct students to ask questions about the examples, facts, and evidence the speaker uses to support the argument; develop their knowledge of and ability to consider whether the speaker manipulates the audience through the use of faulty evidence, flawed syllogisms, or any other fallacies that undermine the speaker's credibility.
- Show students how to identify commonly used propaganda techniques: bandwagon, name-calling, transfer (making an illogical link between two unrelated things), emotional appeals, loaded words, stereotypes, and either/or thinking; when teaching these elements, seek online resources for examples from history and the current era, making additional connections between the spoken forms and print propaganda during, for example, World War II.
- Provide and ask students to generate questions to use when evaluating the rhetoric of a speaker; these

questions would focus on SOAPS as well as the three main rhetorical appeals speakers use to persuade their audience: ethos, logos, and pathos.

To have students assess a speaker's stance, premises, diction, and tone, do the following:

- Distinguish between *stance* (the speaker's attitude toward the audience) and *tone* (the speaker's attitude toward the subject).
- Provide students with (or have them generate) a list of words that can be used to describe stance, tone, and diction in general; then have them choose from these lists those words that apply to the speech, narrowing their selection eventually to just the one or two words that best describe this speech.
- Ask students to identify the major (universal truths) and minor (specific case) premises found in the speaker's arguments; then, show students how to break down the deductive logic to determine whether each premise is true, asking the students to explain why a premise is or is not correct.
- Tell your students which word or words best describe, for example, the tone of the speaker, directing them to find and explain how their examples from the speech support your claim.
- Provide students with a printed copy of the speaker's text they can annotate; after showing them how, tell them to go through the text to evaluate the speaker's diction as it relates to tone, stance, persona, credibility, occasion, audience, and purpose.

To help your English Language Learners, try this one thing:

- Use a speech that students can read (in print), hear (in audio), and watch (as a video). Use these versions in stages to help students understand and evaluate different aspects of the speech. Presidential inauguration and State of the Union speeches are most easily accessed for this purpose, but others are available.

Academic Vocabulary: Key Words and Phrases

Assessing the stance, premises, links among ideas, word choice, points of emphasis, and tone used: That's a lot to assess! Assessing means to evaluate the quality, effectiveness, or value of something; in this case that means assessing the speaker's:

Stance: This refers to the attitude toward the audience, which is different from the speaker's *tone*, which refers to the attitude toward the *subject*.

Premises: This refers to prior comments, claims, or statements made that are used as the bases for inferences or conclusions about a subject.

Links among ideas: This refers to how one idea relates to or affects another in a narrative, persuasive, or descriptive sequence.

Word choice: This refers to what effect the speaker's choice of one word over another has on the tone, content, style, or impact of the speech; this would include not only individual words but also phrases that carry weight in the speech for their grace, emotional impact, or force.

Points of emphasis: This refers to which points the speaker chooses to shine a spotlight on and for what purpose; this includes not only which points speakers emphasize but also when, how, and why they do so.

Tone: The speaker's attitude toward the subject as revealed through his *tone of voice*, gestures, and words. When assessing the speaker's tone, one would also consider the effect the tone has on the content and the audience's perception of and response to that content.

Evidence: This refers to the data, details, quotations, or examples the speaker uses in the presentation or speech and how credible, accurate, and valid it is; in addition, one would evaluate the ways the speaker *uses* this evidence to persuade or otherwise influence the audience.

Exaggerated or distorted evidence: This refers to any evidence that the speaker had "cherry-picked" from the original source to support a position the authors of that evidence did not intend; in addition to such distortion or unethical use of evidence, speakers may overemphasize certain details over others or simply exaggerate the findings or the meaning and significance of those findings to prove an argument for which they were unable to find more reliable evidence.

Fallacious reasoning: This refers to flawed or erroneous logic applied to the connection between claims and evidence; the speaker has said two ideas are related or causal based on incorrect information or a connection that does not exist.

Point of view: Where does the speaker stand in relation to the subject and audience on this occasion? Is the speaker representing her ideas or those of another person or agency? Point of view is vital in terms of any bias the speaker may reveal about the subject; point of view, when inappropriate to the occasion or audience, can dramatically undermine the speaker's credibility or reception.

Reasoning: This refers to the logic of the speaker as it relates to his ideas; it also refers to how well and to what end the speaker's ideas and the reasoning behind them connect with and complement each other to improve the coherence of the speech.

Rhetoric: This refers to the speaker's use of any devices, techniques, or strategies to persuade or otherwise influence how the listener or audience thinks, acts, or feels about the topic being addressed.

Speaking and Listening 4: Present information, findings, and supporting evidence so listeners can follow the line of reasoning and the organization, development, and style are appropriate to task, purpose, and audience.

9–10 English Language Arts and Social Studies, Science, and Technical Subjects	**11–12** English Language Arts and Social Studies, Science, and Technical Subjects
Present information, findings, and supporting evidence clearly, concisely, and logically such that listeners can follow the line of reasoning and the organization, development, substance, and style are appropriate to purpose, audience, and task.	Present information, findings, and supporting evidence, **conveying a clear and distinct perspective,** such that listeners can follow the line of reasoning, **alternative or opposing perspectives are addressed,** and the organization, development, substance, and style are appropriate to purpose, audience, and **a range of formal and informal** tasks.

Note that no distinction is made between the speaking and listening standards for English Language Arts, Social Studies, History, Science, and other technical subjects.

Source: Copyright © 2010. National Governors Association Center for Best Practices and Council of Chief State School Officers. All rights reserved.

What the **Student** Does

9–10 English Language Arts and Social Studies, Science, and Technical Subjects	**11–12** English Language Arts and Social Studies, Science, and Technical Subjects
Gist: Deliver presentations in clear and concise language that highlights key details, results, or supporting evidence in a logical way, revealing to the audience the thinking and structure of those ideas whose substance the speaker embellishes in a style chosen for that purpose, audience, and task.	**Gist:** Deliver presentations using language that establishes and communicates a cogent, specific viewpoint whose logic the audience grasps, even as it considers additional or conflicting arguments. In addition, students organize and refine all information, details, and evidence in a style and manner appropriate to their objective and audience and a variety of both formal and informal tasks.
• What are the subject, purpose, occasion, and audience of your presentation? • What evidence (or other information) do you have (or need) to support your claim or develop your ideas? • What style, format, or approach should you use to present this information (as a list, in a diagram, in words; on paper, on a screen, or just orally)? • How can you help listeners better understand and follow what you are saying: color, a more visual format, an accompanying handout?	• What are the subject, purpose, occasion, and audience of your presentation? • What evidence (or other information) do you have (or need) to support your claim or develop your ideas? • What aspects help to make your perspective clear and distinct? • What other or opposing perspectives should you address?

What the **Teacher** Does

To have students present information and findings so that listeners can follow, do the following:

- Identify for students the key elements that they should include, address, or accomplish in the speech they will give.
- Give students a tool, such as a storyboard organizer, or a technique, such as outlining, they can use to plan out their speech in a way that listeners will follow; they should only use this tool or technique, however, after they have generated many possible ideas about what they might say about their findings on this topic.
- Introduce students to the range of ways to make findings and information easier to grasp, including organizing patterns such as cause–effect, compare–contrast, problem–solution, chronological, and narrative; see Common Core Speaking and Listening Standard 5 for more detail about one of the best approaches: using visual or graphic formats, including tables, charts, and graphs.

To have students present evidence in ways that listeners can follow, do the following:

- Ask students to determine first what evidence they have or need to obtain to best support the claim they wish to make, or if they have evidence but no claim yet, ask them then to draw whatever conclusions the evidence supports as a first step.
- Suggest that students identify a question their speech will attempt to answer and gather the evidence needed to support their answer to that question.
- Show students a range of ways to organize information and evidence (e.g., order of importance or classification); have them apply several of these different approaches to their information.
- Model for students how to map a speech for its logic using "chunking," a technique that is less structured and formal than outlining, allowing students to focus more on the structure and logic of the information and evidence they provide.
- Assess and provide feedback on the logic and quality of their evidence; another option would be to create

a rubric students can use to evaluate their use of evidence in their speech.

To have students help listeners follow the reasoning and organization, do the following:

- Evaluate students' use of signal words or phrases that provide transitions from one idea to another, specifically those that clarify and reinforce reasoning and organization.
- Explain the idea of points of emphasis in a speech and how the speaker can organize the content and use their voice to reinforce certain information, ideas, or perspectives on the topic.
- Require students in the upper-grade levels to include in their speech competing interpretations or alternative points of view as a way to help listeners better understand the speaker's claim through contrast with others.

To ensure students' organization, development, and style are appropriate, do the following:

- Ask students to analyze their speech in light of organization and development (i.e., details, examples, evidence, and the subsequent discussion of the meaning and importance of these), explaining why they organize their content as they do and why they think it is the most effective approach for their speech.
- Give students a printed text of a speech they can annotate and view in class, as well; after guiding students through an analysis of the speaker's style (e.g., figurative language, diction, syntax, imagery, and tone), have them conduct a similar analysis to their speech once they show an acceptable mastery of the ideas.

To help your English Language Learners, try this one thing:

- Encourage (or even require if it seems best) your students to create an outline of the speech, doing this in stages, so that you can assess the structure, development, and content of the speech as they build it throughout this early stage of the process.

Academic Vocabulary: Key Words and Phrases

Alternative or opposing perspectives: This refers to opinions, ideas, or points of view different from yours or, if similar, from others to show your ideas are broadly supported or not in conflict as some would argue. These alternative or competing views would also be used to acknowledge these other positions if one were presenting an argument.

Appropriate to the task, purpose, and audience: This refers to how one organizes, develops, or speaks varies depending on the objective, their actual purpose, and the audience to whom they are speaking.

Concisely: This means to state in as few words as possible, though not to the point of simplicity. People want an engaging speech that takes no longer than necessary to accomplish its purpose.

Conveying a clear and distinct perspective: This refers to a position, conclusion, or finding that uses examples, evidence, or data to clarify and distinguish its ideas for the intended audience in ways that are compelling or substantial in a fresh or unique way to the audience.

Development: This refers to the examples, ideas, details, and commentary the speaker adds to ensure the ideas are thoroughly expressed and effectively delivered, anticipating and responding to any questions the audience might have.

Findings: This refers to conclusions drawn from observations, investigations, experiments, or inquiries about questions or problems.

Formal and informal tasks: The tone of the speech and nature of the ideas depend a great deal on the context in which they are spoken; thus, if it is an informal, small-group, or class conversation, the speaking task is likely to involve simply explaining what one thinks a text or some other content means. If it is a more formal occasion such as a debate, formal presentation of research, or other serious address, the task is likely to involve argument, interpretation, or some other more evidence-based speaking.

Line of reasoning: The speaker links a series of ideas in some meaningful and clear way as they speak, sort of a connect-the-dots approach that links all the connections to show why one thinks as he or she does and/or how he or she arrived at a conclusion or argument.

Logically: When presenting information or findings and the evidence that supports them, as well as any subsequent discussion of the meaning of those findings, speakers must ensure that the ideas connect to each other in ways that enhance clarity and further the speaker's claims or explanations.

Organization: An appropriate and effective structure is vital to the speaker's success; whether organized to show cause–effect or problem–solution, from least to most important, or from past to present, the ideas put forth by the speaker require a clear organizing structure so listeners can hear and process the ideas presented.

Present: When people are merely *speaking*, they can be standing at a podium telling a story, explaining what a text means, or discussing what they learned from an experience. When people *present*, they have a more specific purpose such as to persuade the audience to think or act in a certain way. To achieve this outcome, the presenter often uses evidence from a range of established sources, different media, or presentation software such as Keynote or PowerPoint.

Substance: This refers to the content of the presentation—the ideas, the arguments and evidence—it is what you present and use to support your ideas.

Supporting evidence: This refers to data, information, quotations, examples, or other information that the speaker uses to back up whatever they are saying or presenting.

Speaking and Listening 5: Make strategic use of digital media and visual displays of data to express information and enhance understanding of presentations.

9–10 English Language Arts and Social Studies, Science, and Technical Subjects	11–12 English Language Arts and Social Studies, Science, and Technical Subjects
Make strategic use of digital media (e.g., textual, graphical, audio, visual, and interactive elements) in presentations to enhance understanding of findings, reasoning, and evidence and to add interest.	Make strategic use of digital media (e.g., textual, graphical, audio, visual, and interactive elements) in presentations to enhance understanding of findings, reasoning, and evidence and to add interest.

Note that no distinction is made between the speaking and listening standards for English Language Arts, Social Studies, History, Science, and other technical subjects.

Source: Copyright © 2010. National Governors Association Center for Best Practices and Council of Chief State School Officers. All rights reserved.

What the **Student** Does

9–10 English Language Arts and Social Studies, Science, and Technical Subjects

Gist: Incorporate various digital media (e.g., textual, graphical, audio, visual, interactive elements) in strategic ways that improve listeners' understanding of and engagement with ideas, results, or other evidence presented. Students format and design content in presentations (i.e., on screens created for a range of purposes, audiences, devices), using color, size, and fonts, as well as the arrangement and display of any content, to communicate the substance and meaning of their ideas and findings.

- What are you trying to accomplish with or say about this subject?
- Which elements of your presentation are most important to convey?
- What types or features of digital media would make your presentation more engaging, the content more clear, the evidence more effective?
- What is the problem that using video, audio, and interactive elements will address or solve?
- How would the use of color, fonts, arrangement, or digital media (e.g., audio or video) improve your presentation?

11–12 English Language Arts and Social Studies, Science, and Technical Subjects

Gist: Incorporate various digital media (e.g., textual, graphical, audio, visual, interactive elements) in strategic ways that improve listeners' understanding of and engagement with ideas, results, or other evidence presented. Students format and design content in presentations (i.e., on screens created for a range of purposes, audiences, devices), using color, size, and fonts, as well as the arrangement and display of any content, to communicate the substance and meaning of their ideas and findings.

- What are you trying to accomplish with or say about this subject?
- Which elements of your presentation are most important to convey?
- What types or features of digital media would make your presentation more engaging, the content more clear, the evidence more effective?
- What is the problem that using video, audio, and interactive elements will address or solve?
- How would the use of color, fonts, arrangement, or digital media (e.g., audio or video) improve your presentation?

What the **Teacher** Does

To have students make strategic use of digital media and visual displays of data, do the following:

- Outline and illustrate for students the four principles most commonly emphasized in all books about digital and visual design: contrast, repetition, alignment, and proximity; have them then apply these notions to their digital designs.
- Create and require students to follow a set of principles or guidelines for all presentation slides and visual displays (e.g., graphs, charts, infographics, diagrams) you incorporate into your slides; provide a range of samples you assemble in a presentation of your own that embodies the principles of effective presentation design.
- Provide contrasting examples of different presentation slide designs with the same content to illustrate the effect of different fonts, layouts, colors, and content on presentations.
- Direct students to sites like Duarte's (duarteshop.com) and Abela's (extremepresentation.com) for examples and guidelines for effective use and creation of visual displays of information.
- Do not allow students to incorporate distracting animations, wacky fonts, extended video clips, degraded or otherwise lower-grade images, useless sound effects, or any other elements that will detract from the effective presentation of the information; this is an important opportunity to *teach* design, which is an ever-increasing part of effective communication and composition now.

To have students express information and enhance understanding of their ideas, do the following:

- Emphasize to students the role and uses of story in any presentation and how they can use different elements—images, numbers, data, their voice, gestures, or storytelling itself—to convey their ideas with clarity and emphasis to make a more emotional impact on the audience while also enhancing understanding.

- Stress the importance of reducing any content that competes with or otherwise distracts from the content or point you are trying to make in your presentation.
- Encourage students to play with visual explanations (graphs, charts, or diagrams) and visual narratives (images, video, diagrams, or cartoons) as well as color, font, and composition to convey the relationships between different parts of their subject more clearly and effectively—without adding distraction and confusion through extraneous elements.

To have students make strategic use of digital media to add interest and impact, do the following:

- Take time to teach students more about the principles of effective design so they can take time in planning and designing their presentations with the greatest impact.
- Walk students through the process of finding, choosing, formatting, editing, and embedding digital content—images, video, or audio—into their presentations, giving them feedback as they work through the design and delivery process.
- Give students a tour of the different presentation applications—PowerPoint, Keynote, Google Presentation, and Prezi, and any others that come along—then let them choose the one they want to use for their presentation.
- Allow students the option of creating a stand-alone digital presentation (i.e., one that has a voice-over and can be uploaded and viewed online) instead of presenting to the class; a variation of this idea would be to require students to create digital media–based presentations that you and the class can view on tablets if that is an option in your classroom.

To help your English Language Learners, try this one thing:

- Take time to be sure they know how to use all these digital tools and have access to them to do what you are assigning; if they do not, make time in class for all to work on this assignment.

Notes

Academic Vocabulary: Key Words and Phrases

Add interest: One can add interest through content itself or certain effects that create a wow factor in the audience. Selective use of images, video, audio, or mixed media adds power, entertainment, and the possibility of emotional impact. One needs to be sure that any material included to add interest also complements the content; otherwise, it is mere fluff that adds to the length of the presentation and either distracts or frustrates the audience.

Audio elements: Recorded content embedded in the presentation such as voice-over or featured content as in an interview (e.g., image of the person interviewed shown while audio interview plays). Music and sound effects (that serve a real purpose and enhance content) can be effective if used sparingly and in the right way. Other audio content can be made available through hotlinks to primary source recordings of, for example, presidential addresses.

Data: This refers to quantitative, measurable information that has been or could be analyzed and used as evidence to support a claim or to illustrate a point the speaker is trying to make in his or her presentation.

Digital media: This includes presentation software applications such as PowerPoint, Keynote, Google Presentation, and Prezi; also, it refers to digital images, screen captures of online material, stand-alone or embedded video, and audio and mixed media formats.

Enhance understanding: This refers to using all available media and methods—images, audio, multimedia, words, and graphs—in ways that make the abstract more concrete, more visual, more comprehensible. Through charts, images, graphs, or video, the speakers illustrate the processes, concepts, or procedures they are discussing, using these as tools to help the audience *see* what they are saying.

Express information: This means to put forth, to convey, or to relate data, ideas, details, and content to the audience in the clearest way possible.

Graphic elements: This means the use of such elements as diagrams, graphs, tables, and any other graphic elements that help the audience to understand more easily and fully certain procedures or abstract ideas the speaker is discussing.

Interactive elements: Such elements would include handheld devices used to "vote" or otherwise interact with content the speaker displays to the audience; additional interactive features would include hotlinks that connect to content on other sites, video, images, or audio. If the presentation is being made through a tablet or a computer, the prerecorded presentation might have buttons, links, or other options to allow the viewer to interact with the content by choosing different paths or content.

Strategic use of digital media and visual displays: The key term here is *strategic*, for the point the standard emphasizes is that any media in whatever form should be used to *enhance* content and *engage* viewers, not just make it look nice or try to make it fun. Thus, *strategic* in this context means that all such digital media and visual displays are carefully chosen with a purpose in mind and used in specific ways to achieve that purpose or effect in the audience.

Textual elements: This applies to the fonts and typographic elements of the text itself: typeface, size, format, color, and so on. Certain fonts used to convey a feeling or effect might use all uppercase, bold, sans serif fonts from the Helevetica type family to imply strength or force.

Visual displays of data: This refers to tables, charts, graphs, or any other type of infographics used to show to relationship between different data or other such quantifiable information.

Visual elements: This refers to color, shape, size, format, arrangement, and other elements that visually illustrate how data, ideas, and information are connected on slides, screens, or other formats used by the presenter.

Speaking and Listening 6: Adapt speech to a variety of contexts and communicative tasks, demonstrating command of formal English when indicated or appropriate.

9–10	English Language Arts and Social Studies, Science, and Technical Subjects	11–12	English Language Arts and Social Studies, Science, and Technical Subjects
	Adapt speech to a variety of contexts and tasks, demonstrating command of formal English when indicated or appropriate. (See grades 9–10 Language standards 1 and 3 for specific expectations.)		Adapt speech to a variety of contexts and tasks, demonstrating a command of formal English when indicated or appropriate. (See grades 11–12 Language standards 1 and 3 for specific expectations.)

Note that no distinction is made between the speaking and listening standards for English Language Arts, Social Studies, History, Science, and other technical subjects.

Source: Copyright © 2010. National Governors Association Center for Best Practices and Council of Chief State School Officers. All rights reserved.

Common Core Speaking and Listening Standard 6

What the **Student** Does

9–10	English Language Arts and Social Studies, Science, and Technical Subjects

Gist: Distinguish between different occasions or situations, shaping their speech—its content, style, tone, and format—according to the student's purpose, and the needs of the audience, which may be a small or large group of people the student does or does not know, depending on the occasion or context of the speech. Students must decide, in light of their purpose and audience, what style or language to use, whether it is best to use more formal diction and syntax or a more informal, familiar tone. Students should at least know the difference between the two and why, for example, a more formal tone is best for job interviews or other situations related to college or the workplace, and why it is always best to speak according to the conventions of formal English (as spelled out in grades 9–10 Language Standards 1 and 3).

- Who are you addressing on this occasion?
- What are the occasion and the purpose for your speech?
- What is the appropriate tone on this occasion as it relates to your audience and purpose?
- How might you best prepare for this particular task or situation?
- How can you ensure that your speech is appropriate and correct according to the conventions of both the situation (e.g., a job interview) and formal English?

11–12	English Language Arts and Social Studies, Science, and Technical Subjects

Gist: Distinguish between different occasions or situations, shaping their speech—its content, style, tone, and format—according to the student's purpose, and the needs of the audience, which may be a small or large group of people the student does or does not know, depending on the occasion or context of the speech. Students must decide, in light of their purpose and audience, what style or language to use, whether it is best to use more formal diction and syntax or a more informal, familiar tone. Students should at least know the difference between the two and why, for example, a more formal tone is best for job interviews or other situations related to college or the workplace, and why it is always best to speak according to the conventions of formal English (as spelled out in grades 11–12 Language Standards 1 and 3).

- Who are you addressing on this occasion?
- What are the occasion and the purpose for your speech?
- What is the appropriate tone on this occasion as it relates to your audience and purpose?
- How might you best prepare for this particular task or situation?
- How can you ensure that your speech is appropriate and correct according to the conventions of both the situation (e.g., a job interview) and formal English?

What the **Teacher** Does

To have students adapt a speech to a variety of contexts and tasks, do the following:

- Discuss with and warn students about those problems or errors most common to language when spoken on formal or otherwise important occasions (e.g., job interviews). These problems include using slang, euphemisms, stereotypes, clichés, and incorrect grammar, usage, or vocabulary.
- Identify and instruct students to also be wary of using any of the following when speaking at a formal occasion: culturally insensitive language or remarks, jokes, sarcasm, irony, and jargon (unless the audience you are addressing would be fluent in such jargon, in which case it is acceptable).
- Remind students that appropriate anecdotes and figurative language can be effective ways to improve their speech and demonstrate their command of the language and make it more clear to the audience; such figurative language includes using analogies, similes, metaphors, hyperbole, and understatement.

To have students demonstrate their command of formal English when appropriate, do the following:

- Have students identify *before* they speak any words, phrases, or parts of the speech that cause them trouble when they speak; once identified, these portions might be replaced with words that are more familiar but no less appropriate for the occasion or audience.

- Have students deliver their speeches, even if they are created on the spot, in different styles, having fun with it but not being in any way disrespectful of those they might be trying to address; follow up with a chance to discuss the differences between the styles, which one is likely to be more effective and why.
- Make time to confer with students to discuss their speeches, making a special effort to identify any flaws that would undermine correctness and, thus, their credibility as a speaker in any situation that required a mastery of formal English.
- Allow time for the discussion with them individually or as a class (if it is a classwide issue) to discuss why this matters to colleges, the community at large, and especially employers.

To help your English Language Learners, try this one thing:

- Meet individually with them or, if appropriate, as a small group to walk through their speech, first editing for content, then for correctness; then have them do a read-through with you so they can get feedback about words, phrases, or sections of the speech that need to be changed. During this session, you might also model for them how to say or emphasize certain words while speaking. This sort of task, giving a speech in front of a group, is near the top of most people's list of anxieties, all the more so if you must give a speech in a language you are still learning, so it is important to do all you can to address the emotional aspect of such an assignment.

Notes

Academic Vocabulary: Key Words and Phrases

Adapt speech: This means to change the language, style of delivery, tone, or format of the presentation or speech as needed to suit the audience, purpose, and occasion. This could mean not using any digital media or presentation software that might interfere with the more intimate setting of the small group to which one is presenting; it might also mean using less formal but still grammatically correct language when presenting to a group the speaker knows or with whom the speaker wants to create a more familiar atmosphere as they speak.

Appropriate: Each presentation or talk has its own unique audience each time one speaks and so one must know how to speak—which words, tone, and style of address—one should use when speaking on each occasion. What is appropriate on one occasion—informal, colloquial speech to a group of people you know—is inappropriate, even offensive, the next time when the occasion is formal and the audience has completely different expectations. Certain things are *never* appropriate: spelling and formatting mistakes on handouts, slides, or other visual aids; slang, foul language, or otherwise rude terms or comments that undermine the speaker's credibility.

Command of formal English: The standards place a clear and consistent emphasis on a command of formal English—grammatically correct, clearly enunciated words delivered with good eye contact—as an essential ingredient in college or career success. This means speaking in ways that would be appropriate when addressing customers, colleagues, classmates, or professors in college.

Communicative tasks: These tasks would include contributing to a discussion group in class, interviewing with a local business or organization for an internship, delivering a formal speech, debating a controversial issue with others, or presenting a formal topic or argument to a group with the idea of persuading them to act, think, or believe a certain way. Increasingly, these tasks and their related contexts will include, for example, conferring with people through online audio and video (or chat) platforms to collaborate, confer, or communicate.

Contexts: This refers to the place as much as the purpose of any speaking; examples include speaking in-class, online, in small and larger groups, to the full class or larger groups, in the community at large, at work with customers and colleagues, or for interviews with bosses or organizations.

Indicated: One is sometimes asked to talk in a specific way to a group on a topic or occasion; thus, one looks to the prompt, directions, adviser, teacher, or other source for indications about how to speak on a given occasion to a particular audience about a particular topic. In the event that it is not indicated, the speaker must learn to determine themselves what is the most appropriate way to speak in a given situation.

Notes

Part 4

The Common Core State Standards

Language

College and Career Readiness Anchor Standards for
Language 9–12

Source: Common Core State Standards

The grades 6–12 standards on the following pages define what students should understand and be able to do by the end of each grade. They correspond to the CCR anchor standards by number. The CCR and grade-specific standards are necessary complements—the former providing broad standards, the latter providing additional specificity—that together define the skills and understandings that all students must demonstrate.

Conventions of Standard English

1. Demonstrate command of the conventions of standard English grammar and usage when writing or speaking.
2. Demonstrate command of the conventions of standard English capitalization, punctuation, and spelling when writing.

Knowledge of Language

3. Apply knowledge of language to understand how language functions in different contexts, to make effective choices for meaning or style, and to comprehend more fully when reading or listening.

Vocabulary Acquisition and Use

4. Determine or clarify the meaning of unknown and multiple-meaning words and phrases by using context clues, analyzing meaningful word parts, and consulting general and specialized reference materials, as appropriate.
5. Demonstrate understanding of figurative language, word relationships, and nuances in word meanings.
6. Acquire and use accurately a range of general academic and domain-specific words and phrases sufficient for reading, writing, speaking, and listening at the college and career readiness level; demonstrate independence in gathering vocabulary knowledge when considering a word or phrase important to comprehension or expression.

Note on Range and Content of Student Language Use

To be college and career ready in language, students must have firm control over the conventions of standard English. At the same time, they must come to appreciate that language is at least as much a matter of craft as of rules and be able to choose words, syntax, and punctuation to express themselves and achieve particular functions and rhetorical effects. They must also have extensive vocabularies, built through reading and study, enabling them to comprehend complex texts and engage in purposeful writing about and conversations around content. They need to become skilled in determining or clarifying the meaning of words and phrases they encounter, choosing flexibly from an array of strategies to aid them. They must learn to see an individual word as part of a network of other words—words, for example, that have similar denotations but different connotations. The inclusion of language standards in their strand should not be taken as an indication that skills related to conventions, effective language use, and vocabulary are unimportant to reading, writing, speaking, and listening; indeed, they are inseparable from such contexts.

Source: Copyright © 2010. National Governors Association Center for Best Practices and Council of Chief State School Officers. All rights reserved.

College and Career Readiness Anchor Standards for

Language

The College and Career Readiness (CCR) anchor standards are the same for all middle and high school students, regardless of subject area or grade level. What varies is the sophistication of the language—grammar, vocabulary, and figurative language—at subsequent grade levels in each disciplinary domain. The fundamental language skills should not change as students advance; rather, the level at which they learn and can perform those skills should increase in complexity as students move from one grade to the next.

Conventions of Standard English

Simply put, students should know and use the proper forms of English—spelling, grammar, usage, and conventions—when speaking or writing for public purposes or audiences such as at work or school. The emphasis here is on the crucial role that such attention to correctness plays in college and the workplace, where first impressions matter and the smallest error can cost customers or money. This becomes all the more important in light of social media trends where businesses communicate more and more online, through social media, chat, and text messages.

Knowledge of Language

This standard not only recognizes the range of functions language plays in creating style, voice, and meaning, but also, it emphasizes the importance of diction, syntax, and other factors as they relate to the writer's or speaker's ethos and general effect on the audience in a given context. One must, in other words, give serious thought to which words, which order, for which audience, and which purpose if one is to convey the meaning with maximum effect.

Vocabulary Acquisition and Use

Vocabulary, so instrumental in reading, writing, and speaking/listening, is divided into several domains in these standards. First are those words that are unknown or have many possible meanings, the proper one(s) determined by the occasion or context in which they are used. An essential part of this standard involves using general and specialized reference materials in print or online to determine the etymology of words and learn more about their different meanings and usages. In addition to these words, students add to their word bank the way language is used figuratively, as well as through word relationships that suggest some association, connotation, or nuance depending on how it is used. Finally, students should pay most of their attention to those words that will help them understand or complete their assignments for school; this means learning those domain-specific words and phrases unique to each discipline that students routinely encounter when they read, write, speak, or listen. Over time, students should actively gather and work to grow their knowledge of and ability to use the words and phrases in each subject area to accommodate the increasing complexity of the texts and tasks they face at each subsequent grade level.

Language 1: Demonstrate command of the conventions of standard English grammar and usage when writing or speaking.

9–10 English Language Arts and Social Studies, Science, and Technical Subjects	11–12 English Language Arts and Social Studies, Science, and Technical Subjects
Demonstrate command of the conventions of standard English grammar and usage when writing or speaking. a. Use parallel structure. b. Use various types of phrases (noun, verb, adjectival, adverbial, participial, prepositional, absolute) and clauses (independent, dependent; noun, relative, adverbial) to convey specific meanings and add variety and interest to writing or presentations.	Demonstrate command of the conventions of standard English grammar and usage when writing or speaking. a. **Apply the understanding that usage is a matter of convention, can change over time, and is sometimes contested.** b. **Resolve issues of complex or contested usage, consulting references (e.g., *Merriam-Webster's Dictionary of English Usage*, Garner's *Modern American Usage*) as needed.**

Source: Copyright © 2010. National Governors Association Center for Best Practices and Council of Chief State School Officers. All rights reserved.

What the **Student** Does

<table>
<tr>
<td>

9–10 English Language Arts and Social Studies, Science, and Technical Subjects

Gist: Show, whether writing or speaking, that they know and can follow the conventions of standard English grammar and usage. Also, students communicate ideas and achieve certain effects by using parallel structure and a variety of types of phrases (noun, verb, adjectival, adverbial, participial, prepositional, absolute) and clauses (independent, dependent, noun, relative, adverbial), all of these different constructions enhancing the writer's or speaker's ability to engage the audience.

- How might techniques such as parallel structure—in your sentences, on your slides, or on any lists you might include in this document or speech—strengthen your message and its effect?
- What specific types of phrases or clauses would show a command of the language that would not only engage but persuade your reader, thereby helping you communicate your idea(s) to their fullest effect?
- Why are you using, for example, a series of noun (appositive) phrases in a given situation? Does this choice add both substance *and* style to your writing—or do the phrases merely distract from your message?

</td>
<td>

11–12 English Language Arts and Social Studies, Science, and Technical Subjects

Gist: Show, when writing or speaking, that they know and can apply the conventions of standard English grammar and usage. In addition, students realize that usage can evolve, making what was a convention now seem antiquated or unnecessary, though such changes are often points of contention, which students should learn to resolve, along with other matters of usage, by consulting established sources such as Garner's *Modern American Usage* and *Merriam-Webster's Dictionary of English Usage*.

- What are the conventions or matters of usage you struggle with and so should always look for when writing or speaking?
- What questions of usage or conventions have evolved over time—for example, ending a sentence with a preposition, the use of *their* as a gender-neutral singular noun—but are still frequently contested?
- What sources do you consult to resolve or learn more about conventions when writing or speaking?

</td>
</tr>
</table>

Common Core Language Standard 1

What the **Teacher** Does

To have students demonstrate command of standard English grammar and usage, do the following:

- Teach students the various conventions appropriate to whatever type of writing they are doing, studying, or reading, providing a rich and varied array of examples of how these conventions are used in the world and by real writers.
- Cultivate an environment of respect and wonder relative to language in general and specific aspects of it in particular, one that invites students into language instead of inspiring fear of it; this can be done by bringing in real-world writing (or articles about such writing) that captures the power of language to shape our thinking and convey ideas.
- Invest in and continually add to your knowledge about language, grammar, and usage as these relate to the subjects you teach; share this learning with your students to establish and reinforce your authority when working with language.
- Try *always* to model the virtue of correctness when writing and speaking to your students; this means seeing every handout, every email to the class, and every homework assignment posted online for your students as an occasion to reinforce the importance of communicating clearly and correctly at all times.
- Use this three-step process to teach conventions: (1) Provide direct, separate instruction in the concept, what it is, how it works, why they should know and use it. (2) Create opportunities to practice and refine their knowledge of the concept through simulations and feedback. (3) Apply the knowledge and use the learning in an actual piece of writing to demonstrate a full understanding of the concept, refining their use as needed through your feedback.
- Require that students *use* these conventions and constructions in their writing both to reinforce and to further develop their knowledge of these conventions in their writing; a necessary adjunct to this

requirement to use what they learn would be that you provide targeted, constructive feedback on their use, with the opportunity to revise in light of your comments so they might refine their knowledge and use of these conventions until they become habits and their rules internalized.
- Find the latest version of "The 20 Most Common Errors in Undergraduate Writing," an ongoing study of college writing conducted by Andrea Lunsford that lists the most frequent errors and provides information about their causes and remedies; it serves as a useful guide to your studies of language conventions by narrowing your focus. See also, *Getting It Right*, by Michael W. Smith and Jeffrey D. Wilhelm.
- Provide mentoring texts that show how students should write certain constructions; however, make a point of finding or creating texts that are similar to the type of writing you want your students to do (i.e., sentences that show effective parallel structure written in an academic style as opposed to a sentence from Hemingway using the same convention).
- Use these four sentence-composing techniques to improve students' confidence, fluency, and correctness when teaching different types of sentences and their related conventions: (1) unscramble sentences dissembled for the purpose of studying their construction, (2) imitate specific forms and conventions of writing your students are studying, (3) combine multiple sentences into one as a way to learn a specific convention or construction, and (4) expand on sentences, beginning with a base or stem sentence and then adding to it those forms you are studying.

To help your English Language Learners, try this one thing:

- Provide many models and opportunities to practice when teaching these more advanced constructions and conventions.

Notes

Academic Vocabulary: Key Words and Phrases

Absolute phrase: This modifies the whole sentence; it also begins with a noun that functions as a subject for which there is no actual verb, though sometimes there is a verbal. **Example:** Roosevelt delivered his Four Freedoms speech prior to our entry into WWII, <u>his words preparing the nation for the war on the horizon.</u>

Adjectival phrase: A phrase beginning with an adjective that is separate from the noun or noun phrase it modifies. Example: Lincoln, <u>calm and sure of his purpose after much reflection</u>, signed the Emancipation Proclamation.

Adverbial clause: This is a dependent clause that modifies, qualifies, or defines a verb, an adjective, or another adverb by telling readers where, when, why, how, or under what circumstances an action occurred. Such clauses are headed by a subordinating conjunction and contain a subject–verb pair. **Example:** <u>Although alternative explanations are available</u>, only Zakaria's statements about the causes of dissent are viable, <u>as they come with the evidence to support them.</u>

Adverbial phrase: This is a small group of words that modify or qualify a verb, adjective, or another verb, explaining when, where, or how something happened. **Example:** The balance of power between the two leaders shifted <u>after a time</u>.

Clause: This is a group of words with a subject *and* a predicate; there are two types: dependent (cannot stand alone) and independent (functions as a complete sentence). **Dependent:** The policies of the past, <u>which undermined small businesses</u>, still appeal to many. **Independent:** <u>The economic policies of that period protected small businesses</u>, which had often felt undermined by previous legislation.

Contested: This is any use of language that causes another person to challenge the usage or construction as incorrect or flawed; a traditional example would be ending sentences with prepositions.

Conventions: This is a way of doing or using something—in this case, words, punctuation, or grammar—as established and endorsed by a group that has agreed to observe certain practices or techniques.

Grammar: The study of words and their component parts and how they combine to form sentences; the structural relationships in language that contribute to the meaning of the words and sentences.

Interest: As used here, the word suggests that choosing one word or set of words over another, and arranging them in a certain style will intrigue or otherwise have an impact on the reader.

Noun: This is a single word that names a person, place, object, concept, or action. More specific forms include common nouns, proper nouns, collective nouns, and count and noncount nouns.

Noun clause: This is a dependent clause consisting of a group of words that include a subject and predicate and functions as a noun in the sentence. **Example:** <u>The cause of the Great Depression</u> eluded most economists, each of whom offered a different theory.

Parallel structure: Items included in a pair or series consist of the same grammatical unit and function in a unified way within the sentence. **Example:** Churchill spoke of "<u>blood</u>, <u>sweat</u>, and <u>tears</u>." (three nouns)

Participial phrase: This functions as an adjective and includes a present participle (the falling market) or past participle (the broken machine).

Phrase: This is a group of words that functions as one unit but lacks a subject or verb—or both. **Example:** <u>The conclusion we reached</u> hinted at the need for further research into the role of humor and healing.

Prepositional phrase: This is words that begin with a preposition and end with its object; it can function as an adjective, an adverb, or a noun.

Usage: This refers to how one uses language or whether a specific usage of language is permitted.

Verb: A word that names an action or state of being; verbs change form to indicate tense, number, voice, or mood.

Notes

Language 2: Demonstrate command of the conventions of standard English capitalization, punctuation, and spelling when writing.

9–10 English Language Arts and Social Studies, Science, and Technical Subjects	11–12 English Language Arts and Social Studies, Science, and Technical Subjects
Demonstrate command of the conventions of standard English capitalization, punctuation, and spelling when writing. a. Use a semicolon (and perhaps a conjunctive adverb) to link two or more closely related independent clauses. b. Use a colon to introduce a list or quotation. c. Spell correctly.	Demonstrate command of the conventions of standard English capitalization, punctuation, and spelling when writing. a. **Observe hyphenation conventions.** b. Spell correctly.

Source: Copyright © 2010. National Governors Association Center for Best Practices and Council of Chief State School Officers. All rights reserved.

What the **Student** Does

English Language Arts and Social Studies, Science, and Technical Subjects

Gist: Know and observe the established rules of standard English when writing in general and especially with regards to capitalization, punctuation, and spelling. In addition, students exhibit their command of conventions such as the semicolon by joining multiple independent clauses which share a connection, and the colon when introducing a list or inserting a quotation. Finally, students show their knowledge of and commitment to correct spelling at all times when writing for anyone but their close friends.

- Which sources (*Merriam-Webster's, American Heritage*) do you use to get the most current information about spelling and conventions such as capitalization or use of semicolons?
- What ideas throughout your paper might be better expressed using a semicolon to signal they share a connection?
- Which ideas, quotations, or details would be better expressed as a list following a colon?
- Which misspelled words are most likely to be missed by your spellchecker (e.g., to/too, they're/their)?
- Which of Andrea Lunsford's "Top Twenty Most Common Errors" do you frequently make when writing?

English Language Arts and Social Studies, Science, and Technical Subjects

Gist: Know and observe the established rules of standard English when writing in general and especially with regards to capitalization, punctuation, and spelling. In addition, students exhibit their command of conventions such as the hyphen by using them correctly (to *join*) and not confusing the hyphen with the dash, which separates; they consult established sources like *Merriam-Webster's* and grammarbook.com to resolve questions of correctness. Finally, students show their knowledge of and commitment to correct spelling at all times.

- What editing and proofreading strategies—e.g., using the search function for specific words, colons, or other elements—do you use besides the grammar and spelling check on your word processor?
- Which source (*Merriam-Webster's, American Heritage*) do you use to get the most current information about spelling and conventions such as hyphens and dashes?
- Which words do you use a hyphen on which may not require it (e.g., *hard drive*)?
- Which misspelled words are most likely to be missed by your spellchecker (e.g., to/too, they're/their)?
- Which of Andrea Lunsford's "Top Twenty Most Common Errors" do you frequently make when writing?

What the **Teacher** Does

To develop students' command of the conventions of Standard English, do the following:

- Emphasize, reinforce, and teach students how to capitalize, punctuate, and spell as needed within the context of your larger writing curriculum; for example, when teaching them how to construct and use different modifiers such as appositives, teach students how to punctuate those specific constructions.

- Routinely point out how the writers your students study use these conventions to achieve clarity and convey relationships by using punctuation such as the semicolon or conjunctions to link two or more closely related independent clauses.

- Use multiple and contrasting models to illustrate the proper and incorrect use of conventions such as colons and hyphens, using these models to show when, how, where, and why to use the colon versus the semicolon, the hyphen instead of the dash.

- Honor at all times, in all your writing and speaking directed to students, the value of correctness; treat every assignment, email to students, and homework directions posted online as an opportunity to reiterate the importance of correctness.

- Teach conventions using this three-step approach: (1) Provide direct instruction in the concept, explaining what it is, how it works, and why they should know and use it. (2) Create opportunities to practice and refine the lesson through simulations and feedback. (3) Demonstrate what they learned in an actual piece of writing that shows they understand the concept.

- Provide targeted, constructive feedback to students about their use of these conventions, and the opportunity to revise in light of your comments.

- Require students keep their own lists of conventions they need to learn or improve their use of; to these, they might add samples of correct—or incorrect—usage;

they might consider extending their learning online by using sites like noredink.com to practice and improve their grammar skills.

- Use mentor texts similar to the type of writing you want your students to do (i.e., sentences that show how writers use punctuation in general and specific forms such as the hyphen, semicolon, or colon in particular).

- Limit the number of grammatical terms you actively teach so the focus remains on how to write better instead of what to remember; you can reinforce the terms by routinely using them when discussing them.

- Generate with students a range of possible punctuation marks (e.g., a dash, colon, parentheses, or comma) they might use in certain circumstances (e.g., when punctuating certain types of appositives); then try them out, discussing each as you display them on the screen; an alternative approach would be to generate different punctuation strategies to create a particular effect (e.g., emphasis, distinction between, link between related ideas or elements) in a sentence.

- Use these four sentence-composing techniques to improve students' confidence, fluency, and correctness when teaching different types of sentences and their related conventions: (1) unscramble sentences dissembled for the purpose of studying their construction, (2) imitate specific forms and conventions of writing your students are studying, (3) combine multiple sentences into one as a way to learn a specific convention or construction, and (4) expand on sentences, beginning with a base or stem sentence and then adding to it those forms you are studying.

To help your English Language Learners, try this one thing:

- Try to limit the number of new conventions you introduce at any one time to avoid overwhelming your ELL students.

Notes

Academic Vocabulary: Key Words and Phrases

Capitalization: Use uppercase letters not only to signal where sentences begin, but also to indicate that a word is a title, a person's name, a product or brand name, or some other form of proper noun. This is especially important in light of trends to ignore capitalization when texting and carry that over into the workplace or classroom when writing more formal documents.

Colon: Typically, writers use a comma to introduce a quotation; they can also use a colon when the quotation is a complete sentence. **Example:** One line in particular rose above all the others in Gehrig's speech: "I am the luckiest man alive."

Conjunctive adverb: This means using an adverb as a conjunction; examples include *however*, *furthermore*, *therefore*, and *likewise*, among others. Writers use these to link ideas that are connected but located in two independent clauses. **Example:** Some suggest that Cormac McCarthy incorporates concepts from physics in his novels; however, this should not surprise people given that he is on the staff of the Santa Fe Institute, a think tank for scientists.

Conventions: This refers to those rules about which punctuation marks to use, how, when, why, and where to use them when writing different types of documents in various media.

Hyphenation conventions: Often mistaken for a dash, the hyphen is made by hitting the hyphen key *once*; to make an em dash, hit it *twice*, at which point many word processors will reformat it as one long dash (—). One of the most common errors made by college writers, the hyphen *joins* words or parts of them to create compound words and numbers. A common source of confusion—and mistakes—is the evolution of words that begin hyphenated (e-mail) and eventually are not hyphenated (email). We hyphenate compound adjectives that come *before* a noun (five-course meal) but not after (meal had five courses).

Independent clause: This is group of words that contains a subject and predicate and is able to function on its own as a complete sentence.

Punctuation: All the marks—period, comma, colon, semicolon, dash, hyphen, quotation and question marks, parentheses, exclamation points, and others—that writers use to be clear, to make connections, and to create a style that suggests how the text should be read. It is, as some say, what makes the music of the writing happen in ways similar to musical notations that signal where, when, and how long to stop or speed up, where to pause and what to emphasize.

Quotation: One most often uses a comma leading into a quotation; one can, however, also use a colon when the quotation is a complete sentence (see Colon). **Example:** One line in particular rose above all the others in the speech: "I have a dream that my four little children will one day live in a nation . . . where they will not be judged by the color of their skin but by the content of their character."

Semicolon: Some describe the semicolon (which looks like this;) as half period and half comma; more officially, however, a semicolon creates a pause that is more pronounced than a comma and implies a connection between complete ideas related to each other in the same sentence. Writers use semicolons to join or suggest a connection between two ideas; they also use them to extend, restate, or otherwise comment on or provide a point of contrast to what comes before the semicolon. **Example:** Many argue that Smith's notion of the "invisible hand" suggests government should play no role but simply let everything take its course; yet Smith's writings on morality clearly suggest we have a moral obligation to care for others.

Standard English: This refers to English as it should be written and spoken in the mainstream workplace or college classroom.

Notes

Language 3: Apply knowledge of language to understand how language functions in different contexts, to make effective choices for meaning or style, and to comprehend more fully when reading or listening.

9–10 English Language Arts and Social Studies, Science, and Technical Subjects	11–12 English Language Arts and Social Studies, Science, and Technical Subjects
Apply knowledge of language to understand how language functions in different contexts, to make effective choices for meaning or style, and to comprehend more fully when reading or listening.	Apply knowledge of language to understand how language functions in different contexts, to make effective choices for meaning or style, and to comprehend more fully when reading or listening.
a. Write and edit work so that it conforms to the guidelines in a style manual (e.g., *MLA Handbook*, Turabian's *Manual for Writers*) appropriate for the discipline and writing type.	a. **Vary syntax for effect, consulting references (e.g., Tufte's *Artful Sentences*) for guidance as needed; apply an understanding of syntax to the study of complex texts when reading.**

Source: Copyright © 2010. National Governors Association Center for Best Practices and Council of Chief State School Officers. All rights reserved.

What the **Student** Does

9–10 English Language Arts and Social Studies, Science, and Technical Subjects	**11–12** English Language Arts and Social Studies, Science, and Technical Subjects

Gist: Draw on their knowledge of language—how it creates meaning, achieves various effects, shapes a message or convey a style—when reading, writing, speaking, or listening. Here, language refers not only to the surface conventions of grammar, usage, and mechanics, but to diction, syntax, and grammar, and how they combine to create a writer's style and achieve certain effects when read or spoken. Also, students learn which style manual to consult when writing for different disciplines. In general, humanities papers follow the guidelines laid out by the Modern Language Association (MLA) format; social sciences, education, and business use the American Psychological Association (APA) format; and many other fields, including those already listed, use the *Chicago Manual of Style* (sometimes called *Turabian*). Science and mathematics use those style guides specific to their discipline.

- What is the context or occasion for which the text was written—and how does that context affect the choice and arrangement of words in this text?
- How does the context or purpose affect the choice and arrangement of words in this text?
- How do the writer's words affect the meaning and style of the writing?
- Which of the different style manuals (APA, MLA, Chicago, or some other such guide used by math or science) should you consult when writing, editing, or formatting this document?

Gist: Draw on their knowledge of language—how it creates meaning, achieves various effects, shapes a message or convey a style—when reading, writing, speaking, or listening. Here, language refers not only to the surface conventions of grammar, usage, and mechanics, but to diction, syntax, and grammar, and how they combine to create a writer's style and achieve certain effects when read or spoken. Also, students learn not only to vary their syntax to achieve specific effects such as emphasis when writing, but also to use that same knowledge when reading those texts written by authors whose style shows great syntactic complexity.

- What is the context or occasion for which the text was written—and how does that context affect the choice and arrangement of words in this text?
- How does the context or purpose affect the choice and arrangement of words in this text?
- How do the writer's words affect the meaning and style of the writing?
- How would you characterize the syntax in your writing here (i.e., do you tend to use the same syntactic patterns or vary them to achieve specific effects)?

What the **Teacher** Does

To have students understand how language functions in different contexts, do the following:

- Stress to students that one can write well in one genre but not necessarily another; it is a craft that must, and can be, learned; this validates the struggle of learning something they declare they already know how to do very well (write) but is, in fact, different in form and function (write an argument essay).

- Direct students to read the assigned texts closely, focusing their attention on the ways the author uses language—specifically through the diction, imagery, syntax, and grammar—to create meaning or a style that contributes substance to the text; this might lead to such strategies as parsing the sentences to help students see the spatial relationship between parts of the sentences, or using color-coding functions on the computer when displaying the passages being analyzed.

- Use a range of contrasting models that clarify and extend students' understanding of how language can function within a text; this might mean showing them examples of the same passage modified to show the effect of it written as a series of simple sentences versus more sophisticated sentences in light of the topic or their purpose; it might also mean having them read a poem, story, essay, and encyclopedia entry about the same topic so they can see how differently each one writes about the same subject as a function of its genre and conventions.

- Expose students to a wide variety of texts and authors, styles and genres, forms and formats, so they not only learn from these practitioners the full range of choices they can make as writers, but also so they can learn how to read these different types of writing.

To help students make effective choices for meaning or style, do the following:

- Provide feedback on their drafts throughout the process, offering them suggestions about the different choices they can make to join, emphasize, or subordinate certain ideas, events, or other details in the text.

- Create a slide show or handout that shows different iterations of the same idea or subject in various sentence formats, each one written to emphasize some different element or achieve a slightly different effect on the reader; have students evaluate these—on their own or by conferring with classmates—and agree on the one they think is best, providing a rationale for their selection.

To enable students to write and edit as appropriate for a discipline, do the following:

- Introduce them to the established conventions specific to the writing of that discipline or genre as defined by the *MLA Handbook* or whatever other style guide sets the standards for that discipline or genre.

To improve students' knowledge of and ability to vary syntax, do the following:

- Give them a rubric with different traits on it related to syntax and style that they can use to assess their own or another's writing.

- Teach students a range of different syntactical constructions—see Tufte's *Artful Sentences: Syntax as Style* for an excellent guide—and require them to use those throughout their writing and analyze their use in the writing of others.

To help your English Language Learners, try this one thing:

- Provide them with a set of examples—of whatever aspect of style you are teaching—that show, through small incremental steps, the different changes; then ask them to explain the difference between each, to discuss what they notice and how the changes seem to affect the meaning or experience of the text.

Notes

Academic Vocabulary: Key Words and Phrases

Complex texts: This refers to those texts, informational or literary, that employ a variety of stylistic or rhetorical techniques, use different and sophisticated sentence structures, and contain challenging words or familiar words used in unfamiliar ways.

Conforms to guidelines: Documents in different disciplines all have conventions about format, structure, and other elements that affect style and content. When writing a paper for an English or a social studies class, for example, students would conform to those guidelines outlined in the *MLA Handbook* about how to cite sources, lay out a page, and format a works cited list.

Discipline: Synonymous in this case with *subject* or *course*, the word signals to the reader and writer that certain conventions—for format, layout, even style and content—apply to the text from a specific discipline (or subject) for which you are reading or writing it.

Edit: The emphasis here is on satisfying your reader's expectations for a clean and corrected final draft of whatever you wrote—whether on paper, smartphone, tablet, or big screen—whether for school, work, or a public audience online. This means taking time to check and, as needed, repair or revise grammar, punctuation, mechanics, spelling, as well as citation and formatting problems you encounter.

Effective choices for meaning or style: Drawing on such elements as syntax, rhetoric, and diction, among others, writers choose words and other elements such as punctuation, then arrange those to some purpose (meaning) or effect (style).

How language functions in different contexts: We are always writing a specific type of text for an audience, on some occasion, for some purpose. How we write, what features or format we choose, which words or sentence types we include, what tone or style we adopt, all relate to the context in which that document is written and must be considered whether we are the writer, the speaker, the reader, or the listener.

Knowledge of language: This refers to all its forms and functions, including vocabulary, grammar, usage, syntax, rhetoric, diction, and style.

MLA Handbook: The *Modern Language Association Handbook for Writers of Research Paper* is the standard reference for writing humanities papers in particular and research papers in general. A new edition is published every few years to reflect the latest changes, most of them a result of technology.

Syntax: This refers to the rules by which we combine words and other elements in the sentence to make grammatical sentences or the way we arrange words and other elements within a sentence to create or affect the meaning of that sentence. It is an important element of a writer's style.

Turabian's *Manual for Writers*: Associated with the *Chicago Manual of Style* (an alternative to the MLA guidelines), the *Manual for Writers* was written by Kate Turabian in 1937, and then a secretary in the dissertation office at University of Chicago. She created a guide to help all students format their papers according to the department standards.

Writing type: This applies to the genre or type of text within that genre and all the conventions for style and format that accompany it. If the "writing type" is a traditional research paper, then the guidelines for that are in the Turabian or the MLA style guides, or some other such book required by your teacher; if the student is composing within the emerging hybrid forms that blend media, they can consult the *Yahoo! Style Guide* or some other authoritative source with questions about format, layout, or features.

Notes

Language 4: Determine or clarify the meaning of unknown and multiple-meaning words and phrases by using context clues, analyzing meaningful word parts, and consulting general and specialized reference materials, as appropriate.

9–10 English Language Arts and Social Studies, Science, and Technical Subjects	**11–12** English Language Arts and Social Studies, Science, and Technical Subjects
Determine or clarify the meaning of unknown and multiple-meaning words and phrases based on grades **9–10** reading and content, choosing flexibly from a range of strategies.	Determine or clarify the meaning of unknown and multiple-meaning words and phrases based on grades **11–12** reading and content, choosing flexibly from a range of strategies.

9–10

a. Use context (e.g., the overall meaning of a sentence, paragraph, or text; a word's position or function in a sentence) as a clue to the meaning of a word or phrase.
b. Identify and correctly use patterns of word changes that indicate different meanings or parts of speech (e.g., *analyze, analysis, analytical; advocate, advocacy*).
c. Consult general and specialized reference materials (e.g., dictionaries, glossaries, thesauruses), both print and digital, to find the pronunciation of a word or determine or clarify its precise meaning, its part of speech, or its etymology.
d. Verify the preliminary determination of the meaning of a word or phrase (e.g., by checking the inferred meaning in context or in a dictionary).

11–12

a. Use context (e.g., the overall meaning of a sentence, paragraph, or text; a word's position or function in a sentence) as a clue to the meaning of a word or phrase.
b. Identify and correctly use patterns of word changes that indicate different meanings or parts of speech (e.g., **conceive, conception, conceivable**).
c. Consult general and specialized reference materials (e.g., dictionaries, glossaries, thesauruses), both print and digital, to find the pronunciation of a word or determine or clarify its precise meaning, its part of speech, its etymology, **or its standard usage**.
d. Verify the preliminary determination of the meaning of a word or phrase (e.g., by checking the inferred meaning in context or in a dictionary).

Source: Copyright © 2010. National Governors Association Center for Best Practices and Council of Chief State School Officers. All rights reserved.

What the **Student** Does

9–10 | English Language Arts and Social Studies, Science, and Technical Subjects

Gist: Apply a range of strategies to discern or illuminate the meaning of any unfamiliar or multiple-meaning words found in grades 9–10 texts. Among these strategies, four are especially effective and important to know well: using context clues, noting how words change when used, consulting reference sources, and confirming one's initial sense of the word's meaning. Also, students note how words change to reflect tense or type (past/present, verb/noun); this allows them to break down a word's meaning and connotation (as they track *declaration* and *declarative* from *declare*). While looking into *declare*, students might also consult a good dictionary, one with the etymologies of most words; this would allow them to develop that deeper understanding of the concept of *declaring*, which stems from Latin by way of *thoroughly* (de-) and *to make clear* (*clarare*). In addition to using the dictionary, students make intelligent use of other sources such as the thesaurus and glossary for alternative words or guidance in how to use, speak, or better understand a given word.

- Which words or phrases in a sentence do you not understand—or prevent you from understanding other portions of the text?
- Which words have many different meanings or connotations? Of the different meanings and implications of this word or phrase, which one seems most fitting in the context used in this text?
- What does this word's location within the sentence, the general subject or point of the paragraph in which it appears, and the word's purpose in the sentence tell you about its likely meaning?
- What other variations or conjugations of this word (e.g., *inspiration, inspire, spirit; synthesis, synthesize*) come to mind that might be more familiar to you?
- What reliable, authoritative sources might you consult to get more information about the word's meaning, its history, and its classification (what part of speech)?
- What is your initial hunch or prediction about the meaning of this word or phrase in this context? How does your guess compare with the dictionary's definition?

11–12 | English Language Arts and Social Studies, Science, and Technical Subjects

Gist: Apply a range of strategies to derive or elucidate the meaning of any unfamiliar or multiple-meaning words found in grades 11–12 texts. Among these strategies, four are especially effective and important to know well: using context clues, noting how words change when used, consulting reference sources, and confirming one's initial sense of the word's meaning. Also, students observe how words change to reflect tense or type (past/present, verb/noun); this allows them to break down a word's meaning and connotation (as they track *declaration* and *declarative* from *declare*). While looking into *declare*, students might also consult a good dictionary, one with etymologies and usage notes (e.g., *American Heritage Dictionary*); this would allow them to develop a deeper understanding of the concept of *declaring*, which stems from Latin by way of *thoroughly* (de-) and *to make clear* (*clarare*). In addition to using the dictionary, students make intelligent use of other sources such as the thesaurus and glossary for alternative words or guidance in how to use, speak, or better understand a given word.

- Which words or phrases in a sentence do you not understand—or prevent you from understanding other portions of the text?
- Which words have many different meanings or connotations? Of the different meanings and implications of this word or phrase, which one seems most fitting in the context used in this text?
- What does this word's location within the sentence, the general subject or point of the paragraph in which it appears, and the word's purpose in the sentence tell you about its likely meaning?
- What other variations or conjugations of this word (e.g., *inspiration, inspire, spirit; synthesis, synthesize*) come to mind that might be more familiar to you?
- What reliable, authoritative sources might you consult to get more information about the word's meaning, its history, and its classification (what part of speech), or conventions for use?
- What is your initial hunch or prediction about the meaning of this word or phrase in this context? How does your guess compare with the dictionary's definition?

What the **Teacher** Does

To have students determine or clarify the meaning of unknown words and phrases, do the following:

- Teach students a range of strategies to choose from, including using context clues, word parts, reference works, and available resources such as indexes, glossaries, sidebars, footnotes, and other texts you may be using as part of the unit.
- Model for students by thinking aloud how you handle unknown words when reading, noting that you first acknowledge that you do not know a word and wonder if you need to know it to understand the text; having decided you do, you would then try one of the strategies listed previously in an effort to infer its meaning; in the event that you cannot, you would actually turn to a dictionary to show them how you use it to decide which, of the many different definitions, is the one that best fits.
- Use this procedure developed by Robert Marzano in *Building Background Knowledge for Academic Achievement* for teaching words you want students to know or that they have determined they do not understand but must learn if they are to comprehend the assigned text: (1) You describe, explain, or provide an example of the new term in association with the specific word you want them to learn. (2) Students then explain the new term, paraphrasing your description in their own words. (3) Students next represent the term in some graphic way that helps them understand and remember the word. (4) Students revisit the term over time, encountering it through various activities and contexts designed to deepen their fluency with that word. (5) You ask students to return to and discuss these target words with each other periodically. (6) You engage students in activities or games that invite them to interact with these terms to reinforce and deepen their understanding and fluency.

To have students determine or clarify word meanings by analyzing word parts, do the following:

- Work with students to identify the suffixes, prefixes, and roots that make up a particular word; sometimes it is best to ask them if the root calls to mind other, more familiar, words that can help them access the word's meaning.
- Model for students how you go about understanding a word such as *indomitable* by analyzing its parts, looking to the prefix for some clue (e.g., *in-* meaning *not*), then the base or root (*domitare* meaning *to tame*, which you note calls to mind the word *dominate*), and finally the suffix (*able*, which means *able to be*), concluding for the class that it means unable to be controlled.

To have students learn how to consult general and specialized reference materials, do the following:

- Guide your students through different reference works related to vocabulary, including books like *Garner's Modern American Usage*, *The Synonym Finder*, and unabridged and specialized dictionaries for phrases, allusions, etymologies, and aphorisms; these will only be useful if students are engaged in the sort of close, analytical reading that requires such detailed information.

To have students determine or clarify words and phrases with multiple meanings, do the following:

- Help students learn to identify which words likely have multiple meanings in the context in which they are used; then break out the dictionary and, working in pairs, have them determine which of the eight possible definitions of *fair* apply to the passage where the author uses it repeatedly but never quite the same way.

To help your English Language Learners, try this one thing:

- Confirm that they have access to an appropriate ELL dictionary in their primary language at school and at home; then work with them to develop a set of the most important words for them to know in your class—words the other students are likely to know to varying degrees—and help them learn them as needed.

Notes

Academic Vocabulary: Key Words and Phrases

Choose flexibly: This is needed as the situation requires or the purpose demands; the emphasis here is on the choosing *flexibly*, which is to say that students' judgment is a key part of this process showing how able they are to think strategically.

Consult general and specialized reference materials: This includes everything from a dictionary to usage handbooks such as *Garner's Modern American Usage*, or other sources that focus on specialized aspects of words and phrases such as etymologies and allusions, as well as the *Oxford English Dictionary* to examine the word in depth.

Content: This refers to texts other than a page of words being "read"; this includes mixed media, as well as digital and visual texts (infographics).

Context clues: One makes an informed guess about the meaning of a word after looking at all the words around it, the way it is used (to determine its part of speech), how it is used in this context, and its place in the sentence and/or paragraph.

Determine and clarify the meaning of unknown and multiple-meaning words: Students cannot afford to ignore or not know many words in complex texts they read at this level; lacking such understanding, they cannot understand the texts read, especially when these words appear in discipline-specific texts as specialized terms related to a field of study they are trying to learn. As for "multiple-meaning" (polysemic) words they may encounter in literary texts, they must look these up in specialized or unabridged dictionaries with etymologies and the full range of definitions available.

Etymology: This refers to the study of a word and its origins, how it has evolved in its meaning across time. This includes examining the word's roots. **Example:** *Character* derives from Middle English *carecter*, meaning imprint on the soul; Old French and Greek *kharacter* meaning to inscribe; and Greek, *kharak*, which means the pointed end of stick.

Inferred meaning: This refers to the meaning we derive from taking what we learn from the text or about the word as it is used in context and adding that to what we already know; this adds up to an inference. That is, what we learn + what we already know = the inferred meaning.

Parts of speech: This refers to what function a word serves in its context in a given sentence: verb, noun, pronoun, preposition, conjunction, adjective, and adverb; subject or predicate.

Patterns of word changes: This is one of the vocabulary strategies listed here, it involves considering a word as it is conjugated in this specific context. So for example, if the word is *advocate*, is the writer using that as a noun (*advocate*) or a verb (*advocate*); in another tense or form (*advocacy*, *advocation*, or *advocator*).

Precise meaning: When words can be used to mean different things, it is important to determine which, of all the possible meanings, applies to this word as it is being used.

Range of strategies: The emphasis here is on the *students* knowing and using a "range of strategies," looking up individual words in the context of use, examining those words around the word for clues, skimming to find words they should look up and learn about *before* reading the text, and collecting and looking up words as they read to generate their own definitions of frequently seen and misunderstood words.

Standard usage: This refers to how a word or phrase would be used in the workplace or a college class, the newspaper or a textbook, or as defined by *Garner's Modern American Usage*.

Word's position or function in a sentence: Where a word appears in a sentence and how it functions—its part of speech—offer abundant information about its meaning, purpose, and importance.

Language 5: Demonstrate understanding of word relationships and nuances in word meanings.

9–10 English Language Arts and Social Studies, Science, and Technical Subjects	**11–12** English Language Arts and Social Studies, Science, and Technical Subjects
Demonstrate understanding of figurative language, word relationships, and nuances in word meanings. a. Interpret figures of speech (e.g., euphemism, oxymoron) in context and analyze their role in the text. b. Analyze nuances in the meaning of words with similar denotations.	Demonstrate understanding of figurative language, word relationships, and nuances in word meanings. a. Interpret figures of speech (e.g., **hyperbole, paradox**) in context and analyze their role in the text. b. Analyze nuances in the meaning of words with similar denotations.

Source: Copyright © 2010. National Governors Association Center for Best Practices and Council of Chief State School Officers. All rights reserved.

What the **Student** Does

9–10	English Language Arts and Social Studies, Science, and Technical Subjects

Gist: Show they know and can apply their knowledge of figurative language, word relationships, and nuances in the words they use when writing, speaking, and especially reading those complex texts they encounter in grades 9–10. Students use a range of sources and strategies to make sense of the figures of speech (e.g., euphemism and oxymoron) in the context of their reading, going beyond merely defining these words to analyze how they function within the larger text to shape meaning and style. A similar process takes place as students examine the nuances of those words which share denotative meanings (e.g., *fair, just, right, correct*).

- What examples of figurative language does this author use in this text?
- What effect is the writer or speaker seeking to achieve by using a given form of figurative language?
- What nuance of meaning does this author attempt to achieve by choosing one word (e.g., *elegant*) over another (e.g., *fancy*) with the same denotative meaning?

11–12	English Language Arts and Social Studies, Science, and Technical Subjects

Gist: Show they know and can apply their knowledge of figurative language, word relationships, and nuances in the words they use when writing, speaking, and especially reading those complex texts they encounter in grades 11–12. Students use a range of sources and strategies to make sense of the figures of speech (e.g., hyperbole and paradox) in the context of their reading, going beyond merely defining these words to analyze how they function within the larger text to shape meaning and style. A similar process takes place as students examine the nuances of those words which share denotative meanings (e.g., *fair, just, right, correct*).

- What examples of figurative language does this author use in this text?
- What effect is the writer or speaker seeking to achieve by using a given form of figurative language?
- What nuance of meaning does this author attempt to achieve by choosing one word (e.g., *elegant*) over another (e.g., *fancy*) with the same denotative meaning?

What the **Teacher** Does

To help students understand word relationships, do the following:

- Provide them with a set of words from the text that are somehow related; how subtle the relationship is should depend on the class and grade level. Students reading in a social studies class about American history, for example, might get words such as *liberty, freedom, independence, free will, laissez-faire, self-determination,* and *license.* Those reading a novel such as Conrad's *Heart of Darkness* might get a list of words such as *gloomy, dark, shadow, night, mourning,* and *subterranean.* The task of any such group would be to determine the relationship between these different words and how it relates to and affects the meaning of the text when the words are used together.

- Extend the previous activity, or use it in more advanced contexts (upper grades), so that you provide the students with the idea (the West as a source of enlightenment and civilization bringing light to the darkness, as Conrad suggests), and then tell them to find words and phrases related to that idea from the text, presenting them and explaining their connection to this motif.

- Offer more open-ended opportunities at different points in the study of a text or topic, and invite students to generate a group of words that are related by a concept such as fear; this can be done to prepare students to read a text or to enrich their reading of a text that treats this topic in some depth. You can also add conditions, such as that all words must be a particular part of speech. Consider trying this same activity using visualthesaurus.com to see what associations it comes up with when a word like *fear* is entered.

- Examine some critical writings about the subject or text you are teaching, looking for the sort of nouns, verbs, and adjectives used to discuss that particular topic. Create a three-column organizer and, as you read, copy the relevant nouns, verbs, and adjectives into the respective columns; if time allows, take verbs such as *character* from the noun column and add *characterize* in the verb column, and *characteristic* and *caricature* to the noun column, and so on. Use these lists as seems appropriate when students are writing about or discussing the topic or texts.

To have students interpret and analyze figures of speech in context, do the following:

- Use a graphic organizer that allows you to analyze the associations between the core word and its associated words; for example, you could draw a line and write *Literal* on the top and *Figurative* underneath it, defining a word used figuratively in the text (e.g., the word *swerve* used in a William Stafford poem) first in its literal or denotative meaning; below that, on this two-tier organizer, you would generate with students all the different connotations of the word *swerve* in the figurative, metaphorical sense, and then discuss how these might apply to the poem.

- Try a range of other structured activities or note-taking tools such as semantic mapping, semantic feature analysis, and concept ladders; a related activity for individual words is to create short sentence templates that allow students to better understand words while practicing their writing. An example of such a template would be something like: (the word) is/means (the def); however, it is not/does not mean (the antithesis) .

To have students analyze the nuance of words with similar denotations, do the following:

- Draw a continuum on the board and have students place a set of related words (e.g., all words related to *civilized*) along the continuum with *civilized* at one end and the others arranged as students see fit, though they must be prepared to explain the rationale for their placement.

To help your English Language Learners, try this one thing:

- Do anything you can to make what is very abstract and elusive more visual and concrete for these students.

Notes

Academic Vocabulary: Key Words and Phrases

Analyze the role (of figures of speech) in the text: After interpreting what the figures of speech mean, students then analyze how each one contributes to or affects the meaning of the text as a whole. This might mean examining the imagery used in an analogy in light of the author's purpose or other imagery used in the text to see how they complement each other and shape the meaning of the text.

Denotations: This refers to the literal or dictionary meaning of a word (as opposed to its connotative meaning, which includes all the more nuanced, subtle meanings of a word as we use and understand them). It is often the nuanced or connotative meaning of words that undermine comprehension, especially for English Learners or those without exposure to the other uses of the word.

Euphemism: This is a polite, neutral, or sometimes jargon word that replaces another harsh or blunt term that seems inappropriate to use in this context or with this audience (e.g., Instead of "firing" people, the company said it was merely "downsizing" its workforce.)

Figurative language (figures of speech): This refers to the use of more visual, associative language to help readers "see" what one is saying or otherwise convey a deeper idea or emotion through such figures of speech as metaphor, simile, analogy, and allusion; clichés and mixed metaphors are also figures of speech, but they are more often weak points the writer should have revised or otherwise rewritten.

Hyperbole: This is one of the most commonly used—some would say *overused*—rhetorical devices. It exaggerates some aspect of a subject in a way that the reader or listener is clearly meant to notice and not take literally. When used effectively, it allows the writer to distinguish between two or more subjects; add energy to the text through its sometimes amusing but extreme comparisons; and, more important, emphasize some aspect of the subject through exaggeration.

Interpret: This means to make sense or explain the meaning of different figures of speech such as those listed here: oxymoron and euphemism.

Nuance: Related to connotative meaning (see Denotations), this word reminds us of the subtle meanings of some words as we use and come to know them. In its etymology, the word *nuance* derives from *to shade* something; thus, as readers we discern the veiled or implied meanings of a word and as writers attend to these degrees of meaning as we choose which words to use.

Oxymoron: A figure of speech in which two seemingly contradictory words are used in conjunction with each other in an implied relationship (e.g., jumbo shrimp, friendly fire, half empty).

Paradox: This is a statement that seems logical but upon closer inspection reveals itself to be self-contradictory (e.g., The more Hamlet insists he is not mad, the more mad he appears to be).

Word relationships: This refers to how two or more words might be related grammatically, rhetorically, conceptually, or in some other meaningful way as they are used in this text. Included in this category of words are figures of speech such as metaphors, analogies, and similes, which are based entirely on associations and relationships between words and ideas.

Notes

Language 6: Acquire and use accurately a range of general academic and domain-specific words and phrases sufficient for reading, writing, speaking, and listening at the college and career readiness level; demonstrate independence in gathering vocabulary knowledge when considering a word or phrase important to comprehension or expression.

9–10	English Language Arts and Social Studies, Science, and Technical Subjects

Acquire and use accurately general academic and domain-specific words and phrases, sufficient for reading, writing, speaking, and listening at the college and career readiness level; demonstrate independence in gathering vocabulary knowledge when considering a word or phrase important to comprehension or expression.

11–12	English Language Arts and Social Studies, Science, and Technical Subjects

Acquire and use accurately general academic and domain-specific words and phrases, sufficient for reading, writing, speaking, and listening at the college and career readiness level; demonstrate independence in gathering vocabulary knowledge when considering a word or phrase important to comprehension or expression.

Source: Copyright © 2010. National Governors Association Center for Best Practices and Council of Chief State School Officers. All rights reserved.

What the **Student** Does

9–10 English Language Arts and Social Studies, Science, and Technical Subjects

Gist: Learn and use the language of discourse appropriate to the subject, discipline, or context, whether writing, speaking, reading, or listening, some of which are specific to the subject being studied (e.g., specialized terms such as *synecdoche* (English), *evolution* (science) or general academic terms such as *analyze* and *evaluate*). In addition, students gather knowledge of words and how to use them when writing, speaking, or listening to others discuss these texts and subjects.

- What are the most frequently used academic words you hear when writing about or discussing a text, topic, or task?
- What are the key words or sentence frames used to express (when writing or speaking) the "thinking moves" in this subject area (e.g., X caused Y to mutate as a result of Z)?
- What is the difference between these different words as they apply to any particular subject: *assess, evaluate, determine, identify; summarize, synthesize, paraphrase; analyze, synthesize, examine, explain*?
- What strategy do you have for determining which words you should look up, attempt to understand, and remember for future use and success in this subject area or school in general?

11–12 English Language Arts and Social Studies, Science, and Technical Subjects

Gist: Learn and use the language of discourse appropriate to the subject, discipline, or context, whether writing, speaking, reading, or listening, some of which are specific to the subject being studied (e.g., specialized terms such as *synecdoche* (English), *evolution* (science) or general academic terms such as *analyze* and *evaluate*). In addition, students gather knowledge of words and how to use them when writing, speaking, or listening to others discuss these texts and subjects.

- What are the most frequently used academic words you hear when writing about or discussing a text, topic, or task?
- What are the key words or sentence frames used to express (when writing or speaking) the "thinking moves" in this subject area (e.g., X caused Y to mutate as a result of Z)?
- What is the difference between these different words as they apply to any particular subject: *assess, evaluate, determine, identify; summarize, synthesize, paraphrase; analyze, synthesize, examine, explain*?
- What strategy do you have for determining which words you should look up, attempt to understand, and remember for future use and success in this subject area or school in general?

What the **Teacher** Does

To help students acquire and use academic and specialized words, do the following:

- Gather a list of words—academic vocabulary words—used in directions, prompts, and assignments for classes or subject areas such as yours; these are words students need to know to do what you assign them and that have often slight but significant differences (e.g., between *evaluate* and *analyze*). These are not the same as specialized academic words, which the Common Core document calls "Tier Three" words, such as *iambic pentameter* (English), *moral hazard* (economics), or other "domain-specific words . . . specific to a domain or field of study (*lava, carburetor, circumference, aorta*) that are key to understanding a new concept within a text" (Common Core Appendix A, p. 33).
- Ask students at the beginning to assess their knowledge of the specialized words important to know in your class; they can do this most efficiently by taking a list of words you prepare and scoring themselves as follows: (1) have never heard or seen it, (2) heard of it but don't know it, (3) recognize it as somehow related to _____, (4) know it when I read it but not sure I can use it correctly when writing or speaking, or (5) know it and can use it as a reader, writer, speaker, and listener.

To help students acquire words and phrases for college and career, do the following:

- Think of these words as arrayed along a continuum with generalization (the ability to define it) on one end and accessibility (the ability to access and use the word with precision and fluency while reading, writing, speaking, thinking, and taking tests) on the other end.
- Focus on what the Common Core calls "Tier Two" words, which it defines as "general academic words . . . [that] are far more likely to appear in written texts than in speech, [including] informational texts (words such as *relative, vary, formulate, specificity,* and *accumulate*), technical texts (*calibrate, itemize, periphery*), and literary texts (*misfortune, dignified,*

faltered, unabashedly). [These] Tier Two words often represent subtle or precise ways to say relatively simple things—*saunter* instead of *walk*, for example" (Common Core State Standards, Appendix A, p. 33).

To have students use these words when reading, writing, speaking, and listening, do the following:

- Preview the text students will read, write about, and discuss, looking for those words that carry more meaning, more weight in the passage, linked as they are to the central ideas whether literary or informational texts. These are the words *as concepts* in the text that students must know as they are essential to the author's ideas and argument(s).

To help students acquire and use academic and specialized words, do the following:

- Use the words as often and in context as you can, incorporating them into assignments, directions, prompts, and your discussion of the content; prompt students to do the same during discussions, restating their observations if necessary so they can hear what they just said in the more precise language of the discipline (e.g., "So what you seem to be saying is that he is a mere caricature rather than a fully formed, dynamic character.").
- Create and incorporate into the class whenever possible sentence templates anchored in and built from these academic words specific to our disciplines (e.g., X argues, through her repeated reference to _____, that Y is, in fact, not _____ but _____, which refutes her initial claim that _____.).

To help your English Language Learners, try this one thing:

- Check that they always know the essential academic terms needed for that night's homework (e.g., Write a *paragraph* about the *causes* of westward expansion and its *effect* on those who remained, *comparing* the lives of one with the other.).

Notes

Academic Vocabulary: Key Words and Phrases

Acquire and use accurately: The emphasis here is on adding words to one's vocabulary so students are prepared for any text they might read or write about. To "acquire" words, one must attend to the words they see but do not know and then make an effort both to learn and to remember them for future use. The added emphasis on using words *accurately* reminds us that the difference between one word and another is often crucial to full and deeper comprehension.

College and career readiness level: Upon entering any postsecondary career or classroom, students immediately realize they are either ready to meet the demands of that situation or not. Those not ready for the demands of college-level reading most often have to take one or more remedial classes, which cost time and money—and often momentum—for those trying to pursue a college degree.

Comprehension: It means understanding what you read, but full, robust comprehension demands the reader take in *all* the details of a text and examine them in light of the occasion, purpose, and audience to see if there other or deeper meanings to the text.

Expression: As it is used here, *expression* refers to writing; it is saying that it is important to know what a word or phrase means before one chooses to include it in something he or she is writing.

General academic and domain-specific words: These are the general words students encounter in all subjects—*analyze, evaluate, describe, compare, contrast,* and so on—and the specialized vocabulary they face in specific course or subject areas—*gravity, force, evolution, inflection point,* and the many words specific to literature and other subject areas.

Independence in gathering vocabulary knowledge: For students to grow their vocabulary, a person must take pains to look up words and note those meanings so he or she can draw on them in the future as a reader and a writer. This independence comes from jotting down and looking up words that either interest or confuse the reader and merit further efforts to understand and distinguish them from others.

Words and phrases sufficient for college level: This is similar to the entry for college and career readiness level; however, the difference here is the emphasis on being able to use words and phrases appropriate to the college-level classroom. This means using refined, specific, and appropriate language when writing about or discussing a topic in a class. One must learn to master the discourse patterns common to a specific subject area or topic on which the student might be writing or doing research.

Notes

Resources

Common Core Recommended Reading Lists

The following links take you to places that showed a commitment to building on the initial reading lists provided by the Common Core State Standards document itself. I include this short list to help you explore other sources for rich texts for your students:

Common Core Curriculum Maps

http://commoncore.org/maps

Cooperative Children's Book Center

http://www.education.wisc.edu/ccbc/books/commoncore.asp

North Carolina Department of Public Instruction

http://www.dpi.state.nc.us/docs/acre/standards/common-core-tools/exemplar/ela.pdf

Official Common Core State Standards 9–12 Text Exemplars

Grades 9–10 Text Exemplars

Stories

Achebe, Chinua. *Things Fall Apart*

Álvarez, Julia. *In the Time of the Butterflies*

Bradbury, Ray. *Fahrenheit 451*

De Voltaire, F. A. M. *Candide, or The Optimist*

Henry, O. "The Gift of the Magi"

Gogol, Nikolai. "The Nose"

Homer. *The Odyssey*

Kafka, Franz. *The Metamorphosis*

Lee, Harper. *To Kill a Mockingbird*

Olsen, Tillie. "I Stand Here Ironing"

Ovid. *Metamorphoses*

Shaara, Michael. *The Killer Angels*

Steinbeck, John. *The Grapes of Wrath*

Tan, Amy. *The Joy Luck Club*

Turgenev, Ivan. *Fathers and Sons*

Zusak, Marcus. *The Book Thief*

Drama

Fugard, Athol. *Master Harold . . . and the boys*

Ibsen, Henrik. *A Doll's House*

Ionesco, Eugene. *Rhinoceros*

Shakespeare, William. *The Tragedy of Macbeth*

Sophocles. *Oedipus Rex*

Williams, Tennessee. *The Glass Menagerie*

Poetry

Auden, Wystan Hugh. "Musée des Beaux Arts"

Baca, Jimmy Santiago. "I Am Offering This Poem to You"

Cullen, Countee. "Yet Do I Marvel"

Dickinson, Emily. "We Grow Accustomed to the Dark"

Donne, John. "Song"

Houseman, A. E. "Loveliest of Trees"

Johnson, James Weldon. "Lift Every Voice and Sing"

Poe, Edgar Allan. "The Raven"

Shakespeare, William. "Sonnet 73"

Shelley, Percy Bysshe. "Ozymandias"

Walker, Alice. "Women"

Informational Texts: English Language Arts

Angelou, Maya. *I Know Why the Caged Bird Sings*

Hand, Learned. "I Am an American Day Address"

Henry, Patrick. "Speech to the Second Virginia Convention"

King, Jr., Martin Luther. "I Have a Dream: Address Delivered at the March on Washington, D.C., for Civil Rights on August 28, 1963"

Lincoln, Abraham. "Gettysburg Address"

Lincoln, Abraham. "Second Inaugural Address"

Martin Luther. "Letter From Birmingham Jail"

Reagan, Ronald. "Address to Students at Moscow State University"

Roosevelt, Franklin Delano. "State of the Union Address"

Smith, Margaret Chase. "Remarks to the Senate in Support of a Declaration of Conscience"

Washington, George. "Farewell Address"

Wiesel, Elie. "Hope, Despair and Memory"

Quindlen, Anna. "A Quilt of a Country"

Informational Texts: History/Social Studies

Brown, Dee. *Bury My Heart at Wounded Knee: An Indian History of the American West*

Connell, Evan S. *Son of the Morning Star: Custer and the Little Bighorn*

Dash, Joan. *The Longitude Prize*

Gombrich, E. H. *The Story of Art*, 16th Edition

Haskins, Jim. *Black, Blue and Gray: African Americans in the Civil War*

Kurlansky, Mark. *Cod: A Biography of the Fish That Changed the World*

Mann, Charles C. *Before Columbus: The Americas of 1491*

Thompson, Wendy. *The Illustrated Book of Great Composers*

Informational Texts: Science, Mathematics, and Technical Subjects

Cannon, Annie J. "Classifying the Stars"

Devlin, Keith. *Life by the Numbers*

Euclid. *Elements*

Hakim, Joy. *The Story of Science: Newton at the Center*

Hoose, Phillip. *The Race to Save Lord God Bird*

Nicastro, Nicholas. *Circumference: Eratosthenes and the Ancient Quest to Measure the Globe*

Preston, Richard. *The Hot Zone: A Terrifying True Story*

U.S. EPA/U.S. Department of Energy. *Recommended Levels of Insulation*

Walker, Jearl. "Amusement Park Physics"

Grades 11–CCR Text Exemplars

Stories

Austen, Jane. *Pride and Prejudice*

Bellow, Saul. *The Adventures of Augie March*

Borges, Jorge Luis. "The Garden of Forking Paths"

Brontë, Charlotte. *Jane Eyre*

Chaucer, Geoffrey. *The Canterbury Tales*

Chekhov, Anton. "Home"

de Cervantes, Miguel. *Don Quixote*

Dostoevsky, Fyodor. *Crime and Punishment*

Faulkner, William. *As I Lay Dying*

Fitzgerald, F. Scott. *The Great Gatsby*

Garcia, Cristina. *Dreaming in Cuban*

Hawthorne, Nathaniel. *The Scarlet Letter*

Hemingway, Ernest. *A Farewell to Arms*

Hurston, Zora Neale. *Their Eyes Were Watching God*

Jewett, Sarah Orne. "A White Heron"

Lahiri, Jhumpa. *The Namesake*

Melville, Herman. *Billy Budd, Sailor*

Morrison, Toni. *The Bluest Eye*

Poe, Edgar Allan. "The Cask of Amontillado"

Drama

Hansberry, Lorraine. *A Raisin in the Sun*

Miller, Arthur. *Death of a Salesman*

Molière, Jean-Baptiste Poquelin. *Tartuffe*

Shakespeare, William. *The Tragedy of Hamlet*

Soyinka, Wole. *Death and the King's Horseman: A Play*

Wilde, Oscar. *The Importance of Being Earnest*

Wilder, Thornton. *Our Town: A Play in Three Acts*

Poetry

Bishop, Elizabeth. "Sestina"

Collins, Billy. "Man Listening to Disc"

Dickinson, Emily. "Because I Could Not Stop for Death"

Donne, John. "A Valediction Forbidding Mourning"

Dove, Rita. "Demeter's Prayer to Hades"

Eliot, T. S. "The Love Song of J. Alfred Prufrock"

Frost, Robert. "Mending Wall"

Keats, John. "Ode on a Grecian Urn"

Li Po. "A Poem of Changgan"

Neruda, Pablo. "Ode to My Suit"

Ortiz Cofer, Judith. "The Latin Deli: An Ars Poetica"

Pound, Ezra. "The River Merchant's Wife: A Letter"

Tagore, Rabindranath. "Song VII"

Wheatley, Phyllis. "On Being Brought From Africa to America"

Whitman, Walt. "Song of Myself"

Informational Texts: English Language Arts

Anaya, Rudolfo. "Take the Tortillas Out of Your Poetry"

Chesterton, G. K. "The Fallacy of Success"

Emerson, Ralph Waldo. "Society and Solitude"

Hofstadter, Richard. "Abraham Lincoln and the Self-Made Myth"

Jefferson, Thomas. The Declaration of Independence

Mencken, H. L. *The American Language*, 4th Edition

Orwell, George. "Politics and the English Language"

Paine, Thomas. *Common Sense*

Porter, Horace. "Lee Surrenders to Grant, April 9th, 1865"

Tan, Amy. "Mother Tongue"

Thoreau, Henry David. *Walden*

United States. The Bill of Rights (Amendments One through Ten of the US Constitution)

Wright, Richard. *Black Boy*

Informational Texts: History/Social Studies

Amar, Akhil Reed. *America's Constitution: A Biography*

An American Primer. Edited by Daniel J. Boorstin

Bell, Julian. *Mirror of the World: A New History of Art*

Declaration of Sentiments by the Seneca Falls Conference

Douglass, Frederick. "What to the Slave Is the Fourth of July? An Address Delivered in Rochester, New York, on 5 July 1852"

FedViews by the Federal Reserve Bank of San Francisco

Lagemann, Ellen Condliffe. "Education"

McCullough, David. *1776*

McPherson, James M. *What They Fought For 1861–1865*

The American Reader: Words that Moved a Nation, 2nd Edition, Edited by Diane Ratich

Tocqueville, Alexis de. *Democracy in America*

Informational Texts: Science, Mathematics, and Technical Subjects

Calishain, Tara, and Rael Dornfest. *Google Hacks: Tips and Tools for Smarter Searching*, 2nd Edition

deGrasse. "Gravity in Reverse: The Tale of Albert Einstein's 'Greatest Blunder'"

Gawande, Atul. "The Cost Conundrum: Health Care Costs in McAllen, Texas"

Gibbs, W. Wayt. "Untangling the Roots of Cancer"

Gladwell, Malcolm. *The Tipping Point: How Little Things Can Make a Big Difference*

Fischetti, Mark. "Working Knowledge: Electronic Stability Control Tyson, Neil

Kane, Gordon. "The Mysteries of Mass"

Kurzweil, Ray. "The Coming Merger of Mind and Machine"

Paulos, John Allen. *Innumeracy: Mathematical Illiteracy and Its Consequences*

U.S. General Services Administration. Executive Order 13423: Strengthening Federal Environmental, Energy, and Transportation Management

Text Complexity Tool

Title:	Author:		Date:
Appropriate Grade Level:	Length:	Text Type/Genre:	
	Too Simple	Just Right	Too Complex
QUANTITATIVE FACTORS			
Word Length			
☐ What is the average length of a word in this text?			
☐ Do the words tend to have one or many meanings?			
Sentence Length			
☐ How long is the average sentence?			
☐ Do sentences tend to be all the same length or vary as a function of style?			
☐ Do the sentences have a range of syntactical complexity—or do they tend to follow the same pattern?			
Word Frequency			
☐ Which words are used frequently?			
☐ Are these words known/familiar?			
Text Cohesion			
☐ How well does this text hold together or flow (thanks to signal words such as transitions)?			
☐ Does the text use other techniques such as repetition, concrete language to improve cohesion?			
☐ Does the text lack cohesion as a result of having no signal words?			
QUALITATIVE FACTORS*			
Levels of Meaning or Purpose			
☐ If *literary*, does the text have more than one obvious meaning?			
☐ If *informational*, is the purpose explicitly stated or implied?			
☐ Does the text explore *more* than one substantial idea?			
Text Structure			
☐ Does the text use simple, predictable structures such as chronological order?			
☐ Does the text use complex literary structures such as flashbacks or, if informational, sophisticated graphics and genre conventions?			
☐ Does the text use other features—layout, color, graphics—in ways that might confuse or challenge some readers?			
Language Conventions and Clarity			
☐ Is the language literal, clear, modern, and conversational?			
☐ Is the language figurative, ironic, ambiguous, archaic, specialized, or otherwise unfamiliar?			
Knowledge Demands			
☐ Does the text make few assumptions about what you have experienced or know about yourself, others, and the world?			
☐ Does the text assume you know about this topic or text based on prior experience or study?			
READER AND TASK CONSIDERATIONS			
Motivation, Knowledge, and Experience			
☐ How motivated is this student to read this text?			
☐ How much does this student know about this topic or text?			
☐ How much experience does the student have with this task or text type?			
Purpose and Complexity of the Assigned Task			
☐ Is this student able to read and work at the assigned level?			
☐ Are these questions the student will know how to answer?			
☐ Is the student expected to do this work alone and without any support—or with others and guidance?			
☐ Is this text or task appropriate for this student at this time?			
☐ Is this text or task as, less, or more complex than the last one?			

Created by Jim Burke. Visit www.englishcompanion.com for more information.

* The CCSS states that "preference should likely be given to qualitative measures of text complexity when evaluating narrative fiction for students in grade 6 and above" (8).

Resource C

July Planning Calendar

Sunday	Monday	Tuesday	Wednesday	Thursday	Friday	Saturday

August Planning Calendar

Sunday	Monday	Tuesday	Wednesday	Thursday	Friday	Saturday

September Planning Calendar

Sunday	Monday	Tuesday	Wednesday	Thursday	Friday	Saturday

October Planning Calendar

Sunday	Monday	Tuesday	Wednesday	Thursday	Friday	Saturday

November Planning Calendar

Sunday	Monday	Tuesday	Wednesday	Thursday	Friday	Saturday

December Planning Calendar

Sunday	Monday	Tuesday	Wednesday	Thursday	Friday	Saturday

January Planning Calendar

Sunday	Monday	Tuesday	Wednesday	Thursday	Friday	Saturday

February Planning Calendar

Sunday	Monday	Tuesday	Wednesday	Thursday	Friday	Saturday

March Planning Calendar

Sunday	Monday	Tuesday	Wednesday	Thursday	Friday	Saturday

April Planning Calendar

Sunday	Monday	Tuesday	Wednesday	Thursday	Friday	Saturday

May Planning Calendar

Sunday	Monday	Tuesday	Wednesday	Thursday	Friday	Saturday

June Planning Calendar

Sunday	Monday	Tuesday	Wednesday	Thursday	Friday	Saturday

About the Author

Jim Burke currently teaches English at Burlingame High School, a public school where he has worked for more than 20 years. In addition to *The Common Core Companion: The Standards Decoded* (Corwin 2013), Jim is the author of more than 20 books, including an entirely new edition of *The English Teacher's Companion* and *What's the Big Idea?* both published by Heinemann. He is a senior consultant for the Holt McDougal *Literature* program. Jim has received several awards, including the 2000 NCTE Exemplary English Leadership Award. In 2009, he created the English Companion Ning, an online community for English teachers, which has been awarded the Best Social Network for Teachers several times. More recently, he was appointed to the AP English Course and Exam Review Commission and the PARCC Consortium, where he serves on the Content Technical Working Groups, which advise the PARCC Leadership Team and the Operational Working Groups.

STANDARDS-BASED TEACHING

The key to raising school- and district-wide achievement is purposeful, potent, standards-based instruction—all year long in every classroom. That's where the Your Literacy Standards Companion series can help. Series creator Jim Burke and an all-star team of authors walk you step by step through what the standards mean and how to teach them. Ensure that every student in your district has the critical skills they need to succeed on test day, in school, and in life.

Grades K–2
978-1-5063-8682-9

Grades 3–5
978-1-5063-8700-0

Grades 6–8
978-1-5063-8553-2

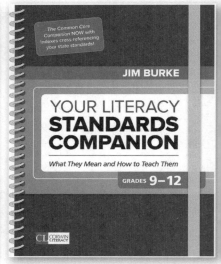

Grades 9–12
978-1-5063-8552-5

www.corwin.com/literacy